PLATE IX

Poster art by Kāẓem Čalipa depicting Khomeini watching over five Iranian soldiers of different ethnicities, emphasizing national unity against the background of the "imposed war" with Iraq. *Source*: Middle Eastern Posters Collection, Box 3, Poster 70, Special Collections Research Center, University of Chicago Library.

other occasions (see *Ṣaḥifa-ye Emām*, XIII, pp. 237, 291, 408), but without substantial effect. Iraqi soldiers certainly never showed the same devotion and fervor as their Iranian counterparts, and, at key points in the war, they were taken prisoner in the thousands, but only a negligible few heeded Khomeini's call to turn on Saddam. A number of Iraqis did, however, seek refuge in Iran, and they were welcomed by Khomeini (*Ṣaḥifa-ye Emām*, XIII, p. 275).

While predicting ultimate victory, Khomeini asserted that the war, in and of itself, brought blessings, for among other things it served the "export of the revolution," and its triumphant outcome would open the way to the "liberation" of Jerusalem (*Ṣaḥifa-ye Emām,* XIII, pp. 331, 483, 513). Messages combining condolence with congratulation were regularly addressed to families whose sons had died in the war, sometimes collectively, sometimes individually (*Ṣaḥifa-ye Emām*, XIII, pp. 182, 513, 530). When victories were achieved, such as breaking the sieges of Ābādān in September 1981 (*Ṣaḥifa-ye Emām*, XV, p. 254) and of Dezful in March 1982 (*Ṣaḥifa-ye Emām*, XVI, pp. 155, 200), Khomeini issued congratulations to the armed forces and those who had supported them (*Ṣaḥifa-ye Emām*, XIII, 354). When Khorramshahr was liberated on 24 May 1982, he congratulated the armed forces on achieving this divinely enabled triumph: Regional states should now be aware that Iran was speaking from a position of strength and abandon their unquestioning obedience to America: Hosni Mubarak of Egypt, King Hussein of Jordan, and King Fahd of Saudi Arabia should remember what had become of the shah (*Ṣaḥifa-ye Emām*, XVI, pp. 257-59).

In these and many other messages, Khomeini warned against factions and personalities, generally left unnamed, who subversively nurtured pessimism concerning the outcome of the war and were opposed to continuing it. By way of response, the slogan "War, war until victory!" (*jang, jang, tā piruzi*) began to gain currency. It was, Khomeini declared, precisely those who had suffered most from the war who demanded that it be continued (see his address to the people of Gilān-e Ḡarb on 18 August 1983, *Ṣaḥifa-ye Emām*, XVIII, pp. 47-49). The same insistence continued during the territorial stalemate and what became known as the "war of the cities," the bombing raids on major cities exchanged between Iraq and Iran beginning in February 1984.

The home front was by no means tranquil during the war years. Some six months into the war, a conspiracy led by Ṣādeq Qoṭbzāda to take over the state and assassinate Khomeini was alleged to have been discovered (Moin, p. 252). Qoṭbzāda had left Iran in 1959 after a time in the shah's jails, studied at Canadian and American universities, and resided in Algeria, Egypt, and Syria, in turn, before settling in Paris. It was there that he met Khomeini, whom he accompanied on the historic flight returning to Tehran. Linked earlier to the Freedom Movement, he was appointed to membership on the Revolutionary Council, and during his term as acting foreign minister from November 1979 to August 1980, he showed opposition to the occupation of the US embassy. Already on 7 November 1980, he had been arrested for plotting against the state, but was released days later. He was re-arrested on 8 April 1982, and in the course of the trial that began in August, leading to his execution on 15 September, he pleaded guilty and asserted that Ayatollah Šariʿatmadāri had been aware of his plans; this was confirmed by Šariʿatmadāri in a televised statement, as a result of which he remained under house arrest until his death in 1986, and the party that had operated under his auspices, chiefly in Azerbaijan, the Ḥezb-e jomhuri-e ḵalq-e mosalmān, was banned. This outcome was perhaps not surprising: Šariʿatmadāri's support for the revolution had been tentative and ambiguous.

As the war continued, international assistance to Iraq intensified. France supplied Iraq with missiles and Mirage and other warplanes, and the Soviet Union provided MiG fighter aircraft. The American Airborne Early Warning and Control System (AWACS) conveyed the coordinates of Iranian targets to Iraq, enabling them to be struck with chemical weapons acquired from West Germany. American warships in the Gulf struck Iranian oil installations in the Persian Gulf and bombed an Iranian warship. What has been termed "the quasi-war" between Iran and America was reaching its climax in late 1987 (Crist, p. 329). The "war of the cities" that had begun in 1984 was intensified. More egregious than all the foregoing was what followed in the summer of the following year. On 3 July 1988, the USS *Vincennes* shot down an Iranian Airbus over the Persian Gulf, killing all 290 aboard. The plane had been in Iranian airspace and was not descending menacingly in the direction of the American ship, as was initially asserted, apart from which it was clearly a civilian, not a military, plane. Neither a convincing explanation nor an apology was forthcoming from the United States. This atrocity was inevitably seen in Tehran as confirmation of American resolve to prevent an Iranian victory in the war, at whatever cost.

On 20 July 1988, Khomeini announced with great reluctance Iran's acceptance of UN Resolution 598 calling for a ceasefire between Iraq and Iran; it was for him like "draining a chalice full of poison." It was also the anniversary of the slaughter of Iranian pilgrims making the Hajj in Mecca in 1987 (see below, p. 563), which had been motivated, he asserted, by the slavish desire of the Saudis to serve "the Great Satan," i.e., the United States. He believed that neither that atrocity nor the pain inflicted on Iran by the war would extinguish the flame of resistance: It would not always be the case that the Americans could shoot down an Iranian passenger plane; it was possible that the sons of the revolution might someday send their warships plunging to the bottom of the Gulf. He exalted those who had fought or been martyred in the war. Khomeini said he was embarrassed before the Iranian people to accept the ceasefire, although the national interest (*maṣlaḥat*) required that he do so. If one test was now over, others awaited, and all should take care that the revolution not fall into the hands of the unworthy (*nā-ahlān*). Long-term developments could not be foreseen; and the Iranian people should be ready to fend off any new aggression (*Ṣaḥifa-ye Emām*, XXI, pp. 74-100).

While the war was still underway, structural problems had persisted; the resignation of Bāzargān and the dismissal of Bani-Ṣadr had not sufficed to eliminate disagreement among different organs of the state. The Majles had approved a number of measures relating to economic concerns, especially the limitation of legally acquired land holdings, only to have them vetoed by the Council of Guardians. In October 1981 and January 1983, Rafsanjāni, who had become chairman of the Majles, requested Khomeini to arbitrate decisively, drawing on the prerogatives inherent in *welāyat-e faqih*, in order to break the deadlock. He was reluctant to do so, preferring that a consensus should emerge, and it was not until 6 January 1988, in a letter addressed to Khamenei, that Khomeini put forward a far-reaching definition of *welāyat-e faqih*, now termed "absolute" (*moṭlaqa*), which made it theoretically possible for the leadership to override all conceivable objections to the policies it supported. Governance, he proclaimed, is the most important of all divine ordinances (*aḥkām-e elāhi*), and it takes precedence over secondary divine ordinances (*aḥkām-e farʿiya-ye elāhiya*). Not only does the Islamic government permissibly enforce a large number of laws not included in those ordinances, such as the prohibition of narcotics and the levying of customs dues, it can also suspend the performance of a fundamental religious duty, such as the Hajj, when this is necessitated by the higher interest of the Muslims (*Ṣaḥifa-ye Emām*, XX, pp. 451-52). The specific mention of the Hajj was due, no doubt, to the killing of Iranian and other pilgrims by the Saudis in 1987. Use of the adjective "absolute" might appear to be a justification for unlimited individual rule by the leader, but it was more a clarification of the concept of *welāyat-e faqih* than an expansion of it. In any event, in February 1988, Khomeini delegated these broadly defined prerogatives to a body cumbersomely entitled the Assembly for the Determination of the Interest of the Islamic Order (Majmaʿ-e taškiṣ-e maṣlaḥat-e neẓām-e eslāmi) (*Ṣaḥifa-ye Emām*, XX, p. 463). It comprised six jurists from the Council of Guardians and seven other figures, including the then-president, Khamenei (Schirazi, p. 82, n. 19). It was empowered to rule decisively on bills passed by the Majles but rejected by the Council of Guardians. It issued no fewer than fifty-four rulings during the first ten years of its functioning (*Majmuʿa-ye moṣawwabāt-e Majmaʿ-e taškiṣ-e maṣlaḥat-e neẓām-e eslāmi*, pp. 47-209).

Even this measure did not suffice to bring sufficient order to the functioning of the government. Factional disputes were a perennial problem, in addition to which the delineation of executive power between president and prime minister had for long been a subject of dispute, and, as the war with Iraq was ending, it became particularly acute. To address this and other concerns, on 18 April 1989, members of the Majles requested Khomeini to order a revision of the constitution that had been approved in December 1979. A week later, he agreed, and assigned the task to a committee, the Council for the Revision of the Constitution (Majles-e bāznegāri-e qānun-e asāsi); it consisted of eighteen religious scholars and two others appointed by Khomeini, plus five others elected by the Majles. It first met on 29 April, electing Ayatollah ʿAli Meškini, president of the Council of Experts, as its chair. It was not until after the death of Khomeini that the process of revision was completed, on 9 July; the revised constitution was approved nineteen days later in a popular referendum. The most significant change was contained in Chapter Eight, articles 107 to 112, relating to the selection of a *rahbar*. Unlike the Constitution of 1979, it did not specify that he be a *marjaʿ-e taqlid*, only that he possess sufficient knowledge to issue *fatwā*s, "a correct vision of political and social concerns" (*bineš-e ṣaḥiḥ-e siāsi va ejtemāʿi*), courage, and adequate strength for the task of *rahbari*. In the event that more than one person should be so qualified, the one whose credentials in the knowledge of *feqh* and political concerns are the strongest is to be preferred (*Qānun-e asāsi-e Jomhuri-ye Eslāmi*, pp. 54-55). The deletion of *marjaʿiyat* from the qualifications for the position of *rahbar* was in conformity with a statement from Khomeini on 9 May to the effect that recognition simply as a *mojtahed-e ʿādel* should suffice (*Ṣaḥifa-ye Emām*, XXI, p. 371). Relevant to this statement was no doubt the resignation of Ayatollah Montaẓeri from the succession, a few months earlier, on 27 March.

For several years, Khomeini had viewed the Hajj as having always had a political dimension; it was now an occasion to foster unity among the Muslim peoples and awaken them to the threats confronting them, primarily American imperialism and Israel. Thus on 7 August 1986, he had addressed a lengthy message to the pilgrims, Iranian and otherwise, who were about to depart on the Hajj. He prefaced it with Qur'an, 9:3: "A declaration from God and His Messenger to the people on the day of the supreme pilgrimage: That God and His Messenger abjure and renounce the *mošrekin* [polytheists]." The injunction contained in the verse is still valid, for the *mošrekin* have their modern counterparts, and it is incumbent on the pilgrims to abjure them. Khomeini also used the occasion to reject calls for the acceptance of what he called an "imposed peace" (*ṣolḥ-e taḥmili*) to end the "imposed war" (*jang-e taḥmili*) (*Ṣaḥifa-ye Emām*, XX, pp. 86-99).

Similar in content and extremely lengthy was the message he addressed to all pilgrims, Iranian and other, exactly one lunar year later, on 28 July 1987. It was in one sense celebratory, for Iran had been able to defend itself against the aggression from Iraq, and the hopes of the superpowers that the Islamic Republic would collapse in a matter of months or a year had come to naught. Again citing Qur'an, 9:3, Khomeini enjoined on the pilgrims renunciation of the contemporary counterparts of the *mošrekin* (polytheists), "the practitioners of global arrogance headed by criminal America." This they were to do by engaging in demonstrations and marches in organized fashion under the supervision of Mehdi Karrubi. In error were those who claimed that political concerns should not be raised on the Hajj (*Ṣaḥifa-ye Emām*, XX, pp. 311-47). What followed three days later, on 31 July 1987, while the war with Iraq was still raging, was the slaughter of some 400 pilgrims, mostly Iranian, by armed Saudi police, as they demonstrated in the courtyard of the Kaʿba. The tragedy became known as "the Friday of blood" (*jomʿa-ye ḵunin*).

Khomeini reacted vigorously to the atrocity. It was, he declared, deliberate and pre-planned, the result of a conspiracy imposed on "the idiot Saudi dynasty," resulting in their disgrace. With the exception of a few groups, the Hijazis themselves had not been involved. King Fahd, Khomeini continued, had sent him a message at the beginning of the Hajj season thanking him for enjoining peaceful conduct on the Iranian pilgrims, so that after the atrocity the Saudis could claim that they had been well-intentioned. The Saudis claimed that the Iranians were planning to set fire to the Kaʿba and make a new Kaʿba in Qom. It was rather they, the Saudis, who had violated the sanctity of the Kaʿba, a crime concerning which the

Muslims would not remain silent. Far from being "the servant of the Ḥaramayn" (*ḵādem al-Ḥaramayn*), Fahd was a "traitor to the Ḥaramayn" (*ḵāʾen al-Ḥaramayn*). The day on which the atrocity occurred should never be forgotten, particularly during the month of Moḥarram; Imam Ḥosayn had, after all, left Mecca to confront his enemies elsewhere lest harm befall the Kaʿba (*Ṣaḥifa-ye Emām*, XX, pp. 368-71).

The following year, on 8 April 1988, he issued a similar although briefer declaration as 150,000 Iranian pilgrims were preparing to depart on the Hajj. It was not possible, Khomeini proclaimed, that our pilgrims should go on the Hajj and not demonstrate against "global arrogance" (*estekbār-e jahāni*). Failure to perform this political duty would invalidate the Hajj. If the Saudis tried to prevent it, they would find all the Muslims in the world arrayed against them; it would be to their benefit not to do so (*Ṣaḥifa-ye Emām*, XXI, p. 22). As it happened, the Saudis limited the number of pilgrims they were prepared to admit from Iran to 45,000, a restriction that was found unacceptable and resulted in a boycott of the Hajj that year.

Toward the end of the war with Iraq, the Mojāhedin-e Ḵalq reappeared on the scene in a murderous episode that had consequences for the succession to Khomeini. Persuaded to leave France, where the group had been in exile, for Iraq in 1986 as part of a deal for the liberation of French hostages held in Lebanon by Ḥezb-Allāh, the Mojāhedin placed themselves at the disposal of the Baathist regime. On 18 June 1988, Iraqi forces attacked the Iranian frontier town of Mehrān, flying no fewer than 530 sorties against it and launching attacks with nerve gas. When the town fell to the Iraqi forces, some 3,000 Mojāhedin accompanied the Iraqi troops, inflicting heavy casualties on the enemy. After three days, the Iraqi forces withdrew, leaving the Mojāhedin to fend for themselves. They were thoroughly defeated when the town was recaptured by Iran in an operation known as Merṣād (Hiro, 1989, p. 312). Despite this stunning defeat, on 26 July 1988, before the U.N. ceasefire came into effect, a detachment of Mojāhedin advanced suddenly across the border into Iran, taking and destroying the city of Eslāmābād-e Ḡarb. Their advance was swiftly repelled, with the loss of close to 4,500 lives. A significant consequence of their incursion was the execution of numerous members of the organization in Iranian jails, and others who had previously been released. The number of those executed is a matter of dispute, but it was certainly in the thousands. Prisoners who undertook to fight against their erstwhile comrades, designated "penitents" (*tawwābun*) by vague analogy with an early movement in Shiʿism, are said to have been spared this fate.

Ayatollah Montaẓeri criticized this response to the incursion by the Mojāhedin. Conventionally eulogized as "esteemed jurisprudent" (*faqih-e ʿāliqadr*), he had been selected in November 1985 by the Assembly of Experts (Majles-e ḵobragān), after deliberations lasting for more than two years, as successor to Khomeini as leader of the Islamic Republic. He was a firm believer in *welāyat-e faqih*, a subject on which he wrote a multivolume study (*Derāsāt fi Welāyat al-faqih*), and had been appointed by Khomeini as the first *emām-e jomʿa* (q.v.) of Tehran soon after the revolution. Later, however, he distanced himself from various aspects of government policy, and, in the fall of 1986, he found himself obliquely and involuntarily involved in the turgid dealings of the Iran-Contra affairs (q.v.).

Mehdi Hāšemi, the brother of Montaẓeri's son-in-law, Hādi Hāšemi, active in the "export of the revolution" and influential among certain groups in Lebanon, had come to learn about the Iran-Contra arms deal and publicized it, first by distributing pamphlets in Tehran and then by providing the information to the Lebanese monthly journal *al-Šerāʿ*, which published it on 3 November 1986. The news also reached Montaẓeri, and, in addition, Manučehr Qorbānifar, the principal arms dealer involved, had informed him via an intermediary of the clandestine visit to Tehran of Robert McFarlane, the US national security adviser (Montaẓeri, 2001, pp. 338-39). Mehdi Hāšemi was arrested on 12 October 1986 on charges of treason and executed on 28 September 1987 before the verdict was publicly announced; Hādi Hāšemi was also put on trial. Moḥammad Reyšahri, the minister of intelligence, affirmed in his memoirs that Mehdi Hašemi had been guilty of a whole range of nefarious activities unconnected to the Iran-Contra affair—smuggling, maintaining his own armed militia, and spreading corruption and immorality (Reyšahri, p. 136). Montaẓeri claimed to have suffered from guilt by association; he denied that either Mehdi or Hādi Hāšemi had operated out of his headquarters in Qom, and he believed the whole affair to have been concocted in order to sabotage his succession to Khomeini (Montaẓeri, 2001, p. 338).

More serious than all the preceding was Montaẓeri's condemnation of the mass executions that followed the Mojāhedin incursion; he estimated their number to be between 2,800 and 3,000, men and women, including some who fasted and prayed. He promptly sent his representatives to the prisons where Mojāhedin were being held prior to execution, and even voiced objections to the long-standing designation of the Mojāhedin as "hypocrites" (*monāfeqin*) (Montaẓeri, p. 349). Despite attempts to discourage him, in early March 1989, Montaẓeri sent a letter to Khomeini, citing six reasons why he viewed the indiscriminate executions as unacceptable, and three days later recused himself from all *šarʿi* functions (Montaẓeri, pp. 352-55). This put paid to his succession to the leadership. On 26 March 1989, Khomeini dismissed him officially, writing that were he to succeed him, he would hand the country over to the "liberals," meaning presumably Bāzargān and the Freedom Movement, and through them to the *monāfeqin*. The number of those executed was "very small," and the concerns Montaẓeri had raised were not worth answering. He was a "simpleton" (*sāda-lawḥ*) whose appointment he had come to regret, just as he regretted the appointments of Bāzargān and Bani-Ṣadr; in all three cases, he had been persuaded by "friends," whom he leaves unnamed (*Ṣaḥifa-ye Emām*, XXI, 330-32). Montaẓeri responded submissively and respectfully, stating that he had been reluctant in the first place to accept succession to the leadership (Montaẓeri, pp. 336-37).

However, Montaẓeri doubted the authenticity of the letters, for Khomeini was stricken with cancer at the time and inaccessible to visitors; Aḥmad Khomeini, he recalled, acted as his intermediary, and according to ʿAli Fallāḥiān, deputy minister of intelligence at the time, it was he who responded to questions posed by officials, but the answers he gave were presented as the words of Khomeini himself (Montaẓeri, p. 369). On 8 September 1988, Aḥmad had indeed requested Khomeini to entrust him with supervising all his written communications to ensure their accuracy, and his father had agreed (*Ṣaḥifa-ye Emām*, XXI, 125-27). A collection of eighty-four letters from Khomeini to Aḥmad, ranging in date from 1971 to 1989, relate to a wide array of matters, including the political (*Waʿda-ye didār*, Tehran, 1997). In his own memoirs, Aḥmad relates in considerable detail the ways in which he assisted his father, first in Iran, then in Iraq and in Paris, and finally back again in Iran, down to the time of his death (Aḥmad Ḵomeyni, *Dalil-e āftāb*, passim). That Aḥmad should have brazenly usurped his father's authority on so important a matter as the succession is nonetheless extremely doubtful. Although it is true that, on 29 April 1989, Aḥmad sent Montaẓeri a lengthy screed with the title *Ranj-nāma*, many of his complaints, especially those relating to Montaẓeri's attitudes to the Mojāhedin, reflected the long-standing concerns of his father.

While these internal developments were unfolding, Khomeini came anew to global attention in two unrelated and contrasting ways. On 11 December 1988, as the Soviet Union was advancing toward implosion, Khomeini composed a lengthy message to Mikhail Gorbachev advising him to abandon communism and not be tempted by capitalism, another form of materialism. Instead, he should study Islam, paying particular attention to the works of Fārābi, Ebn Sinā, Sohravardi, Mollā Ṣadrā, and Ebn al-ʿArabi (*Ṣaḥifa-ye Emām*, XXI, pp. 220-26). In the first week of January 1989, the message was delivered in person to Gorbachev in Moscow by Ayatollah ʿAbd-Allāh Javādi Āmoli, accompanied by Javād Lārijāni and Marżiya Ḥadidči from the Foreign Ministry.

Of far greater impact was the *fatwā* Khomeini issued on 14 February 1989 calling for the execution of Salman Rushdie, author of *The Satanic Verses*, and all those who, aware of its contents, were involved in its publication (*Ṣaḥifa-ye Emām*, XXI, p. 263). The book had already enraged Muslims across the world, not only because of the alleged episode in the life of the Prophet that furnished its title, but also because of its depiction of a brothel staffed by women bearing the names of his wives as well as other offensive material hiding behind a veneer of fiction in the novel. Four days later, Rushdie issued a statement from London regretting the offence that he had caused to Muslims. Immediately, on the very same day, Khomeini emphasized that the *fatwā* still stood, and it could not be rescinded even if Rushdie repented and became the most pious man of the age (*Ṣaḥifa-ye Emām*, XXI, p. 268). The *fatwā* was acclaimed throughout the Muslim world and never rescinded.

On 22 February 1989, eight days after issuing the *fatwā* condemning Rushdie, Khomeini addressed a lengthy message to all the strata of the religious institution—the *marājeʿ*, the *ṭalaba*, the leaders of congregational and Friday prayer; it was entitled *Manšur-e ruḥāniyat*. Part of its content was, however, obliquely addressed to the public at large. It combines laudation with admonition, and retrospection with warning.

Khomeini began by praising those of the religious classes who fought in the war with Iraq; their efforts were not in vain, even if they were not martyred. It is the religious scholars who have always preserved Islam; they were at the forefront of the uprising of 15 Ḵordād. This should not be taken as a comprehensive defense of all religious scholars, including those of the present. "Pseudo-saintly idiots" are still combating "pure Muhammadi Islam" (*Eslām-e nāb-e Moḥammadi*) and propagating "American Islam." This they do by claiming that religion should be separate from the state, and that entry into the political sphere is beneath their dignity. If you were to tell them "the shah is a traitor," they would respond, "but the shah is a Shiʿi!" or "the shah is the shadow of God." Another argument they would make is that just government is unattainable before the advent of the Twelfth Imam. Khomeini noted that he himself had suffered greatly at their hands during his years of study in Qom, additionally because his engagement with philosophy and *ʿerfān* was taken as a symptom of *šerk*, to the degree that the glass from which his son drank water was deemed polluted. Even after the revolution, the *ḥawza* is still subject to two conflicting approaches, and it is imperative that the younger generation not be contaminated by the "idiots" who continue to be opposed to political engagement—their file has not yet been closed. Although they claimed to distance themselves from politics, they supported attempted coups d'état such as those in Qom and Tabriz (an allusion to the violent demonstrations organized by the Ḥezb-e jomhuri-e ḵalq-e mosalmān in 1979 on the pretext of protecting Ayatollah Šariʿatmadāri) and that launched from the Nuža airbase on 10 July 1980. Some of the same class accused politically engaged *ʿolamāʾ* of being Wahhabi or inspired by communism. Also engaged in sabotaging the revolution were the Ḥojjatiya (q.v.), an organization founded in 1953 with the twin aims of refuting Baha'ism and hastening the advent of the Twelfth Imam, before which all attempts at establishing Islamic government are illicit, and the Welāyatis, who claim that the Islamic Republic has made the *ḥalāl*, *ḥarām*, and vice versa. To deal properly with all these "turban-wearers," who act as channels of foreign influence, is not an easy task. The unity of the revolutionary *ʿolamāʾ* and the *ṭalaba* must be preserved, and whatever criticism arises within the religious institution should be measured (*Ṣaḥifa-ye Emām*, XXI, pp. 273-82).

Important, too, Khomeini continued, is to remember that ten years after the triumph of the revolution, most of its aims had been achieved. Even in the war, Iran was victorious in the sense that it repelled the Iraqi aggression. True, if it had had more resources at its disposal, it would have

PLATE X

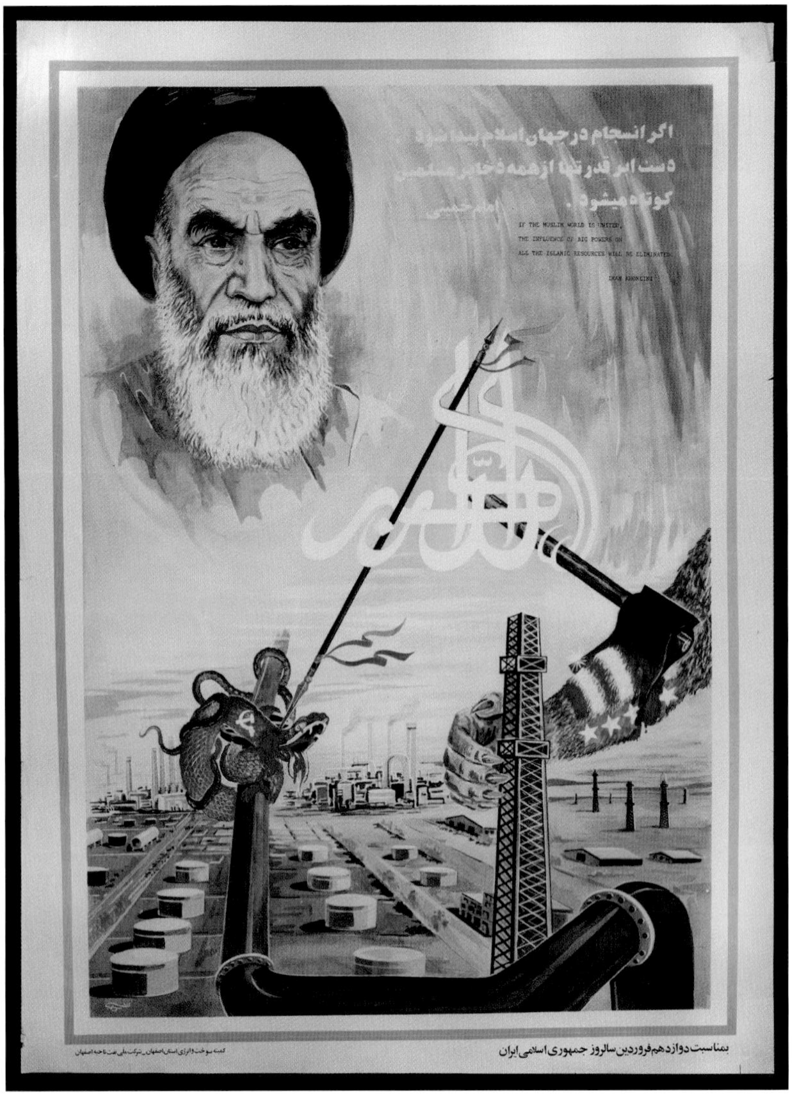

Anti-imperialist poster, with a portrait of Khomeini and quoting his call to protect Iran's resources from the control of the superpowers. Issued by the Petroleum Company for the Area of Isfahan (Komita-ye sok̲t va enerži-ye ostān-e Eṣfahān, Šerkat-e naft-e nāḥiya-ye Eṣfahān) on the occasion of the 12 Farvardin anniversary of the Iranian Revolution. *Source*: Middle Eastern Posters Collection, Box 4, Poster 198, Special Collections Research Center, University of Chicago Library.

achieved higher aims, but the war aided Iran in exporting its revolution, in coming to know its friends and its enemies, and in proving to the people of the region that resistance to the superpowers was possible. The next step, Khomeini optimistically proclaimed, will be the liberation of Palestine. Accepting the UN resolution calling for a ceasefire was a matter of expediency (*maṣlaḥat)* needed to preserve the revolution (*baqā-ye enqelāb*); it did not signify a fundamental shift in policy (*Ṣaḥifa-ye Emām*, XXI, pp. 283-84).

The *ṭalaba* should beware not only of the pseudo-saintly but also of "pseudo-revolutionaries," by whom he presumably meant "liberals" such as Bāzargān and his associates. Immediately after the revolution, Khomeini confessed, he had appointed to important positions persons who did not believe in *Eslām-e nāb-e Mohammadi*; he did so reluctantly, on the advice of friends left unnamed. As for the present, some people ask why he implemented God's command against the *monāfeqin*, an obvious reference to Montaẓeri's objections to the mass executions that followed the Mojāhedin incursion of 26 July 1988. As long as he was alive, Khomeini affirmed, he would not allow the government to fall into the hands of the liberals and the *monāfeqin* and thereby destroy the Islam of the Iranian people (*Ṣaḥifa-ye Emām*, XXI, pp. 285-86).

Khomeini noted that another problem afflicting the *ḥawza* was the attempt to create a division between those who adhere to "traditional *feqh*" (*feqh-e sonnati*) and those who propagate what they call "exploratory *feqh*" (*feqh-e puyā*). Khomeini did not, at least on this occasion, make a clear distinction between the two. It seems, however, that the former takes as its point of departure the Qur'an and Sunna before engaging in *ejtehād* (q.v.), while the latter first engages in rational consideration and then attempts to reconcile the results with the Qur'an and Sunna. Khomeini claimed that the true motive of the proponents of *feqh-e puyā* was to sideline revolutionary *modarresin* and put the pseudo-saintly in control of the *ḥawza*. Among the numerous services of the "traditionalists" was denouncing a claimant to *marjaʿiya* who had distanced himself from the revolution (here again, it is Šariʿatmadāri who was intended). If debate is to take place between adherents of the two tendencies, it should be done with moderation. His own preference, Khomeini made clear, was for the exercise of *ejtehād* in accordance with *feqh-e sonnati*, a discipline which itself has claims to being *puyā*, for variations in time and place are always taken into consideration, and the *mojtahed* must be aware of the political, social, economic, and cultural complexities of the age. Properly understood, *feqh* is the means for regulating man's life "from cradle to grave." Important, therefore, is that *feqh* should not remain in the books of the scholars, but also be *ʿamali*, acted upon (*Ṣaḥifa-ye Emām*, XXI, pp. 287-89, 292). It is precisely *feqh-e sonnati*, cultivated and implemented by the *ruḥāniyat*, that is seen by foreign enemies as a danger; it is this, rather than concern for the person of Rushdie, that explains their denunciation of the *fatwā*. Further, they propagate the notion that those scholars are responsible for the shortages and problems afflicting the masses, rather than the economic blockade of Iran and the war. By way of conclusion, Khomeini appealed to competent members of the *ḥawza* to accept executive and judiciary positions as a "sacred concern" (*amr-e moqaddas*) (*Ṣaḥifa-ye Emām*, XXI, pp. 286-89).

Testament and death. Khomeini's will and testament (PLATE XI), entitled *Ṣaḥifa-ye enqelāb: Waṣiyat-nāma-ye*

PLATE XI

Cover and frontispiece for the English translation of Khomeini's *Waṣiyat-nāma*, published and distributed by the Interests Section of the Islamic Republic of Iran, Embassy of the Democratic and Popular Republic of Algeria, Washington, D.C., n.d.

siāsi-elāhi, bears the date 15 February 1983, presumably the day on which he completed it, some six years before his demise. On 14 July 1983, it was sealed with his stamp and entrusted to the Assembly of Experts (Majles-e ḵobragān). In the following years, Khomeini made some changes and arranged for one copy to be archived at the Majles-e ḵobragān and the other to be sent to the Āstān-e Qods-e Rażawi (q.v.) in Mashhad; this took place on 10 December 1987. Although when writing his testament he had some six years left to live, Khomeini described himself in it as taking his "last breaths," clearly not in a literal sense, but rather as anticipating his death, perhaps as the result of a diagnosis made during his hospitalization (*Ṣaḥifa-ye enqelāb: Waṣiyat-nāma-ye siāsi-elāhi*, in *Ṣaḥifa-ye Emām*, XXI, pp. 393-452). It consists primarily of prolix, often repetitive, exhortations and admonitions addressed to the various segments of Iranian society, and others to the Muslim world at large; it has much in common with the *Manšur-e ruḥāniyat*, delivered some two years after its composition. Throughout, Khomeini displays an acute awareness of actual and potential threats, of opposition and discontent; the Islamic Republic is portrayed as a work in progress. His testament also serves as a summary of the history of the Islamic Republic as he viewed it.

It begins on a gnostic note. In what may be called a preamble, Khomeini examines *al-Ṯaqalayn*, the hadith in which the Prophet proclaims the Book of God and his descendants, the Ahl al-Bayt (see AHL-E BAYT), to be the two entities of supreme value that constitute his legacy and shall remain interconnected until they enter *al-ḥawż* ("the pond"); this, Khomeini suggested, means "the station wherein the drops are absorbed into the sea," or "the union of multiplicity with unity." Next, in a lengthy invocation of blessings on the Prophet and the Ahl al-Bayt, he describes them as "the treasuries of Your Book, in which absolute unity is manifested with all of Your names, including even the reserved name (*al-esm al-mostaʾṯar*)." He had already discussed the concept of "the reserved name" in his *Šarḥ doʿā al-saḥar*. According to a tradition of Imam Jaʿfar al-Ṣādeq, this name, also known as "the supreme name" (*al-esm al-aʿẓam*), consists of seventy-three letters; knowledge of varying quantities of these letters had been bestowed on the prophets, culminating in the Prophet Moḥammad, to whom knowledge of seventy-two letters was revealed—one short of the full total. It is in this sense that "the supreme name" is reserved (*Šarḥ doʿā al-saḥar*, pp. 85-86). On this occasion, Khomeini does not explain the meaning of the term, nor does he attempt to examine the gnostic implications of the hadith of *al-Ṯaqalayn*: his intention is rather to examine what has befallen the two, the Book of God and the Ahl al-Bayt, after the death of the Prophet. Important to what follows is that the hadith in question, although more commonly invoked by Shiʿis, is to be found in the six authoritative books of the Ahl al-Sunna, so that its sense is binding on all Muslims.

Beginning with the martyrdom of Imam ʿAli, the Qur'an was effectively laid aside, and the possibility of just government annulled. Distortions and deviations continually proliferated, thanks to the tyrants (*ṭāḡutihā*) and "vile akhunds" (*āḵundhā-ye ḵabiṯ*; see ĀḴUND). Recitation of the Qur'an was confined to funerals, and anyone who spoke of Islamic government was denounced as a sinner. Fine, ornate printings of the Qur'an were made by the shah, for which certain *āḵund*s praised him, and then by King Fahd of Saudi Arabia, to aid in propagating the superstitious creed of Wahhabism. However, the message of the Qur'an has now been saved from extinction thanks to the Iranian people's devotion. Second only to the Qur'an is the *Nahj al-balāḡa*, adherence to which is a source of pride. Pride, too, is to be taken in the uprising of all ranks of the people for the sake of just government, and the direct participation of qualified and capable women in the defense of Islam—something opposed by "friends of ours unacquainted with the rules of Islam"—as well as the stoic endurance of mothers whose sons had been martyred. America, "the terrorist state" par excellence, has set the world on fire, together with its allies: Zionism; King Hussein of Jordan; Hosni Mubarak of Egypt, "who shares a trough with Israel"; and Saddam Hussein of Iraq.

The people should remain impervious to foreign propaganda and committed to the straight path, neither that of "the atheist East nor the oppressive West," and they should be on watch at all times for "agents, foreign or domestic," the latter being worse than the former. All Muslims should follow the teachings of the Imams and the *feqh-e sonnati* deriving therefrom, not listen to the "whisperers insinuating evil" (*waswāsān-e ḵannāsān*), an expression drawn from Qur'an, 114:4. Crucial in this respect are attending Friday prayer and congregational prayers; observing the ritual mourning on ʿĀšurāʾ (q.v.); cursing those who oppressed the Ahl al-Bayt, above all the Omayyads; resisting the United States and the Soviet Union and their dependents (PLATE X), above all the Saudis, who have betrayed the Ḥaramayn—they should be cursed loudly (*Ṣaḥifa-ye Emām*, XXI, pp. 393-400).

The testament proper begins with an enumeration of the obstacles which, with divine help, have been surmounted by the revolution. For a hundred years, a propaganda war had been waged against Islam, by writers sowing discord among the people in the mass media, meetings and gatherings held to subvert belief, the proliferation of debauchery and immorality, and the consumption of drugs and alcohol. Worse still was the situation in universities and high schools, where most instructors were enamored of either the West or the East. True, there was among them a small committed minority that proclaimed itself "nationalist" (*melli-gerā*), but it was unable to accomplish anything. Here, Khomeini is doubtless alluding to Bāzargān and like-minded persons. It was only with divine aid, he continues, that these multiple obstacles were surmounted, setting apart the Islamic Revolution of Iran from all other revolutions. Incumbent now on the people of Iran is safeguarding the Islamic order (*Ṣaḥifa-ye Emām*, XXI, p. 402).

Next, and throughout his testament, Khomeini warns of ongoing threats and challenges, both from abroad and within the country. The aim of the revolution must always be kept in mind to avoid division and disunity, an aim promoted by incessant propaganda. The leaders of some

Muslim countries submissive to the United States, joined by pseudo-clerics (*ruḥāni-namāhā*) within Iran, suggest that Islam as a fourteen-century-old religion cannot cope with the challenges of modern government. Then there are those who claim that the concern of Islam is only with the spiritual realm and that participation in government is sinful. The first of these groups is ignorant of the nature of government, and imagines that justice and the rules for its implementation are outdated. The second group is unaware that the Qur'an contains more rulings concerning government than any other subject; even those relating to worship have a political dimension (*Ṣaḥifa-ye Emām*, XXI, pp. 406-7).

More harmful than the foregoing, Khomeini noted, are the rumors, widespread throughout the country, but especially in the provinces, that the Islamic Republic has accomplished nothing for the people, that they are now in the thrall of a regime worse than the one they overthrew: The prisons are full of young men, and the torture they endure is worse than that practiced under the Shah! Executions take place every day in the name of Islam! The diffusion of these complaints is in itself proof of a conspiracy: A complaint is made somewhere in the country, and then it is repeated in taxis and buses. Certain clerics are also involved. Neither the problems that inevitably occur after revolutions nor the positive developments that have taken place should be ignored (*Ṣaḥifa-ye Emām*, XXI, p. 408). Islam is like a newborn infant, surrounded by enemies; it deserves mercy and sympathy.

There follows a clear acknowledgement of existing shortcomings: "I have never said, nor do I say now, that everything has been done in accordance with Islam or that no one, out of ignorance, has acted contrary to the regulations of Islam, but the three branches of government are striving to make this country fully Islamic, enjoying the support of tens of millions of its people. If the fault-finding minority were to join them, problems would be solved more swiftly and easily" (*Ṣaḥifa-ye Emām*, XXI, pp. 409- 10). Those loyal millions are better than the people of the Hijaz in the time of the Prophet and those of Iraq in the time of Imam ʿAli; they would disobey them under some pretext or other. All branches of the Iranian armed forces manifest extreme devotion, and the families of the martyrs show fortitude. Listen to the tape recordings circulating in the country, Khomeini counsels the youth, those made by the hypocrites and the opportunist deviants who want the Islamic Republic to collapse, and then compare them with those made by the martyrs, and see which group truly supports the deprived and the oppressed (*Ṣaḥifa-ye Emām*, XXI, pp. 411-12)

Khomeini next addresses a frequently recurring concern: The often hostile dichotomy between universities and the religious institution that had been fostered by the Pahlavis. University professors were selected from the "Westoxicated" and the "Eastoxicated," both categories presenting Islam as reactionary; committed believers were a small minority among them. Religious scholars for their part came to fear the universities and the government officials they produced as irreligious, and the religiously inclined masses were fully alienated from the state. The divide between *dānešgāhi* and *ruḥāni* resulted in a plundering of the country and its resources. Professors and university students should now establish ties of friendship with the religious scholars and their students, and expel from their midst those who act in contrary fashion (*Ṣaḥifa-ye Emām*, XXI, p. 414). Somewhat later, alluding to the cultural revolution (*enqelāb-e farhangi*) that was still underway at the time, Khomeini exhorts students and faculty alike to resist those who wish to alienate them from the *ruḥāni* (*Ṣaḥifa-ye Emām*, XXI, pp. 418-19).

Another persisting affliction had been a sense of inferiority and alienation from the country's own culture, instilled in the people by the Pahlavis, as if they could never engage in useful innovation or attain self-sufficiency. The result was an imported culture of consumerism and immorality; the youth wasted its time in places of vice and entertainment. Now, however, despite the embargoes imposed on Iran, or perhaps even because of them, some progress to self-sufficiency has been made; Iranian factories, for example, can now manufacture aircraft parts. Useless consumer goods must no longer be imported, and competent technical experts should be encouraged (*Ṣaḥifa-ye Emām*, XXI, pp. 415-17).

After the Constitutional Revolution of 1907, particularly under the Pahlavis, the Majles had been controlled by a corrupt majority that did the bidding of Britain and America; the constitution was never properly observed. Now that the situation is different, people should elect representatives who are acquainted with the rulings of Islam, "not persons inclined to deviant schools of thought (*maktabhā-ye enḥerāfi*)." If deviant elements are nonetheless elected, their credentials should immediately be withdrawn. The religious scholars, particularly the *marājeʿ*, also have a duty in this respect. It was they who brought about the constitution of 1907 and then left the political scene. Indifference now to politics and the affairs of the Muslims would be an unpardonable sin. Everyone should participate in elections, whether for the president, the Majles, or the Council of Guardians (*Ṣaḥifa-ye Emām*, XXI, pp. 419-21).

Khomeini continued by stating that the judiciary stands in need of committed persons, well trained in *feqh* at one of the *ḥawzas*, especially Qom; those without such qualifications should be removed. The *ḥawzas* must guard against infiltration by deviant saboteurs, including "nationalists" (*melligerāhā*), fraudulent intellectuals, and sympathizers of the Mojāhedin-e ḵalq, the Fedāʾiyān-e ḵalq, and the Tudeh party. *Feqh-e sonnati* must be preserved as the basis for all research and investigation, but this does not preclude innovative methods of teaching and discussion. Necessary, too, is training in moral refinement (*tahḏib-e nafs*) and spiritual progress toward God (*sayr o soluk*), this being the supreme jihad (*Ṣaḥifa-ye Emām*, XXI, pp. 424-26).

The Foreign Ministry should exercise care in appointing ambassadors. Particularly sensitive are relations with other Muslim countries, most of which are hostile to the Islamic Republic; unity with their peoples should be promoted, by

PLATE XII

Khomeini with grandson in Jamārān, late 1980s. After http://english.khamenei.ir/d/2015/09/19/3/281.jpg (original source unknown).

means of appropriate publications. The Ministry of Guidance ought similarly to improve its efforts to counter the propaganda waged against the Islamic Republic by the superpowers. If university students are to be sent abroad, it should be to industrially advanced countries, but not to the United States or the Soviet Union (*Ṣaḥifa-ye Emām*, XXI, p. 427).

Iranians abroad opposed to the revolution should come to their senses, and return to Iran unless they have committed a crime deserving punishment. Leftist groups should admit that communism has failed, and the only result of their efforts to gain autonomy for the Kurds and the Baluch has been to prevent economic aid from reaching them. There are those who oppose the government because of some of its errors, but they should realize that certain mistakes are inevitable in the aftermath of revolutions. The war imposed numerous hardships, and government institutions were infiltrated by people seeking to sabotage the Islamic Republic. Above all, the sacrifices made by those who fought and gave their lives at the front should not be forgotten (*Ṣaḥifa-ye Emām*, XXI, 436-49). In conclusion, Khomeini proclaims: "With a tranquil heart and joyful spirit, I take my leave of my sisters and brothers, and set out for the eternal resting-place," asking God and the people to accept his apologies for his shortcomings (*Ṣaḥifa-ye Emām*, XXI, p. 450).

Appended to the testament were three admonitions; it is unclear whether they were added immediately after he had completed writing it or later, at some point before his death. Either way, they bear witness to developments that he found disturbing at the time. The first disowned statements or pronouncements attributed to him unless they had been written by him and bore his seal, were authenticated by experts (*kāršenāsān*), or had been broadcast on state media. Second, "certain persons" had been claiming to have arranged his move to Paris after he had been turned back at the frontier with Kuwait, whereas it was in consultation with his son, Aḥmad, and him alone, that he had chosen Paris as his destination. The "certain persons" may have been from the Freedom Movement, among them in

PLATE XIII

Tomb of Ruhollah Khomeini, Tehran, 9 April 2017, by Gilbert Sopakuwa, Flickr, licensed under CC BY-NC-ND 2.0.

particular Ebrāhim Yazdi; the general view was indeed that it was Yazdi who made this extremely important proposal (Chehabi, p. 242). Its attribution to Aḥmad may reflect the important role he played in his father's last years. Finally, he confessed to having praised in the course of the revolution hypocrites whose deceitfulness he had later discovered; the criterion for assessing everyone should be their current posture (*ḥāl-e feʿli*). No names are given in this connection, perhaps Bāzargān, Bani-Ṣadr, and Montaẓeri are intended and people who might come to resemble them in the future. This last admonition clearly betrayed anxiety for the future welfare of the Islamic Republic (*Ṣaḥifa-ye Emām*, XXI, pp. 451-2). Significant, perhaps, was this warning, extracted from his declaration accepting the ceasefire, posted next to his mausoleum, that was seen by the present writer on his visit in June, 2009: "Do not permit the revolution after me to fall into the hands of the unworthy (*nā-ahlān*)."

Khomeini passed away shortly before midnight on 3 June 1989, after suffering a series of heart attacks. The next day, the seal on his testament was broken. He had stipulated that Aḥmad was to read it aloud, but, overcome by grief, he was unable to do so; it therefore fell to Khamenei to accomplish the task. Mass demonstrations of mourning filled the streets of Tehran, and when, on 5 June, Khomeini's body was taken to the Moṣallā in the hills to the north of the city to be prepared for burial, crowds massed there as well. It was then placed in a helicopter to be conveyed to the Behešt-e Zahrā cemetery, but once there, the burial shroud was torn to pieces by mourners, and it became necessary to take the body back to the Moṣallā to be shrouded anew under the supervision of Ayatollah Golpāyagāni. The crowds had not diminished when it was returned to the cemetery for burial. The scenario was appropriately reminiscent of his arrival from Paris, when similarly accompanied by vast numbers of supporters, he had proceeded from the airport to Behešt-e Zahrā. Thus was he laid to rest, in proximity to those who had given their lives for the Islamic Republic he had led and inspired. The construction of a mausoleum, intended to be the center of a complex of buildings, was begun on 18 July 1989 (PLATE XIII). Buried in it are also Khomeini's son, Aḥmad (d. 16 March 1995), and his widow, Ḳadija Ṭaqafi (d. 21 March 2009).

Bibliography: Works of Khomeini cited in this entry: *Ādāb al-ṣalāt: Ādāb-e namāz*, Tehran, 1994. *Divān-e Emām: Majmuʿa-ye ašʿār-e Emām Ḳomeyni*, Tehran, 1994. *Ḥokumat-e eslāmi*, n.p., 1971 (English translation by Hamid Algar in *Khomeini, Islam and Revolution*, Berkeley, Calif., 1981, pp. 27-149). *Kašf al-asrār*, Tehran, n.d. *Kawṯar*, 2 vols., Tehran, 1984. *Ṣaḥifa-ye Emām: Bayānāt, payāmhā, moṣaḥeba-hā, aḥkām, ejāzāt-e šarʿi va nāma-hā*, 21 vols., Tehran, 1999. *Šarḥ doʿā al-saḥar*, ed. Aḥmad Fehri, Tehran, 1983. *Serr al-ṣalāt: Meʿrāj al-sālekin wa salāt al-ʿārefin*, Tehran, 1996. *Tafsir-e sura-ye ḥamd*, Tehran, 1996. *Taḥrir al-wasila*, 2 vols., Qom, 1970. *Tawżiḥ al-masāʾel*, n.p., n.d. *Waʿda-ye didār*, Tehran, 1997.

Documentary sources. *Majmuʿa-ye moṣawwabāt-e Majmaʿ-e taškiṣ-e maṣlaḥat-e neẓām-e eslāmi*, Tehran, 1997. *Qānun-e asāsi-ye Jomhuri-ye Eslāmi-ye Irān hamrāh bā eṣlāḥāt-e Šurā-ye bāznegari-ye Qānun-e asāsi*, Tehran, 1991. *Sayr-e mobārezāt-e Emām Ḳomayni ba rewāyat-e asnād-e SĀVĀK*, 22 vols., 2nd. ed, Tehran, 1987.

Primary sources. Javādi Āmoli, *Bonyān-e marṣuṣ-e Emām Ḳomeyni*, Qom, 1997. Ḥamid Anṣāri, *Mohājer-e qabila-ye imān*, Tehran, 1996. *Āšnāʾi bā Majles-e šurā-ye eslāmi: Kār-nāma-ye 1361*, Tehran, 1984. Asad-Allāh Bādāmčiān and ʿAli Benāʾi, *Hayʾathā-ye moʾtalefa-ye eslāmi*, Tehran, 1983. *Baḥṯi dar bāra-ye marjaʿiat va ruḥāniat*, Tehran, 1972. ʿAqiqi Baḵšāyeši, *Yak-ṣad sāl mobāreza-ye ruḥāniat-e Šiʿa*, 3 vols., Qom, 1982. Abol Hassan Bani-Sadr (Abu'l-Ḥasan Bani-Ṣadr), *L'Espérance Trahie*, Paris, 1982. Mehdi Bāzargān, *Enqelāb-e Irān dar do ḥarakat*, Tehran, 1984. Hedāyat-Allāh Behbudi, *Šarḥ-e esm: Zendagi-nāma-ye Āyatollāh Sayyed ʿAli Ḳāmenaʾi*, Tehran, 2012. *Biografi-ye Pišvā*, Tehran, n.d. Moḥammad Taqi Bušehri, "Ruh-Allāh Musawi Ḳomeyni: Ṭofuliat, ṣabāwat, va šabābat," *Češmandāz* no. 5, 1368 Š./1989, pp. 12-37. Idem, "Ruḥ-Allāh Musawi Ḳomeyni: Dawrān-e taḥṣil va taʿallom dar Dār al-amān-e Qom," *Češmandāz* no. 10, 1371 Š./1992, pp. 38-41. Idem, " Ruḥ-Allāh Musawi Ḳomeyni: Taʿallom dar ḥawza-ye ʿelmiya-ye Qom," *Češmandāz* no. 11, 1371 S./1992. Idem, " Ruḥ-Allāh Musawi Ḳomeyni: Moʿallemān va ostādān," *Češmandāz* no. 12, 1372 Š./1993, pp. 44-57. Idem, "ʿĀref-e Kāmel Mirzā Moḥammad ʿAli Šāhābādi: Moʿallem va morād-e Ruḥ-Allāh Musawi Ḳomeyni," *Češmandāz* no. 13, 1373 Š./1994, pp. 32-41. ʿAli Davāni, *Nahżat-e ruḥāniān-e Irān*, 10 vols., Tehran, n. d. M. Dehnavi, *Qiām-e ḳunin-e 15 Ḳordād be rewāyat-e asnād*, n.p., 1982.

Moḥammad Moḥammadi Gilāni, *Emām-e rāḥel wa feqh-e sonnati*, Tehran, 1994. *Ḥamāsa-āfarinān-e Qom va Tabriz*, 3 vols., n.p., n.d. *Ḥekāyat-e mehr, yādmān-e sālgard-e reḥlat-e yādgār-e gerāmi-e Emām Ḳomeyni*, Tehran, 1996. ʿAli Reżā Ḥosayni, *Āʾina-ye dānešvarān*, Tehran, 1934. ʿAli Rabbāni Ḳalḳāli, *Šohadā-ye ruḥāniyat dar yak-ṣad sāl-e aḳir*, n.p. 1982. Ṣādeq Ḳalḳāli, *Ḳāṭerāt az ayyām-e ṭalabagi tā dawrān-e ḥākem-e šarʿ-e dādgāhhā-ye enqelāb-e eslāmi*, Tehran, 2001. Aḥmad Ḳomeyni, *Ranj-nāma*, Tehran, 1989. Idem, *Pedar ʿalamdār-e maktab-e maẓlum*, Tehran, 1993. Moʾassasa-ye tanẓim va našr-e āṯār-e Ḳomeyni, *Maḥżar-e nur: Fehrest-e didārha-ye Emām Ḳomeyni*, 2 vols., Tehran, 1995. Idem, *Dalil-e āftāb: Ḳāṭerāt-e yādgār-e Emām*, Tehran, 1996. Ḥosayn ʿAli Montaẓeri, *Derāsāt fi Welāyat al-faqih*, 2 vols., Beirut, 1989. Idem, *Ḳāṭerāt*, Los Angeles, 2001. Moḥammad Morādiniā, *Saṭr-e awwal: Ḳāndān, rejāl, va ḥawādeṯ-e bist sāl-e naḳost-e zendagi-ye Emām Ḳomeyni*, Tehran, 2006. Mortażā Moṭahhari, *ʿElal-e gerāyeš ba māddigari*, Tehran, 1978. *Omid-e Eslām: Šahid Āyat-Allāh Ḥājj Sayyed Moṣṭafā Ḳomeyni be rewāyat-e asnād-e SĀVĀK*, Tehran, 2009. Mortażā Pasandida, *Ḳāṭerāt*, ed. Moḥammad Morādiniā, Tehran, 1995. *Qiām-e ḥamāsa-āfarin-e Qom va Tabriz*, 3 vols., n.p., 1977-78. Moḥammad Ḥasan Rajabi, *Zendagāni-ye siāsi-ye Emām Ḳomeyni az āğāz tā tabʿid*, Tehran,

1991. Moḥammad Reyšahri, *Ḵāṭerahā*, Tehran, n.d. Moḥammad Šarif Rāzi, *Āṯār al-ḥojja*, 2 vols., Qom, 1954. Ḥamid Ruḥāni, *Nahżat-e Emām Ḵomeyni*, 18th ed., 4 vols., Tehran, 2001. Ruḥāniun-e mobārez-e ḵārej az kešvar, *Šahidi digar az ruḥāniyat*, Najaf, n.d. Ayatollah Moḥammad ʿAli Šāhābādi, *Šaḏarāt al-maʿāref*, Tehran, 1982. ʿAbd al-Karim Soruš, ed., *Yād-nāma-ye ostād-e šahid Mortażā Moṭahhari*, Tehran, 1981. Fāṭema Ṭabāṭabāʾi, *Eqlim-e ḵāṭerāt*, Tehran, 2011. *Terurism-e żedd-e mardomi: baḥṯi pirāmun-e māhiat va ahdāf-e ḥarakat-e mosallaḥāna-ye monāfeqin*, Tehran, 1982. *U ba tanhāʾi yak ommati bud*, Tehran, 1982 (a collection of speeches by Ayatollah Behešti with materials for his biography). Moṣṭafā Vejdāni, ed., *Sargoḏašthā-ye viža az zendagi-e Hażrat-e Emām Ḵomeyni*, Tehran, 1989. *Viža-nāma-ye Ostād-e Šahid Mortażā Moṭahhari*, n.p., n.d. *Yādegār-e Emām: Ḥojjat-al-Eslām Ḥājj Sayyed Aḥmad Ḵomeyni be rewāyat-e asnād-e SĀVĀK*, Tehran, 2009.

Other sources. Pejman Abdolmohammadi, "Il Repubblicanesimo Islamico dell'Ayatollah Khomeini," *Oriente Moderno*, n.s. 89, 2009, pp. 87-100. Ervand Abrahamian, *Iran between Two Revolutions*, Princeton, 1983. Idem, *The Iranian Mojahedin*, New Haven, 1989. Idem, *Khomeinism: Essays on the Islamic Republic*, London and New York, 1993. Arshin Adib-Moghaddam, ed., *A Critical Introduction to Khomeini*, Cambridge, 2014. Ṣādeq Āhangarān, ed., *Lāla-hā-ye ḵunin-e enqelāb*, Tehran, 1983. Moṣṭafā Alamuti, *Irān dar ʿaṣr-e Pahlavi*, 10 vols., London, 1988-91. Hamid Algar, "The Oppositional Role of the Ulama in Twentieth-Century Iran," in N. Keddie, ed., *Scholars, Saints and Sufis*, Berkeley and Los Angeles, 1972, pp. 231-55. Idem, tr., *Constitution of the Islamic Republic of Iran*, Berkeley, 1980. Idem, tr. and annotated, *Islam and Revolution: Writings and Declarations of Imam Khomeini*, Berkeley, 1981. Idem, *Roots of the Islamic Revolution in Iran*, London, 1983. Idem, "Imam Khomeini, 1902-1962: The Pre-Revolutionary Years," in Edmund Burke and Ira Lapidus, eds., *Islam, Politics, and Social Movements*, Berkeley and Los Angeles, 1988, pp. 263-88. Idem, "Religious Forces in Twentieth-Century Iran," in Peter Avery, Gavin Hambly, and Charles Melville, *The Cambridge History of Iran* VII*: From Nadir Shah to the Islamic Republic*, Cambridge, 1991, pp. 732-64. Idem, "A Short Biography," in Abdar Rahman Koya, ed., *Imam Khomeini: Life, Thought and Legacy, Essays from an Islamic Movement Perspective*, Kuala Lumpur, 2009, pp. 19-60. Ḥamid Anṣāri, *Ḥadiṯ-e bidāri*, Tehran, 1995. Said Amir Arjomand, *The Shadow of God and the Hidden Imam*, Chicago, 1984. Idem, *Authority and Political Culture in Shi'ism*, Albany, 1988a. Idem, *The Turban for the Crown: The Islamic Revolution in Iran*, New York and Oxford, 1988b. Ahmad Ashraf, "Charisma, Theocracy and New Men of Power in Postrevolutionary Iran," in M. Weiner and A. Banuazizi, eds., *The Politics of Social Transformation in Afghanistan, Iran, and Pakistan*, Syracuse, 1994, pp. 101-55. Ahmad Ashraf and Ali Banuazizi, "The State, Classes, and Modes of Mobilization in the Iranian Revolution," *State, Culture, and Society* 1/3, 1985, pp. 3-40. Fakhreddin Azimi, "Khomeini and the 'White Revolution,'" in A. Adib-Moghaddam, ed., *A Critical Introduction to Khomeini*, Cambridge, 2014, pp. 19-42.

Shaul Bakhash, *The Reign of the Ayatollahs: Iran and the Islamic Revolution*, New York, 1986. Maziar Behrooz, "Factionalism in Iran under Khomeini," *Middle Eastern Studies* 27, 1991, pp. 597-614. Christian Bonaud, *L'Imam Khomeyni, un gnostique méconnu du XXe siècle*, Beirut, 1997. Daniel Brumberg, *Reinventing Khomeini: The Struggle for Reform in Iran*, Chicago, 2001. Norman Calder, "Accommodation and Revolution in Imāmi Shiʿi Jurisprudence: Khumayni and the Classical Tradition," *Middle Eastern Studies* 18, 1982, pp. 3-20. Cengiz Çandar, *Dünden yarına İran*, Istanbul, 1981. Houchang Chehabi, *Iranian Politics and Religious Modernism: The Liberation Movement of Iran under the Shah and Khomeini*, Ithaca, N.Y., 1990. Ronen A. Cohen, *Revolution under Attack: The Forqan Group of Iran*, New York, 2016. Elvire Corboz, "Khomeini in Najaf: The Religious and Political Leadership of an Exiled Ayatollah," *Die Welt des Islams* 55, 2015, pp. 221-48. David Crist, *The Twilight War*, New York, 2012. Stephanie Cronin, *Reformers and Revolutionaries in Modern Iran: New Perspectives on the Iranian Left*, London, 2004. Hamid Dabashi, "Ayatollah Khomeini: The Theologian of Discontent," in idem, *Theology of Discontent: The Ideological Foundation of the Islamic Revolution in Iran*, New York, 1993, pp. 400-484. Joanna De Groot, *Religion, Culture, and Politics in Iran: From the Qajars to Khomeini*, London, 2007. E. A. Doroshenko, *Shiitskoe Dukhovenstvo v Sovremennom Irane*, Moscow, 1975. Diede Farhosh-van Loon, "The Fusion of Mysticism and Politics in Khomeini's Quatrains," *International Journal of Persian Literature* 1, 2016, pp. 59-88. Vali-Allāh Fawzi, *Ḥamāsahā-ye eslāmi-e mellat be rahbari-e Emām Ḵomeyni*, Qom, n.d. Moḥammad Ḥosayn Fażl-Allāh, *Taʾammolāt fi'l-fekr al-ḥaraki wa'l-siāsi wa'l-manhaj al-ejtehādi ʿend al-Emām al-Ḵomeyni*, Beirut, 2000. Michael M. J. Fischer, *Iran: From Religious Dispute to Revolution*, Cambridge, Mass., and London, 1980. Moḥammad Moḥammadi Gilāni, *Esm-e mostaʾṯar dar waṣiyat-nāma-ye Emām wa zaʿim-e akbar*, Tehran, 1991. Idem, *Emām-e rāḥel va feqh-e sonnati*, Tehran, 1995.

Sayyed Sadegh Haghighat, ed., *Six Theories about the Islamic Revolution's Victory*, Tehran, 2000. Moḥammad Reżā Ḥakimi, *Tafsir-e Āftāb*, Tehran, n.d. Dilip Hiro, *Iran under the Ayatollahs*, London, 1985. Idem, *The Longest War: The Iran-Iraq Military Conflict*, Ann Arbor, 1989. Idem, *The Iranian Labyrinth*, New York, 2005. Moḥammad-Ṣādeq Ḥosayni, *al-Ḵomeyni fi rasāʾel al-eṣlāḥ wa'l-taḡyir*, Beirut, n.d. [2009]. Nura Hossainzadeh, "Ruhollah Khomeini's Political Thought: Elements of Guardianship, Consent, and Representative Government," *Journal of Shi'a Islamic Studies*, 7/2, 2014, pp. 26-44. Idem, "Democratic and Constitutional Elements in Khomeini's *Unveiling of Secrets* and *Islam-*

ic Government," *Journal of Political Ideologies*, 21/1, 2016, pp. 26-44. Fahmi Howaydi, *Irān men al-dākel*, Cairo, 1988. Asaf Hussain, *Islamic Iran: Revolution and Counter Revolution*, New York, 1985. Moṣṭafā Izadi, *Gozari bar zendagi-ye Āyat-Allāh Montaẓeri faqih-e ʿaliqadr*, 2 vols., Tehran, 1987. ʿAli Kamāli, *Enqelāb*, Tehran, n.d. Nikki R. Keddie, *Roots of Revolution: An Interpretive History of Modern Iran*, New Haven and London, 1981. Idem, ed., *Religion and Politics in Iran: Shi'ism from Quietism to Revolution,* New Haven, 1983. Sayyed Hādi Ḵosrawšāhi, *al-Ṯawra al-eslāmiya wa al-emberiāliya al-ʿālamiya*, Rome, n.d. Abdar Rahman Koya, ed., *Imam Khomeini: Life, Thought and Legacy, Essays from an Islamic Movement Perspective*, Kuala Lumpur, 2009. Flynt Leverett and Hillary Mann Leverett, *Going to Tehran: Why the United States Must Come to Terms with the Islamic Republic of Iran*, New York, 2013. Vanessa Martin, *Creating an Islamic State: Khomeini and the Making of a New Iran*, London, 2003. Hamid Mavani, *Religious Authority and Political Thought in Twelver Shi'ism*, London and New York, 2013. Mohsen M. Milani, *The Making of Iran's Islamic Revolution*, Boulder, San Francisco, and Oxford, 1994. Baqer Moin, *Khomeini: Life of the Ayatollah*, London, 1999. Sayyid Amjad Hussain Shah Naqavi, *The Mystery of Prayer: The Ascension of the Wayfarers and the Prayer of the Gnostics*, Leiden, 2015 (tr. with introd. and annotations of Khomeini's *Serr al-ṣalāt*). Graeme Newman, "Khomeini and Criminal Justice: Notes on Crime and Culture," *Journal of Criminal Law and Criminology* 73, 1982, pp. 561-81. ʿAli Qāderi, *The Life of Imam Khomeini,* Tehran, 2001.

Farhang Rajaee, *Islamic Values and World View: Khomeyni on Man, the State and International Politics*, New York and London, 1983. R. K. Ramazani, ed., *Iran's Revolution: The Search for Consensus*, Bloomington, Ind., 1990. Qahhār Rasuliān, *Rasul-e bidāri-e šarq: Majmuʿa-ye maqālat-e dānešmandān-e tājik dar bāra-ye Emām Ḵomeyni*, Tehran, 2008. Māšāʾ-Allah Razmi, *Āḏarbāyjān va jonbeš-e ṭarafdārān-e Šariʿatmadāri dar sāl-e 1358*, Stockholm, 2000. L. A. Reda, "*Khatt-e Imam*: The Followers of Khomeini's Line," in Adib-Moghaddam, ed., pp. 115-148. Yann Richard, "Ayatollah Kashani: ein Wegbereiter der islamischen Republik?," *Religion und Politik im Iran*, Berlin, 1981, pp. 277-305. Lloyd Ridgeon, "Hidden Khomeini: Mysticism and Poetry," in A. Adib-Moghaddam, ed., *A Critical Introduction to Khomeini*, Cambridge, 2014, pp. 193-210. Saiyid Athar Abbas Rizvi, *A Socio-Intellectual History of the Isnā ʿAshari Shiʿis in India*, 2 vols., Canberra, 1986. Kishwar Rizvi, "Religious Icon and National Symbol: The Tomb of Ayatollah Khomeini in Iran," *Muqarnas* 20, 2003, pp. 209-24. Oliver Scharbrodt, "Khomeini and Muḥammad al-Shīrāzī: Revisiting the Origins of the 'Guardianship of the Jurisconsult'," *Die Welt des Islams* 60, forthcoming. Asghar Schirazi, *The Constitution of Iran: Politics and the State in the Islamic Republic*, London and New York, 1997. Sayyed Sebṭ-e Ḥasan, *Enqelāb-e Irān*, Karachi, 1988. Asghar Seyed-Gohrab, "Khomeini the Poet Mystic," *Die Welt des Islams* 51, 2011, pp. 438-58. Gary Sick, *October Surprise*, New York, 1991. ʿAli Širḵāni, *Ḥamasa-ye 29-e Bahman-e Tabriz*, Tehran, 2000. *Tā ṣobḥ-e ešrāq: Gozida-ye šeʿr dar manaqabat va sug-e Ḥażrat Emām Ḵomeyni*, Tehran, 1997. ʿAli Tasḵiri, *Derāsāt fi al-fekr al-siāsi le'l-Emām al-Ḵomeyni*, Qom, 1995. Sinā Vāḥed, *Qiām-e Gowhar-šād*, Tehran, 1987. Waheed-uz-Zaman, *Iranian Revolution: A Profile*, Islamabad, 1985. Linda Walbridge, ed., *The Most Learned of the Shi'a: The Institution of the Marjaʿ Taqlid*, New York, 2001. Sepehr Zabih, *The Left in Contemporary Iran*, Stanford, 1986. Dmitrii Zhukov, *Imam Khomeini: Ocherk Politicheskoi Biografii*, Moscow, 1998. Sadegh Zibakalam, "To Rule, or Not to Rule? An Alternative Look at the Political Life of Ayatollah Khomeini between 1960 and 1980," in A. Adib-Moghaddam, ed., *A Critical Introduction to Khomeini*, Cambridge, 2014, pp. 256-74.

(HAMID ALGAR)

ii. WORKS

Prodigiously erudite and energetic, Ruhollah Khomeini left as part of his legacy a vast and varied corpus of written work. The emphases reflected in it changed or were modified at various stages in his scholarly and political career, but insofar as his spiritual and intellectual personality remained stable throughout, it will be appropriate to examine his writings by category rather than chronology. Inevitably, there is a certain overlap between some categories, given the permeation of many of Khomeini's works by the concerns of *ʿerfān* (q.v.). For a listing of twenty-seven of his works in order of publication see *Ḥożur*, Ḵordād 1376/June-July 1997, p. 126.

ON RITUAL PRAYER (*NAMĀZ*) AND SUPPLICATORY PRAYER (*DOʿĀʾ*)

(1) *Serr al-ṣalāt: Meʿrāj al-sālekin wa ṣalāt al-ʿārefin* (in Persian; completed in 1939). A relatively compact exposition of the occult mysteries or inward meanings of prayer, this work has been characterized as "the most difficult of all texts by the Imam" (Bonaud, p. 123), in part because of the complex terminology employed. It is self-evident, Khomeini proclaims (pp. 10-11), that the prayer of the wayfarer (*sālek*) to the divine presence is quite different from that of "the perfect friend of God" (*wali-e kāmel*) who has completed his spiritual ascension (*meʿrāj-e ruḥi*). He discusses in turn the various degrees of the presence of the heart (pp. 3-33); ritual purity (pp. 34-54); the place where the prayer is performed (pp. 55-59); the times for which prayer is prescribed (pp. 60-64); orientation to the Kaʿba (pp. 65-66); standing as the prayer is about to begin (*qiām*) (pp. 72-73); the forming of intention (*niyat*) (pp. 74-76); the raising of the hands at the beginning of the prayer (pp. 76-80); the seeking of protection from God (*esteʿāḏa*) (pp. 83-85); the Qur'anic verses to be recited, with particular attention to *al-Fāteḥa* (pp. 85-93); genuflection (*rokuʿ*; pp. 94-99); prostration (*sojud*; pp. 99-107);

uttering the profession of faith (*tašahhod)* and the *salām* that conclude the prayer (pp. 108-15); and the threefold *takbir* that follows its termination (pp. 116-17). It was first published in *Yād-nāma-ye šahid Mortażā Moṭahhari* (ed. ʿAbd al-Karim Soruš, Tehran, 1981, pp. 31-106), followed by a preliminary edition published in Qom (n.d.) under the title *Asrār-e namāz*. Sayyed Aḥmad Fehri's *Parvāz dar malakut yā Asrār-e maʿnawi-e namāz* (Qom, 1981) incorporates much of Khomeini's work. The definitive edition is that published in Tehran in 1996; it has an introduction by ʿAbdollāh Jawādi Āmoli and includes the autograph manuscript of Khomeini (xxx+169+96 pp.).

(2) *Ādāb al-ṣalāt*: *Ādāb-e namāz* (in Persian; completed in 1942). Its subject and purpose is much the same as that of *Serr al-ṣalāt:* the exposition of the esoteric meanings of prayer. The earlier work was, however, relatively concise and written in the language of the gnostic elite, "not suited to the commonalty. I decided therefore to write a few lines concerning the states of the heart in that spiritual ascension, in the hope that my brothers in faith reflect upon them with benefit to their hardened hearts" (Tehran edition of 1991, p. vii). "The few lines" occupy a total of 381 pages. The first section of the work discusses the inward norms (*ādāb*) that must be observed in all acts of worship—awareness of God's omnipotence, humility toward Him, protecting oneself from the wiles of Satan, inward serenity (*ṭomaʾnina*), and presence of the heart and preventing its disruption by worldly attachment (pp. 7-53). The second section deals with the preliminaries to the prayer—ritual purity, clothing to be worn during prayer, the place where prayer is performed, the times at which prayer is mandatory, and orientation to the Kaʿba and its connection to man's primordial nature (*feṭrat*) (pp. 55-120). The third and lengthiest section, divided into thirty-eight chapters, analyses each component of the prayer with reference to relevant verses of the Qurʾan and their esoteric meaning; particular attention is paid to the chapters *al-Fāteḥa, al-Ek̲lāṣ*, and *al-Qadr* (pp. 120-369). Prefaced to the 1991 edition are letters Khomeini wrote in 1984 to his son, Aḥmad, and his daughter-in-law, Fāṭema Ṭabāṭabāʾi (whom he affectionately addresses as "Fāṭi" on this as on other occasions), exhorting them to read and benefit from the work; it was presumably a manuscript copy he placed at their disposal (pp. xiii-xvii).

(3) *Sarḥ doʿā al-saḥar* (in Arabic; completed in 1929). A commentary on the supplicatory prayer recited by Imam Moḥammad al-Bāqer (q.v.) before the onset of dawn throughout the month of Ramadan. In it, the Imam invokes twenty-three divine qualities; thus, the first supplication reads as follows: "O my God! I ask of You by Your most splendid splendor—and all of Your splendor is the most splendid—I request of You all Your splendor." Each separate manifestation of a divine attribute is, by definition, the most perfect manifestation of the entire attribute (1983 ed., p. 21). Khomeini completed this work when he was a mere twenty-seven years of age and had just begun studying with Mirzā Moḥammad ʿAli Šāhābādi soon after the gnostic's arrival in Qom (see KHOMEINI i. LIFE, p. 545). He refers to him reverentially as "our shaikh" at several points in the book, and cites also a wide range of earlier authorities, including Mirzā Jawād Maleki (d. 1925), ʿAbd-al-Razzāq Kāšāni, Mir Dāmād (q.v), and Mollā Ṣadrā (q.v.). The work was first published in 1980 in a Persian translation by Aḥmad Fehri (Tehran, 280 pp.); three years later, Fehri oversaw the publication of the Arabic original (Tehran, 168 pp.).

ON *ʿERFĀN*

(1) *Meṣbāḥ al-hedāya elā'l-k̲elāfa wa'l-welāya* (in Arabic; completed in 1930). It was published in Tehran in 1993, edited and with a prologue in Persian by Jalāl-al-Din Āštiāni (d. 2005) that is far lengthier than the work itself (pp. 11-167); Khomeini's text, separately paginated, occupies a mere seventy-nine pages (pp. 11-90).

The title of the work, *Meṣbāḥ al-hedāya* ("The Lamp of Guidance"), alludes to Qur'an, 24:35, *Āyat al-nur*: "The similitude of His light is a niche wherein is a lamp." The text is accordingly divided into two "niches" (*meškāt*), the first of which contains no fewer than fifty-six "lamps" (pp. 13-42). The first of those fifty-six "lamps" seeks to "unveil some of the mysteries of the Vicegerency of Moḥammad (*al-k̲elāfat al-moḥammadiya*) and the Loyal/Intimate Friendship of ʿAli (*al-welāyat al-ʿalawiya*) in the realm of knowledge, together with an infinitesimal fragment of the station of prophethood, conveyed by means of the symbols and allusions employed by the masters of gnosticism among the truest followers (*k̲ollaṣ)* of the Ahl al-Bayt" (p. 13).

The second "niche" is devoted to expounding "the mysteries of *k̲elāfa, welāya*, and *nobowwa* on the plane of the unseen and the worlds of command and creation" (p. 43). In it are placed three "lamps"; the first seeks to illumine "the inflaming of the heart by breezes from the World of Command proceeding from the breath of the All-Compassionate (*al-nafas al-raḥmāni*)," expounded in twenty-one "lights" (pp. 43-58). The second of the three "lamps" in this second "niche" shines light on "the mystery of *k̲elāfa, nobowwa,* and *welāya* that the plane of the unseen and the lights of the divine intellect disclose to you; it contains within it truths relating to faith and luminous paths of ascension (*maṭāleʿ*), permitting you gradually to attain the perfections of humanity"; the "paths of ascension" set forth are thirteen in number (pp. 59-81). The third and last of the "lamps" sheds light on "the mysteries of *k̲elāfa, nobowwa,* and *welāya* on the manifest plane of creation, as well as the occult purpose (*serr*) for the sending of the prophets, upon whom be peace, and their rank with respect to our Prophet, peace and blessings be upon him and his family." This purpose is accomplished by twelve *wamiż* ("flashes of lightning") (pp. 81-90).

Setting forth a highly complex metaphysical scheme, replete with arcane terminology, this work is clearly intended for a specialized readership. It is not without reason that Āštiāni, the editor, encourages the reader to study his own lengthy introduction before engaging with the text itself. Khomeini himself emphasizes as a prerequisite for its understanding acquaintance with the works of Avicenna (q.v.), Ebn ʿArabi (q.v.), Mollā Ṣadrā, and other authorities, all of whom he cites frequently. At the same time, he promises the reader new doctrinal insights (p. 86). Perhaps anticipating criticism precisely of those insights, Khomeini warns his readers, "beware of revealing these mysteries to the unqualified" (p. 90). Given the complexities of the text, it is unlikely that the ordinary believer would even have attempted to embark on its study. What may have been on his mind was, perhaps, the hostility to *ʿerfān* still prevailing in Qom at the time, despite the presence there of Mirzā Moḥammad ʿAli Šāhābādi.

(2) *Taʿliqa ʿalā Šarḥ Foṣuṣ al-ḥekam* (in Arabic; completed in 1936). This provides notes on the *Maṭlaʿ ḵoṣuṣ al-kalem fi maʿāni Foṣuṣ al-ḥekam*, a commentary by Dāʾud Qayṣari (d. 751/1350) on the *Foṣuṣ al-ḥekam* of Ebn ʿArabi.

(3) *Taʿliqa ʿalā Meṣbāḥ al-ons* (in Arabic). This provides notes on *Meṣbāḥ al-ons* (more fully, *Meṣbāḥ al-ons bayn al-maʿqul wa'l-mašhud fi šarḥ Meftāḥ al-ḡayb*) by Moḥammad Fanāri (d. 834/1431), commonly known as Mollā Fenāri. As the full title indicates, *Meṣbāḥ al-ons* is a commentary on the *Meftāḥ al-ḡayb al-jamʿ wa'l-wojud* of Ṣadr al-Din Qonavi (d. 673/1274), one of the principal associates of Ebn ʿArabi. Khomeini studied this work and the preceding one with Šāhābādi, and his notes on the two have been published together in one volume as *al-Taʿliqāt ʿalā Šarḥ Foṣuṣ al-ḥekam wa Meṣbāḥ al-ons* (Tehran, 1985, repr. 1989, 322 pp.). Numerous passages have been translated with extensive commentary by Christian Bonaud (passim).

Noteworthy is Khomeini's complex analysis of the five divine "Presences" (*ḥażarāt*) and their difference from the "Worlds" (*ʿawālem*); the former relate to the divine dimension of the universe, and the latter to its earthly dimension. Presence is the prerogative of the Truth (*al-ḥaqq*), while manifesting something is a quality of creation (*al-ḵalq*). Each of the Worlds is a locus for the manifestation of one of the Presences, and both Presences and Worlds can be enumerated in corresponding series of five. The five Presences are the following: *al-ḡayb al-moṭlaq*, absolute hiddenness, this being the hidden dimension of the supreme name (*al-esm al-aʿẓam*); *al-aḥadiya al-ẓohuriya*, manifested oneness, i.e., the manifested dimension of the supreme name; *al-wāḥediya al-ḡaybiya*, the hidden dimension of the divine names (*al-ḡayb al-możāf*); *al-wāḥediya al-ẓohuriya*, the manifested dimension of the divine names; and *al-šahāda al-moṭlaqa*, the manifested aspect of the "sacred emanation" (*al-fayż al-aqdas*). As for the Worlds, they are *al-serr al-wojudi*, the existential secret; *al-kawn al-jāmeʿ*, the all-inclusive being; *al-ensān al-kāmel*, the perfect man; *al-aʿyān al-ṯābeta*, the hidden dimension of the fixed archetypes; and *al-aʿyān al-ṯābeta al-ʿelmiya*, the manifest dimension thereof (*al-Taʿliqāt*, pp. 32-4; see also Kiashemshaki, pp. 239-40).

(4) *Leqāʾ Allāh* (in Persian). This is a brief undated essay on the occasions and modalities of "meeting with God". This was published as a supplement to the *Resāla-ye Leqāʾ Allāh* of Ḥājj Mirzā Jawād Maleki, edited with an introduction and footnotes by Sayyed Aḥmad Fehri (Tehran, 1981); another edition, prepared by Ṣādeq Ḥasanzāda, includes also a brief treatise on the subject by Fayż-e Kāšāni (q.v.; d. 1679) in addition to that by Khomeini (Tehran, 1992). Referring his readers to Maleki's work for a fuller treatment of the subject, Khomeini argues that certain scholars and exegetes have blocked the path to meeting with God; they deny the witnessing of the manifestations of the divine essence and attributes, motivated in so doing by a wish to protect the divine transcendence. They interpret all the relevant verses and traditions as referring exclusively to the hereafter and the day on which reward and punishment will be dispensed. Their error is proven by Qurʾan, 53:8, which describes the ascension (*meʿrāj*) of the Prophet to the divine presence, and the purport of the *Monājāt-e šaʿbāniya*, the whispered invocation of God made by Imam ʿAli and the other Imams of the Ahl al-Bayt during the month of Šaʿbān. It is necessary in such matters to transcend formal knowledge (*ʿelm*), failing which it will act as a barrier (*Leqāʾ Allāh*, pp. 253-60).

(5) *Ḥāšiya bar Asfār* (in Persian; marginal notes on the *Asfār al-arbaʿa* of Mollā Ṣadrā). The attribution to Khomeini of a work with this title is uncertain. A hadith *qodsi*, found in both Sunni and Shiʿi sources, reads as follows: "I hesitate (*ma taradadtu*) in nothing that I do except the death of My believing servant who does not wish to die; I, too, dislike his predicament." In this *Ḥāšiya*, Khomeini is said to have taken issue with Ṣadrā's interpretation in the *Asfār* of the divine "hesitation" (*taraddod*), but since it has never been published the nature of his objection is unclear (Moḥammad Ḥasan Aḥmadi Faqih-e Yazdi, "Mafhum-e taraddod dar aḥādiṯ," *Kayhān-e andiša* 18, Ḵordād-Tir 1367/June-July 1988, p. 40). It is likewise unknown whether the *Ḥāšiya* extended to more than this one criticism, but given Khomeini's engagement with the *Asfār* during his early years in Qom, it seems likely that he did indeed compile a series of notes on the work.

COMMENTARIES ON QURʾAN AND HADITH

(1) *Tafsir-e Sura-ye ḥamd* (in Persian). This consists of the text of five lectures delivered on the Iranian television program, *Qorʾān dar ṣaḥna*, between 17 December 1979 and 11 January 1980; they were discontinued when a petition protesting against their *ʿerfān*-oriented content was launched by Javād Tehrāni, a cleric in Mashhad (see KHOMEINI i. LIFE, p. 558). By the time of their curtailment, Khomeini had not proceeded beyond the first two verses of this, the opening chapter of the Qurʾan. Several editions exist of this work, including one with a preface by ʿAli-Aṣḡar Rabbāni Ḵalḵāli and an introduction by Sayyed Mehdi Lājvardi: *Tafsir-e Sura-ye mobāraka-ye ḥamd* (Tehran, 1989; 131 pp.). Preferable, however, is the Tehran, 1996 edition, which supplements the text of his lectures (pp. 93-193) with extracts from his other works, such as *Serr al-ṣalāt* and *Ādāb al-ṣalāt*, to provide a complete commentary on *Surat al-fāteḥa*.

By way of prelude, Khomeini disclaims any intention of providing a comprehensive or authoritative treatment of this *sura*, warning at the same time against biased interpretations of the Qur'an by various categories of the unqualified, who seek to portray it as concerned exclusively either with the affairs of this world or with spiritual concerns. He then examines in detail the *basmala* ("In the Name of God"; see BESMELLĀH), the phrase that stands at the beginning of every *sura* with the exception of the ninth, *al-Tawba*. It is probable, he suggests, that it is not simply an opening formula, but syntactically connected to the verses that follow it, in this and other *suras*. The names of God are signs of His Sacred Essence, something that lies beyond the reach of man; His Essence is unknown to all but Itself. They may be understood at different levels, corresponding to the spiritual capacities of individuals. A name, moreover, is not only verbal, for the whole world is composed of signs, effectively names, that point to the divine essence, in that nothing comes into existence by itself and is dependent on that intrinsically existent Essence; contingent being points to necessary being. The divine perfections are reflected in all beings, even the inanimate and the material; by virtue of their mere existence, they glorify God. All things are, in this sense, names of God—every breath that one takes, every heartbeat and movement of the pulse (pp. 93-103).

As for the name "Allāh," it is a comprehensive manifestation of God that embraces all other manifestations, and the attributes *al-Raḥmān al-Raḥim* that follow it in the *basmala* are manifestations of that manifestation. Taken together, these first two verses of *Surat al-fāteḥa* indicate, then, that all instances of praise and admiration, including those made by individuals, inanimate objects, and heavenly bodies, ultimately revert to God; *al-ḥamd* is generic in meaning. Rational perception of the foregoing does not suffice; it must be conveyed to the heart for it to have an effect on one's life, to raise man from his defective state to one that befits him (pp. 103-13).

Given the fact that the *basmala* does not simply introduce each *sura* but is syntactically connected to it, its precise meaning varies in each instance. In the case of *al-Fāteḥa*, it may therefore be interpreted as the instrument whereby praise is offered: "Praise be to God *by means of* the name of God." Every instance of praise, by whomever it is uttered, takes place by means of God's name, and it is effectively He who is praising Himself. Another possibility is that *al-ḥamd* is not generic, but absolute praise without condition or limitation, which in its nature is beyond the abilities of man; the sense of *al-ḥamdu le'llāh* then becomes, "God, and God alone, praises Himself as He deserves."

Comprehension of much of the foregoing depends on "migrating" from the self toward God and "being overtaken by death," i.e., losing all awareness of self. This constitutes the "greater jihad" (*jehād-e akbar*), which is a prerequisite for the "lesser jihad" (*jehād-e aṣḡar*), i.e., armed conflict with the enemy (pp. 114-31).

God's relation to creation is not analogous to that of a father with his son, or of the sun with its rays, but one of manifestation, as indicated by Qurʾan, 8:17: "When you cast the dust, you did not cast it; rather God cast it." This, together with the two interpretations of praise, generic and pertaining to God alone, can be understood by inductive reasoning, but it ranks lower than the perceptions and visions of the prophets and the *awliāʾ* (q.v.). The language of the Qurʾan has seven or even seventy levels of meaning, and it is only the lowest thereof that is addressed to the commonalty. The Qurʾan, indeed, is not verbal in essence; it was "sent down on the Night of Power" (Qurʾan, 97:1) in the sense that it assumed a verbal form entrusted to the heart of the Prophet, in a visionary experience, for him to convey to mankind (pp. 132-55).

It is in the nature of things, however, that mankind cannot grasp the full meaning of the divine message. Formal knowledge, moreover, whether it be *feqh* (q.v.), gnosticism, philosophy, or the natural sciences, if pursued as a goal in its own right, leads to arrogance and presents a further obstacle to true comprehension of the divine word. What is needed is to "rise up for God" (Qurʾan, 34:46), i.e., to awaken from love of the self and all to which it is attached. Prayer, correctly understood and performed, and supplicatory invocations such as the *Doʿā-ye Komayl* (see DOʿĀ), are the most effective means for so doing (pp. 132-55).

Returning to the analysis of the *basmala*, Khomeini emphasizes that the *bāʾ* is not causative, for God's manifestation is not a matter of cause and effect, nor is His praise caused by His name. He briefly considers a tradition attributed to Imam ʿAli in which he identifies himself with the dot under the *bāʾ*, before analyzing the series of divine names mentioned in Qurʾan, 59:23. Those names fall into three categories with respect to their relationship with the name *Allāh: Allāh* stands for the Essence as such, and the names following it are in apposition to it; *Allāh* stands for the manifestation of the Essence, and the names following it are the means for that manifestation; and *Allāh* stands for the active manifestation of the Essence by means of the divine acts, and the names following it indicate those acts. Similarly complex is the understanding of two apparently contradictory pairs of attributes: "the First and the Last, the Outward and the Inward" (Qurʾan, 57:3). Whatever the mode and degree of understanding man may attain, the matter is simple: "there is nothing other than God; whatever is, is He" (p. 146). As for "the Most Beautiful Names" (Qurʾan, 17:110), they are present in all the divine attributes in absolute fashion. Another pair of terms germane to the discussion is "the unseen and the manifest" (*al-ḡayb wa'l-šahāda*). It may mean that even the natural world has a dimension that is "unseen," imperceptible to all but the prophets and the *awliāʾ*. After a final discussion of *al-Raḥmān al-Raḥim* and their connection to *Allāh*, Khomeini warns against denial of that which lies beyond one's immediate understanding and perception and is expounded by the mystics and gnostics. The Qurʾan is like a banquet of which all can partake according to their capacities and appetites (pp.156-74).

He repeats the same metaphor in the fifth and final lecture, aware, no doubt, of the growing unease his philosophical-gnostic approach was causing in some quarters. By way of further clarification, he cites the celebrated story in Rumi's *Maṯnawi* about an Arab, a Persian, and a Turk arguing, each in his own language, over what fruit they should eat, until it turns out they all wanted some grapes. Somewhat analogously, the philosophers, the mystics, and the *foqahā'* use different terminologies for that which lies beyond verbal encapsulation—the nature of reality. The closest thereto is the terminology deployed by the gnostics, grounded as it is in the supplicatory prayers of the Imams of the Ahl al-Bayt, particularly the *Doʿā-ye Šaʿbān*, which was recited by all of them. "Manifestation," for example, is preferable to the notions of causality used by the philosophers. This being the case, mysticism may not be casually dismissed. When he first went to Qom, Khomeini reminisces, the exponents of *ʿerfān* were viewed with much suspicion, but Šāhābādi, his principal instructor in the subject, insisted on addressing a group of visiting merchants on some of its topics. In similar fashion, Khomeini now finds it "incorrect to divide people into categories and pronounce some incapable of understanding these matters" (pp. 175-93). The fifth lecture turned out, however, to be the last. (An annotated translation by Hamid Algar is in Khomeini, *Islam and Revolution*, pp. 365-434.)

(2) *Tafsiri az sura-ye ʿalaq* (in Persian; n.p, n.d, 26 pp). This is a lecture on the first four verses of Qur'an, 96. The strictly exegetical part of the text is brief; it serves as point of departure for declaring that Islam is not properly understood or known by the secular jurists who have opposed the declaration of an Islamic Republic (pp. 12, 15). Its laws are immutable, and the executions it ordains are a form of mercy, comparable to the amputation of a decaying limb by a surgeon in order to preserve the life of the body (p. 13). As for the Westerners who denounce the nascent Islamic Republic, their concept of freedom is the ability to engage in gambling while half-naked (p. 26).

(3) *Taʿliqa ʿalā Šarḥ hadiṯ ra'r al-jālut,* also known as *al-Taʿliqa ʿalā al-Fawā'ed al-rażawiya* (in Arabic; Qom, 1996, 190 pp.). This is probably identical with the *Šarḥ ḥadiṯ ra's al-jālut* that Khomeini is said to have completed in 1929 (see Rāzi, *Āṯār al-ḥojja*, II, p. 45, and Dašti, p. 46). This consists of notes by Khomeini appended to the commentary by Qāżi Saʿid b. Moḥammad Mofid Qomi (q.v.; d. ca. 1107/1695) on a curious hadith recording an exchange between Imam Reżā and the exilarch (*ra's al-jālut*), head of the Jewish community in the Abbasid realm (see POLEMICS i. BETWEEN SHIʿITES AND JEWS); precisely when or where these meetings took place is unclear. The exilarch is said to have asked the Imam: "What are unbelief and faith (*imān*); what are the two forms of unbelief (*kofrān*); what are paradise and the fires (*nirān*); and what are the two satans (*al-šayṭānān*) both of whom are desired (*marjowān*)?" He then claimed that all the foregoing are mentioned in *Surat al-Raḥmān*. This clearly not being the case, the Imam chose initially to ignore the question, which emboldened the exilarch to pose another query: "What is the one, the self-multiplier, the multiple that singularizes itself, the created that creates, the fluid that is solid, the defective that is superfluous?" The Imam then decided to respond to both questions, assigning meaning even to the terms absent from *Surat al-Raḥmān*. Duly impressed, the exilarch forthwith professed his belief in Islam (text of the exchange, pp. 45-76). Qāżi Saʿid's commentary explains each of the terms involved, and Khomeini's comments on his commentary, printed in the form of lengthy, unnumbered footnotes to the text, offer further elucidation. Thus, "the self-multiplier, the multiple" (*al-motakaṯṯer al-mowaḥḥed*) is the world of the first entification (*al-taʿayyon al-awwali*) which despite its intense luminosity and the perfection of its essence, does not lack multiplicity within itself. However, at the same time, it is exalted above matter and transcends all forms of attachment, as well as spatiality and temporality (pp. 98-100).

(4) *Šarḥ-e čehel ḥadiṯ (Arbaʿin ḥadiṯ),* a commentary on forty hadith, (Tehran, 1992, 800 pp.). Completed in 1939, this is the first and lengthiest book Khomeini wrote in Persian; it is not known when he embarked on it. The title refers to a tradition found in both Sunni and Shiʿi sources, with slightly variant wording. The following is that cited by Khomeini at the very beginning of his work: "Whosever from my community preserves/memorizes (*ḥafeẓa*) forty hadith beneficial to it will be raised by God on the Day of Resurrection as a jurist and scholar" (p. 1). Khomeini was by no means the first Shiʿi scholar to select forty traditions deemed to meet the criterion of general utility; in this, he had been preceded by, among others, Shaikh Ṣaduq Ebn Bābawayh, (q.v.; d. 381/991) in *al-Keṣāl* (Qom, 1983, pp. 541-43). However, it was Khomeini who for the first time not only selected a body of forty traditions, complete with chains of transmission, but also analyzed their implications in prolix and exhaustive detail in this, one of the most voluminous of all his works. Each hadith is followed by a number of segments (*foṣul*) detailing its implications, many of them involving the citation of other hadiths.

Only the very first of the forty hadith is an injunction by the Prophet; of the remaining thirty-nine, thirty are narrated from Imam Jaʿfar al-Ṣādeq, and nine from other Imams of the Ahl al-Bayt. In the opening hadith, the Prophet is reported to have congratulated a group of believers returning from battle on fulfilling their duty of "the lesser jihad" (*al-jehād al-aṣḡar*) while exhorting them now to engage in "the greater jihad" (*al-jehād al-akbar*). When asked about the meaning of the "greater jihad," he responded: "it is the jihad against the appetitive soul" (*jehād al-nafs*) (pp. 3-27). This definition serves as prelude to the citation and examination of ten hadith identifying vices and errors that need to be combated: *riyā* (hypocrisy), *ʿojb* (arrogance), *kebr* (pride), *ḥesādat* (envy), *ḥobb-e donyā* (love of the world), *ḡażab* (anger), *nefāq* (duplicity), *ʿaṣabiat* (tribalism), *hawā-ye nafs* (capricious impulses of the lower self), and *derāzi-ye ārzu* (long-term or unrestrained desires) (pp. 35-178).

Of the remaining twenty-nine hadith interpreted by Khomeini, eleven relate to virtues and desirable practices, suggesting, perhaps, that once the vices and errors have been repelled, the way will be clear for moral and spiritual advancement. The eleven are: *tafakkor,* reflection (pp. 189-212); *tawakkol*, placing one's trust in God (pp. 213-20); *ḵawf wa rajā',* fear and hope (pp. 221-33); *emteḥān*, the endurance of divine testing (pp. 235-52); *ṣabr*, patience (pp. 253-70); *tawba*, repentance (pp. 221-

86); *ḏekr-e ḵodā*, the remembrance of God (pp. 287-97); *eḵlāṣ*, sincerity (pp. 321-35); *šokr*, thankfulness (pp. 337-55); *ʿebādat wa hożur-e qalb*, worship with the presence of the heart (pp. 425-49); and *yaqin wa reżā*, certainty and contentment (pp. 557-65).

The others relate to a variety of moral and creedal concerns: *karāhat az marg*, abhorrence of death (pp. 357-65); *aṣnāf-e juyandagān-e ʿelm*, categories of those who seek knowledge (pp. 367-83); *aqsām-e ʿelm*, the divisions of knowledge (pp. 385-97); *šakk wa waswās*, doubt and uncertainty (pp. 399-410); *fażilat-e ʿelm*, the excellence of knowledge (pp. 411-23); *leqāʾ Allāh*, the meeting with God (pp. 451-66); *waṣāyā-ye rasul be amir al-moʾmenin*, the testamentary counsels of the Prophet to the Commander of the Believers, ʿAli b. Abi Ṭāleb (pp. 467-524); *aqsām-e qolub*, different types of hearts (pp. 525-37); *ʿolum-e maʿrefat-e ḥaqiqi*, the sciences of true cognition (pp. 539-56); *welāyat wa aʿmāl*, trustworthiness in one's deeds (pp. 567-80); *maqām-e moʾmen nazd-e Ḥaqq-e Taʿālā*, the station of the believer in the view of God (pp. 581-96); *maʿrefat-e asmāʾ-e Ḥaqq wa masʾala-ye jabr wa tafwiż*, knowledge of the divine names and the question of predestination and free will (pp. 597-604); *ṣefāt-e Ḥaqq*, the attributes of God (pp. 605-20); *maʿrefat-e Ḵodā wa rasul wa uli'l-amr*, the knowledge of God, the Messenger, and the holders of authority (pp. 621-29); *āfarineš-e Ādam bar ṣurat-e ḵodāvand*, the creation of Adam in the form of God (pp. 631-37); *ḵayr o šarr*, good and evil (pp. 639-48); *sura-ye tawḥid wa āḡāz-e sura-ye ḥadid* a commentary on Sura 112 (*al-Eḵlāṣ*) and the opening verses of Sura 57 (*al-Ḥadid*) (pp. 649-61).

(5) *Mobāraza bā nafs yā jehād-e akbar* (in Persian). In October 1972, shortly before the beginning of Ramadan 1392, Khomeini gave a series of lectures to the religious students (*ṭollāb*) of Najaf on the same subject, the greater jihad, that he discussed first among the *Forty Hadith*. He exhorted his listeners to ponder on the hadith that the fasting believers are the guests of God during the month of Ramadan. Further, he reminded them of the enduring need to transcend the technical niceties of *feqh* in order to struggle against both the appetitive self and the plots of the imperialists. The transcript of the lectures was first published in Najaf soon after their delivery under the title *Mobāraza bā nafs yā jehād-e akbar*; numerous other editions also exist, the most recent published in Tehran in 1992 (71 pp.)

(6) *Šarḥ-e ḥadiṯ-e jonud-e ʿaql wa jahl* ("Commentary on the Hadith of the Battalions of Intelligence and Ignorance"; in Persian; Tehran, 1998, 503 pp.). Khomeini completed this work in 1944 in Maḥallāt, a cool and windy city where, according to his annotation at the very end of the book (p. 429), he had gone to escape the extreme heat prevailing in Qom.

In this lengthy hadith, Jaʿfar al-Ṣādeq depicts intelligence and ignorance as personified entities, deploying their forces against each other in unending combat; recognizing them is a source of guidance for the believers. Asked for an explanation, Imam Jaʿfar clarifies that intelligence is the first being created by God from His own light, to the right of His throne; when He told it to turn away, it did so; and when He told it to turn toward Him, it did so. He then informed intelligence that He had exalted it over all His creation. Next, He created ignorance from a salt-laden, dark sea, and addressed it with the same two commands He had given intelligence, but ignorance failed to obey, so God cursed it. Seventy-five battalions were accorded to intelligence, a favor that aroused envy in ignorance, who protested that, like intelligence, although its exact opposite, he too was part of God's creation and therefore deserved his own seventy-five battalions. There then follows a complete enumeration of the seventy-five battalions deployed by each side, pairs of opposing attributes such as justice and injustice, and compassion and anger (pp. 17-19).

In a series of sections, subsections, and chapters, Khomeini's somewhat diffuse and terminologically complex commentary covers a broad range of topics relating directly or indirectly to the hadith, most of them focusing on questions of spiritual or moral advancement. The work can be characterized as a complex manual of ethical self-improvement. Less tightly organized than his commentary on the forty hadith, but like it, this work often discusses opposing pairs of conduct and character. On the title page (p. 73), Khomeini disclaims any intention to be exhaustive, and on its last page (p. 429), he expresses the hope to return to the topic at some time in the future.

Among the topics he discusses at some length is the meaning of *imān* (faith); it is distinct from knowledge and perception, for they relate to intelligence while *imān* relates to the heart. The attainment of knowledge of God, the angels, the prophets, and resurrection does not suffice to qualify one as a believer, for Satan also had this knowledge and God calls him an unbeliever. Likewise, a philosopher may employ philosophical proofs for the oneness of God and its degrees, but this does not make of him a believer because those proofs have not established themselves in his heart. Intelligence, therefore, can serve only as a prelude to belief. The very word *imān* lexically implies "confidence" (*eṭmeʾnān*) and "humility" (*ḵożuʿ*), these being qualities of the heart (pp. 87-89).

None of this means, as Khomeini makes clear in a later section of this work, that knowledge is worthless. But its highest form is the knowledge of the divine names, for God taught them to Adam as a title of his superiority to the angels (cf. Qur'an, 2:31-33). It is not a form of knowledge obtained by deduction, by recourse to various abstract concepts, for such a process would not explain the exalting of Adam above the angels. It is rather a knowledge of the reality of the names, an awareness of the evanescence of the created in the Ultimate Reality (*roʾyat-e fanāʾ-e ḵalq dar Ḥaqq*). Khomeini then adduces a further series of Qur'anic verses in elucidation of the primordial knowledge bestowed on man (pp. 263-68).

The *nafs* is the battleground for the battalions of intelligence and ignorance, so tempering the instincts and impulses of the self (*taʿdil-e qowā-ye nafsāniya*) is extremely important; failure to do so will result in great and irreparable loss. It may take place at any time that man is in the natural realm (*ʿālam-e ṭabiʿat*), but it is best that it begin in childhood, for a child is like a blank sheet of paper that passively accepts whatever is inscribed on it. Primarily responsible are the father and mother, particularly the former, for he has to choose a pious and observant teacher for his offspring. Habits and characteristics acquired in childhood will for better or worse have their impact on society as a whole. If correction or reform is required, then it is best to undertake the task while still possessing the vigor of youth, but the possibility of redemption remains even in old age (pp. 155-57).

A particularly significant pair of opposites is light (*nur*) and darkness (*ẓolumāt*), the former being singular in a number of Qur'anic verses and the latter, plural. Thus Qurʾan, 2:257, "God is the Protector of those who believe; He brings them forth from darkness into light"—when taken in conjunction with Qurʾan, 39:69, "the earth will shine with the light of its Lord"—may be taken to mean the following: the various forms of darkness that beset man's earthly existence will be dispelled by the absolute light of God's absolute oneness (pp. 270-71). Other diametrically opposed pairs are understanding (*fahm*) and idiocy (*ḥomq*) (pp. 269-76); humility (*tawāżoʿ*) and arrogance (*takabbor*) (pp. 333-55); prudent reticence (*ṣamt*) and empty, meaningless talk (*hadayān*) (pp. 385-96); patience (*ṣabr*) and disquiet or anxiety (*jazaʿ*) (pp. 409-23).

ON FEQH

(1) *Resāla fi taʿyin al-fajr fi'l-layāli al-moqmera* ("Determining the Onset of Dawn on Moonlit Nights"; in Arabic). This is a twenty-two-page essay, published in Qom in 1988. The date of its composition is uncertain.

(2) *Manāhej al-woṣul elā ʿelm al-oṣul* (in Arabic). Completed in 1941, this detailed work on the principles and methodology of *feqh* was published in two volumes in Tehran in 1994, with an introduction and notes by Ayatollah Fāżel Lankarāni (d. 2007), who had studied the subject with him in Qom and praises him for his innovative methods. Khomeini frequently cites the views of other scholars, both past and present, sometimes respectfully taking issue with them.

The first volume is devoted primarily to questions of language as they affect the discipline of *ʿelm al-oṣul*. After a definition of the discipline (I, pp. 45-50) come a whole series of clarifications, such as the need to take into account changes in the sense of words and expressions, and the lack of an essential connection between words and their meanings, for changes take place and complexities emerge as human life develops, and words may acquire a plurality of meanings (I, pp. 51, 55). The significance of particles, or the lack thereof, must also be taken into consideration (I, p. 57). The purpose is to establish rules whereby the divine ordinances and practical duties may be deduced from words and expressions. Topics that arise in this connection are the meanings of letters, and the problem of words that may be understood either as metaphorical (*majāz*) or taken in their literal sense (*ḥaqiqa*), a problem capable of solution by establishing the sense in which a word is commonly understood (I, pp. 102-5). Important, too, is distinguishing between the meanings of a word occurring both in the *šariʿa* and in common usage (*ʿorf*). Even apart from this distinction, words may be used in more than one sense (I, pp. 170-80). The derivation of words from the same root (*ešteqāq*) does not necessarily imply a uniformity of significance (I, p. 187). Next to be addressed is the question of whether an imperative is a simple command or implies an obligation (*wājeb*) (I, pp. 235-41). Connected to questions of language is the nature of reward and punishment in the hereafter (I, pp. 378-84).

The second volume opens with a consideration of whether the command to perform a certain act implies the prohibition of its opposite (II, pp. 7-58). Then, there is an examination of what in its own right constitutes a prohibition, one consideration being whether some form of corruption (*fasād*) is at issue (II, pp. 103-79). Also important is the distinction between the general (*al-ʿāmm*) and the specific (*al-ḵāṣṣ*) in terms of applicability, and that between the absolute (*al-moṭlaq*) and the specific (*al-moqayyad*) (II, pp. 229-307, 313-39).

(3) *Al-Rasāʾel* (in Arabic). This is a collection of five treatises written by Khomeini between 1949 and 1954, each relating to one of the subjects he taught in his lectures on *oṣul-e feqh*. Edited and annotated by Mojtabā Tehrāni (d. 2013) with the approval of Khomeini, it was published in Qom in 1964 in two sections bound together in a single volume, with each section separately paginated.

The first treatise, completed in 1949, deals with the principle of *lā żarar* (more fully, *lā żarar wa lā żerār*), neither inflicting harm on another nor retaliating for harm inflicted on one, a principle derived from a hadith of the Prophet (pp. 6-68). The same treatise was published separately in Qom in 1993 in 176 pages under the title *Badāʿi al-dorar fi qāʿedat nafy al-żarar*. The second treatise is devoted to *esteṣḥāb*—the presumption of continued validity for a ruling related to a pre-existing situation, unless it can be proven that a newly emerging situation negates or invalidates that ruling (pp. 70-358). The third treatise, coming first in the second section of *al-Rasāʾel*, concerns *al-taʿādol wa'l-tarjiḥ*, "balance and preference," the course of action to be taken when confronted with two or more apparently contradictory or incompatible hadith (pp. 4-92). Next come *al-ejtehād wa al-taqlid*, the qualities required in a *faqih* for him to act as a *marjaʿ al-taqlid*, and the prerogatives (*ḏekr šoʾun al-faqih*) that may be exercised by a duly qualified *faqih*, including judgeship and governance, this essentially constituting an early adumbration of *welāyat al-faqih*, the doctrine central to the foundation of the Islamic Republic (pp. 94-172). This treatise, written in 1951, was also published separately in Qom in 1979. Finally, *al-taqiya*, "prudential dissimulation or concealment," because of either fear or caution, is discussed, including the circumstances under which it is obligatory, permitted, or forbidden (pp. 174-210). Of particular interest is the consideration of the validity of prayer performed in a congregation of Sunnis (*al-ʿāmma*) p. 198-201, a topic that gained Khomeini's attention anew after the revolution (see below, *Esteftāʿāt*).

(4) *Taʿliqa ʿalā Kefāyat al-oṣul* (in Arabic). These are glosses on *Kefāyat al-oṣul* by Āḵund Moḥammad-Kāẓem Ḵorasāni (q.v.; d. 1911), written in 1948.

(5) *Taʿliqa ʿalā al-ʿOrwa al-woṯqā* (in Arabic). This provides glosses on *al-ʿOrwa al-woṯqā* by Sayyed Moḥammad-Kāẓem Yazdi, a collection of legal rulings that he compiled in 1919, the year of his death. Khomeini completed this work in 1955, and it was published soon thereafter in Qom, in 345 pages. To avoid hostile scrutiny of the work by the shah's regime, Khomeini was identified on the title page simply as "Ḵ".

(6) *Taʿliqa ʿalā Wasilat al-najāt* (in Persian). *Fatwā*s (q.v.) of Khomeini are arranged to form a commentary on *Wasilat al-najāt* by Sayyed Abu'l-Ḥasan Eṣfahāni (q.v.; d. 1946), an *ʿālem* politically active in both Iraq and Iran during World War I and its immediate aftermath. When Khomeini finished this work is unknown. It was first published separately in Qom (n.d., in 225 pp.) and then together with the *Wasilat al-najāt* itself.

(7) *Ketāb al-ṭahāra* (in Arabic). This four-volume work in Arabic on ritual purity originated in classes given by Khomeini in Qom between 1954 and 1957. The first volume deals with *najāsāt* (objects intrinsically unclean); volume two, with *al-demāʾ al-ṯalāṯa* (menstrual, extra-menstrual, and postnatal bleeding); volume three, with *tayammom* (ritual purification with clean earth or soil); and volume four, with *aḥkam al-najāsāt* (rulings concerning unclean objects). The complete work was published in Najaf in 1969 in 1,202 pages. Ṣādeq Ḵalḵāli's *al-Demāʾ al-ṯalāṯa* (Qom, n.d., 479 pp.), is based on the notes he took in Khomeini's class on this subject; several years later, it was reviewed and approved for publication by Khomeini himself.

(8) *Resāla-ye najāt al-ʿebād* (in Persian). This consists of three volumes on the rulings of *feqh*. The second volume, on subjects ranging from *makāseb-e moḥarrama* (forbidden modes of earning) to divorce, was published in Qom in 1961, in 155 pages.

(9) *Ḥāšiya bar Resāla-ye erṯ* (in Persian). Khomeini's *fatwā*s on the topic of inheritance are arranged to form a commentary on a work dealing with the subject by Mollā Hāšem Ḵorāsāni. It was published in Qom (n.d., 120 pp.).

(10) *Al-Makāseb al-moḥarrama* ("Forbidden Modes of Earning /Lucrative Activities"; in Arabic). Completed in 1961, this two-volume work was first published in Qom the following year; the Tehran 1995 edition, copiously annotated with references to earlier authorities, runs to a total 1,023 pages in two volumes.

The first four sections prohibit trading in objects intrinsically impure (*najes al-ʿayn*, I, pp. 9 158); in things intended for illicit use (I, pp. 161-236); in things that serve no purpose (I, pp. 237-50); and in that which is intrinsically illicit (*mā howa ḥarām fi nafseh*) or held to be so (I, pp. 251-70). This fourth segment is, perhaps, the most interesting, for some of the rulings Khomeini puts forth in it count as innovative. This applies, for example, to the topic of *taṣwir*, the making of images, either in the form of statues or by way of pictorial representation. Traditions prohibiting the making of idols cannot be taken as outlawing all forms of sculpture, Khomeini argues; if the Prophet forbade sculpture even after the destruction of the idols in the courtyard of the Kaʿba, it was because the Arabs had not yet been fully purged of their idolatrous tendencies. Statues produced in modern times form a completely different category (I, pp. 268-70). Busts and statues of cultural heroes such as Ferdowsi have indeed remained in place after the revolution, and they have been joined by others, such as Biruni (q.v.) and Sohrawardi. As for painting, its permissibility can be deduced from Khomeini's declaration that "there is no proof for the prohibition (of *taṣwir*) of other than statues" (I, p. 267).

Next comes an extremely prolix discussion of *ḡenāʾ*, a term that, though commonly taken to mean "singing," defies a one-word translation (I, pp. 299-356). It opens with an analysis of *Rawżat al-ḡenāʾ*, a treatise on the subject by Shaikh Moḥammad-Reżā Eṣfahāni (d. 1943), who had been one of Khomeini's instructors in Qom (see translation by Reżā Ostādi, "Tarjoma-ye Resāla-ye rawżat al-ḡenāʾ," *Kayhān-e Andiša* 18, Ḵordād-Tir 1367/May-June 1988, pp. 104-16). The primary meaning of *ḡenāʾ* is a pleasant or melodious voice, a manifestation of beauty that induces *ṭarab* in the hearer, a state of joy or excitement. Insofar as *ṭarab* may be frivolous or even immoral in nature, Qurʾan, 22:30, "shun the word that is false (*qawl al-zur*)," has been cited as proof for the prohibition of *ḡenāʾ*; this, however, is rejected by Khomeini (I, pp. 306-7). Similarly, Qurʾan 31:6, "There are those who buy frivolous talk (*lahw al-ḥadiṯ*) in order to lead people astray from the path of God, taking it as an object of ridicule; they shall suffer a humiliating torment," cannot be taken as grounds for the impermissibility of all *ḡenāʾ*. Distinct from frivolous talk are homilies, elegies, *ḏekr* and Qurʾanic recitation, all of which count as *ḡenāʾ* if performed in a pleasing voice (I, p. 317). Similarly permissible is *ḡenāʾ* on ʿId al-Feṭr (see FASTING) and ʿId-al-Ażḥā; this may be extended to certain national holidays (*baʿż al-aʿyād al-qawmiya*) (I, p. 330). Beyond the devotional context, singing when accompanying a bride to the home of her groom (*al-zefāf*) is unobjectionable (I, p. 330). Unconditionally forbidden is the playing of wind instruments (*mezmār*), for they may induce a descent into merriment (*tafriḥ*) (I, p. 329). Likewise to be avoided, as a matter of caution, are "certain types of frivolous songs to which people in the bazaar (*ahl al-suq*) now listen, since they may form a forbidden category of *ḡenāʾ*" (I, p. 369).

In July 1979, the broadcasting on radio and television of music other than traditional religious chants and revolutionary anthems (*sorudhā-ye enqelābi*) was banned. Later, however, in a somewhat vague and perhaps deliberately ambiguous *fatwā* dated 19 March 1987, Khomeini decreed that most musical performances were not "reprehensible" (*makruh*), and instruments that could be used for either legitimate or illegitimate purposes (*ālāt-e moštaraka*) should not be banned (see Schirazi, p. 67). Persian classical music has enjoyed particular favor on state radio and television.

The first volume concludes with a minute and detailed examination of what constitutes slander or backbiting (*ḡayba*), an appropriate topic for inclusion among the forbidden modes of earning insofar as a desire for material gain may be the aim of the offender (I, pp. 381-480).

Intrinsically illicit and therefore prohibited are also all forms of gambling and games of chance. This extends to chess and backgammon, even when not accompanied by gambling, for the term *maysar*, interpreted to include these two, is coupled in Qurʾan, 2:219 and 5:90, 91, with wine drinking as a major sin. It is also forbidden for children to compete with each while playing with nutshells. On the other hand, pigeon racing, archery, and competitions to see who can throw camel shoes or arrowheads the farthest are licit, as long as no betting is involved (II, pp. 7-47). After the revolution, chess was banned for about a decade, but its popularity remained, and Khomeini was asked "if chess entirely discards its aspect of gambling and, as is the case today, serves the purpose of mental exercise, is playing it permitted?" He answered: "If there is no loss or gain involved, it is unobjectionable" (undated *fatwā* in *Esteftāʾāt*, II, p. 10). Iran now fields a national chess team that competes in international tournaments.

After a detailed examination of gains to be made by lying in a transaction (II, pp. 48-141) comes a list of prohibitions relating to the public and political sphere. It is impermissible to earn income or benefit from service to a "tyrant" (*jāʾer*), which may be taken to mean any illegitimate ruler (II, pp. 142-58), or from exercising authority on his behalf (*al-welāya men qebal al-jāʾer*). Exemptions may be permitted if under certain circumstances such conduct secures a benefit for the general public (II, pp. 159-254). Awards made by a tyrannical ruler or his agents may be permissible, again under certain circumstances (II, 235-414). Categorically impermissible is profiting from doing that which in its nature is obligatory (II, pp. 256-331).

(11) *Tawżiḥ al-masāʾel* (in Persian). This work began as a re-editing of Ayatollah Ḥosayn Borujerdi's (q.v.; d. 1961) book with the same title. Even in Borujerdi's lifetime, it was felt by a number of the *ʿolamāʾ* in Qom that Borujerdi's text deserved to be refashioned in order to make it more accessible to the common believers, and two of them, Ḥājj Šayḵ ʿAli Karbāsči and ʿAli-Aṣḡar Faqihi, undertook the task. After Borujerdi's death, Khomeini wrote a commentary (*ḥāšiya*) that was then merged with Borujerdi's text and published as *Tawżiḥ al-masāʾel-e Emām Ḵomeyni*. This completed the process of declaring his availability as a *marjʿa-e taqlid* after the demise of Borujerdi. Some early editions omitted Khomeini's name on the title page to avoid censorship by the shah's regime. Since 1962, it has been re-published many times by different organizations, often with neither place nor date of publication; sometimes it bears the title *Resāla-ye aḥkām* (e.g., the edition published in Tehran in 1980).

Tawżiḥ al-masāʾel may be described as a handbook for the conscientious follower (*moqalled*); proofs from the Qurʾan and hadith are accordingly left unmentioned. In keeping with the tradition of the genre of this type of manual, detailed rules are supplied for all the situations the believer might ever encounter, however unlikely some of them may seem, the purpose being to demonstrate the comprehensive applicability and the practical utility of *feqh*. The number of topics (*masʾala*) varies slightly from one edition to another; thus, the Tehran edition of 1980 covers 2,785 topics; another, also entitled *Resāla-ye aḥkām*, but without place or date of publication, includes 2,887; and yet another, published in Tehran and undated, covers 2,890. Given the broad audience to which it was addressed, the attention it paid to their practical concerns, and the numerous editions in which it appeared, it is probable that it received more attention than any other of his works.

The first section deals with the incumbent nature of *taqlid* and the means whereby the common believer can determine the "most learned" (*mojtahed-e aʿlam*) to follow (1980 Tehran edition, pp. 1-3). Lengthy and extremely detailed is the section devoted to *ṭahārat* (ritual cleanliness or purity): objects and substances that count as unclean (*najes*) are enumerated, and instructions are provided for dealing with various anatomical conditions and bodily discharges (pp. 4-80). Then come regulations for *namāz* (pp. 80-168), complete with a Persian translation of the Qurʾanic *suras* and formulae recited during the prayer (pp. 123-24); for fasting (pp. 168-87); for the calculation and payment of *ḵoms* (pp. 188-98); the types of property on which *zakāt* is payable and the uses to which it should be put (pp. 199-217); and the performance of the hajj (pp. 218-19).

Next come a whole series of economic and financial situations: buying and selling (pp. 220-31); the formation and functioning of companies, even if they consist of only two people (pp. 232-34); *ṣolḥ*, in the sense of voluntarily assigning one's property to another person (pp. 235-36); renting (pp. 237-41); *joʿāla*, the promise of recompense to someone for undertaking a given task (pp. 242-43); *mozāraʿa*, meaning that a landowner permits a farmer to cultivate his land for a share of the crop (pp. 244-45); *mosāqāt*, the undertaking by an owner of fruit trees to give someone a share of the fruit in exchange for keeping the trees watered (pp. 246-47); *wekāla*, managing the property of children who have not attained puberty and that of the mentally disabled (pp. 248-50); loans (pp. 251-52); *ḥawāla*, the transfer by the creditor of a debt to someone other than the original borrower (pp. 253-54); *rahn*, the lien placed on a borrower's property (pp. 255-56); *żāmen*, serving as guarantor for the repayment of a debt (pp. 257-58); *kafālat*, undertaking to pay someone's debt on his behalf whenever the borrower demands that he do so (p. 259); *wadiʿa*, entrusting one's property to someone else for safe keeping (pp. 260-62); and *ʿāria*, loaning one's property to another free of charge (pp. 263-64). These rulings pertained to practices prevalent in Iranian society at the time.

Of more general relevance are the minute regulations on marriage and childbearing (pp. 265-78), including the provision of a suitable wetnurse for an infant when the mother is unable to lactate (p. 277); and on divorce (pp. 279-84).

Next come detailed regulations concerning the usurpation of property (*ḡaṣb*), a major sin (pp. 285-87); what to do with property the owner of which is unknown (pp. 288-90); slaughtering animals for consumption and hunting them, using either firearms or dogs, and fishing (pp. 291-97); the conditions under which locusts may permissibly be eaten (p. 297); which birds it is permissible to eat and which liquids it is permissible to drink (pp. 298-300); how to make a formal vow to undertake a good deed (*naḏr*; 301-3); the penalties incumbent on one who violates an oath (pp. 304-5); and conditions for establishing a charitable foundation (*waqf*, pp. 306-8).

Most editions of *Tawżiḥ al-masāʾel* include an appendix (*molḥaqāt*) consisting of rulings on modern topics of concern (*masāʾel mostaḥdaṯa*) as well as innovative solutions to other, longstanding problems (see, for example, the Tehran edition of 1980, pp. 321-36). The source is *Taḥrir al-wasila*, a work in Arabic completed by Khomeini in 1969 and intended for scholars of *feqh*; the rulings are expounded there in great detail, with the citation of proofs from the Qur'an and hadith (see below, *Taḥrir al-wasila*). The purpose for including them, in Persian and simplified form, in *Tawżiḥ al-masāʾel* was plainly to make them available to the *moqalledin*. The *molḥaqāt* are also said to have been published separately.

First comes a re-examination of "enjoining the good and forbidding the evil" (*amr be maʿruf wa nahy az monkar*; see AMR BE MAʿRUF). It is a duty that must be fulfilled, either individually or collectively; if a verbal reminder to the offender does not suffice, it is permissible to beat him, but not too harshly (p. 321-25). At issue, however, is far more than sins committed by the common man, such as the consumption of alcohol. The forms of evil to be forbidden include the receipt of monies by the *ʿolamāʾ* or their students in the madrasas from *awqāf* administered by the state; such interference by the state is the prelude to the destruction of the foundations of Islam in accordance with the desires of the imperialists, as has already happened or is about to happen in all Muslim countries (p. 322).

Comparable in tone and purport to the preceding is the section relating to defense (*defāʿ*), broadly defined to extend beyond repelling military aggression. For Khomeini, it is certainly the duty of all Muslims, whether individually or collectively, to defend any Muslim land that comes under attack, but beyond that they should resist all plans by foreigners leading to their dominance in any Muslim land; prevent any expansion of foreign political, economic or commercial influence liable to result in the domination of a Muslim land; oppose political relations between a Muslim government and a foreign power leading to domination by the latter; and combat all forms of commercial relations with a foreign power liable to damage the national economy. If a Muslim country establishes commercial or political relations detrimental to the interest of Islam and the Muslims, all Muslim states must force the government in question to sever those ties. Finally, commercial and political dealings with "certain countries" that are pawns in the hands of Israel must be opposed by whatever means necessary as they are traitors to Islam; the same applies to merchants that deal with Israel (pp. 326-27). This set of injunctions may be regarded as a blueprint for Iranian foreign policy after the revolution.

In another significant ruling, Khomeini condemns as a violation of Islam dictated by foreign powers the Family Protection Law of 1967, revised in 1975, that deprived husbands of the unilateral right to divorce their wives and assigned to civil courts the right to dissolve a marriage at the request of either a husband or a wife. The aim, he declared, was to destroy the Muslim family; if a woman, after obtaining a court-ordered divorce, remarried, she would count as an adulteress (p. 328). The regulations that came into effect after the revolution in September 1979 were not, however, totally dissimilar from the earlier law: they provided for the appearance before a special civil court of a couple seeking divorce from each other; if the court was unable to reconcile them with each other, the divorce was granted (see, DIVORCE iv. DIVORCE IN MODERN PERSIA).

Not all the rulings contained in the *Molḥaqāt* have political implications. Several relate to financial dealings, such as *softa*, a promissory note; *sarqofli*, the unrefundable payment made by the renter of a property to its owner to secure the lease; banking transactions; and insurance (pp. 329-33). Lotteries (*baḵtāzmāʾi*) are categorically forbidden as a form of gambling, even if disguised by the state as a form of charitable expenditure (*eʿāna-ye melli* "national assistance"; pp. 333-34). Of greater practical importance, perhaps, are Khomeini's rulings on artificial insemination (*talqiḥ*), permissible on condition that it is the husband's semen that is injected into the womb (p. 334); and the dissection of corpses—those of non-Muslims may legitimately be dissected, but those of Muslims only if non-Muslim corpses are unavailable, and then only to save the life of a Muslim, not for purposes of anatomical instruction (pp. 335-36; also discussed at greater length in *Taḥrir al-wasila*, below).

Ḵātema, the concluding section of the *molḥaqāt*, includes a prohibition of eating the meat of animals mechanically slaughtered or imported from non-Muslim countries (p. 336). Strongly discouraged or even forbidden in the circumstances prevailing at the time is the possession of radio and television sets, for that which is broadcast consists largely of music, the propagation of laws contrary to Islam, and the praise of "traitors and tyrants" (p. 336).

A Clarification of Questions (Boulder, Colo., 1984), J. Borujerdi's translation of *Tawżiḥ al-masāʾel*, with an introduction by Michael Fischer and Mehdi Abedi, suffers from misspellings, a clumsiness of diction, and an insistence on the misleadingly literal rendering of Persian idioms; thus, *namāz gozārdan* (performing prayer) is repeatedly translated as "laying a prayer" (pp. 175-89).

(12) *Zobdat al-aḥkām* (in Arabic; Tehran, 1983, 273 pp.). This is composed of selected rulings from the *Taḥrir al-wasila* and other works; no editor or compiler is mentioned.

(13) *Taḥrir al-wasila* (in Arabic). Having already written a commentary on the *Wasilat al-najāt* of Sayyed Abu'l-Ḥasan Eṣfahāni while in Qom, Khomeini decided dur-

ing his period of exile in Turkey to merge his commentary with the text itself and to add to it several chapters lacking in the original. It was first published in Najaf in 1969, in two volumes with a total of 1,309 pages. It has subsequently been reprinted many times (e.g., in Beirut, 1982) and translated into Persian by Moḥammad-Bāqer Musavi Hamadāni. After the revolution, it became a textbook regularly taught in the *ḥawza*, and, for the benefit of a less specialized readership, a selection of the rulings it contained was published, in Arabic, under the title *Zobdat al-aḥkām* (mentioned above).

The first volume details the standard prescriptions of *feqh*: the *taqlid* incumbent on the common believer (*al-ʿāmmi*) and his obligation to choose the "most learned" (*al-aʿlam*; I, pp. 5-11); ritual purity (*ṭahāra*; I, pp. 12-134); prayer (I, pp. 135-274); fasting (I, pp. 278-310); *zakāt* (I, pp. 311-50); *ḵoms* (I, pp. 352-69); and hajj (I, pp. 370-461).

Next, the duty of "enjoining the good and forbidding the evil" (*al-amr be'l-maʿruf wa'l-nahy ʿan al-monkar)*, as expounded in Qur'an, 3:104 and 9:71, is discussed in some detail as "the most exalted and honorable of duties" (I, pp. 462-84). There are varying degrees of evil, and the danger that may be incurred by those combating them needs to be weighed against the expected benefit. The oppressiveness of rulers, counting as a major form of evil, must always be opposed, especially by the religious scholars, even if their opposition does not yield an immediate result; failure to do so would be a disgrace (I, pp. 473-75). In society at large, "forbidding the evil" is to be undertaken by expressing disapproval, or in some cases coercive intervention; the implementation of *šarʿi* penalties is, however, reserved for duly qualified scholars of the law (I, pp. 476-84).

Such is the importance of "enjoining the good and forbidding the evil" that after the revolution it was incorporated in the Constitution of the Islamic Republic. Article Eight reads in part: "Summoning men to good by enjoining good and forbidding evil is a universal and mutual duty that must be fulfilled by the people with respect to each other, by the government with respect to the people, and by the people with respect to the government. The conditions, limits, and nature of this duty will be specified by law." In order to implement the principle, very soon after the revolution, patrols known as Gašt-e Ṯaʾr-Allāh ("God's Vengeance Patrols") began policing the streets of Tehran; their primary concern was monitoring women's observance of *ḥejāb*. Less fearsome in name but identical in function is the Gašt-e Eršād ("Guidance Patrol"), active since the early 2000s.

Distinctive is Khomeini's discussion of "defense" (*defāʿ*) in this context of basic religious duties, for it goes beyond and precedes the right to defend one's person and property. Incumbent on the believers as a collective duty is the defense of Muslim lands, even during the occultation of the Imam and without seeking the permission of his deputy. This duty extends to combating the entrenchment of all foreign political or economic influence detrimental to the interests of the Muslims, in whatever Muslim state it may be (I, pp. 485-87). It is only after the expounding of this collective duty that Khomeini turns his attention to the defense of one's person and property (I, pp. 487-92)

The final topic of volume one is "modes of earning and trading" (*al-makāseb wa al-matājer*) (I, pp. 493-656). First comes a section on forbidden modes of earning (*al-makāseb al-moḥarrama*), a subject Khomeini had expansively addressed seven years earlier in his book with that title (I, pp. 493-503). The discussion of *taṣwir* and *ḡenāʾ* (I, pp. 496-97) reflect in concise form the relatively lenient views expressed earlier in *al-Makāseb al-moḥarrama* (I, pp. 496-97). Categorically forbidden is magic in all its forms, such as summoning the jinn and the angels, fortune telling, predicting rainfall or draught, and recourse to astrology (I, pp. 498-99). Then follow regulations for thirty-seven types of financial and commercial transactions, organized under twelve headings (I, pp. 504-656).

The exhaustive discussion of the traditional topics of *feqh* continues in the second volume. Included are, for example, regulations concerning *ṣadaqa* (charitable donations) (II, pp. 90-93); questions relating to marriage, such as the permissibility of anal intercourse, reprehensible though it may be (II, p. 241); the impermissibility of marriage to non-Muslims (II, pp. 285-87); the upkeep (*nafaqa*) owed by a husband to his wife, offspring, and other relatives (II, pp. 313-24); the modalities of divorce (II, pp. 325-47); inheritance (II, pp. 363-402); the qualities that must define a judge (II, pp. 404-10); and the compensation (*dia*, q.v.) to be paid for various types of bodily injury (II, 570-86).

Of greater interest and originality than the foregoing is the section on *al-masāʾel al-mostaḥdaṯa* ("questions relating to modern concerns") (II, pp. 608-39). Here, Khomeini discusses in detail, with supporting evidence, some of the questions relating to financial dealings later included in the *Molḥaqāt* in summary form. In addition, he rules on insurance (permitted; II, p. 608) and a variety of banking transactions (II, pp. 616-19)

Entirely innovative are his rulings concerning medical procedures such as artificial insemination, permitted on condition it is the husband's sperm that is inserted into the womb of the wife (II, 621). The dissection of a dead Muslim is forbidden, but that of a non-Muslim, *ḏemmi* or other, is permissible; if a non-Muslim corpse is unavailable, then that of a Muslim may be dissected, but only to save the life of a Muslim, not for purposes of medical instruction or research. The topic acquired a certain urgency in the course of the revolution when the supply of corpses from India used for instruction in medical schools dried up. Grafts and organ transplantation are, however, permitted under certain conditions (II, p. 624).

Sex change is permitted, if a person has inclinations contrary to his or her biological gender. If both a husband and wife undergo the relevant procedure and reverse roles, it is advisable that they remarry each other. The guardianship of a minor child born of the first marriage should be assigned to the paternal grandfather (II, pp. 626-28). It may be noted in this connection that, after the revolution, Khomeini was visited by a male who sought transformation into a female; he is said to have given him/her a letter authorizing the procedure, which ultimately took place in 1997 (see "The Ayatollah and the Transsexual," *The Independent,* 25 November 2004). Sex-reassignment surgery is now even subsidized by the state.

Radio, television and tape recorders have both legitimate and illegitimate uses. It is permissible to listen to the news and to sermons and to view images of permitted objects such as "the wonders of creation, at sea and on dry land," and impermissible to listen to music and other matters forbidden by the *šariʿa* and harmful to public morality (II, pp. 629-31).

Then come complex questions relating to the duties of prayer and fasting as affected by long-distance travel by jet plane (II, pp. 631-39). Prayer is permitted while flying, on condition that the plane is oriented to the *qebla*; if it deviates therefrom after the worshipper has completed all verbal recitation, his prayer is valid (II, p. 631). Then there is the case of a traveler who, missing the dawn prayer before taking off from Tehran, arrives in Istanbul an hour later, half an hour before sunrise. If he immediately performs the dawn prayer, will he count as having done so at the prescribed time, or as having made up for missing it in Tehran (II, p. 632)?

In the concluding section, a transition is accomplished from the actual to the hypothetical, from earth to outer space. Among the questions that may arise in the future are differences in gravity affecting weight, and the nature of plants and animals existing on other planets. If human beings are found there, they are to be treated like their terrestrial counterparts, and if there are creatures having a different form from humans but like them are endowed with perception and intelligence, they are to be treated as human, to the extent that marriage with them will be permissible, and they will be subject to all divine prescriptions. The way in which they fulfil those prescriptions, such as ablution, may however be determined by the number of arms they have (II, pp. 639-40). Khomeini's purpose here is no doubt to emphasize the enduring relevance of the *feqh-e sonnati* he espoused and to refute the claims of those who regard the whole discipline as a historical artefact.

(14) *Ketāb al-bayʿ* (in Arabic; five volumes, written between 1961 and 1976). This work represents the contents of the courses Khomeini taught on the subject, first in Qom and then in Najaf. Regulations for the buying and selling of property are the theme of all five volumes. Volume one was published in Najaf in 1961 in 450 pages, and volume two, which includes a discussion of *welāyat-e faqih*, was written in Najaf in 1962 and published there the same year in 575 pages. Volume three, in 485 pages, was completed in 1972, also in Najaf. The topic of volume four, published in Najaf in 1974 in 452 pages, is *ḵeyārāt,* (the legal ability of either party to a contract to annul its provisions); and volume five, published in Najaf in 1977 in 402 pages, completes the discussion of *keyārāt* and then deals with transactions in cash, credit, and the seizure of property. This final volume is the last work to be written or completed by Khomeini during his years in Najaf.

(15) *Esteftāʾāt* (10 vols., Tehran, 1996-2019). This compiles a total of 12,387 *fatwā*s, Khomeini's answers to requests for a binding judgement on matters of law, most of them relating to the period after the revolution. The names of the questioners, if private citizens, are omitted; the text of their queries is followed by brief responses, in keeping with the nature of the genre. Other requests for *fatwā*s were made by duly-named government officials, and the answers they received were more detailed. Before being incorporated in this collection, most of these had already appeared in *Ṣaḥifa-ye Emām*, the twenty-two-volume assemblage of Khomeini's public declarations.

One *fatwā* clearly relating to the immediate post-revolutionary situation is the following: Question: "If a duly qualified *mojtahed* issues a binding command for jihad or some other matter, is obedience to his command incumbent on those who are not his *moqalleds*?" Answer: "The command of the *wali al-amr* is binding on everyone, including other *mojtaheds*" (I, p. 19). At issue here is the opposition of certain *mojtaheds*, primarily Moḥammad-Kāẓem Šariʿatmadāri, although his name is not mentioned, to a number of government policies. Of more general and lasting importance are the *fatwā*s declaring the permissibility of praying behind a Sunni imam. In a locality left unnamed by the questioner, Sunnis and Shi'is had come together to build a mosque, but it was a Sunni who customarily led the prayer; it was permissible, Khomeini proclaimed, for the Shiʿis to pray behind him, on condition that in prostration they place their foreheads on the clay tablet known as *torba* or *mohr* (I, p. 279). Another questioner inquired whether Shiʿis can pray behind a Sunni imam on occasions other than the Hajj; Khomeini replied, "they can" (I, p. 279). Other *fatwā*s addressed concerns of a more personal nature, such as those of a religiously observant wife unable to persuade her husband to pray regularly (I, pp. 486-87).

KALĀM

Ṭalab wa erāda ("Demand and Will"; in Arabic). The subject of this work, freewill vs. predetermination, while belonging to *kalām*, relates also to *oṣul-e feqh*, for *amr*, the divine command, is a foundational concept of that discipline. Khomeini therefore touched upon it in his classes on *oṣul*, but recognized it as a subject calling for detailed treatment in its own right (p. 5). Khomeini completed this work on 25 Ramadan 1371/20 June 1952 while in Hamadan, having gone there presumably to escape the extreme heat prevailing in Qom.

The Arabic text was published in Tehran in 1983 together with a Persian translation by Sayyed Aḥmad Fehri. As if the terminological density of the work were not enough of a challenge for the reader, Fehri's version frequently expands on the Arabic original without acknowledgement, and confusingly intermingles it with a detailed commentary and footnotes. The structure of the original text is also unclear. After a preface and introduction (pp. 10-37) comes the first *maṭlab* (topic), an examination and refutation of the theological arguments advanced by Abu'l-Ḥasan Ašʿari (q.v.; pp. 37-53), leading the reader to expect a series of other *maṭlabs*. Instead, what follows are several unnumbered *foṣul* (chapters) (pp. 53-129). In the most significant of these *foṣul*, the arguments of both the Aš^ʿariya (q.v.) and Moʿtazeli schools of thought are refuted, and the cryptic formula, "something in between" (*amron bayn al-amrayn*), i.e., between free will and predetermination, is explained and put forward as the truth of the matter (pp. 62-77). After the *foṣul* comes a succession of five separately numbered *maṭlab*s (pp. 129-58). The topic of the first is the true nature of felicity and wretchedness (pp. 129-32). The second establishes that the contingent attributes of existence do not pertain to its essence (pp. 133-35). The third demonstrates that since all contingent quiddities lack reality in their essence, they are incapable of independent causation (pp. 135-36). The fourth provides a definition of what is commonly regarded as felicity, the permanent availability of all the pleasures desired by the appetitive soul, and what truly constitutes it (pp. 136-40). The fifth refutes the idea that the inclination of an individual soul to either good or evil is determined by its innate disposition (*ṭina*) (pp. 141-58).

POLEMICS AND POLITICAL WORKS

Many of the works surveyed in other categories contain elements that are either polemical or political or both, but it seems appropriate to single out two works for separate treatment under this heading.

(1) *Kašf al-asrār* (in Persian; Qom, 1945, 334 pp.). It does not appear to have been republished after the revolution, perhaps because most of the concerns it addresses had been superseded by others. The work is nonetheless of historical value, for it demonstrates Khomeini's view of the dire situation in which Iran, and the religious institution in particular, found themselves after twenty years of Pahlavi rule. The title, *Kašf al-asrār* ("The Uncovering of Secrets"), refers in the first place to the objectionable book, *Asrār-e hazārsāla*, he sought to refute (see KHOMEINI i. LIFE, p. 548), but it also alludes to a coalition of forces plotting against Iran and Islam.

Early in the book, he addresses an unnamed individual, saying, "we know you better than anyone … you have not read the Qurʾan even once" (p. 8). But nowhere does he dignify with explicit mention by name either the *Asrār-e hazārsāla* or its author, ʿAli-Akbar Ḥakamizāda. (By contrast, he does mention by name a writer expressing views similar to those of Ḥakamizāda, Aḥmad Kasravi [q.v.], twice denouncing him as an opium addict [pp. 133, 302], and he also condemns Reżāqoli Šariʿat-Sanglaji, a clerical deviant like Ḥakamizāda [p. 333]).

Instead, Khomeini launches his book with the warning that "certain idiots are striving with all their might to sow corruption, chaos, and disunity, and to destroy the foundations of society; at a time when the whole world is aflame, they aim their blows at religion and the religious scholars" (p. 2). Whatever they have to say derives from the Wahhabis, "the ghouls of the desert of Najd … a band of camel-herders…one of the most abominable peoples in the world" (p. 4). Similar execrations of the Wahhabis recur later in the book (e.g., pp. 10, 27, 39). That Wahhabi teachings should be propagated in Iran during the rule of Reżā Khan is no surprise, for he wished to silence the *ʿolamāʾ* as he set about destroying the country (p. 9). Even after his dethronement, matters have not substantially improved.

Khomeini addresses serially the Wahhabi-inspired accusations circulating at the time. First comes the charge that a whole series of distinctively Shiʿite practices constitute *šerk* and an infraction of *tawḥid*: seeking favors from the Prophet and the Imams; the attribution of miracles to them and seeking their intercession; prostrating on clay tablets from Karbala; and the construction of domes. His answer is extremely lengthy, touches on a number of additional topics, and cites philosophers as well as Islamic scholars (pp. 11-105). He accuses his adversaries, among other things, of wishing clandestinely to promote a return to Zoroastrianism (p. 74).

Second comes the question of the Imamate, and the claim that it is not explicitly mentioned in the Qurʾan. After adducing rational proofs for the innate necessity of government as such, Khomeini affirms that for twenty-five years the Prophet strove to establish a just government for enforcing divine law. As for scriptural proofs, Qurʾan 4:59 makes of obedience to "the possessors of authority" (*ulu'l-amr*) a corollary of obedience to God and His Messenger (pp. 107-11). Reżā Khan and Atatürk do not qualify for this title, nor do the sultans and caliphs of the past. In fact the usurpation of authority can be traced back to the rule of the first two caliphs, Abu Bakr and ʿOmar; not yet inclined to ecumenical relations with Sunnis, Khomeini enumerates the deviations of which they were allegedly guilty, such as the prohibition of *motʿa* (temporary marriage) by ʿOmar (pp. 112-17). This, in turn, leads to the discussion of numerous hadith concerning the Imamate; the reasons for commemorating the martyrdom of Imam Ḥosayn (q.v.); the nature of the Imamate having been governmental as well as spiritual from the outset; the meaning of Qurʾan, 5:3 "this day I have perfected for you your religion" (p. 135), which he takes as referring to the Prophet's nomination of ʿAli as his successor at the Pool of Ḵomm (see ḠADIR ḴOMM). After adducing other Qurʾanic verses alluding to the Imamate, Khomeini counters the arguments made against Shiʿism in *Toḥfa-ye Eṯnā-ʿašariya*, a lengthy, well-known polemical work by Shah ʿAbd-al-ʿAziz Moḥaddeṯ Dehlavi (q.v.; d. 1824), citing approvingly its refutation by Ḥāmed Ḥosayn Musawi (d. 1888) in his *ʿAbaqāt al-anwār fi emāmat al-aʾimmat al-aṭhār*.

Especially pertinent to the future of Iran was Khomeini's tentative exposition of what he calls *welāyat-e faqih* or *welāyat-e mojtahed*, "the viceregency of the *mojtahed*" (pp. 185-90), in support of which he cites four hadith (pp. 187-88). He takes care to stress that the doctrine does not mean the religious scholars should assume ministerial or administrative positions, but rather form or oversee an assembly to select a "just ruler" observant of divine law; such an assembly would be totally at variance with the Constituent Assembly (Majles-e moʾassesān) that, "formed at bayonet point," had substituted the Pahlavi for the Qajar dynasty. Many great scholars of the past, such as Naṣir-al-Din Ṭusi (q.v.; d. 1274) and Moḥammad-Bāqer Majlesi (q.v.; d. 1699), while preserving their independence, had even collaborated with kings in order to promote the welfare of the people. "Even though all sovereignties other than the sovereignty of God (*joz' salṭanat-e Ḵodā'i hama-ye salṭanathā*) are oppressive and contrary to the public welfare, and all laws other than divine law are invalid and useless (*bi-huda*), they (the religious scholars) observe these laws and do not seek to abolish them until a better political system can be established" (p. 186). This may be read both as a warning and as a statement of intention. Indeed, part of what follows somewhat later is a clarification of how an Islamic state would draw up a budget; what taxes it would impose; how endowments (*awqāf*) would be administered; and the functions that would be undertaken by its "office of propagation" (*edāra-ye tabliḡāt*) (pp. 255-58, 279).

Compulsory military service as instituted by Reżā Khan is harmful to the people, paralyzing the industrial and agricultural sectors. Unless their impoverished families can afford to pay a bribe, young men are taken away from them for two years to be spent in "centers of vice and depravity," where they are liable to be infected by venereal diseases while sauntering on the boulevards of Tehran (p. 244). "If fornicating men and women were to receive a hundred lashes, these devastating diseases would not occur" (pp. 274-75). The prohibition of *ḥejāb* (*kašf-e ḥejāb*) is likewise an assault on public morality (pp. 223, 283). Likewise reprehensible is the peaked hat known as "the Pahlavi hat" (*kolāh-e pahlavi*), closely resembling the French kepi, that was imposed on men in 1927 in order to give them a European appearance (p. 224).

Much of what is advocated by the so-called reformists as conducive to "a true Islam" and is being enforced by the Pahlavi state derives from a misplaced admiration of Europe, "a Europe which has no purpose other than bloodshed, slaughter, and devastation ... that has annihilated millions of its own people, crushing them with tanks and artillery" (p. 272). By contrast, Muslim countries that were at least partly implementing Islamic laws displayed the highest level of civilization for several centuries, as acknowledged by Gustave Le Bon in his book, *La civilisation des arabes* (p. 273). The universities established by the state in Iran are one example of the blind imitation of Europe (what would later be derided, by Khomeini and others, as *ḡarbzadagi*, "Westoxication"); they had failed to produce competent physicians, while at the same time ignoring traditional medicine (*ṭebb-e qadim*; pp. 281-82). Another reprehensible innovation is the state-controlled press: scarcely a household could be found in which newspapers were not kept; they ought to be stacked up and burnt in town squares (pp. 283-84).

The rest of *Kašf al-asrār* consists of a repetition of points made earlier in the book and later elaborated in the Najaf lectures on *welāyat-e faqih*. Thus, legislation is the prerogative of God alone, so that all existing governments are inherently illegitimate (p. 288); the law of Islam has perennial validity (p. 291); and the distortion of Islam is the work of the Europeans, who have recruited to this end "the idiot Reżā Khan and the moron Atatürk" (pp. 330-31).

(2) *Welāyat-e faqih, Ḥokumat-e eslāmi*. This began with the transcript of four lectures delivered in Najaf to an audience of mostly young students in late January and early February 1970; the text was published there the following year. Numerous other editions exist, the most recent appeared in Tehran in 1996. The citations given here are from an undated reprint of the Najaf edition; the material has been slightly rearranged, however, for the sake of greater coherence and to avoid repetition—hence the lack of serial order to the page references. When Khomeini gave these lectures, twenty-five years had elapsed since the publication of *Kašf al-asrār*. He now had a more specialized audience than the intended readership of that book and accordingly supplied detailed proofs from the Qur'an and hadith for the vicegerency of the *faqih*. In order to forestall any misinterpretation, he carefully examines the precise wording of each hadith that he cites. Moreover, much in the political situation had changed: America had replaced Britain as the principal enabler of the Pahlavi regime, and the state of Israel had come into existence, with consequences for Iran. The establishment of Islamic government was no longer a hypothetical possibility, but an urgent necessity.

At the very outset, Khomeini affirms the indisputable validity of the principle of *welāyat-e faqih*; the lack of attention paid to it derives from the circumstances prevailing in society at large and the teaching institutions in particular. These are, in turn, due to the hostility with which Islam has been confronted from the outset, beginning with the Jews (by whom he presumably means the Jewish tribes in Medina at the time of the Prophet, primarily the Bani Qorayẓa, mentioned by name on p. 111), and continuing with the Crusaders and the European imperialists (pp. 6-7). Their influence has penetrated educational institutions, including even those devoted to religious scholarship, with the result that Islam is thought to be nothing but a series of regulations concerning ritual purity and is deprived of its revolutionary aspect. The great majority of Qur'anic verses and hadith pertain, however, to the gestation of society; it is therefore incumbent on the younger generation of religious students to pursue the revival of Islamic governance, in whatever way they find most beneficial. The legal system practiced in Iran is of foreign origin and corrupt in its application, and in no way does it serve to check vices such as the consumption of alcohol and promiscuity. The laws of Islam are comprehensive and of lasting validity; what is required is their implementation, a duty first performed by the Prophet and then passed on to his successors. Through writing and preaching, people need to be made aware of the beneficial effects of Islamic law on society; "know that it is your duty to establish an Islamic government," Khomeini commands his young audience (pp. 7-23).

The Prophet exercised all the functions of government, and his appointment of a successor indicates that they were to continue after his passing. After his death, no one disputed the need for government; they disagreed only on who should head it. Even after the beginning of the Greater Occultation (see ḠAYBA), all the laws of Islam remain valid. Islam provides a complete social system and has regulations for family life, trade, and agriculture (pp. 26-29). Similarly, it has its own distinct taxation system consisting of *ḵoms, jezya, ḵarāj,* and *zakāt*, each intended for specific forms of expenditure. Incumbent on the state is the provision of health care, education, and economic development (pp. 34-37). Equally important is the maintenance of forces to defend the lands of Islam, in accordance with Qurʾan 8:60: "Prepare against them whatever force you can muster." It is the neglect of this injunction as well as pure incompetence that has led to the loss of Palestine (pp. 37-38).

The corruption of government began with the Omayyads and continued with the ʿAbbasids and all the monarchical governments succeeding them, the result being "the proliferation of corruption on earth" (Qurʾan, 5:33, on p. 39). A further consequence has been the splintering of the Islamic homeland by the imperialists and their agents, a prime example being the dismembering of the Ottoman state, which despite its defects represented a form of unity (pp. 41-42).

Thanks to the imperialists and their puppet governments, corruption and oppression prevail everywhere (pp. 43-50). The corruption is at one and the same time moral, financial, and political. The imperial regime is responsible for the proliferation of prostitution and alcoholism, and spends money from the religious endowments (*awqāf*) on building cinemas (p. 57). Public funds are embezzled; money is wasted on royal ceremonies; expensive armaments are imported; oil and other natural resources are exploited by foreigners; and Phantom jets are bought from Israel, making Iran a base for the Zionists (pp. 59-60, 160, 167-68, 194). It is to prevent these forms of corruption, as well as the diffusion of heretical concepts, that an Islamic government is needed; this is the conclusion to be drawn from a lengthy hadith of Imam Reżā, the essence of which is the lasting necessity of a divinely appointed trustee (p. 45; text in Shaikh Ṣadduq Ebn Bābawayh, *ʿElal al-šarāʾeʿ*, Qom 1958, I, 183).

This is but one of the many hadiths Khomeini cites, with the intention both of clarifying the nature of Islamic government and of identifying the class of scholars, namely the *foqahāʾ*, whose duty it is to establish one. The wording on each occasion is meticulously analyzed in order to refute possible misinterpretations or objections. For example, Imam ʿAli is reported to have asked the Prophet: "Who are those that succeed you?" to which he replied, "Those who come after me, transmit my traditions and practice, and teach them to the people after me." Khomeini argues that "teaching," even if narrowly interpreted, implies training those who are taught to implement what they learn (pp. 80-81). Closer to being explicit is a tradition from Imam Musā al-Kāẓem that describes the *foqahāʾ* as "the fortress of Islam," which implies active engagement against the enemy. If a *faqih* sits passively in some nook, not enforcing the penal code or guarding the frontiers of Islam, a crack will have appeared in the wall of the fortress (pp. 82-84). Somewhat similarly, the Twelfth Imam advised the believers to consult the *foqahāʾ* concerning situations newly arising (*ḥawādeṯ-e wāqeʿa*) during his occultation; each of them will count as "a proof of Islam" (*ḥojjat al-Eslām*). From this hadith, Khomeini concludes that "just as the Most Noble Messenger was the proof of God—the conduct of all affairs being entrusted to him so that whoever disobeyed him had a proof advanced against him—so, too, are the *foqahāʾ* the proof of the Imam ... to the people." The conclusion to be drawn from these and other hadiths serves to clarify the meaning of Qurʾan, 4:59: "O you who believe, obey God and obey the Messenger and the holders of authority among you (*uli'l-amre menkom*)" (pp. 104-6).

The duty or right of a *faqih* to exercise governmental power is not a matter of spiritual status, but of knowledge and justice: "If a worthy individual possessing these two qualities arises and establishes a government, he will possess the same authority as the Most Noble Messenger in the administration of society, and it will be the duty of all people to obey him" (p. 66). He will implement the same penalties as did the Prophet and Imam ʿAli, including one hundred lashes for the fornicator—a provision Khomeini singles out for mention several times because of its perceived urgency, for example on p. 93—and stoning for the adulterer; their implementation cannot be postponed until the return of the Twelfth Imam. (These penalties have, in fact, been frequently imposed after the foundation of the Islamic Republic). The *faqih* will also collect religiously mandated taxes as did the Prophet and Imam ʿAli (pp. 64-65).

An Islamic government, by contrast with all other forms of rule, will be constitutional only in the sense that those presiding over it are bound by the conditions set out in the Qurʾan and Sunnah; legislation belongs to God alone, so that "a simple planning body will take the place of a legislative assembly" (pp. 52-53). Similarly, in his final lecture, Khomeini asserts that "the entire system of government and administration, together with the necessary laws, lies ready for you.... There is no need for you, after establishing a government, to sit down and draw up laws.... All that remains is to draw up ministerial programs, and that can be accomplished with the help and cooperation of consultants and advisers who are experts in different fields, gathered together in a consultative assembly" (pp. 190-91).

In the meantime, it is incumbent on duly qualified *foqahāʾ* to exercise the function of judges. Imam Jaʿfar al-Ṣādeq was once asked how two Shiʿis should resolve a disagreement between them, and he instructed them to seek out one learned in the traditions and accept him as judge (pp. 117-19). This assignation of judgeship to the scholars, together with all the extrinsic functions of the Imam, is permanent, a view already expressed by Mollā Aḥmad Narāqi (d. 1829) and, more recently, Mirzā Moḥammad-Ḥosayn Nāʾini (d. 1936) (p. 98).

A number of other hadiths are then reviewed, culminating in a lengthy sermon addressed to the scholars of his time by Imam Ḥosayn not long before his martyrdom, in which he reproaches them for their failure to "enjoin the good and forbid the evil," as demanded by Qurʾan, 9:71 (pp. 144-68). The least they could have done was to speak out; Khomeini accordingly instructs his listeners not to remain silent: "If they strike you on the head, cry out in protest. Do not submit to oppression; such submission is worse than oppression itself" (pp. 156-69).

At the conclusion of this, the penultimate lecture, Khomeini cites as scholars who issued rulings based in effect on *welāyat-e faqih* Mirzā Ḥasan Širāzi (q.v.; d. 1895), who in December 1891 decreed a boycott of tobacco as long as its production and marketing in Iran remained the monopoly of a British company; Mirzā Moḥammad-Taqi Širāzi (d. 1921), who proclaimed jihad against the British occupiers of Iraq at the end of World War I; and Moḥammad Ḥosayn Kāšef-al-Ḡeṭā (q.v.; d. 1954), also politically active in Iraq (p. 172).

In his final address, Khomeini exhorts the students and scholars of the religious sciences to mobilize the masses to work for the establishment of an Islamic government. Propagation and instruction are the first steps to take. The imperialists and their agents are engaged everywhere in distorting the truths of Islam, endeavoring to alienate the youth from religion; they take aim particularly at university students, who are, however, opposed to tyranny and eager to learn the truths of Islam. Gatherings such as congregational prayer, the Friday prayer, the Hajj, and the commemoration of ʿĀšurāʾ are occasions for fixing the issue of government in the minds of people; rousing and impassioned speeches should be delivered, even if the ultimate goal cannot be reached in the foreseeable future; what is needed, in fact, is nothing less than a replication of ʿĀšurāʾ (pp. 179-82). Despite the unfavorable circumstances of his time, Imam Jaʿfar al-Ṣādeq laid out a pattern of government for future implementation (pp. 184-86).

An urgent need at present is the reform of the religious teaching institution. Apathy, depression, and laziness have infected Najaf, Qom, and Mashhad, where all too many are content simply to give their opinions on religious law and believe government lies beyond their purview. Too many have fallen prey to the imperialist propaganda that concern with politics, an intrinsically dirty affair, is beneath the dignity of a religious scholar; they may be thought of as saintly, but in reality they are only pseudo-saints (*moqaddas-namā*; p. 188). Khomeini then recalls a meeting he had at his house in Qom, on an unspecified date, with Ayatollah Borujerdi and three other senior scholars, imploring them to deal with this pestilence of the pseudo-saintly (p. 197). If rational efforts to disabuse these deviants do not succeed, it will become obvious that they are in the service of the state and count as "akhunds of the court" (*āḵundhā-ye darbāri*); they must—literally—be stripped of their turbans (pp. 201-2). *Feqh* must indeed be studied and taught in the religious institution, but at the same time the truths of Islam and the nature of Islamic government must be conveyed to the general public (pp. 200-201). This involves the severance of all relations with the existing government and proclaiming its illegitimacy (p. 203).

Khomeini closes this final lecture with a supplicatory prayer for the success of the *foqahāʾ* in establishing an Islamic government (p. 208).

There is a translation of this work in Algar, *Islam and Revolution*, pp. 27-165.

POETRY

Given the command of Persian verse that Khomeini displayed at various points in his life, albeit intermittently, it can be assumed that already in his youth, or even as a boy, he had studied and memorized a large body of poetry. An unlikely interlocutor, Nāder Nāderpur (q.v.; d. 2000), modernist poet who chose exile in Los Angeles after the revolution, relates that when, in the early 1960s, he met Khomeini in Qom, "for four hours we recited poetry; every single line I recited from any poet, he recited the next" (cited by Moin, p. 315).

Two of the earliest surviving examples of Khomeini's poetry are political in content: one ridicules the claim of Reżā Shah to patriotic glory for abolishing capitulations granted to foreign powers; and the other, when Nowruz coincided with the birth anniversary of the Occulted Imam, calling for his aid in overthrowing tyrants (Algar, 1988, p. 275). Given Khomeini's spiritual disposition and the long-standing consanguinity in Persian literature between poetry—particularly the *ḡazal* (q.v.)—and gnosticism, there can be little doubt, however, that from his youth onward the bulk of his verse consisted of gnostically inspired *ḡazals*. Fairly early in life, he is said to have kept with him a notebook in which he wrote down his poems; it was lost, however, in the course of his travels. A similar fate befell two other notebooks, in one of which his wife Ḵadija had transcribed his poems. Other manuscript poems were lost or destroyed when SAVAK ransacked his home in Qom in the aftermath of the uprising of 15 Ḵordād (preface to *Divān-e Emām: Majmuʿa-ye ašʿār-e Emām Ḵomeyni*, Tehran, 1993, p. 31). It was not until considerably later that, at his home in Jamārān, on the insistence of Aḥmad Khomeini's wife, Fāṭema Ṭabāṭabāʾi, he is known to have resumed the regular composition of poetry. Her primary interest was initially in philosophy, a discipline from which he gently sought to redirect her to *ʿerfān* in a succession of quatrains. Reciprocally, she was able to persuade him to compose verse as frequently as possible (her introduction to *Divān-e Emām*, pp. 33-35).

Some of his poems were first published in five small collections: (1) *Rah-e ʿešq* (Tehran, 1990), prefaced by the facsimile of a letter to Fāṭema Ṭabāṭabāʾi; (2) *Noqṭa-ye ʿaṭf* (Tehran, 1990), which includes the text of a hortatory letter addressed to Aḥmad; (3) *Maḥram-e rāz* (Tehran, 1990), consisting of twenty-six ghazals and fourteen quatrains written between 1984 and 1986 and preceded by another letter to Aḥmad, dated 9 December 1987; (4) *Bāda-ye ʿešq* (Tehran, 1989), twenty-four ghazals and forty-one quatrains composed between 1984 and 1988 in response to Fāṭema Ṭabāṭabāʾi's request (translated with commentary by Muhammad Legenhausen as *The Mystic Verse of Imam Khomeini*, Qom, 1992); and (5) *Sabu-ye ʿešq*, published on the fortieth day after Khomeini's death on 3 June 1989, consisting of eight ghazals written between 1986 and 1989. All these poems are included in the *Divān-e Emām*, together with others that had survived in private hands and were donated to the Institute for the Compilation and Publication of the Works of Imam Khomeini (Moʾassasa-ye tanẓim wa našr-e āṯār-e Emām Khomeyni).

The poems in the *Divān* are arranged according to genre: *ḡazal*s (139); quatrains (120); *qaṣida*s (3); *mosammaṭ* (2); *tarjiʿband* (1); *qeṭaʿāt* (31). It is the *ḡazal*s that form the core of the *Divān*, arranged in traditional form according to the *radif*, eliminating the possibility of assigning them a date with the exception of those included in *Bāda-ye ʿešq*; the same applies to the quatrains, except those referring to the Islamic Republic (see pp. 193, 195, 197, 206) and others addressed to "Fāṭi" (fifteen occurrences; see index of proper names in the *Divān*, p. 343), which plainly relate to the last ten years of his life.

Noteworthy is that, although Khomeini generally makes no use of a *maḵlaṣ*, on two occasions he identifies himself as "Hendi." This occurs once in a *qeṭʿa* with the following opening line: "your alluring stature in the rose bed of beauty/is a cypress not to be found in Kāšmar" (*Divān-e Emām*, p. 299). Kāšmar (or Kašmar) was one of two locations in Khorasan where Zoroaster is said to have planted cypress trees endowed with lasting miraculous qualities

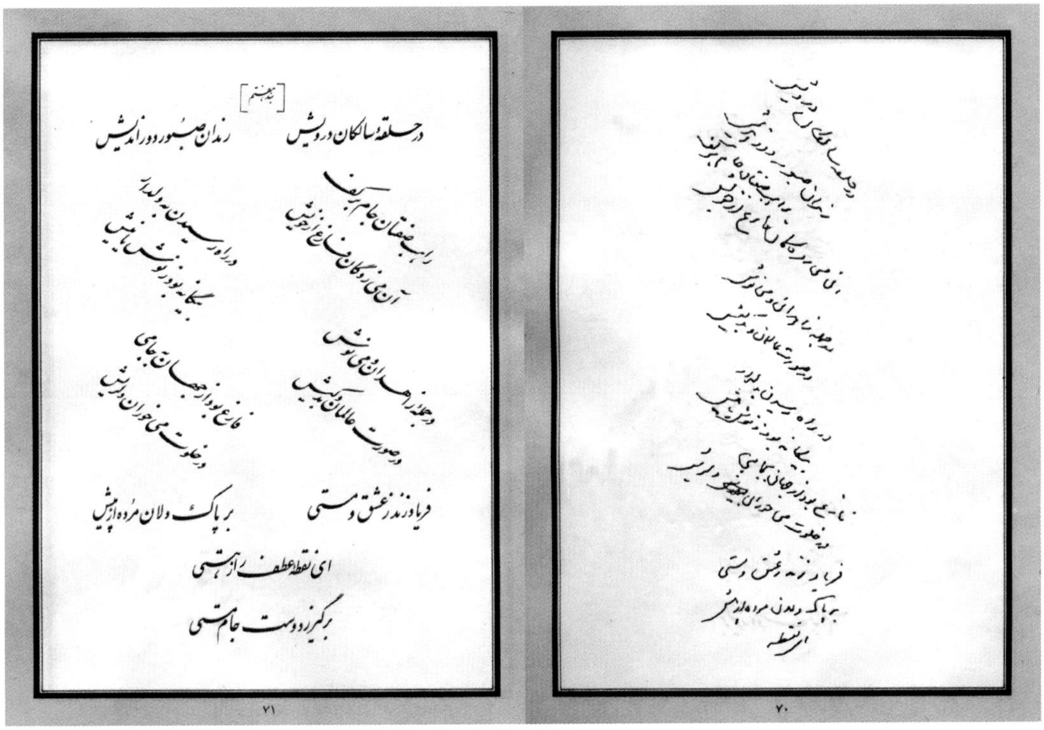

Figure 1. Autograph text of the seventh strophe of the *tarjiʿ-band* by Khomeini (right) and a version by the calligrapher Nāṣer Jawāherpur (left). After *Noqṭa-ye ʿaṭf: Ašʿār-e ʿārefāna-ye Emām Ḵomeyni*, Tehran, 1990, pp. 70-71. Translation:

In the circle of penniless wayfarers,
The far-sighted forbearing rakes,
Hermit-like, clasping a cup,
Inebriated, free from their selves,
In the company of ascetics, yet sipping wine
In the garb of the learned, yet heretics
In the journey to reach the beloved,
A stranger to pleasure as well as pain,
Oblivious to the world, through a single cup
Amidst wine-drinkers with wounded hearts,
He cries out, driven by intoxicated love
To those pure of heart, dead to the world:

O Pivot of the Mystery of Being,
Accept the cup of intoxication from the Friend.

(see ʿAli b. Zayd Bayhaqi, *Tāriḵ-e Bayhaq*, ed. Aḥmad Bahmanyār, Tehran, n.d., pp. 281-82). It is unclear why Khomeini should have used the *maḵlaṣ* Hendi on this occasion.

The opening line of the other ghazal where Khomeini uses the *maḵlaṣ* "Hendi" reads as follows: "Tonight as you sleep beside me like a bride / let it not be that you deny me an embrace and a kiss, " and its final line, "Hendi has come all the way from India to your dwelling / that he might surrender his heart to the realm of Shiraz and the empire of Tus" (*Divān-e Emām*, p. 128). He "has come all the way from India" in the sense that two generations separate him from the Indian sojourn of his ancestors, and he has come to Shiraz and Tus in the sense that he wishes to emulate Hafez and Ferdowsi. The influence of Hafez (q.v.), and to a lesser extent Saʿdi, does indeed pervade his poetry; traces of Ferdowsi are far rarer.

It is above all Hafez from whom he draws inspiration. The opening line of one of Khomeini's *ğazal*s reads as follows: "O cupbearer (*alā yā ayyohā'l-sāqi*), take away the sorrow from our hearts / for with your cup all problems are solved" (*Divān*, p. 46). It calls to mind, as no doubt it is intended to do, the celebrated *maṭlaʿ* of the very first *ğazal* in the *Divān* of Hafez: "O cupbearer (*alā yā ayyohā'l-sāqi*), pass the cup around and proffer it / for love appeared easy at first, and then problems arose" (*Divān-e Šams-al-Din Moḥammad Ḥāfeẓ*, ed. Parviz Nātel Ḵānlari, Tehran, 1983, I, pp. 18-19). A further echo of the same poem comes in the fifth line of Khomeini's *ğazal*: "From the flowers in the garden of the friend, what have you glimpsed of that idol? / Remote are you now from that garden, separated by whole oceans and shores (*sāḥelhā*)." The corresponding line from the first *ğazal* by Hafez reads: "A dark night, fear of the waves, an awesome whirlwind— / What know they of our state, those lightly laden on the shore (*sāḥelhā*)?" The sense of danger and deprivation is common to both lines.

More significant than precise parallels with the *ğazal*s of Hafez is Khomeini's regular deployment of the same metaphors concerning wine and its consumption that suffuse the verse of Hafez. The subject has been examined by Aḥmad Faršbāfiān; he has identified numerous verses by Khomeini and Hafez in which the same metaphors occur, and goes to great pains to clarify their roots in *ʿerfān*. While conceding Hafez's superiority as a poet, he ranks Khomeini higher as an *ʿāref* (*Mašrab-e ʿerfāni-ye Emām Ḵomeyni va Ḥāfeẓ*, n.p., 1997). Slightly different in motivation is Moḥsen Binā's *Šamʿ-e jamʿ: Šarḥ va tafsiri bar bakši az ğazaliyāt-e Ḥażrat-e Emām Ḵomeyni* (Tehran, 1995). Before commenting in great detail on eight of Khomeini's *ğazal*s, he expresses concern that common readers unfamiliar with the metaphors employed might understand them in their literal meaning, thus taking the tavern to mean a wine store and wine to mean the drink forbidden by the *šariʿa* and now officially banned. (It might of course be argued that the viability of the metaphor of wine as mystical love presumes acquaintance with, or at least awareness of, its liquid analogue). He upbraids other, more educated critics of Khomeini's poetry for their failure to study poetic tradition (*Samʿ-e jamʿ*, p. 5).

The political is, for the most part, lacking in the *Divān*. There are, however, exceptions. A lengthy undated *qaṣida* in praise of the Occulted Imam (*wali ʿaṣr*) laments the persistence of royal tyranny, ruthlessly reinforced by the British: "Until when shall the unbelievers continue to quaff the blood of the believers, / these wolves to prey on the sheep? ... Until when are we to endure oppression by the British, / they who are unique and unchallenged in their cruelty?" He then appeals to the Occulted Imam: "Make of the center of learning (*ḥawza-ye ʿelmiya*) of Qom a banner to the world, / so that the firmament turns to the salvation of the Muslims!" (*Divān*, pp. 263-67). Dating from a much later time, when the desired transformation of Qom had taken place, is this simple quatrain: "Our republic is the ensign bearer of Islam, / the foul plans of the seditious are in vain. The nation thrusts forth on its way, / Ṣaddām has cast himself into a hundred traps (*ṣad dām*)" (*Divān*, p. 195). The present writer recalls seeing this quatrain prominently displayed at various sites in Tehran during the Iran-Iraq War.

Bibliography (mostly given in the text; see also the bibliography for KHOMEINI i. LIFE for titles not given here).

Lists of Khomeini's works have been provided by Reżā Ostādi, "Ketābhā va āṯār-e ʿelmi-ye Emām Ḵomeyni," *Kayhān-e Andiša* 29, Farvardin-Ordibehešt 1369, pp. 143-61, Ṣadr-al-Din ʿEmād Dašti, "Ketābšenāsi-ye mawżuʿi-e tawṣifi-ye āṯār-e emām-e rāḥel," *Ḥożur*, Ḵordād 1376/June 1995, pp. 40-53. More recent and authoritative is the listing of Khomeini's published works to be found online at www.imam-khomeini.ir/fa/page/206/; online copies of many of them can be accessed from this website.

In addition, mention may be made of anthologies of his writings and proclamations on different subjects extracted from various books; *Simā-ye zan dar kalām-e Emām Ḵomeini* (Tehran, 1986) and *Emām dar barābar-e ṣahyunizm* (Tehran, 1983) may be mentioned as examples. Many of his works in Persian have been translated into Arabic. A listing of translations into a wide range of languages is to be found on pp. 179-86 of *Fehrest-e ketābhā-ye Moʾassesa-ye tanẓim va našr-e torāṯ-e Emām* (Tehran, 1997); the website www.imam-khomeini/ir/EN may also be consulted.

Studies of Khomeini's works: (a) On *ʿerfān*. Christian Bonaud, *L'Imam Khomeini: Un gnostique méconnu du XXe siècle*, Beirut, 1997; Alexander Knysh, "*Irfan* Revisited*:* Khomeini and the Legacy of Islamic Mystical Philosophy," *Middle East Journal* 46/4, Autumn 1992, pp. 631-54. (b) On *tafsir*. *Tafsir va šawāhed-e Qorʾāni dar āṯār-e Emām Komeyni*, Tehran, 1991.

Other secondary sources: Michael Cook, *Commanding Right and Forbidding Wrong in Islamic Thought*, Cambridge, 2001, pp. 531-48. Abulfadhl Kiashemshaki, "The Universal Degrees, Manifestations and Presences of Existence in Ibn ʿArabi's School of Mysticism," *Ishrak: Ezhegodnik Islamskoĭ Filosofii* 3, 2012, pp. 230-46.

(HAMID ALGAR)

KHORASAN, a historical region with varying boundaries, as well as a provincial region comprising the northeastern part of Iran in modern times. The term Khorasan, country of the "rising sun," had a much wider designation in pre- and early-Islamic times, covering parts of what are now Russia, Central Asia, and Afghanistan. Since 2004, Khorasan has been divided administratively into three smaller provinces: Ḵorāsān-e Rażawi, Ḵorāsān-e Šemāli, and Ḵorāsān-e Jonubi, with their administrative capitals at Mashhad, Bojnurd, and Birjand (qq.v.), respectively. This series of articles survey the history of Khorasan in the broad sense of "Greater Khorasan" as well as the history and culture of Iranian or "Inner Khorasan."

See also entries on relevant cities, districts, and geography (e.g., ABARŠAHR, ABIVARD, ĀLĀ DĀḠ, ALLĀHO AKBAR, ANDARĀB, ASFEZĀR, ATRAK, ĀZĀDVĀR, BĀḴARZ, BALḴ, BAYHAQ, BESṬĀM, BIDOḴT, BINĀLUD, BIRJAND, BOJNURD, BUKHARA, ČĀČ, ČAḠĀNIĀN, DANDĀNQĀN, DARRAGAZ, ESFARĀYEN, FARĀVA, FARḠĀNA, FĀRYĀB, FARYUMAD, FERDOWS, FIRUZKUH, FUŠANJ, GAZNI, GĀZORGĀH, GONĀBĀD, ḠUR, HERAT, JĀM, JOVAYN, JOWZJĀN, KALĀT-E NĀDERI, ḴOTTAL, MARV, MASHHAD, NISHAPUR, OSTOVĀ).

i. *The concept of Khorasan.*
ii. *Pre-Islamic history.*
iii. *Historical geography in the late Sasanid-early Islamic periods.*
iv. *The Arab conquest and Omayyad period.*
v. *History in the ʿAbbasid period.*
vi. *History in the Taherid and Samanid periods.*
vii. *History from the Ghaznavids to the Mongol conquest.*
viii. *History from the Mongol conquest to the Timurids.* See Supplement; see also ČENGĪZ KHAN; IL-KHANIDS.
ix. *History in the Timurid period.* See Supplement.
x. *History in the Safavid and Afsharid periods.*
xi. *History in the Qajar and Pahlavi periods.*
xii. *History in the Islamic Republic period.* See Supplement.
xiii. *Khorasan in modern Islamist ideology.*
xiv. *Ethnology of Qajar and Pahlavi Khorasan.*
xv. *The Babi-Baha'i community in Khorasan.*
xvi. *The Jewish community of Khorasan.* See BUKHARA vii. BUKHARAN JEWS; MASHHAD.
xvii. *The Kurdish communities of Khorasan.*
xviii. *Physical geography of Khorasan.*
xix. *Linguistic features of Khorasani Persian.*
xx. *Khorasani style of poetry.*
xxi. *Jewish dialects of Khorasan.*
xxii. *Arabic dialects of Khorasan.* See IRAN vii. NON-IRANIAN LANGUAGES: ARABIC (9.12).
xxiii. *Turkic dialects of Khorasan.*
xxiv. *Monuments of Khorasan.*
xxv. *Clothing of Khorasan.* See CLOTHING XX. CLOTHING OF KHORASAN.
xxvi. *Music of Khorasan.*
xxvii. *Folklore of Khorasan.*
xxviii. *Newspapers of Khorasan.*

i. The Concept of Khorasan

Movsēs Xorenacʿi (q.v.) in his *Geography* divides Khorasan into 26 districts stretching from Gorgān (q.v.) and Qumes in the southeastern Caspian region to Badaḵšān (q.v.) and Ṭoḵārestān on the upper Oxus and Bāmiān in the Hindu Kush (Marquart, 1901, pp. 16-17, 47ff.).

In the past, Khorasan could often be associated with a territorial entity more than an administrative one. According to recent archaeological and historical discoveries (Rante and Collinet, 2013; Rante, 2015, pp. 9-25), Khorasan should be considered concretely as a large quarter of the Sasanian empire (q.v.) from the mid-6th century CE.

It was, in fact, considered by the Sasanians as one of the four quarters of the empire, that of the east, and traditionally divided into four administrative provinces: Nishapur, Herat, Marv, and Balḵ (Figure 1; Gyselen, 1989, p. 85; and 2003; see also Daryaee, pp. 13-18).

Regarding the frontiers of Khorasan, Ernst Herzfeld (q.v.) described the limits of Khorasan during the last part of the Sasanian period (Figure 2): "Eastern Tehran, at the 'Caspian Gates,' beginning the eastern parts of the Alborz Mountains, to the southeastern corner of the Caspian Sea, today's Russian-Persian border at Atrek, along the Trans-Caspian railway to about Loṭfābād; [then] after a line through the desert, including the oases of Marv and Tejen, up to the Āmu Daryā at Karki, the Āmu Daryā itself to about Ḥażrat Emām, then west of Badaḵšān to the south into the Hindu Kush mountains, thence west to the high ridge of the Hindu Kush and continuing along its western extensions, south past Herat, [by] a salt lake on the Afghan-Persian border, continuing through Kuhestān south of Ḵᵛāf and Toršiz and along the northern edge of the great Dašt-e Kavir desert back to the starting point at the Caspian Gates" (Herzfeld, p. 109).

While the "concept" of Khorasan in the early and Middle-Sasanian period could have been popularly intended to start from Ray, or from Hamadān (Herzfeld, p. 108), eastwards to the "place where the sun rises," it would seem more probable that the limits of western Khorasan would have corresponded to the "whole Abaršahr" (Gyselen, 1989, p. 85). It is therefore probable that in the Sasanian epoch Khorasan excluded Ray and some other provinces mentioned in later historical sources. Qumes, often associated with the Gorgān region (Gyselen, 1989, p. 84), was likely the western frontier of the Abaršahr. The problem is that the "whole Abaršahr" remains hard to circumscribe today. The Sasanian extension of this region could correspond, as attested by Josef Markwart (q.v.), to the area where the Aparni originally settled, corresponding to the area of Tajan (1901, p. 74; Lecoq, p. 151).

The Sasanian occupation of eastern Iran was *de facto* ephemeral (Gyselen, 2003, p. 166), thus rendering it difficult today to have a precise and conclusive idea of the eastern boundaries. Nonetheless, if an administrative Khorasanian entity had existed before the 6th century, its eastern boundaries probably would have corresponded to the Morḡāb River (q.v.; Rante, 2015, p. 10, n. 3). Concerning the south, the large Iranian deserts and Sistān (q.v.) could have been the limits of Khorasan.

During the Arab Islamic invasion, Khorasan seems to correspond to an abstract geographical entity. The Arab armies did not limit their conquest to the boundaries of Sasanian Khorasan, but rapidly passed the Oxus River (q.v.) through the Kara Kum desert and advanced through Sogdiana (q.v.) toward the northeast, to stop later on the Talas River around 750 CE. This could certainly also explain the chaotic administration of the first years of Arab occupation (Daniel, p. 19). At that time, the administrative framework pointed out by a Middle Persian source, *Šahrestānīhā ī Ērānšahr* (q.v.), dated to the ʿAbbasid time, saw Khorasan divided into twelve capitals (Marquart, 1931, pp. 8-13; Daryaee, p.18): Samarkand, Navarak, an unnamed city of K̲ʷārazm (Chorasmia, q.v.), Marv-rud, Marv, Herat, Bušanj (Fušanj, q.v.), Ṭus, Nishapur, Qāʾen, Gorgān and Qumes. The province west of Qumes seems to have been attached to Iraq. This area, between Mesopotamia and Khorasan, was the military outpost to subdue the eastern lands.

Despite the former geographical limitation, which looks furthermore to be an indication of the conquered countries, it seems in any case that at the time of the Arab invasion, between the second half of the 7th century and the beginning of the 8th century, the real northeastern and the western boundaries of Khorasan were respectively the Oxus River and Qumes. The southern ones were Sistān and Kerman (q.v.) provinces, obviously not included in Khorasan. Regarding the eastern frontier, at the time of the conquest its limits would still have been ephemeral. In fact, even if its reign was destroyed and its people dispersed between southeastern Iran and Afghanistan, the territory of the Hayṭāl (Hephthalites, q.v.) is still mentioned at the time of the Arab Muslim conquest and after. Maqdesi describes the Oxus River as being the frontier between the Hayṭāl and Khorasan (see Miquel, p. 286, n. 8). Therefore, in the period corresponding to the Islamic conquest and the Umayyad dynasty (end of the 7th and 8th centuries), the frontiers proposed by Herzfeld would be a good geographical framework of Khorasan, although with strong doubts concerning Badak̲šān.

In the Islamic period, one of the first descriptions of the territory of Khorasan is that of the geographer Yaʿqubi, in the 9th century. In his *Historiae* (I, p. 201), Yaʿqubi lists the districts governed by the *spāhbed* (q.v.) of Khorasan: (1) Nishapur, (2) Herat, (3) Marv, (4) Marv al-Rud̲, (5) Fāryāb, (6) Ṭālaqān, (7) Balk̲, (8) Bukhara,

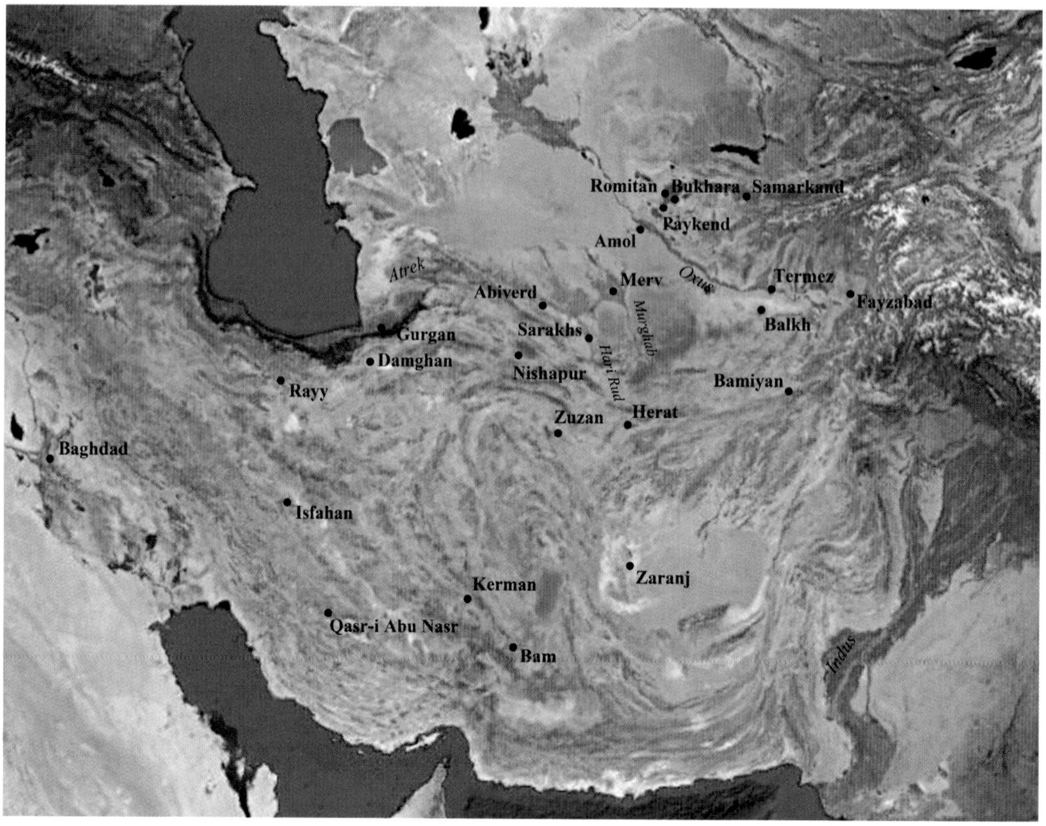

Figure 1: Geographical map showing cities of Khorasan and adjacent areas in an anachronistic way, in order to provide different points of reference through the epochs. (Map courtesy of the authors.)

(9) Bāḏḡis, (10) Bāvard (Abivard, q.v.), (11) Ḡaršestān, (12) Ṭus, (13) Saraḵs, and (14) Gorgān. The same author, in *Ketāb al-boldān*, discussing Balḵ, moreover defines the region as extending from Ray to Farḡāna (q.v.), and identifies its center in Balḵ: between Ray and Balḵ there was a distance of thirty days, the same as between Balḵ and Farḡāna (Yaʿqubi, tr. Wiet, 1937, p. 101). Toward the east there was Turkestan, which surrounds Khorasan and Sistān. The western boundary was Qumes: "of which Dāmḡān was the first city of Khorasan" (Yaʿqubi, tr. Wiet, 1937, p. 80). Yaʿqubi seems also to include Ṭabarestān in Khorasan; the sovereign called himself the "Eṣbahbaḏ [*spāhbed*] of Khorasan" in his correspondence with the caliphs al-Maʾmun and al-Moʿtasem (Yaʿqubi, tr. Wiet, 1937, p. 81).

During the latter part of the 9th century, Abu Ḥanifa Dinavari (q.v.), relating the political and geographical situation of late antiquity and early medieval eastern territories in his *Aḵbār al-ṭewāl* (q.v.), located the city of Āmuya, or Āmul (Āmol), in Khorasan, on the western side of the Oxus (Dinavari, p. 367). He thus also included in this region the area between the Marv oasis and the Oxus. It seems, additionally, that Dinavari excludes Bukhara from the boundaries of Khorasan (Dinavari, pp. 66, 55, 86, 78). Concerning the western frontiers, Dinavari (p. 90) appears to include Qumes and Gorgān in Khorasan. This affirmation seems to be contradictory with the following one describing Besṭām (Besṭām o Bendōy, q.v.) as governor of Khorasan, Qumes, Gorgān, and Ṭabarestān, listed separately (Dinavari, p. 93).

In the same century, Balāḏori (q.v.) proposed a geographical framework of Khorasan that is totally different from those mentioned above. He also included Ḵᵛārazm, Ṭoḵārestān, Sistān, and Transoxiana within the frontiers of Khorasan. According to Yāqut's commentary (Barbier de Meynard, 1861, p. 199), all these countries were mentioned because they were under the authority of the governor of Khorasan, while remaining outside the regional limits of Khorasan. However, Balāḏori did not draw up any official geographical list of the countries included within Khorasan (see also Herzfeld, pp. 108-9).

In the 9th century, it is difficult to understand and delimit the eastern and the northeastern limits of Khorasan, unlike its western and southern ones. The historical sources report different geographical borders of Khorasan, sometimes expanding it up to the frontiers with China and the Turkic people. Nonetheless, Khorasan at that epoch constituted a well-established politi-

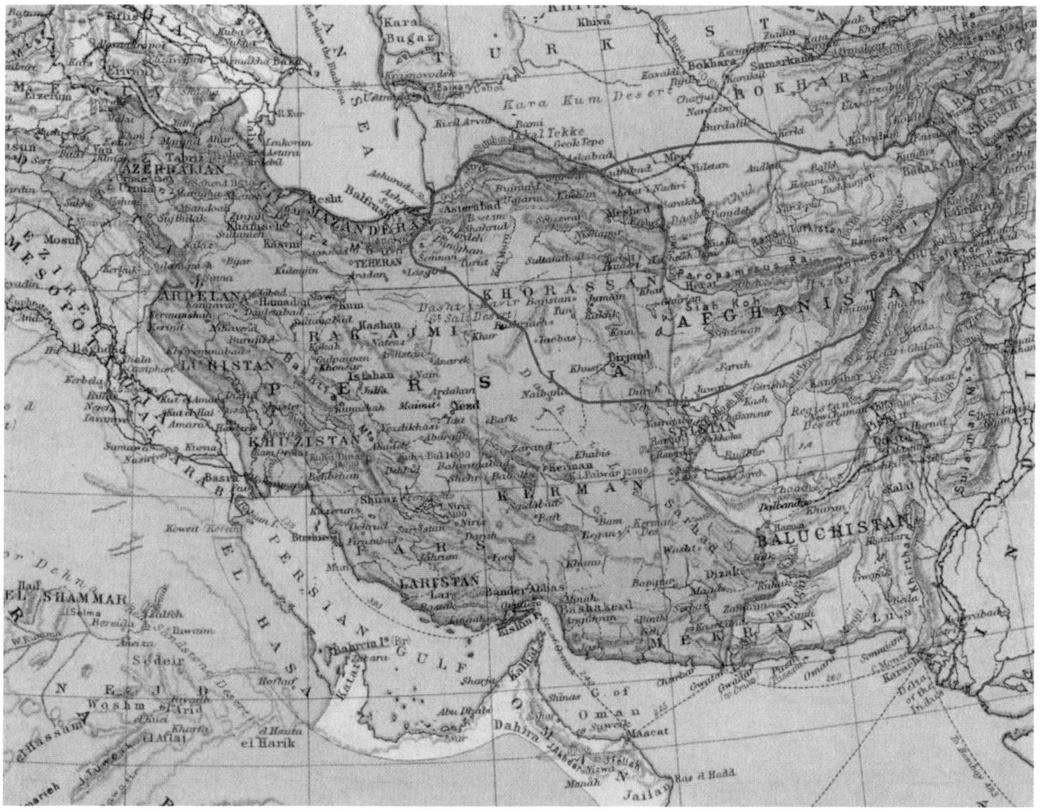

Figure 2: Herzfeld's boundaries of Khorasan as proposed in his 1921 article, imposed on an original map from that same period by the London Geographical Institute (1920).

cal entity due to the advent of the Taherid (q.v.) dynasty in 821 CE. Without diminishing the importance of the unification of Khorasan and the Mā warāʾ al-nahr (q.v.) under the Samanid dynasty, already established in Transoxiana, the Taherids had the merit of having extended their sovereignty to a part of Transoxiana that was still not completely Islamized (Bosworth, 1975, pp. 90-135). If the numismatic evidence reflects a political presence in that area, then it can be assumed that the Taherid sphere extended from Iranian Khorasan to the north and the east covering the oasis of Ḵᵛārazm, Čāč (q.v.), as well as to the west of Ray (Rante, 2015, pp. 13-14). The largest extension of Taherid power, and thus the largest expansive phase of the culture of Khorasan, was established in the 9th century, perhaps more precisely during the short reign of Ṭalḥa b. Ṭāher, governor of Khorasan (822-28). Qodāma b. Jaʿfar (ca. 873-932/948) in his book, *Ketāb al-ḵarāj*, compiled about 879 CE, listed the cities of Khorasan as including Bost, Roḵḵaj, Kābol, Zābolestān, Ṭabas, Qohestān, Herat, Ṭālaqān, Bāḏḡis, Bušanj, Ṭoḵārestān, Ṭārqān, Balḵ, Ḵolm, Marv al-Rud, Ṣaḡāniān, Vāšjerd, Bukhara, Ṭus, Fāryāb, Abaršahr, Kār, Samarkand, Šāš [Čāč], Farḡāna, Ošrusana, Ṣoḡd, Ḵojand, Ḵᵛārazm, Esbijāb, Termeḏ, Nasā, Abivard, Marv, Kass, Nušjān, Bottam, Aḵrun, and Nasaf. Qodama estimated the tax of Khorasan as eight million dirhams, which is one of the most important tax revenues sent from an Islamic province (Qodāma, p. 141).

Later, in the 10th century, the Samanid dynasty carried out the "official" unification of Khorasan and Transoxiana. It created, from the new capital Bukhara, an area of interaction between the Far East (China and the Turkic people) of the Islamic lands and the boundaries of western Khorasan, which at that period corresponded to the Buyid (q.v.) territories. Within that period, the frontiers of Khorasan appear clearer. In the middle of the 10th century, Ebn Ḥawqal (q.v.) located the boundaries of northeastern Khorasan at the Oxus River, the eastern ones in Badaḵšān, of which the city of Jarm should have been the eastern limit (p. 102; Barthold, p. 66) and the western ones, as before, in Dāmḡān (Ebn Ḥawqal, II, pp. 413-16). The southern limit was the Sistān province. Masʿudi (par. 312, p. 119) fixes the Kušān region, which would at least correspond to Ṭoḵārestān, between Khorasan and China, later identifying the mine of Pangšir in Khorasan (par. 455, p. 164).

Later, Yāqut located Khorasan within the boundaries of Iraq, Ṭoḵārestān, Ghazna, Sejestān and Kerman (Barbier de Meynard, pp. 197-98). He definitely excluded Transoxiana and Ḵᵛārazm.

From the Sasanian epoch, Khorasan had been a vast territory joining the Iranian cultures with the Far East and India as well as Mesopotamia and the Near East. From the very outset a territory issued by different ancient regions and provinces, its frontiers have always been hard to understand because the historical reports were often contradictory. The limits proposed by Herzfeld (Figure 2) corresponding to the end part of the Sasanian period seem to be likely, although in the light of the recent researches, it would be preferable to situate the eastern boundaries along the Morḡāb River. During the Arab-Muslim conquest and the Omayyad dynasty, this territory would be constituted of all conquered regions eastwards from the province of Ray.

Guy Le Strange (1966, map 1), who produced a map of the eastern provinces of the ʿAbbasid caliphate that still remains useful, left the eastern part of Khorasan without frontiers. Moreover, concerning the western and the northwestern boundaries, he left Qumes, Ṭabarestān, Gorgān, and Qohestān outside Khorasan (for these provinces see Gyselen, 1989, p. 53; Schwarz, pp. 809 ff.). Although Ṭabarestān, Qumes, and Gorgān could be situated outside the western frontiers of Khorasan, at least in the second half of the 8th century, from the 9th century a part of Qumes and Gorgān could be integrated into the boundaries of Khorasan (Bosworth, 1986, p. 378), making Dāmḡān the gate of Khorasan. The eastern boundaries could be situated in the province of Badaḵšān, around the city of Fayżābād (q.v.), where a solid mountain range rises up as natural border and goes down to reach the main ranges of the Hindu Kush.

During the 10th century (Frye, 1975, map 3, p. 139), when Khorasan and Transoxiana were under the control of the Samanids, the western boundaries of Khorasan, according to Ebn Ḥawqal, remained at Qumes, near or in Dāmḡān. The eastern ones excluded Ḡur (q.v.) from the 9th century limits, even if Bāmiān seems to be within the frontiers of Khorasan (Ebn Ḥawqal, p. 416). The south was bordered by Sistān; Qohestān was inside the perimeter of Khorasan. Concerning the northeastern boundaries, even if at that time Samanids ruled over Khorasan and Transoxiana thus making it almost a unique territory, the limit of Khorasan proper continued to be the Oxus, again separating two historically independent regions, which however were from the advent of Islam culturally, and in part politically, united.

There is little doubt that the designation of "Greater Khorasan" is traceable in the Islamic period, during the ʿAbbasid period, more precisely beginning with the Taherid's several decades of government, in the 9th century, even if some would date it to the time of Abu Moslem Ḵorāsāni (q.v.). The following century and the Samanid control contributed to increase and reinforce it.

From the 6th century, Khorasan seems to have been constituted of an original nucleus, or "Khorasan Proper," which has been tentatively located within the Marv oasis, Herat, and Zuzan, following the eastern border of the Iranian Deserts to the south-eastern corner of the Caspian Sea, excluding thus a large part of Qumes, but including the province of Gorgān following the shape of the Great Wall, which in the light of recent research is dated to the 5th-6th centuries (Figure 3). From this nucleus the limits expanded during the Islamic period, firstly including Balḵ and its province, the whole of Qohestān, a part of ancient Hyrcania as far as the Atrek River, and the desert zones between the Marv oasis and the Oxus, which has been a natural frontier over the centuries. A large part of the Zarafšān valley, in Transoxiana, including the Bukhara and Samarkand oases, has been an area of major influences

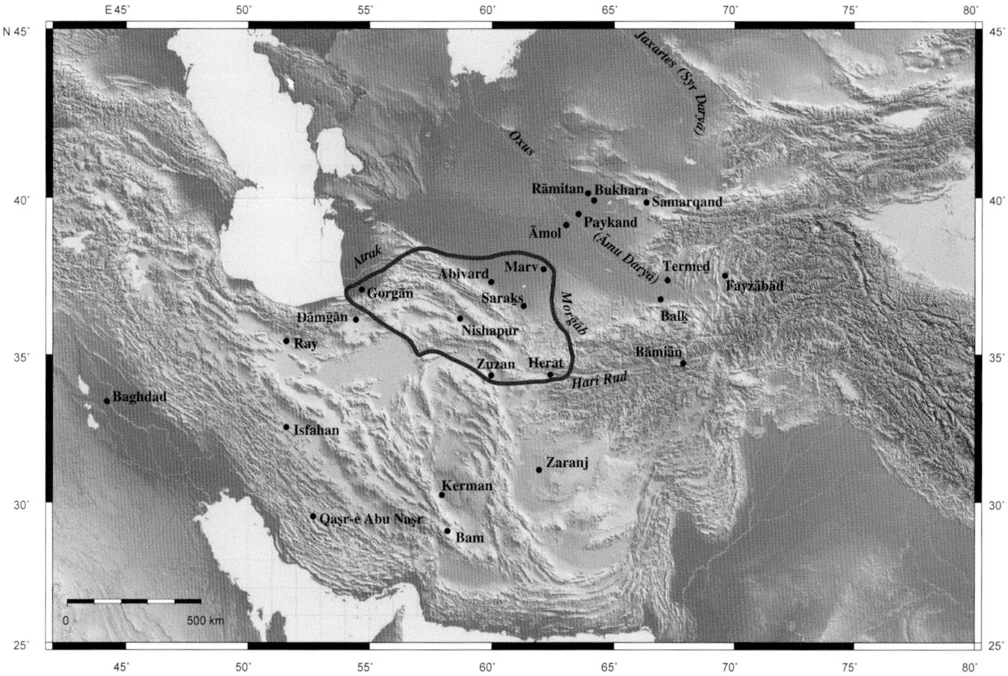

Figure 3: Map proposing the possible frontiers of Khorasan in the 5th-6th centuries CE. (Map created with Generic Mapping Tools and NOAA topographic data.)

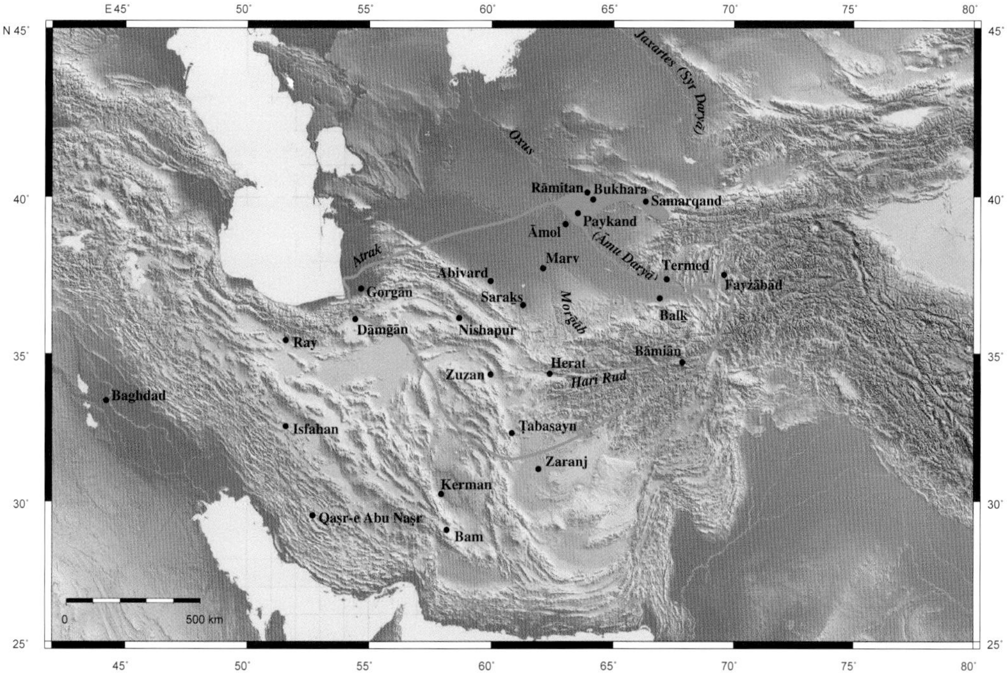

Figure 4: Map proposing the possible frontiers of Greater Khorasan in the 10th century CE. (Map created with Generic Mapping Tools and NOAA topographic data.)

on Khorasan (Figure 4). The standing of this first nucleus of Khorasan, which became "Greater Khorasan," is certainly to be sought in its geographical position at the center of such different lands as Central Asia, China, India, Western Iran and Mesopotamia. This geographical situation formed out of this territory a crossroads through which travelled peoples, cultures, ideas and influences.

Bibliography: Abu'l-ʿAbbās Aḥmad b. Yaḥyā b. Jāber Balāḏori, *Ketāb fotuḥ al-boldān,* tr. by P. K. Hitti as *The Origins of the Islamic State,* part 1, New York, 1916. Charles Barbier de Meynard, *Dictionnaire Géographique, Historique et Littéraire de la Perse et des Contrées Adjacentes, extrait ... du Mo'djem El-Bouldan ... de ... Yaqout,* Paris, 1861. Vaslilii Vladimirovich Barthold, *Turkestan down to the Mongol Invasion,* 3rd ed., London, 1969. C. E. Bosworth, "The Tahirids and Saffarids," *The Cambridge History of Iran* IV, Cambridge, 1975, pp. 90-135. Idem, "Ḳumis," *The Encyclopaedia of Islam* V, Leiden, 1986, pp. 376-78. Elton Daniel, *The Political and Social History of Khurasan under Abbasid Rule, 747-820,* Minneapolis and Chicago, 1979. Touraj Daryaee, *Šahrestānīhā Ī Ērānšahr: A Middle Persian Text on Late Antique Geography, Epic, and History,* Costa Mesa, Calif., 2002. Abu Ḥanifa Dinavari, *al-Aḵbār al-ṭewāl,* ed. Amir ʿAbd-al-Munʿim, Beirut, 1990. Abu'l-Qāsem Ebn Ḥawqal, *Configuration de la Terre,* tr. by J. H. Kramers and G. Wiet, 2 vols., Paris and Beirut, 1964. Richard Frye, "Kushans and Other Iranians in Central Asia," in *Reşid Rahmeti Arat Için,* Türk Kültürünü Araştırma Enstitüsü Yayınlari 19, Ankara, 1966, pp. 244-47. Idem, ed., *The Cambridge History of Iran* IV: *The Period from the Arab Invasion to the Saljuqs,* Cambridge, 1975. Rika Gyselen, *La Géographie Administrative de l'Empire Sassanide,* Paris, 1989. Idem, "La reconquête de l'est iranien par l'empire sassanide au Vie siècle, d'après les sources 'iraniennes'" *Arts Asiatiques* 58, 2003, pp. 162-67.

Ernst Herzfeld, "Khorasan: Denkmalsgeographische Studien zur Kulturgeschichte des Islam in Iran," in *Der Islam* 11, 1921, pp. 107-74. Meysam Labbāf-Ḵāniki, "Ḵorāsān dar ʿasr-e Sāsāni," in Meysam Labbāf-Ḵāniki, ed., *Gozari bar bāstānšenāsi-ye,* Tehran, 2015, pp. 61-67. Pierre Lecoq, "Aparna," *Encyclopædia Iranica* II, London and New York, 1987, p. 151. Guy Le Strange, *The Lands of the Eastern Caliphate; Mesopotamia, Persia, and Central Asia, from the Moslem Conquest to the Time of Timur,* Cambridge, 1930; 3rd ed., London, 1966. Joseph Markwart, Ērānšahr *nach der Geographie des ps. Moses Xorenacci,* Abhandlungen der Königlichen Gesellschaft der Wissenschaften zu Göttingen, phil.-hist. KL. N.F. 3/2, Berlin, 1901. Idem, *A Catalogue of the Provincial Capitals of* Ērānšahr*: Pahlavi Text, Version and Commentary,* ed. Giuseppe Messina, Rome, 1931. Abu'l-Ḥasan ʿAli Masʿudi, *Moruj al-ḏahab,* tr. as *Les prairies d'or* by C. Barbier de Meynard and A. Pavet de Courteille, rev. by Charles Pellat, vol. I, Paris 1962. André Miquel, *La Géographie humaine du monde musulman jusqu'au milieu du 11e siècle,* 4 vols., Paris, 1967-88. Qodāma b. Jaʿfar, *Ketāb al-ḵarāj,* tr. A. Ben Shemesh, Leiden, 1965. Rocco Rante and A. Collinet, *Nishapur Revisited: Stratigraphy and Ceramics of the Qohandez,* Oxford, 2013. Rocco Rante, "'Khorasan Proper' and 'Greater Khorasan' within a Politico-Cultural Framework," in idem, ed., *Greater Khorasan: History, Geography, Archaeology and Material Culture,* Boston, 2015, pp. 9-25. P. Schwarz, *Iran im Mittelalter nach den arabischen Geographen,* Leipzig, 1896-1921, repr. Hildesheim and New York, 1969. Aḥmad b. Abi Yaʿqub Yaʿqubi, *Ketāb al-boldān,* tr. by Gaston Wiet as *Les pays,* Cairo, 1937. Idem, *Taʾriḵ,* ed. M. Th. Houtsma as *Ibn-Wādhih qui dicitur al-Jaʿqubī Historiae,* 2 vols., Leiden, 1883; repr. 1969.

(Meysam Labbaf-Khaniki and Rocco Rante)

ii. Pre-Islamic history

The idea of Khorasan itself goes back to the late Sasanian (q.v.) period, when the term was used to indicate the eastern part of the empire, a vast region whose boundaries were not precisely defined. In fact, the Middle Persian name Xwarāsān (Pers. Ḵorāsān) is attested on the bullae carrying the sealing of the *spāhbeds* (q.v.) of the East, where it occurs in the standard formula ... *wuzurg ērān kust ī Xwarāsān spāhbed* '... grandee, *Ērān spāhbed* of the side of the East' (Gyselen, 2001, pp. 35-36; Gyselen, 2007, pp. 248-54).

Ṭabari (q.v.; d. 923) knew about the quadripartition of the army that he considered to have taken place during the reign of Khosrow I (q.v.; r. 531-79), and he wrote that there was an *iṣbahbadh* of the East, one of the West, one in charge of Nimruz, and one of Azerbaijan (Ṭabari, tr., V, p. 149); similar information is found also in the works of other Islamic historiographers. Thanks to this combined evidence, we know that one of the four mighty armies that defended the empire in late Sasanian times, after the military and administrative reform begun by Kawād I (q.v.; r. 488-531) and completed by Khosrow I, was the army of the East (Xwarāsān), attesting that this name was current in the official language of the Sasanian government. However, chances are that it did not designate any specific region, province or civil administration; rather it is by now clear that it pointed to a specific geographical area in military administration (see already Gnoli, 1985 *contra* Gignoux, 1984).

The "side of the East" is also one of the quarters of the Sasanian Empire according to the Middle Persian geographical treatise *Šahrestānīhā ī Ērānšahr* (q.v.), written well into the Islamic period, under ʿAbbasid (q.v.) rule, though definitely preserving late Sasanian lore. When looking at this text as a whole, one cannot help but notice that the southern quarter is far larger than the other ones, including areas that one may think better placed in Xwarāsān, and that the northern one is comparatively smaller than what one would expect (Marquart, 1931; Daryaee; see also Gyselen, 1988 for a critical evaluation of its contents). The *kust ī Xwarāsān* is the first sector of the empire to be listed in this text. According to its anonymous author, the "East" includes: Samarkand that was in *Sugud ī haft āšyān* 'Sogdiana of the seven abodes', Nawāzag in *Baxl ī bāmīg* 'Splendid Balkh', Xwārazm, Marwrōd, Marw, Harē(w), Pūšang, Tōs, Nēwšābuhr, Kāyēn, Dahestān in Gurgān, and Kūmīs (pars. 2-18).

Moreover, paragraphs 19-20 of the *Šahrestānīhā* contain the name of five cities built by Husraw (Khosrow I): Husraw-šād, Husraw-mūstābād, Wisp-šād-Husraw, Hubōy-Husraw, and Šād-farrox-Husraw, specifying that this conurbation was surrounded by a long wall. Nothing is known about the whereabouts of these cities, but there is no formal reason not to include them in Xwarāsān (Gyselen, 1988, p. 198), though Joseph Marquart (1931, p. 13) and Touraj Daryaee (pp. 40-41) lean toward moving them to the western quarter (*kust ī xwarwarān*). When comparing the toponyms found in the *Šahrestānīhā* with the evidence provided by Sasanian administrative glyptics one immediately notices that only a few of the geographical names mentioned in the *Šahrestānīhā* are also found on seals and sealings and that some of the provinces attested in the Middle Persian text, such as Sogdiana, Bactria or Chorasmia (qq.v.), were not part of the late Sasanian Empire (Gyselen, 1988, p. 193).

Another list of the provinces of Khorasan in the Sasanian era is preserved in a work traditionally assigned to the Armenian geographer and historian Movsēs Xorenacʿi (q.v.; Marquart, 1901, pp. 47-93). The toponyms found in this record only partly coincide with those enumerated in the Middle Persian text. Moreover, both the sequence in which they are listed and some of the toponyms themselves seem to be out of order, suggesting that some mishap may have occurred when writing or copying the *Catalogue*.

Furthermore, Islamic authors such as Ebn K̲ordād̲beh (q.v.; d. ca. 885) knew of a division of Khorasan into four distinct *marzban*ates in Sasanian times (Marquart, 1901, p. 70). Another piece of evidence pointing toward the likelihood of a geographic notion identifying the East in the late Sasanian period comes from numismatics. Coins minted in Umayyad Zāvulistān (Zābolestān) after 687 CE on a Sasanian model carry the legend *tkyn' bg hwtʾy hwlʾsʾn MLKA* (*Tegīn bay xwadāy Xwarāsān šāh* 'Tegin, His Majesty, Lord, King of Khorasan') attesting the title *Xwarāsān šāh* in the very early Islamic period (Gyselen, 2010, p. 237; Rezakhani, 2017, p. 168).

As is well known, Islamic Khorasan includes much of the eastern Iranian world that in the scholarly literature dealing with the pre-Islamic period is typically defined as outer Iran, a region further away from the centers of power of Mesopotamia and Persia that were better known to classical historians due to their closeness to the western world. Nonetheless, the eastern expanse has always been a vital part of the Iranian ecumene. In the Bisotun inscription (q.v.), Darius the Great (q.v.; r. 522-486 BCE) states that he rules over twenty-three countries, among which were the eastern ones of ... *Parθava, Zranka, Haraiva, Uvārazmī, Bāxtriš, Suguda, Gandāra, Saka, Θataguš, Harauvatiš...* '... Parthia, Drangiana, Aria, Chorasmia, Bactria, Sogdiana, Gandāra, Scythya, Sattagydia, Arachosia...' (Schmitt, pp. 49-50), each of which came at some point in history to be considered to be part of Khorasan.

Similar lists are found in other inscriptions by Darius in Susa and Persepolis (qq.v.) as well as of Xerxes I (r. 486-65 BCE; XPh, *daiva* inscription). When the Achaemenid Empire fell under the blows of Alexander (q.v.) and his Macedonians, opening the way for the blossoming of Hellenism in Western Asia, the heartland of Iranism moved toward the East. There, in the flatlands to the east of the Caspian Sea (q.v.), Arsaces rose in revolt against the Seleucids (q.v.), soon to conquer Parthia at the head of his Parni (APARNA, q.v.) kinsmen, taking advantage of the havoc caused by Andragoras' (q.v.) short lived rebellion and of the defeat of the former Seleucid governor. A few years later Diodotus (q.v.), the Seleucid satrap of Bactria-Sogdiana, obtained his independence (Cereti, pp. 236-39). The earlier part of history of the Greek kingdoms of Central Asia and of the kings who later moved toward the territories to the south of the Hindu Kush (q.v.) is only known in its very general outlines (Bernard, pp. 99-101), but these people left an impressive cultural heritage to the Kushans (q.v.), who between the first and third centuries CE became one of the major powers in Eastern Iran and Northern India (Bivar; Falk). The Kushans were able to deal on an equal hand with the Arsacids (q.v.) and were certainly instrumental in keeping alive the Hellenistic heritage while integrating it in the new cultural context, as witnessed among others by the use of the Greek alphabet to write the Bactrian language (q.v.).

Like the Achaemenids, the early Sasanian kings also claimed authority over Eastern Iran. In his renowned trilingual inscription on the Kaʿba-ye Zardošt (q.v.), Šāpur I (q.v.; r. 239-70) mentions the eastern lands of **[Par] θaw (...) ud hamag Parišxwār kōf, Māδ, Wurgān, Marγ, Harēw, ud hamag Abaršahr, Kermān, Sagestān, Tuγrān, Mak(u)rān, Pār(a)dān, Hindestān, Kušānšahr yad fraxš ō Paškabūr ud yad ō Kāš, Suγd ud Čāčestān [ud až hō* (?) *ārag zrē]h Mazū[n]šahr* 'Parthia (...) the entire Alborz chain, Media, Gurgān, Marw, Harēw, the entire Abaršahr, Kermān, Sistān, Turān, Makrān, Pāradān, Hindestān, Kušānšahr up to Pešāwar and to Kāšγar (?), Sogdiana and Taškent and on the other side of the sea the land of Mazūn [Oman]' (Huyse, I, pp. 22-24; the quote follows the better preserved Parthian text). By doing so, he lays claim to lordship over the whole of later Khorasan. Most interesting is Šāpur's mentioning *Kušānšahr*, a province that was then ruled by the Kushano-Sasanian dynasty, probably a cadet branch of the Sasanian family that enjoyed a high degree of autonomy. These dynasts began minting coins almost contemporarily with the Sasanian Ardašīr I (q.v.; d. 242 CE; Rezakhani, pp. 72-86; on Kushano-Sasanian coinage, see Jongeward and Cribb).

The latter part of the Sasanian period was characterized by a growing confrontation of the empire with aggressive eastern foes, who, wave after wave, threatened the oriental frontiers. Unfortunately we have relatively few written documents on the history of the Iranian Huns, Kidarites, Alkhan, Hephthalites, Nēzak (qq.v.), and of the

Turkish groups that followed in their wave (Rezakhani, pp. 87-184), though some information may come from Chinese sources (see Daffinà on Chinese sources for Sasanian history). Nonetheless, numismatic research has made it possible to reconstruct at least the outline of the reigns of these powerful foes of the Sasanian empire, who were deeply influenced by their western neighbor and its culture (Göbl; Vondrovec; Alram and Klimburg-Salter, 1999; Alram et al., 2010).

The Kidarites (ca. 370-467 CE) settled in Bactria already in the 4th century CE and by 370 they were running the administrative divisions of the Sasanian empire in that area. They were followed by a second wave of nomads, the Alkhan (ca. 440-500 CE), who by 380 had taken over the Sasanian mint in Kabulistān to later expand their power to the east and then south toward the Indian plains. Among the Iranian Huns, the Hephthalites (ca. 484-560 CE) were a mighty foe of the Sasanians. In 484 Pērōz (see FIRUZ, r. 459-84) was heavily defeated by this eastern enemy and it was only Khosrow I who avenged this defeat in 560, putting an end to Hephthalite power through an alliance with the western Turks, who were bound to play an important political role in the area in the years to come. The late fifth century also saw the rise of the Nēzak (ca. 480-560 CE) in Zābulistān and then Kabulistān (Alram, 2016, pp. 18 ff.).

This interaction—military, social, and cultural—deeply transformed eastern Iran, preparing the ground for the intellectual *renaissance* that was to take place in the Islamic era.

Eastern Iran was Zoroaster's (q.v.) motherland and the Avesta (q.v.) preserves a wealth of precious information on early society in an area stretching from the Aral Sea to Helmand (qq.v.) province in southern Afghanistan (Skjærvø; on Avestan geography and Zoroaster's homeland see Gnoli, 1980, pp. 59-158; and AVESTAN GEOGRAPHY) that was to have a powerful influence on the development of later Iranian culture and lore. Central Asia has always been a crossroads of different religious traditions and has preserved a rich heritage of Buddhist, Christian, and Manichaean texts written in a variety of languages that have allowed scholars to better understand these religions. It is precisely this multicultural environment that blossomed into a veritable Age of Enlightenment in the Iranian world (Starr). Nor can one underestimate the powerful impact that the Sistanian epic cycle, rich in common Eastern Iranian elements, had on later Persian literature (Hameen-Antilla, pp. 174-199; Gazerani; van Zutphen).

Bibliography: Michael Alram, *Das Antlitz des Fremden: Die Münzprägung der Hunnen und Westtürken in Zentralasien und Indien*, Schriften des Kunsthistorischen Museums 17, Vienna, 2016. Michael Alram and Deborah E. Klimburg-Salter, eds., *Coins, Art, and Chronology: Essays on Pre-Islamic History of the Indo-Iranian Borderlands*, Veröffentlichungen der numismatischen Kommission 33, Vienna, 1999. Michael Alram, Deborah E. Klimburg-Salter, Minoru Inaba, and Matthias Pfisterer, eds., *Coins, Art, and Chronology* II*: The First Millennium C.E. in the Indo-Iranian Borderlands*, Veröffentlichungen der numismatischen Kommission 50, Vienna, 2010. Paul Bernard, "The Greek Kingdoms of Central Asia," in János Harmatta et al., eds., *History of Civilizations of Central Asia* II: *The Development of Sedentary and Nomadic Civilizations 700 B.C. to A.D. 250*, Paris, 1994, pp. 99-129. Adrian David H. Bivar, "Kushan Dynasty i. Dynastic History," *Encyclopædia Iranica,* online edition, 2009. Carlo G. Cereti, "Il mondo iranico dai Parti ai Sasanidi," in Alessandro Barbero and Giusto Traina, eds., *Storia d'Europa e del Mediterraneo*, I. *Il Mondo Antico*, Sez. 3, vol. III/IV, Rome, 2009, pp. 223-62. Paolo Daffinà, "La Persia sassanide secondo le fonti cinesi," *Rivista di Studi Orientali* 57, 1983 [1985], pp. 121-70. Touraj Daryaee, *Šahrestānīhā ī Ērānšahr: A Middle Persian Text on Late Antique Geography, Epic, and History*, Costa Mesa, Calif., 2002. Harry Falk, "Kushan Dynasty iii. Chronology of the Kushans," *Encyclopædia Iranica,* online edition, 2014.

Saghi Gazerani, *The Sistani Cycle of Epics and Iran's National History: On the Margins of Historiography*, Boston and Leiden, 2015. Philippe Gignoux, "Les quatre régions administrative de l'Iran sasanide et la symbolique des nombres trois et quatre," *Annali Istituto Universitario Orientale* 44/4, 1984, pp. 555-72. Gherardo Gnoli, *Zoroaster's Time and Homeland: A Study on the Origins of Mazdeism and Related Problems*, IUO Series Minor 7, Naples, 1980. Idem, "The Quadripartition of the Sasanian Empire," *East and West* 35, 1985, pp. 265-70. Idem, "Avestan Geography," *Encyclopædia Iranica* III, London and New York, 1989, pp. 44-47. Robert Göbl, *Dokumente zur Geschichte der iranischen Hunnen in Baktrien und Indien*, 4 vols., Wiesbaden, 1967. Rika Gyselen, "Les Données de géographie administrative dans le 'Šahrestānīhā-ī Ērān'," *Studia Iranica* 17/2, 1988, pp. 191-206. Idem, *The Four Generals of the Sasanian Empire: Some Sigillographic Evidence,* Conferenze 14, Rome, 2001. Idem, *Sasanian Seals and Sealings in the A. Saeedi Collection*, Acta Iranica 44, Leuven, 2007. Idem, "'Umayyad' Zāvulistān and Arachosia: Copper Coinage and the Sasanian Monetary Heritage," in M. Alram, D. Klimburg-Salter, M. Inaba and M. Pfisterer, eds., *Coins, Art, and Chronology II. The First Millennium C.E. in the Indo-Iranian Borderlands*, Veröffentlichungen der numismatischen Kommission 50, Vienna, 2010, pp. 219-41. Jaakko Hämeen-Anttila, *Khwadāynāmag: The Middle Persian Book of Kings*, Boston and Leiden, 2018. Philip Huyse, *Die dreisprachige Inschrift Šābuhrs I. an der Kaᶜba-i Zardušt (ŠKZ)*, Corpus Inscriptionum Iranicarum 3/1, 2 vols., London, 1999. David Jongeward and Joe Cribb, *Kushan, Kushano-Sasanian and Kidarite Coins: A Catalogue of Coins from the American Numismatic Society*, New York, 2015.

Joseph Marquart (Markwart), *Ērānšahr nach der Geographie des Ps. Moses Xorenacᶜi*, Abhandlungen der königlichen Gesellschaft der Wissenschaften zu Göttingen, phil.-hist. KL. NF 3/2, Berlin, 1901. Idem, *A Catalogue of the Provincial Capitals of Ērānshahr: Pahlavi Text, Version and Commentary*, ed. Giuseppe Messina, Rome, 1931. Khodadad Rezakhani, *ReOrienting the Sasanians:*

East Iran in Late Antiquity, Edinburgh Studies in Ancient Persia 4, Edinburgh, 2017. Prods Oktor Skjærvø, "Avestan Society," in Touraj Daryaee, ed., *The Oxford Handbook of Iranian History*, Oxford, 2012, pp. 57-119. Rüdiger Schmitt, The *Bisitun Inscriptions of Darius the Great: Old Persian Text,* Corpus Inscriptionum Iranicarum Part I, Vol. I, Texts I, London, 1991. S. Frederick Starr, *Lost Enlightenment: Central Asia's Golden Age from the Arab Conquest to Tamerlane,* Princeton, 2013. Ṭabari, *Taʾrik̲*, tr. and annotated by Clifford E. Bosworth, as *The History of al-Ṭabarī* V: *The Sāsānids, the Byzantines, the Lakhmids and Yemen*, Albany, NY, 1999. Klaus Vondrovec, *Coinage of the Iranian Huns and Their Successors from Bactria to Gandhara (4th to 8th Century CE)*, Vienna, 2014. Marjolijn van Zutphen, *Farāmarz, the Sistāni Hero: Texts and Traditions of the Farāmarznāme and the Persian Epic Cycle*, Leiden, 2014.

(Carlo G. Cereti)

iii. Historical Geography in the Late Sasanid-Early Islamic Periods

General Introduction

Khorasan in the Sasanid and early Islamic period included areas that are part of modern-day eastern Iran, Afghanistan, Pakistan, Uzbekistan, Tajikistan, and the eastern portion of Turkmenistan (see KHORASAN i. THE CONCEPT OF KHORASAN). At the time of the Islamic conquests, beginning in the third decade of the 7th century, Khorasan was fragmented geographically, politically, socially, culturally, and ethnically. The population was composed of Persians (Sasanians), Hephthalites (q.v.), Sogdians, and Turks. Regional political elites (the *moluk al-ṭawāʾef*) of this period retained much authority over their localities. When the Arabs arrived in the second half of the 1st/7th century to claim these lands, there were multiple frontiers and mini-states. This complex shatter zone comprised a unique set of geographic features, ecological niches, and different populations. Indigenous populations resisted conquest and rebelled, while significant numbers of localized Muslims established roots in these regions.

In ancient times, these lands were claimed as part of the (Achaemenid) Persian Empire (558–330 BCE). Before 558 BCE, pre-Achaemenid Balk̲ (q.v.) was a major power center. It retained its importance during Achaemenid times and served as the royal capital in the east. It remained the political capital of Bactria under the Greeks (305–125 BCE). Under the Arsacids (Parthians, 250 BCE– 228 CE), Khorasan again rose to preeminence from its regional capital city, Nisa (q.v.; see also CAPITAL CITIES i. PRE-ISLAMIC TIMES; Wiesehöfer, p. 1).

During the latter part of Sasanian rule (590-630), the ongoing wars with Byzantium (309-79, 540, and 590-628) generated a major shift of focus to its western borders. On its Khorasani borders, the Sasanians were defeated by the Hephthalites (465/484) and briefly became tributaries. After 579, major battles with the Western Turks for control of Hephthalite lands resulted in Sasanian defeats and the loss of territorial control of Ṭok̲ārestān/Tocharia (Wiesehöfer, pp. 314-15)

In 39/659 and 41/661 the Chinese (T'ang dynasty) took nominal control of all of the Khorasani lands formerly under the Turks, and bestowed T'ang titles and hereditary offices on their rulers. In 41/661 the T'ang created the Bo-si (Po-ssu, Persia) area command in Sistān and appointed Pērōz (Firuz), the son of Yazdegerd III, as the area commander (Chavannes, p. 172, see CHINESE-IRANIAN RELATIONS i. IN PRE-ISLAMIC TIMES). In 42/662 they gave him the title king of Persia. There are no accounts of this Pērōz in the Arabic chronicles of Ṭabari or Ebn al-Aṯir (qq.v.), but both include short passages referring to *al-šāh* that only make some sense when they are applied to Pērōz (Ṭabari, tr., XIII, p. 175; Ebn al-Aṯir, III, p. 23). Pērōz died in China sometime between 57/676 and 60/679.

Sasanian Khorasan

Geographic divisions. Sasanian Khorasan occupied all of the present-day Iranian province of Khorasan, the northern adjoining non-desert areas of present-day Turkmenistan, including the current capital Ashgabat (Nisa; Ar. Nasā or Nesā), and the northwestern border areas of Afghanistan. The eastern frontier areas had remained under direct Sasanian rule, while neighboring areas were autonomous. There were four distinct geographical areas: the northern piedmont (the Kopet Dāḡ basin or corridor), the Kašaf Rud basin, the Herat valley (the Herat basin), and Qohestān. Ṭabas al-Tamr and Ṭabas al-ʿOnnāb together roughly marked the southern boundary between Qohestān and Kermān. Travel times were long. Marv (Marw al-Šāhejān), in the extreme northeastern corner of the northern piedmont was a twelve-day journey to Ṭus, to the southeast. The travel time from Abaršahr (q.v.; Nishapur) or Ṭus to Herat in the Herat valley was nine days (see Figure 1).

The northern piedmont/Kopet Dāḡ basin. Mountains divided Sasanian Khorasan from the northwest to the southeast. The northern piedmont formed a corridor 375 miles long and 50 miles wide between the mountain slopes and the Qara Qum desert. Nasā and Abivard (q.v.) were the best known and most important settlements during Sasanian and Omayyad times. Beyond this belt lay the Qara Qum desert. Toward the southeastern limits of this rim was the town of Sarak̲s.

Marv in the northeast was situated on a delta formed by the Morḡāb river. Southeast of Marv and also on the Morḡāb river was Marw al-Rud̲, which bordered Bādḡis and Ḡarčestān (q.v.; Ar. Ḡarj al-Šar or Ḡarjestān). Marw al-Rud̲ was on the Sasanian frontier.

Kašaf Rud basin. The Binālud (q.v.) ranges comprised the mountain recesses of Ṭabārestān and Jorjān (Gorgān, q.v.) and meet the Khorasan plateau. Only a narrow, thirty-mile wide strip of land, which began at Qumes, separated this barrier range from the Dašt-e Kavir (see DESERT). This was the only non-desert route into Khorasan. The inner circle of mountains protected the inner region on the north and the east, but it was internally isolated, by salt wastes on the west and southwest.

*Qohestān (Quhestān)***.** The Dašt-e Kavir and Dašt-e Luṭ deserts and the mountains of Qohestān formed an additional physical barrier from Persia proper. To the south, deserts met the mountains of Kermān. The isolated Kermāni frontier sheltered the Kharijites (see KHARIJITES IN PERSIA), who utilized Sistān as a refuge of last resort. Qohestān's north/south mountains (Qāʾen to Birjand) met the deserts on the west and their eastern slopes formed the western boundary to Sistān (Sejestān) and faced the Kuh-e Bābā range. A fertile north-to-south corridor between these two ranges drains southwardly from Herat to Zarang in Sistān.

*The Herat basin***.** The Harirud river watered the Herat valley, flowing from the east to the west out of Ḡur (q.v.). Bušanj (Pušang) was west of Herat where the river flowed north, reaching the Hazār Masjed range. It converged with the Kašaf Rud, flowing out of the southern slopes of the Ālā Dāḡ (q.v.). From there the Harirud flowed past Sarakẖs into the Qara Qum desert.

The Barkut (Šāhjahān) mountains connect the Kopet Dāḡ with the Safid Kuh. The Harirud cut through them. Between the Harirud and the Morḡāb rivers lay the pasturelands of Bāḏḡis and further to the east was Ḡarčestān. The Ālā Dāḡ (q.v.) range in the north and the Afghan Safid Kuh range east of Herat divided Sasanian Khorasan in two, and separated the Iranian plateau from the steppes of Central Asia, and Herat from Bāḏḡis and Ḡarčestān.

Marv and "Inner Khorasan." Nasā, Abivard, Sarakẖs, Marw al-Šāhejān (Marv) and Marw al-Ruḏ comprised the major population centers on the northern piedmont of Sasanian Khorasan. Ṭus and Abaršahr (Nishapur) were the main population centers of the Kašaf Rud basin during the 2nd/7th century. At this time, the irrigation systems most likely limited the populations of these towns to no more than ten thousand (Pourshariati, 1995, p. 9; Christensen, p. 194). Ṭus was the oldest, and Abaršahr was rebuilt during the Sasanian campaigns and wars against the Hephthalites. Smaller settlements in the region of Abaršahr such as Jovayn, Esfarāyen, and Bayhaq (qq.v) rested near the mountains and were stretched out to the western limits of Sasanian Khorasan as far as Qumes. Qāʾen in Qohestān was a small but important place for transiting into and out of Sasanian Khorasan via the desert route to Kermān.

Trade flowed from Ṭokẖārestān, Sogdia, and beyond, either to Sistān or to the Persian Gulf and Kermān through Herat. Northern traders often chose a route through Herat because it was the less difficult one to India. Trade from India also skirted the Hindu Kush through Farāh (q.v.) to Herat and then on to the north or west to Sasanian Kho-

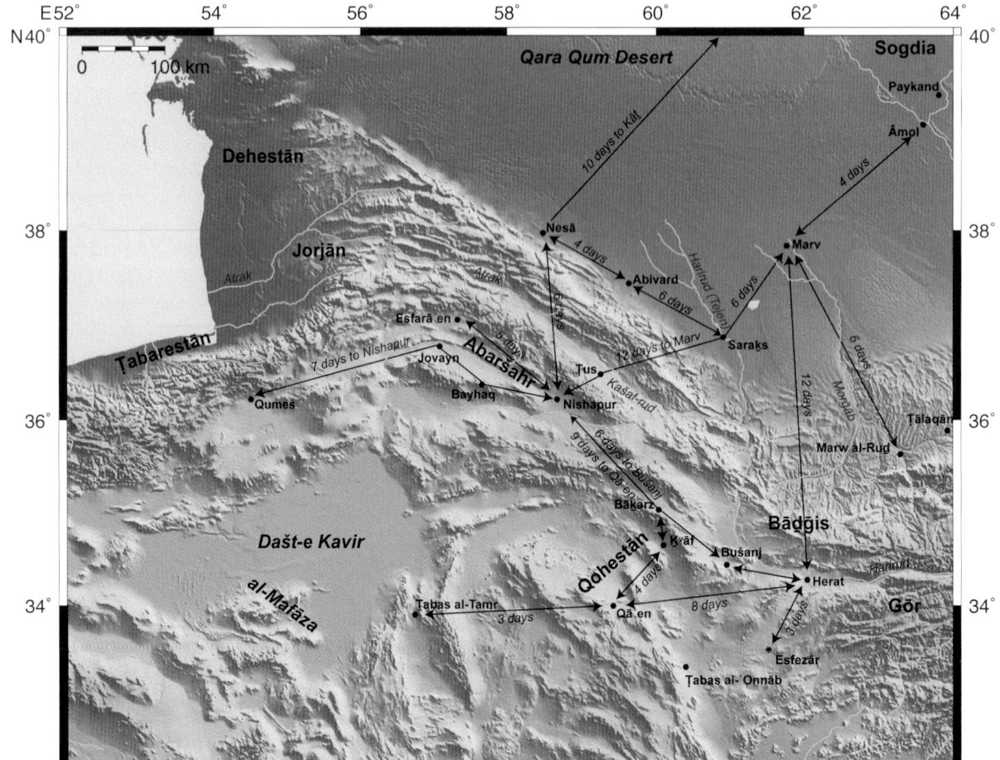

Figure 1. "Sasanian Khorasan" or "Marv and Inner Khorasan." (Map created with Generic Mapping Tools and NOAA topographic data.)

rasan. During the early Islamic conquests, Herat, Bušanj, and the region of Bādḡis negotiated a joint peace treaty with the Arabs. The de facto border of Sasanian Khorasan at the time of the Arab invasions was the Morḡāb river.

ṬOḴĀRESTĀN

Ṭoḵārestān (formerly Bactria, q.v.) was the nexus of the trade routes connecting India with Sogdia and China. The Hephthalites dominated Ṭoḵārestān and Sogdia in the 5th and 6th centuries CE, until they were destroyed politically and militarily by the Western Turks and the Sasanians in 563-66 (Grenet, p. 116; Belenitsky, pp. 110-11). After the Hephthalites were defeated, their lands were divided. The Turks took the territories to the north of the Oxus river (see ĀMU DARYĀ), while the Sasanians took the territories to the south.

Arab geographers delineated the region in a number of ways. (For a detailed explanation of the views of Balāḏori, Ebn Ḵordādbeh, Ebn Rosta, Eṣṭaḵri, Yāqut, and Yaʿqubi concerning Ṭoḵārestān and its divisions, see W. Barthold and C. E. Bosworth, "Ṭukhāristān," in *EI*[2] X, pp. 600-601.) Here, Ṭoḵārestān is defined in its broadest sense to include Ḡarčestān and Jowzjān (q.v.) and includes the river valleys on both sides of the upper Oxus river.

Geographic divisions. Traditionally, Ṭoḵārestān has been divided into an upper region and a lower one, but it is less confusing to rename these two divisions as western and eastern Ṭoḵārestān. The geographical divide between western (lower) Ṭoḵārestān and eastern (upper) Ṭoḵārestān is the Ḵolm river (Kuwayama, pp. 89-134).

Western Ṭoḵārestān was primarily an area of vast plains bounded on the south by the sharp cliffs of the mountains of northern Afghanistan. In the north, the Oxus constituted the boundary. Jowzjān (Gowzgān or Gowzgānān; Ar. Juzjān) was the area between Ḡarčestān and Balḵ. Throughout the Omayyad period, the rulers of Ṭālaqān in Ḡarčestān and Fāryāb and Šoburqān (Šebarḡān) in Jowzjān were important politically. An Omayyad Arab governor lived in Anbār (q.v.), which was a day's journey south of Šoburḡān.

The Arabs called Balḵ the "mother of cities" (Barthold, 1984, p. 33). It was the political and commercial capital of Ṭoḵārestān and a place of religious pilgrimage for both Zoroastrians and Buddhists even in early Islamic times (Barthold, 1968, p. 68). During the governorship of Asad b. ʿAbd-Allāh, in 107/725, Balḵ became the administrative capital of Khorasan (Barthold, 1968, p. 77).

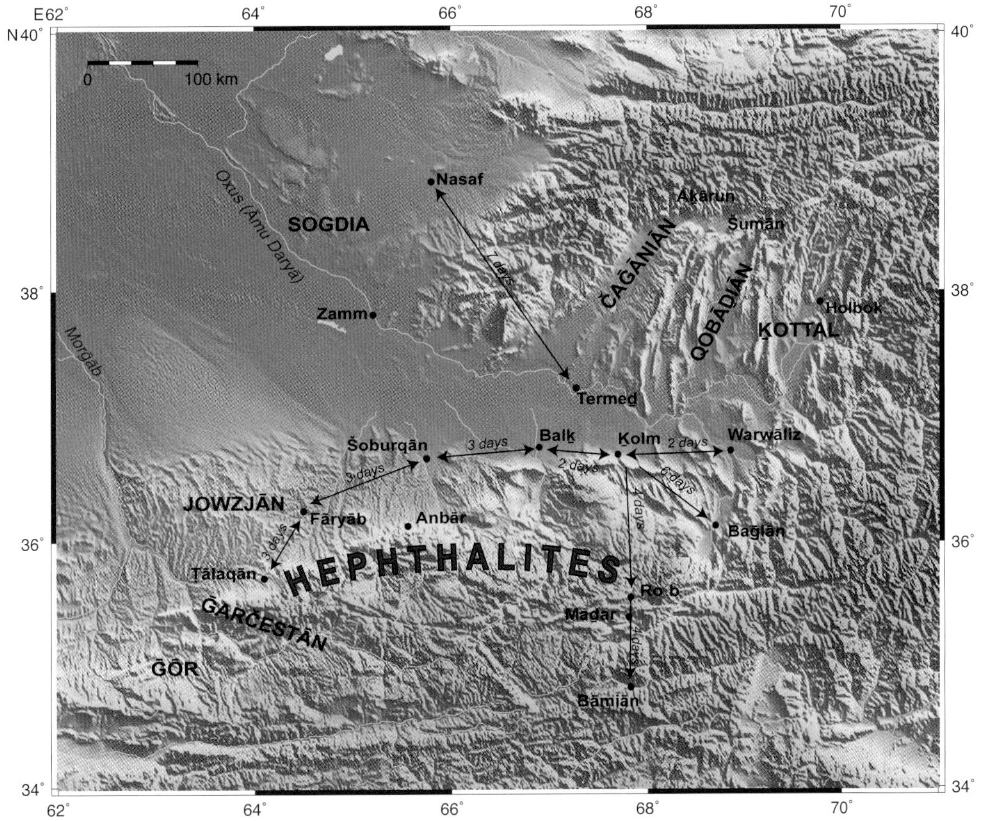

Figure 2. Ṭoḵārestān. (Map created with Generic Mapping Tools and NOAA topographic data.)

As for eastern Ṭoḵārestān, Ḵolm was two-days journey east of Balḵ. Warwāliz (Kunduz) was two days to the east from Ḵolm. From Warwāliz, it was another two days to Ṭālaqān and beyond Ṭālaqān another seven-day journey to Badaḵšān. North of Badaḵšān was the kingdom of Šoḡnān (Šeḡnān). The Ḵāwak and Aq-rabāṭ passes allowed passage through the mountains to the south. The route through Bāmiān was well traveled.

Across the upper Oxus was Ḵottal (q.v.) between the Panj and Waḵš rivers, ruled from Holbok. Ṣaḡāniān (see ČAḠĀNIĀN) in the Sorḵān valley was a four-day journey to the north from Termeḏ, a strong citadel on the Oxus. The small kingdoms of Āḵarun (Ḵarun) and Šumān were situated in the plains of the Sorḵān and Kāfernehān (Qobāḏiān) valleys.

In western Ṭoḵārestān, many of the inhabitants were semi-nomadic and depended on herding. In eastern Ṭoḵārestān, agriculture and trade were dominant. Two major trade routes ran south to India. Ṭālaqān, Fāryāb, Šoburqān, and Anbār in Jowzjān were all connected along the route from Herat to Balḵ or from Marv to Balḵ. Balḵ, Ḵolm and Termeḏ (Termez) had Arab garrisons during Omayyad times.

SOGDIA

Sogdia (see SOGDIANA) lay in Transoxiana (the land beyond the Oxus river up to the Jaxartes (Syr Daryā); see MĀ WARĀʾ AL-NAHR). Culturally, Sogdia was the most potent power in the region, and Sogdian was the lingua franca of traders throughout Central Asia.

Geographic divisions. Sogdia was situated between the Oxus and the Jaxartes. It was bound on the west by Margiana (the region of Marv) and on the north by Ḵᵛārazm (see CHORASMIA), the Qizil Qum desert and Šāš (modern Tashkent; see ČĀČ). Osrušana and Farḡāna (qq.v.) lay to the east, while Ṭoḵārestān lay to the south.

The three major urban centers were Bukhara (q.v.), Samarqand, and Keš (q.v.). The Zarafšān river valley represented the heartland of Sogdia. The Zarafšān river ran 400 miles from east to west, disappearing into the desert forty miles from the Oxus. The valley was extensively irrigated. To the south of the Zarafšān Valley lay the Kaška Daryā river.

The dominant cities on the lower Zarafšān were Paykand and Bukhara, and on the middle course were Samarqand and Panjikant (q.v.). Keš in the Kaška Daryā valley was fifty miles northwest of the Iron Gate, which was the main route into Sogdia from Ṭoḵārestān via Termeḏ.

Ḵᵛārazm, on the lower course of the Oxus river and its delta area, was separated from Sasanian Khorasan by the Qara Qum desert and from Sogdia by the Qizil Qum Desert. The two main towns were Kaṯ on the northern bank of the Oxus and Jorjāniya (Urganj) to the northwest of it.

The eastern frontier. To the east and the northeast lay the lands of Osrušana, Farḡāna, and Šāš (Čāč). Osrušana skirted the Alai mountains. Its capital was Panjikant (Ar.

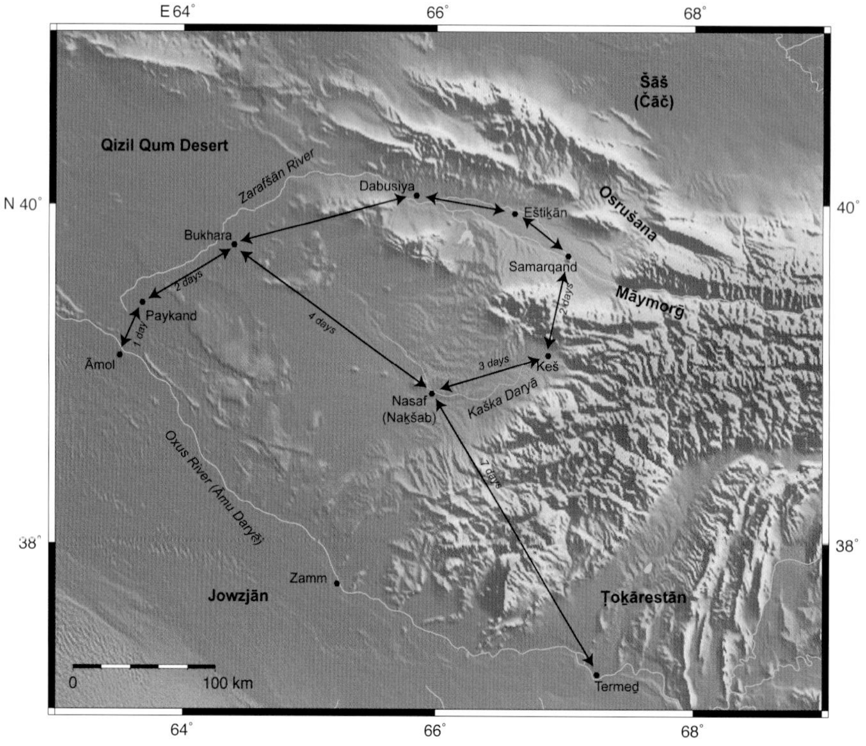

Figure 3. Sogdia. (Map created with Generic Mapping Tools and NOAA topographic data.)

Bonjekaṯ). Farḡāna was situated in a rich river valley and was surrounded on the south, east and north by high mountains (the Tien-shan and Pamirs). Ḵojand (q.v.) was its major city, lying on the Jaxartes (Syr Daryā) bordering Šāš. Both Šāš and Ilāq were bounded by the Jaxartes and the mountains. Benkaṯ, the capital of Šāš, was in the Chirchik (Nahr Tork) river valley, while Ilāq lay in the Āhangarān river valley.

Bukhara was the dominant population center. Paykand (Ar. Baykand) and Wardana were traditional rivals. In 87 or 88/705-6, Qotayba b. Moslem completely destroyed Paykand and held its population for ransom (Ṭabari, tr. XXIII, p. 137; Ebn Aʿṯam, VII, pp. 221-23; Ebn al-Aṯir, IV, pp. 107-9; Naršaḵi, pp. 61-62, tr., pp. 44-45; la Vassière, pp. 268-69). Bukhara emerged as the major city and trade center, but Bukhara's rulers deferred to the ruler of Samarqand. Samarqand, on the middle course of the Zarafšān river, was a major trading emporium linked with the west, with India (via Ṭoḵārestān), and the many routes to China. The city hosted a wide variety of religious communities: Zoroastrians, Christians, Buddhists, Manichaeans and numerous cults. Keš held the dominant position in southern Sogdia. It was situated on the Samarqand to Termeḏ road, a two-day journey from Samarqand and a four-day journey from the Iron Gate. On the lower reaches of the Kaška Daryā lay Nasaf (Naḵšab, Qarši).

Bonjekaṯ, Benkaṯ and Aḵsikaṯ were, respectively, the capital towns of Osrušana, Šāš and Farḡāna in Omayyad times, and constituted the eastern frontier of Omayyad authority. From 86/705 until 96/714, Qotayba b. Moslem waged a campaign of conquest in Sogdia, and these eastern regions became a safe haven from conflict with the Arabs. While Šāš and Farḡāna nominally remained under Arab rule, Omayyad control and authority in reality ended between Samarqand and Osrušana (la Vaissière, p. 266).

THE REGIONAL RULERS (*MOLUK AL-ṬAWĀʾEF*)

The Persian histories and geographies often refer to the local rulers in the East of the pre-Islamic period as the *moluk-e aṭrāf*, which is equivalent to the Arabic *moluk al-ṭawāʾef*. Both the Arabic and Persian expressions are similar in meaning to the middle Persian Sasanian title *marzbān* (warden of the march). Here, the term *moluk al-ṭawāʾef* is used to describe the main local rulers of principalities and mini-states in Ṭoḵārestān, Sogdia, and Sasanian Khorasan (A. Christensen, p. 19; M. Morony, "Moluk al-ṭawāʾif," in *EI*² VII, p. 551; Frye, 1975, p. 9).

The terminology for the titles of these rulers is confusing. Some sources use generic terms such as *dehqān* (q.v.) and *malek*. Other sources use Sasanian terms such as *marzbān* or *spāhbed* (q.v.; Ar. *eṣbahbaḏ*), which denoted administrative or military ranks and titles, respectively. Additionally, most of the *regional rulers* possessed local regnal names (Ebn Ḵordāḏbeh, pp. 39-41 [list of titles]; Balāḏori, *Fotuḥ*, tr., pp. 163, 169, *Ansāb*, V, p. 230; Ḵalifa, *Taʾriḵ* p. 109; Yaʿqubi, *Taʾriḵ*, II, p. 184; Gardizi, p. 103; Ebn al-Aṯir, III, p. 62; Ebn Aʿṯam, II, p. 104; Ṭabari, I, p. 2888, tr., XV, p. 93; Gyselen, pp. 55-56; Rekaya, "Ḳārinids" in *EI*² IV, pp. 644-47l; Table 1).

The regional rulers under the Omayyads retained their positions in exchange for tribute, taxes, and additional obligations. As the leaders of their communities, they maintained the economy and upheld the local beliefs and values. In time, Muslim administrators and governors gradually took over many of the duties as these elites themselves became Muslims. In Ṭoḵārestān and Sogdia, however, the regional rulers resisted Omayyad authority, which represented a period of exploitation and resource extraction.

Peace in Ṭoḵārestān and Zābolestān was never constant because of the shifting loyalties of the three main Hephthalite rulers of these regions: the Nēzak Ṭarḵān in western (lower) Ṭoḵārestān; the Yabḡu (Jabḡuya) in eastern (upper) Ṭoḵārestān; and the Ratbil (or Zunbil) in Zābolestān, one of the most determined opponents of Omayyad authority in Khorasan (Bosworth, 1968, p. 34, following Josef Markwart and others, accepted the form Zunbil as a theophoric title; Bombaci, pp. 58-59, and more recently Sims-Williams, p. 235, have argued for Ratbil or Rotbil, often found in the Arabic sources, as derived from the Turkish title *iltäbir* with metathesis of *l* and *r*, but cf. Afridi, pp. 31-32).

SASANID KHORASAN: STRUCTURES OF THE EMPIRE AND LOCAL NETWORKS

The ruling Parthian families of Sasanian Khorasan controlled vast estates; however, Sasanian dynasts had also acquired large royal estates and appointed elites from other ruling families and transplanted peoples. A blending of centralized and local authority was most visible in the major Sasanian power centers of Marv/Marw al-Ruḏ and Nishapur/Ṭus.

Marv and its dependencies. Abrāz Māhōē (Ar. Māhuya or Māhawayh; see ABRĀZ), the *marzbān* of Marv, is variously described in the sources as the *dehqān* of Marv or as its *marzbān* or its *malek*. His designation *dehqān* by Ṭabari (Ṭabari, I, pp. 2876; tr. XV, p. 83) indicates his standing as a local landed nobleman, while the Sasanian

Table 1
REGIONS AND TITLES OF LOCAL RULERS OF SASANIAN KHORASAN

Mini-States, Regions	Titles
Nesā	Abrāz, Varāz, Erānshāh
Abīward	Bahamna, Vahamna
Saraḵs	Zāḏuya
Marw al-Šahejan	Abrāz, Marzbān
Marw al-Ruḏ	Bāḏām, Kilān
Ṭus	Kanārang
Nišāpur	Kanār
Qohestān	Marzbān
Zarang	Marzbān
Dehestān	Čul (Ar. Ṣul)
Ṭabarestan	Spāhbed (Ar. Eṣbahbaḏ, etc.)
Zābolestan	Ratbil, Rotbil, Zonbil

Source: See Nafisi, *Tāriḵ-e tamaddon-e Irān-e Sāsāni*, pp. 4-5 for a listing of titles.

title/rank *marzbān* indicates an administrative and/or military function. He ruled over Marv and Marw al-Rud̲, its dependency. Additionally, Ebn Aʿt̲am (II, p. 104) names him as the *malek* (king) of Sarak̲s. His local regnal name of Abrāz indicates that he was a leader of the regional elite, and his official designation as the *marzbān* most probably gave him responsibility for the northern piedmont region. Māhōē also was said to have had authority over Ṭālaqān, Jowzjānān and other places. All of these facts, coupled with the information that Māhōē was married to the daughter of the Nēzak Ṭarkān, the Hephthalite ruler of Bādḡis, demonstrates that the Sasanian bureaucracy had successfully stabilized the Sasanian-Hephthalite border.

Māhōē remained the ruler in Marv, subordinate to the Muslim authorities for at least fifteen years. Balād̲ori (*Ansāb* V, p. 230) asserts that Māhōē visited the caliph ʿAli in Kufa and that later the Khorasani governor Rabiʿ b. Ziād Ḥāret̲i escorted Māhōē to meet the governor of Iraq and the East, Ziād b. Abi Sufyān. Yaʿqubi (II, p. 214) acknowledges a correspondence between the caliph ʿAli and Māhōē, ordering Māhōē to recognize ʿAli's appointees and to deliver the *k̲arāj* to them.

There are no records of later *marzbāns* of Marv beyond Māhōē and his son Barāz (Abrāz) until 105/723 under the governorship of Moslem b. Saʿid, who appointed Bahrām Sis, a Zoroastrian, as *marzbān*. Bahrām Sis evidently remained in this position for at least sixteen years, until the governorship of Naṣr b. Sayyār (120-131/738-48), the last Omayyad governor of Khorasan (Ṭabari, II, pp. 1462, 1688, tr. XXIV, p. 193; XXVI, p. 24).

Bād̲ām (Bād̲ān; see Justi, p. 56) is named in the sources as the *marzbān* of Marw al-Rud̲. He was a relative of the former Persian ruler of Yemen. He negotiated a peace treaty with Aḥnaf b. Qays in 31/651. As part of the treaty, Bād̲ām negotiated the exemption of his family from taxes, but he was required to provide *asāwera* (q.v.) as requested.

Abaršahr (Nišāpur)/Ṭus and Qohestān. The *marzbān* of Nishapur is named Aswār by Ebn Aʿt̲am (II, p. 103), but this is most likely a designation meaning the head of the *asāwera*. Nišāburi (paragraph 2,726, p. 204) names him Barzān Jāh, the *marzbān* of the territory (Abaršahr). This could be a corruption of the regnal name Abrāz Šāh (Pourshariati, p. 273, suggests this is a corruption of Borzin Šāh). The *marzbān* of Nishapur fiercely resisted the Muslim siege of the city, but the *kanārang* of Ṭus assisted them and delivered half of the city to the Muslims (Ṭabari, I, p. 2886, tr. XV, pp. 91-92). Balād̲ori represented the *kanārang* of Ṭus as the governor of Khorasan. The narratives concerning the *kanārang* (see *kanārang* in Justi, p. 155, and Frye, 1975, p. 9) are contradictory, but all the reports indicate that he assisted the Muslims in conquering Nishapur and paid tribute to them. Other puzzling reports state that he retained control of half of Nishapur and half of Ṭus and Nasā (see Ṭabari, I, p. 2886, tr., XV, pp. 91-92; Balād̲ori, *Fotuḥ*, tr., pp. 39, 162; Nišāburi, pp. 202-3; Yaʿqubi, *Taʾrik̲*, II, p. 167). In 77/696-7, ʿOmar b. Abi'l-Ṣalt b. Kanārā, a grandson of the *kanārang*, claimed to be the one who killed the Azraqite caliph Qaṭari b. Fojaʾa (Ṭabari, II, p. 1019, tr. XXII, p. 163; see KHARIJITES IN PERSIA). He later fought on the side of Ebn al-Ašʿat̲ during the latter's rebellion (Ṭabari, II, p. 1118, tr. XXIII, p. 63).

Qāren (see KĀRIN) rebelled in Qohestān in 33/653 and marshalled a force of forty thousand from Qohestān, Bādḡis and Herat (K̲alifa, *Taʾrik̲*, p. 107; Ebn al-At̲ir, III, p. 68; Ṭabari, I, p. 2905-6, tr., XV, pp. 108-9). He was killed by forces led by ʿAbd-Allāh b. K̲āzem. The inclusion of troops from Bādḡis and Herat again highlights a joint Sasanian-Hephthalite military effort against the Muslims. Until the colonization of Khorasan in 51/671, there were sporadic rebellions, but the local armies of Sasanian Khorasan were destroyed at this early stage and never re-emerged.

LOCAL RULERS AND THE TʾANG PROTECTORATES

The rulers of Ṭok̲ārestān and Sogdia (Tables 2, 3) included the Yabḡu of Ṭok̲ārestān (see JABḠUYA), the Šad̲ (the ruler of Ṣaḡāniān), the Nēzak Ṭark̲ān of Bādḡis, and the Sabal, the ruler of K̲ottal. The Ratbil of Zābolestān could also be included as Zābolestān was considered subordinate to the Yabḡu, and the Ratbils also later incorporated Kapisa-Kābol into their territories. The terms Yabḡu (Jabḡu) and Šad̲ are pre-Turkish titles of ranks introduced to the region by the Western Turks.

The Chinese *jimi fuzhou* system of frontier regions created the Protectorate of Ṭok̲ārestān and the Protectorate of Sogdia autonomously governed by their own rulers (Twitchett and Wechsler, p. 280; Yihong, pp. 201-2). Throughout the Omayyad period, regional ties remained strong with China, and these states remained loyal to China and requested Chinese military assistance. This quasi-system (*jimi fuzhou*) made no specific tributary demands on the Sogdians and Tocharians. Tʾang military support only manifested itself in the form of the Türgesh (see KHAGAN), whose interests were not altogether altruistic. Chinese military detachments were stationed as far as the Ili valley and Farḡāna (Twitchett, p. 362).

The Nēzak Ṭark̲ān (see NĒZAK) dominated in western Ṭok̲ārestān while the Yabḡu (Jabḡuya, q.v.) dominated in eastern Ṭok̲ārestān. These two men exerted the most influence in the region and served as the main leaders of the many other rulers of small principalities.

The Yabḡu and eastern (upper) Ṭok̲ārestān. Ṭabari (II, p. 1206, tr. XXIII, p. 154) called the Yabḡu the king of Ṭok̲ārestān because all of the local *moluk* (regional rulers) had pledged full allegiance to him and the emperor of China. The major principalities of the Yabḡu comprised Čaḡāniān (Ṣaḡāniān, which included Tirmid̲), K̲ottal (the Wak̲š valley and other valleys to the east), Šomān and Āk̲arun, Rob, Bamiān, Badak̲šān, Kapisa, Kābol and Zābolestān. The Yabḡu resided in Warwāliz (Kunduz).

In 118/736, the Yabḡu gave sanctuary to the Murjiʾite rebel, Ḥāret̲ b. Sorayj, in Badak̲šān. Anticipating the gravity of the threat posed by the joint Türgesh-Sogdian-Tocharian-Murjiʾite alliance, Asad b. ʿAbd-Allāh, the Omayyad governor, moved the capital of Khorasan from Marv to Bal̲k̲ (Ṭabari, II, p. 1591, tr. XXV, p. 128). In 119/737, Ḥāret̲ b. Sorayj, with the K̲āqān and the Yabḡu, attacked K̲olm with 30,000 men and moved across Jowzjān toward Marv. Asad b. ʿAbdullāh defeated them at the battle of Ḵarestān (Ṭabari, II, p. 1604, tr. XXVI, pp. 140-41). After this battle, the Yabḡu ceased to pose a serious threat.

The Šaḏ, Čaḡān (Ṣaḡān) Ḵodā, king of Čaḡānīān. Čaḡānīān served as a Hephthalite buffer principality on the frontier with Sogdia. It lay on a major trade route along the Oxus River. Termeḏ, to the south of Čaḡānīān, was overrun and settled by a rebel Muslim, Musā b. ʿAbd-Allāh, in 72/691. In 85/704, the Čaḡān Ḵodā fought alongside Mofażżal b. Mohallab's forces when Termeḏ was stormed and Musā b. ʿAbd-Allāh was killed. In 86/705, the Čaḡān Ḵodā, Tiš al-Aʿwar, was allied with Qotayba b. Moslem and in 90/708 refused to rebel with the Nēzak Ṭarḵān against Qotayba b. Moslem (Bosworth, 1981, p. 1).

The Sabal, the king of Ḵottal. The Sabal of Ḵottal ruled the Waḵš valley and other valleys to the east and resisted Omayyad authority. However, in an earlier act of solidarity, the Sabal joined the Nēzak, Bukharans, Čaḡānīāns and Modrek b. Mohallab in the assault against Musā b. ʿAbd-Allāh at Termeḏ in 85/704. In 107/725, the Sabal aligned himself with the Murjiʾite rebel Ḥāreṯ b. Sorayj but later left him. The Sabal was defeated along with the Ḵāqān (Türgesh) in the previously mentioned battle of Ḵarestān in 119/737. About this time, an Omayyad governor was appointed to Ḵottal (Ṭabari, II, pp. 1151-53, 1162, 1492-94, 1583-84, tr., XXIII, pp. 96-97, 106, XXV, pp. 30-32, 120-21).

The Nēzak Ṭarḵān and western Ṭoḵārestān. The Nēzak Ṭarḵān figured prominently in the Omayyad period from the earliest times through the governorship of Qotayba b. Moslem (86-96/705-15). He is associated with Bādḡis, a region of high plateau pasturelands with no cities.

In 64/683, the Nēzak Ṭarḵān attacked and defeated the Azdi garrison at Qaṣr Asfād. Not until 84/703 was Yazid b. Mohallab able to force him to pay the *jezya* (q.v.). In 87/705, Nēzak joined forces with Qotayba b. Moslem and the Moslem army in the campaigns into Sogdia. They campaigned together from 88/706 through 90/708. Ṭabari (II, 1204-5, tr., XXIII, p. 153) reports that the Nēzak left the service of Qotayba in 90/709, fearing that he would be killed.

Table 2
REGIONS AND TITLES OF LOCAL RULERS OF ṬOḴĀRESTĀN

Mini-States, Regions	Titles
Bāḏḡis	Tarkhān Nēzak
Herat, Bušanj (Pušang)	Barāzān, Varāzān
Ṭālaqān	Šahrak
Fāryāb	???
Ḡarčestān	Šār
Guzgān (Jowzjān)	Guzgānān Ḵodā
Termeḏ	Termeḏšāh
Čaḡanīān	Čaghān Ḵodā (Šaḏ)
Khottal	Ṣabal, Ḵottalshāh
Roʾb	Roʾb Ḵān, Šāh Samangān
Bamīān	Šir
Warwāliz	Yabḡu, Jabḡuya

Source: See Nafisi, *Tāriḵ-e tamaddon-e Irān-e Sāsāni*, pp. 4-5 for a listing of titles.

Nēzak rebelled with the support of all of the rulers of western Ṭoḵārestān. Tabari (II, pp. 1206, 1218, tr. XXIII, pp. 154-55, 165) lists them as the Eṣbahbaḏ of Balḵ; Bāḏām, the king of Marw al-Ruḏ; Sohrak, the king of Ṭālaqān; Tusek, the king of Fāryāb; and Jowzjāni, the king of Jowzjān. After arranging for possible asylum with the Kābolšāh, Nēzak fled to eastern Ṭoḵārestān, abducted the Yabḡu, and then fortified himself in a fortress in Baḡlān.

Qotayba gathered an army from Abrašahr, Abiward, Saraḵs, and Herat and marched to Marv. From there, he marched east through Tālaqān, Fāryāb and Juzjan to Balḵ subduing the population along the way. The Roʾb Ḵān, the king of Roʾb, helped Qotayba find a way behind Ḵolm pass, which allowed Qotayba to dislodge Nēzak from his secure fortress. Nēzak took refuge in a place called Korz and was besieged for two months until he was enticed to surrender. Nēzak was imprisoned until Qotayba received permission from the governor Ḥajjāj b. Yusof to kill him. During this time, Qotayba allowed the Šaḏ and the Sabal to pledge their fealty to the Yabḡu and depart. Qotayba executed Nēzak and crucified him. Reportedly, an additional 12,000 men were killed (Ṭabari, II, 1218-27, tr., XXIII, pp. 164-74).

This rebellion in 91/710 caused Qotayba to lose a major portion of his local militias and resulted in the extermination of the ruling elites of the area. ʿAmr b. Moslem was posted to Ṭālaqān to maintain order. A member of the tribe of Bāhela was appointed over Fāryāb and ʿĀmer b. Mālek Ḥemmāni over Jowzjān (Ṭabari, II, p. 1218, tr., XXIII, p. 165).

The protectorate of Sogdia. Sogdia was the richest of all the regions of Khorasan. Its established colonies along the trade routes to China allowed it to maintain strong social and economic ties that made the Sogdians natural allies of the Turks and Chinese. Muslim campaigns into Sogdia began in the 50s/670s, but a Muslim presence started only from 90/708 in Bukhara and from 93/711 in Samarqand. This presence was always precarious and never constant.

The Eḵšid (q.v.) or Ṭār of Farḡāna ruled on the upper reaches of the Jaxartes (Syr Daryā) river, and in 38/658, the Chinese emperor Kao-tsung established Farḡāna as the Hsiu-hsün area command and appointed the Eḵšid as the military governor. In 121/738, the emperor Hsüan-tsung

Table 3
REGIONS AND TITLES OF LOCAL RULERS OF SOGDIA

Mini-States, Regions	Titles
Bukhara	Bokārā Kodā
Wardān	Wardānšāh, Wardānḵodā
Samarqand	Eḵšid
Osrušana	Afšin
Farḡāna	Eḵšid
Keš	Bandun
Čāč	Tadon

Source: See Nafisi, *Tāriḵ-e tamaddon-e Irān-e Sāsāni*, pp. 4-5 for a listing of titles. They are frequently called *moluk al-Soḡd* in the Arabic sources.

gave him a princess from the imperial house in marriage (Marshak and Negmatov, p. 274; Bielenstein, pp. 323-24; Ebn al-Aṯir, IV, p. 126).

The Ek̲šid of Farḡāna along with the king of Šāš (Čāč) and the K̲āqān all sent forces to fight the Muslims. Farḡāna and Šāš, both with mixed populations of Sogdians and Turks, supported the Türgesh coalition. The Ek̲šid was forced to shift his capital from Aksikaṯ to Kāšān, and Qotayba b. Moslem captured its chief cities: K̲ojand and Kāšān (Frye, p. 82; Gibb, pp. 467-74).

The Ek̲šid of Sogdia (Samarqand [K'ang-chü]). The Ek̲šid of Samarqand was made a military governor over the K'ang-chü area command created by the T'ang emperor Kao-tsung in 38/658. In 77/696 the empress Wu recognized the king of Sogdia (Tukaspadak) and appointed him "General-in-Chief of the Resolute Guards on the Left."

The Ek̲šid of Sogdia traditionally led a very loose Sogdian confederation of principalities. The four Ekhšids of Samarqand during the Omayyad period were elected and not of royal stock. The Ek̲šid, Ṭark̲un (r. 79- 92/698-710), assisted his neighbors when they needed troops and helped Musā b. ʿAbd-Allāh expel all Omayyad tax collectors from Sogdia in 85/704 (Ṭabari, II, 1147-48, 1152-54, tr., XXIII, pp. 91-92, 96-97; Naršak̲i, pp. 63-65, tr., pp. 45-47). Later, he surrendered to Qotayba and agreed to pay an annual tribute; the Samarqandis were outraged, and Ṭark̲un either committed suicide or was assassinated (Ebn al-Aṯir, IV, p. 262). Ḡurak (r. 92-121/710-738), Ṭark̲un's younger brother, was then elected (Naymark, p. 253).

The Bok̲ār K̲odā and Bukhara. Both Āmol and Paykand were dependencies of Bukhara. Bukhara was made a Chinese commandery in 39/659. The first Muslim campaigns at Bukhara encountered Qabaj K̲ātun. She acted as the regent for her infant son, Ṭoḡšāda, for fifteen years, until Qotayba b. Moslem installed him as the Bok̲ār K̲odā in 91/709. He reigned for thirty years until he was assassinated in 121/738. Ṭoḡšāda appeared to be Muslim and loyal to Omayyad authority. However, once Omayyad authority in Sogdia began to slip away, Ṭoḡšāda, along with the other regional *moluk al-ṭawāʾef*, wrote to the T'ang court pleading for assistance against the Muslims (Frye, "Bukhārā"; Frye, 1975, p. 81; Chavannes, p. 138 n. 2).

Bibliography (see also bibliography for KHORASAN iv.): Gulman S. Afridi, "Etymology of Zhunbil and Identity of the Rulers of Kabul and Zabul in Seventh-Ninth Centuries C.E.," *Journal of Asian Civilizations* 39, 2018, pp. 25-47. Aḥmad b. Yaḥyā Balāḏori, *Ansāb al-ašrāf*, ed. Sohayl Zakkār and Riāż Zerkali, 13 vols. Beirut, 1996. Idem, *Ketāb fotuḥ al-boldān*, ed. M. J. de Goeje, Leiden, 1866, tr. Francis Clark Murgotten, as *The Origins of the Islamic State,* Part II, New York, 1924. W. Barthold, *Turkestan down to the Mongol Invasion,* 3rd ed., London, 1968. Idem, *An Historical Geography of Iran*, tr. Svat Soucek and ed. C. E. Bosworth, Princeton, 1984. A. M. Belenitskiĭ, *Central Asia*, London, 1969. Hans Bielenstein, *Diplomacy and Trade in the Chinese World, 589-1276* Leiden and Boston, 2005. Alessio Bombaci, "On the Ancient Turkic Title Eltäbär," in *Proceedings of the IXth Meeting of the Permanent International Altaistic Conference*, Naples, 1970, pp. 1-66. C. E. Bosworth, *Sīstān Under the Arabs, from the Islamic Conquest to the Rise of the Ṣaffārids (30-250/651-864),* Rome, 1968. Idem, "The Rulers of Chaghāniyān in Early Islamic Times," *Iran* 19, 1981, pp. 1-20. Edouard Chavannes, *Documents sur les Tou-Kiue (Turcs) Occidentaux. Recueillis et commentés, suivi de notes additionnelles*, Paris, 1942. Arthur Christensen, *L'Iran sous les Sassanides*, repr. Osnabrück, 1971. Peter Christensen, *The Decline of Iranshahr: Irrigation and Environments in the History of the Middle East, 500 B.C. to A.D. 1500*, Copenhagen, 1993. Aḥmad Ebn Aʿṯam Kufi, *Ketāb al-fotūḥ*, ed. M. ʿA. Khan et al., 8 vols., Ḥaydarābād (Deccan), 1968-75. ʿEzz-al-Din Ebn al-Aṯir, *al-Kāmel fi'l-taʾrik̲*, 9 vols., Beirūt, 1997. Abu'l-Qāsem Ebn Ḥawqal, *Ketāb ṣurat-al-arż*, ed. J. H. Kramers, 2nd ed., Leiden, 1938-39; repr. as *Ibn Ḥawqal's Kitāb Ṣūrat al-arḍ*: *Opus geographicum*, Leiden, 2014. Ebn K̲ordāḏbeh, *Ketāb al-masālek wa'l-mamālek*, ed. M. J. de Goeje, Bibliotheca Geographorum Arabicorum 6, Leiden, 1889. Ebn Rosta, *Ketāb al-aʿlāq al-nafisa*, ed. M. J. de Goeje, Bibliotheca Geographorum Arabicorum 7, Leiden 1892; tr. G. Wiet, as *Les Atours précieux*, Cairo, 1955.

Richard N. Frye, "Buk̲h̲ārā," in *EI*[2] I, [1960], pp. 1293-96. Idem, *The Golden Age of Persia: The Arabs in the East*, London, 1975. ʿAbd-al-Ḥayy Gardizi, *Zayn al-akhbār*, ed. ʿAbd-al-Ḥayy Ḥabībī, Tehran, 1968. H. A. R. Gibb, "The Arab Invasion of Kashgar in A.D 715," *BSOS* 2/3, 1922, pp. 467-74. Frantz Grenet, "Regional Interaction in Central Asia and Northwestern India in the Kidarite and Hephthalite Period," in Nicholas Sims-Williams, ed., *Indo-Iranian Languages and Peoples,* Oxford, 2002, pp. 203-24. Rika Gyselen, *The Four Generals of the Sasanian Empire: Some Sigillographic Evidence*, Rome, 2001. Abu Ishaq al-Istakhri, *Kitab Masalik al-mamalik*, ed. M. J. de Goeje, Bibliotheca Geographorum Arabicorum 1, repr. Leiden, 1967. Ferdinand Justi, *Iranisches Namenbuch*, repr. Hildesheim, 1963. K̲alifa b. K̲ayyāṭ, *Taʾrik̲ K̲alifa b. K̲ayyāṭ*, ed. Moṣṭafā Najib Fawwāz and Ḥekmat Kešli Fawwāz, Beirut, 1995. Deborah E. Klimburg-Salter, *The Kingdom of Bāmiyān: Buddhist Art and Culture of the Hindu Kush,* Naples, 1989. Shoshin Kuwayama, "The Hephthalites in Tokharistan and Northwest India," *Zinbun: Annals of the Institute for Research in Humanities, Kyoto University* 24, 1989, pp. 89-134. Étienne de la Vaissière, *Sogdian Traders: A History,* Leiden and Boston, 2005. Guy Le Strange, *The Lands of the Eastern Caliphate: Mesopotamia, Persia, and Central Asia from the Moslem Conquest to the Time of Timur*, repr. New York, 1976. B. I. Marshak and N. N. Negmatov, "Sogdiana," in *History of Civilizations of Central Asia* III: *The Crossroads of Civilizations, A.D. 250-750*, Paris, 1996, pp. 237-81. Michael G. Morony, "Mulūk al-ṭawāʾif (a)," in *EI*[2] VII, [1993], pp. 551-52.

Saʿid Nafisi, *Tārik̲-e tamaddon-e Irān-e Sāsāni*, 2 vols., Tehran, 1953-65. Idem, *Tārik̲-e ejtemāʿi-e Irān az enqerāż-e Sāsānian tā enqerāż-e Omawiān*, Tehran, 1964. Moḥammad b. Jaʿfar Naršaki, *Tārik̲-e Bok̲ārā*, ed. M.-T. Modarres Rażavi, 2nd. ed., Tehran, 1984; tr. R. N. Frye, as *The History of Bukhara*, Cambridge, Mass., 1954. Alexsandr Naymark, "Sogdiana, its Christians, and Byzantium: A Study of Artistic and Cultural Connections in Late Antiquity and Early Middle Ages," Ph.D. diss., Indiana University, Bloomington, 2001. Moḥammad b. ʿAbd-Allāh Ḥākem Nišāburi, *Tārik̲-e Nišābur*, tr. Ahmad b. Moḥammad b. Ḥosayn K̲alifa Nišāburi, ed. Moḥammad-Reżā Šafiʿi Kadkani, Tehran, 1996. Parvaneh Pourshariati, "Iranian Tradition in Ṭūs and the Arab Presence in Khurāsān," Ph.D. diss., Columbia University, 1995. Idem, *Decline and Fall of the Sasanian Empire: The Sasanian-Parthian Confederacy and the Arab Conquest of Iran*, London, 2008. M. Rekaya, "K̲ārinids," in *EI*[2] IV, [1978], pp. 644-47. Nicholas Sims-Williams, "Ancient Afghanistan and its Invaders: Linguistic Evidence from the Bactrian Documents and Inscriptions," in idem, ed., *Indo-Iranian Languages and Peoples*, Oxford, 2002, pp. 225-42. Moḥammad b. Jarir Ṭabari, *Taʾrik̲ al-rosol wa'l-molūk*, eds. M. J. de Goeje et al, 15 vols. in 3 series, Leiden, 1879-1901; tr. as E. Yarshater, ed., *The History of al-Ṭabari*, 40 vols., Albany, N.Y., 1985-2007 (translators vary). *Tārik̲-e Sistān*, ed. M.-T. Bahār, Tehran, 1935. Denis Twitchett, "Hsüan-tsung (Reign 712-56)," in idem, ed., *Cambridge History of China* III: *Sui and T'ang China, 589-906 AD*, Cambridge, 1979, pp. 333-463. Denis Twitchett and Howard J. Wechsler, "Kao-Tsung (Reign 649-83) and the Empress Wu: The Inheritor and the Usurper," in Denis C. Twitchett, ed., *Cambridge History of China* III: *Sui and T'ang China, 589-906 AD*, Cambridge, 1979, pp. 242-89. Josef Wiesehöfer, *Ancient Persia from 550 BC to 650 AD*, London and New York, 2004. Aḥmad b. Abi Yaʿqub Yaʿqubi, *Taʾrik̲ al-Yaʿqubi*, Beirut, n.d.; ed. and tr. in Matthew S. Gordon et al., as *The Works of Ibn Wāḍiḥ al-Yaʿqūbī: An English Translation*, 3 vols., Leiden, 2017. Yāqūt ibn ʿAbd-Allāh Ḥamawī, *Moʿjam al-boldān*, Beirut, [1955-57]. Pan Yihong, *Son of Heaven and Heavenly Qaghan: Sui-Tang China and Its Neighbors*, Bellingham, Wash., 1997.

(MARK LUCE)

iv. THE ARAB CONQUEST AND OMAYYAD PERIOD

INTRODUCTION

After the Arabs conquered and colonized Iraq in the early Islamic era, the two garrison towns of Basra and Kufa were established there and soon became cities that experienced massive Arab immigrations. They served as the main bases from which campaigns to the east were launched. Under the caliph ʿOmar (r. 13-23/634-44), raids into Persia commenced. Persian resistance against the Arabs continued through the caliphate of ʿOṯmān (r. 23-35/644-56). The Arabs established garrisons and appointed governors in the major cities and relative calm prevailed. The Arab governors of Iraq administered the eastern lands from Basra and reported to the caliph in Damascus. They were largely responsible for appointing governors in the east. The furthest frontier on the eastern border of the newly emerged Arab Empire was called Khorasan. This region comprised the former Sasanian province of Khorasan as well as Ṭok̲ārestān and lands beyond the Oxus (see MA WARĀʾ AL-NAHR).

The Arabs quickly subdued Sasanian Khorasan and Sistān and raided as far east as Kabul and the Sind (See ʿARAB ii. ARAB CONQUEST OF IRAN). Treaties were negotiated with the individual rulers of the major towns and cities of Khorasan and annual tributes were agreed upon. The local rulers (*moluk al-ṭawāʾef*) were responsible for the collection and payment of tribute. The Arabs did not maintain a large physical presence there during this period (see ʿARAB iii. ARAB SETTLEMENTS IN IRAN; la Vaissière, 2007, 2017, 2018; and Agha, 1999, 2003). Initially, after campaigning, they typically returned to Basra. Due to this and internal Arab upheavals, such as the assassinations of the caliphs ʿOmar, ʿOṯmān, and ʿAli, the Khorasanis frequently used these periods of Arab unrest to rebel. The early raids and garrisons of the Rashidun period (21-40/641-60) were ephemeral. Treaties were concluded, but the Khorasanis rebelled and withheld tribute in locale after locale. The first *fetna* or civil war (36-40/656-60) marked a hiatus for further Muslim advances.

The appointees of the caliph ʿAli (35-40/656-61) experienced multiple problems from both the Khorasanis and the Arab Muslims. Jaʿda b. Hobayra Mak̲zumi, sent to govern Abrašahr (Nishapur) in 37/657 was turned back at the gates. ʿAli's first appointee to Sistān was murdered by bandits, while the second appointee was killed by Ḥasaka b. ʿAttāb, the leader of a renegade Muslim beggar army that occupied Zaranj for two years (36-38/656-58; Balāḏori, *Fotuh*, pp. 394-95, tr., pp. 144-45; K̲alifa b. K̲ayyaṭ, *Taʾrik̲*, pp. 120-21). Only during the reign of Moʿāwia (41-60/661-80) were attempts made to regain and centralize authority in Khorasan (Ṭabari, I, p. 2706, tr. XIV, p. 76; Balāḏori, *Fotuḥ*, p. 396, tr. p. 146-47).

The history of Khorasan in the early Islamic period can be divided into three distinct stages.

First stage. The first stage began with the initial raids under the first three caliphs and ended with the death of Ziād b. Abi Sofyān (d. 53/673), Moʿāwia's governor of Iraq and the East. During the later portion of this stage (54-63/673-82) the Muslims established a presence in former Sasanian Khorasan, Sistān, and Ṭok̲ārestān. The first raids and campaigns into Sogdia began during this phase, which ended with the so-called second *fetna*, namely Ebn Zobayr's rebellion (64-74/683-92). During this period, ʿAbd-Allāh b. K̲āzem ruled Khorasan and was aligned with the counter-caliph Ebn Zobayr (d. 73/692).

Second stage. Factionalism and expansion characterized the second stage (64-96/683-714). Serious Arab tribal conflicts and territorial clashes fostered Muslim disunity and partisanship. The strong neutral authority and intervention of Mohallab b. Abi Ṣofra (gov. 78-82/697-701) and his sons (Yazid, gov. 82-85/701-4; Mofażżal, gov. 85-86/704-5) helped restore Omayyad authority over Khorasan and extended raids into Sogdia. Territorial expansion began and ended with the governorship of Qotayba b. Moslem (gov. 86-96/705-15), who carried out the policies of Ḥajjāj b. Yusof (governor of Iraq and the East, d. 95/714) for activities on the Khorasani frontier. He reclaimed Sistān from the Ratbil (see above), conquered vast areas of Sogdia, and raided beyond the Jaxartes River.

Third stage. The third and final stage of development (97-128/715-45) experienced a period of mis-governance from outsider Syrians and Kufans, who had little understanding of Khorasan and its frontier. Asad b. ʿAbd-Allāh Qaṣri (gov. 106-9/725-27 and 117-20/734-37) initiated reforms and tried to reestablish even-handedness to reduce increasing Khorasani factionalism. Fiscal and administrative reforms implemented by Naṣr b. Sayyār (gov. 120-31/738-49) were followed by social and economic reforms that came too late and culminated with an internal Khorasani uprising led by Abu Moslem K̲orāsāni (q.v.) that toppled the Omayyads and established the ʿAbbasid dynasty.

CONQUEST AND SETTLEMENT (21-64/641-83)

After the imperial Persian army had been defeated in Iraq (see QĀDESIYA) and at Nehāvand (q.v.), the last Sasanian king, Yazdegerd III, fled eastwards to Khorasan and made his last stand at Marv before his betrayal by the local *marzbān* Māhōē and his murder in 31/652 (Ṭabari, I, pp. 2872-84, tr. XV, pp. 78-90; Balāḏori, *Fotuḥ*, pp. 315-16). According to traditional accounts, Arab troops, mainly those based on Basra, had, however, already been raiding toward Khorasan via the Ṭabasayn (Ṭabas al-Tamr and Ṭabas al-ʿOnnāb) in the Great Desert. The first expeditionary forces to Khorasan were reportedly composed of ten thousand men from Baṣra and ten thousand from Kufa. Aḥnaf b. Qays entered Khorasan in 22/642 via Ṭabasayn, the desert route, taking the city of Harāt (Ṭabari, I, p. 2682, tr. XIV, p. 53; Ebn Aṯir, III, p. 16). A brief note in Ṭabari states that in Quhestān a governor and a Muslim judge were appointed and that Quhestān was used as a base for staging attacks into Kermān (Ṭabari, I, p. 2705, tr. XIV, p. 74). The cities of Nišāpur, Ṭus, Marv, Abivard, Nasā, Sarak̲s, and Balk̲ all came under Muslim control. The chronology for these conquests varies but Ṭabari dates the above conquests to 31/651 (Ṭabari, I, pp. 2884-88, tr. XV, pp. 90-93).

Other reports indicate that when ʿAbd-Allāh b. ʿĀmer b. Korayẓ (29-35/649-55 and 41-44/661-64) was governor of Basra and the East, a two-fold attack was launched on Khorasan, with a Kufan army under Saʿid b. ʿĀṣi pushing on the northern route, along the southern rim of the Alborz via Ray, and a Basran army under ʿAbd-Allāh b. ʿĀmer and Aḥnaf b. Qays traveling by the southern route from Fārs through Kerman and the Ṭabasayn. As a result, in 31/651-52 Basran forces under Aḥnaf b. Qays captured Nishapur, and in the next year, the last great fortress of the region, Marw al-Rud, fell. All this took place against the background of resistance by the Sasanian army and by local magnates, such as the *marzbān* of Marw al-Rud, Bāḏām. Bāḏām submitted to the Arabs and received back his lands in exchange for tribute of 60,000 dirhams (Ṭabari, I, pp. 2884-88, 2897-906, tr., XV, pp. 90-93, 102-10; Balāḏori, *Fotuḥ*, p. 406; Markwart, pp. 67-68). Over the following years, however, turmoil in the central lands of the caliphate, with the murder of the caliph ʿOṯmān and the ensuing struggles for power, especially the civil war (35-40/656-61) between ʿAli b. Abi Ṭāleb and Moʿāwia, the tentative Arab control over Khorasan became relaxed. The Iranian landowners and magnates sought the aid of outside powers, such as the Hephthalites of northern Afghanistan, the Western Turks of Türgesh, and even from the Chinese, since the T'ang emperors claimed a distant sovereignty over Tibet and Central Asia to the west of the Tien-shan and Kunlun mountains. But the distances involved meant that practical Chinese aid to the Iranian princes was at best intermittent, and although the Sasanian prince Pērōz, son of Yazdegerd III, was recognized around 661 as vassal prince of *Tsi-ling*, he was speedily driven out by the Arabs and died in China in 672 (Markwart, p. 68). (For a more detailed account of the conquest period, see ʿARAB ii. ARAB CONQUEST OF IRAN).

The continual unrest in Khorasan during this period has muddled the facts and obscured the chronology and the historical records of events there. It appears the Khorasanis rebelled by withholding tribute and expelling Muslims in locale after locale. The small sizes of the Muslim armies and their inability to garrison all towns and cities precipitated a repeated pattern of "capture-rebellion-recapture" (Hill, pp. 135-37). Sistān had a more settled Muslim presence than Sasanian Khorasan and provided Iraq and Syria with 40,000 slaves (Balāḏori, tr., p. 143; Bosworth, 1968, p. 20.) The pacification of the Ratbil in Sistān and the enlargement of the Arab garrison in Marv shifted Muslim priorities to the edges of their new frontier in Ṭok̲ārestān and into Sogdia in Transoxiana (Mā warāʾ al-nahr).

Moʿāwia (r. 41-60/661-80), the founder of the Omayyad dynasty, attempted to centralize authority in Khorasan. Under him, Omayyad Khorasan encompassed Sasanian Khorasan, Sistān, and Zābolestān (the lands of the Ratbil, stretching to Kabul). He re-subdued all of these regions, but much of western (lower) Ṭok̲ārestān resisted Muslim authority (Ṭabari, I, p. 2706, tr., XIV, p. 76; Balāḏori, *Fotuḥ*, tr., p. 137).

TREATIES, TRIBUTE, AND GARRISONS

During this phase, the Muslim armies negotiated treaties with the local elites. The conditions of these treaties varied depending on whether the town or city had been taken by force (*ʿanwatan*) or peacefully (*solḥan*). Those cities taken by force lost everything. In those taken peacefully, all moveable booty was collected and the town and outlying dependencies were put under tribute.

The local rulers (*moluk al-ṭawāʾef*) typically remained in power and collected the tribute for the Muslims, maintaining the existing tax structure. These treaties (*ʿohud*) varied in content but were adhered to by both the Muslims and the Khorasanis. (see Qāḏi, pp. 47-113.) Tribute was paid in cash and in kind. The local rulers during this early period submitted to the Muslims but kept their social hierarchies intact and maintained their privileges. The establishment of Muslim settlements in Khorasan injected a new dynamic that transformed the Muslim presence there from a military force that only extracted resources, to one that shared in its social and economic integration. The principal Muslim garrisons established throughout Khorasan included Abaršahr (Nishapur), Herat, Marv al-Ruḏ, and Marv.

Permanent Settlements (53-64/672-683). The caliph ʿOmar instructed his armies to settle in cities, as urban garrison towns (*meṣr*, pl. *amṣār*). This assured the development of an Islamic zone of control and structured leadership. The *amṣār* provided a safe environment for religious education, adherence to Islamic traditions and beliefs, and concentrated all tribes in a common space that forced them to interact with each other, allowing them to have a sense of community.

A Muslim force of 4,000 under Omayr b. Aḥmar Yaškori remained garrisoned in Marv, the main city in Khorasan, until 32/652 and represented the beginning of a permanent Muslim physical presence in Khorasan (Gardizi, pp. 229-30; Balāḏori, *Fotuḥ*, tr. p. 170). At Marv, the Muslim garrisons rotated in and out until 51/671 when, according to a report by Balāḏori (*Fotuḥ*, p. 410, tr. p. 171), 50,000 families settled around the Marv oasis (for interpretations of this report, see Agha, 1999; la Vassière, 2017). They established themselves in a network of villages along the lines of the five tribal divisions (*aḵmās*) present in Baṣra (Jabali, p. 121; see Figure 1). We know that in addition to Marv, there were garrisons in Nasā, Abivard, Saraḵs, Nishapur, Ṭus, Marv al-Ruḏ, Bušanj, Herat, Ṭālaqān, Fāryāb, and Jowzjān (Ṭabari, I, 2884-904, tr., XV, pp. 90-107). Baruqān, near Balḵ (Yaqut, *Moʿjam*, I, p. 405) and Ḵolm (Samʿani, V, p. 164) are mentioned as being garrisoned much later.

EARLY FRONTIER GOVERNANCE

Under ʿOṯmān, there were five districts (*kowar*) of Khorasan: Marv al-Šāhejān (with Marv al-Ruḏ as a dependency), Balḵ, Herat (with Bušanj and Bādḡis), Ṭus, and Nishapur (see ʿAṭwān, pp. 49-50, and ʿAli). This division mirrors divisions along early (pre-7th century) Sasanian lines. After restructuring, Marv (al-Šāhejān) was administered separately, while Marv al-Ruḏ, on the edge of the former Sasanian-Hephthalite frontier, became the main Muslim administrative center for western (lower) Ṭoḵārestān, which included Ṭālaqān and Fāryāb in Jowzjān to the east, but excluded Balḵ. The district of Herat continued to include both Bādḡis and Bušanj (Balāḏori, *Fotuḥ*, tr. p. 163). The administrative center of Ṭus district was switched to Nishapur, when Oṯmān appointed Qays b. Hayṯām Solami over it and Khorasan (Ṭabari, I, p. 2831, tr., XV, 36; Balāḏori, *Fotuḥ*, p. 404, tr. p. 161).

The caliph ʿOmar had established *šaraf* (nobility) on the basis of Islamic precedence, that is, honoring and granting special privileges to the earliest Muslims. As a consequence, *ṣaḥābis* (Companions of the Prophet) dominated in leadership positions (Ebn al-Aṯir, *Osd al-ḡāba*, I, pp. 68-69; Ḵalifa, *al-Ṭabaqāt*, pp. 95-96; Ebn Ḵallekān, I, pp. 425-28.) All of these Companions of the Prophet represented a segment of the Muslim elite (*ašrāf al-Eslām*), who obtained a high status in society because of their service to Islam and their relationship to the ruling Islamic authorities rather than tribal status or ethnic purity. ʿOṯmān continued this policy while at the same time favoring his relatives. The caliph Moʿāwia (r. 41-60/661–80) ordered

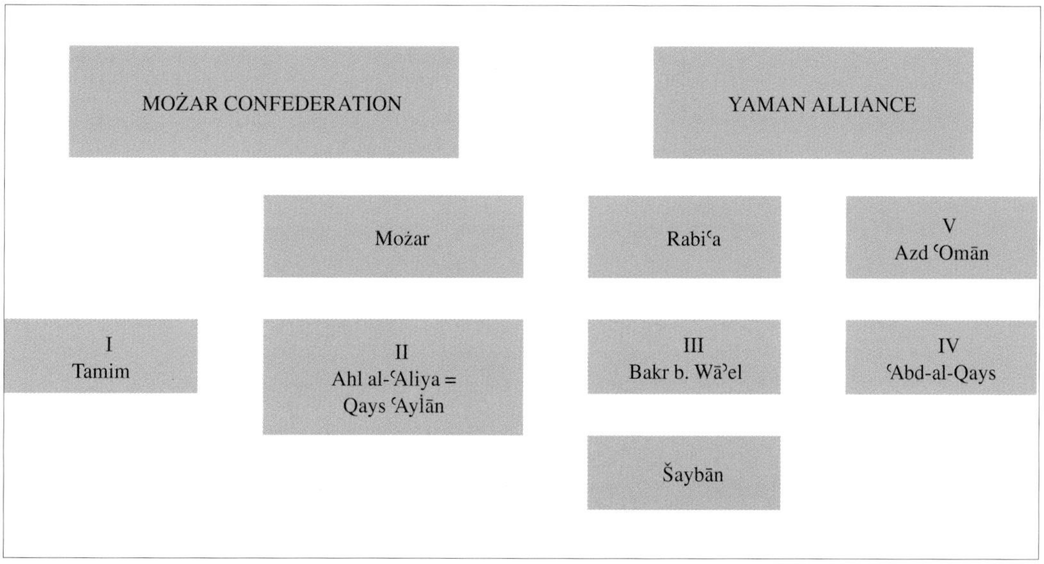

Figure 1. The Arab tribal divisions of Khorasan in the Omayyad Period, with the *aḵmas* marked by roman numerals.

Table 1

GOVERNORS OF KHORASAN DURING THE PERIOD OF RAIDS AND SETTLEMENTS (641-83 CE)

Caliphs	Governors of Iraq	Governors of Khorasan
ʿOṯmān (r. 23-35/644-56)	ʿAbd-Allāh b. ʿĀmer b. Korayz (29-35/649-55 and 41-44/661-64)	
ʿAli (r. 35-40/656-61)		Different District Governors
Moʿāwia b. Abi Sofyān (r. 41-60/661-80)	Ziād b. Abi Sofyān (45-53/665-73)	Different District Governors
		ʿAbd-Allāh b. Ḳāzem[1] (43-45/663-65)
		Ḥakam b. ʿAmr Ḡefāri[2] (47/667?)
		Ḡāleb b. Fażāla Layṯi[3] (48/668)
		Rabiʿ b. Ziād Ḥāreṯi[4] (51-53/671-72)
		ʿObayd-Allāh b. Ziād[5] (53-55/672-74)
	ʿObayd-Allāh b. Ziād (56-67/675-686)	ʿAbd-Allāh and ʿAbd-al-Raḥmān b. Ziād[6]
		Saʿid b. ʿOṯmān b. ʿAffān[7] (56-58/675-77)
		Aslam b. Zorʿa Kelābi[8] (*ḵaraj*)
Yazid b. Moʿāwia (r. 60-64/680-83)		ʿAbd-al-Raḥmān b. Ziād[9] (58-61?/678-80?)
		Salm b. Ziād[10] (61-64/680-83)

Notes: The chronology of the early governors of Khorasan is confusing and extremely difficult to reconstruct up until the governorship of Salm b. Ziād in 61/680.

(1) Both Ebn al-Aṯir (III, p. 210) and Yaʿqubi (II, p. 218) date the beginning of the first governorship of ʿAbd-Allah b. Ḳāzem in 42 AH. Ṭabari, II, p. 65, tr., XVIII, p. 68, places it in 43 AH, the date that Ebn al-Aṯir (III, p. 218) has him leaving that post. Various sources name two companions of the Prophet as having served as governors before Rabiʿ b. Ziād Ḥāreṯi.

(2) Ḥakam b. ʿAmr Ḡefāri and (3) Ḡāleb b. Fażāla Layṯi. Ṭabari (II, p. 85, tr. XVIII, p. 85) and Ebn al-Aṯir (III, p. 224) name Ḥakam as governor in 45 AH, while Yaʿqubi says he was appointed in 44/664. Yaʿqubi also says that he died that year (II, p. 222). Both Ebn al-Aṯir (III, p. 233) and Balāḏori (*Fotuḥ*, p.400) claim that he died in 50/670. Ḡāleb b. Fażāla Layṯi is mentioned by both Ṭabari (II, p. 85, tr., XVIII, p. 93) and Ebn al-Aṯir (III, p. 227) as being appointed in 48/668. Ebn Aʿṯam (IV, p. 202) mentions him following Ḥakam.

(4) Ṭabari (II, p. 155, tr., XVIII, p. 163) and Balāḏori (*Fotuḥ*, p.400) name Rabiʿ b. Ziād Ḥāreṯi as being appointed governor in 51/671, while Yaʿqubi places him there in 44/664 (II, p. 222). Until the second *fetna* all of the governors are from the Banu Ziād except essentially Saʿid b. ʿOṯmān b. ʿAffān, the son of the third caliph.

(5) ʿObayd-Allāh b. Ziād governed Khorasan from 53-56-7/672-675 according to Yaʿqubi (II, pp. 236, 237). Balāḏori mentions his appointment. Ṭabari contradicts this, stating he started in 54/673 (II, p. 167, tr., XVIII, p. 176).

(6) Between the govenorship of ʿObayd-Allāh b. Ziād and that of (7) Saʿid b. ʿOṯmān b. ʿAffān, ʿAbd-Allāh and ʿAbd-al-Raḥmān b. Ziād, two sons of Ziād b. Abi Sofyān, filled in when ʿObayd-Allāh b. Ziād became the governor of Iraq upon the death of his father. Ebn al-Aṯir says they were dismissed in 56/675 (III, p. 253) while Yaʿqubi has them in the position in 57/676 (II, p. 237). Ṭabari (II, p. 177, tr., XVIII, p. 187), Ebn Aʿṯam (IV, pp. 184-85), Ebn al-Aṯir (III, p. 253) and Balāḏori (*Fotuḥ*, p. 400) all agree that Saʿid b. ʿOṯmān b. ʿAffān was appointed in 56/675.

(8) Aslam b. Zorʿa Kelābi was over the *ḵaraj* most likely during Saʿid's governorship. His appointment is confirmed by Ṭabari in 56/676 (II, pp. 179-80, tr., XVIII, p. 190), Ebn Aʿṯam (IV, p. 199), Ebn al-Aṯir [55/674](III, p. 248), Ya'qubi (II, p. 237) and Balāḏori (p. 403).

(9) Ebn al-Aṯir (III, p. 256) states that ʿAbd-al-Raḥmān b. Ziād jailed Aslam when he was appointed governor in 59/678 (Ṭabari XVIII:199; Ebn al-Aṯir 3:256).

(10) After 59/678, no other governor is discussed until the appointment of Salm b. Ziād in 61/680 (Ṭabari, II, pp. 391-92, tr., XIX, p. 184; Ebn Aʿtham, V, p. 254; Ebn al-Aṯir, III, p. 304, Ya'qubi, II, p. 252 and Balāḏori, *Fotuḥ*, p. 403).

Ziād b. Abi Sofyān (gov. of Iraq 42-53/662-73) to select Ḥakam b. ʿAmr Ḡefāri, a *ṣaḥābi* (first-generation Muslim) to be governor of Khorasan in 44/664-65 (Yaʿqubi, II, p. 222). Ḥakam died in office in Marv 50/670 71, and then, after a succession of deputies, Rabeʿ b. Ziād Ḥāriṯi (gov. 51-53/671-72), another *ṣaḥābi*, was appointed governor. Under Moʿāwia, a second generation of administrators emerged who were better equipped to deal with matters of state in Khorasan than the aging first generation *ṣaḥāba* (Companions of the Prophet). For a period of ten years, the east was almost exclusively ruled by Ziād's sons (ʿAbd-al-Raḥmān, ʿObayd-Allāh, ʿAbbād). Yazid b. Moʿāwia (60-64/680-83) continued his father's policy by appointing his "cousins," (Salm b. Ziād [61-64/680-83] and Yazid b. Ziād [killed 61/680]). This Sofyānid corporate dynasty thus ruled, and the only exception was the two-year appointment of the third caliph ʿOṯmān's son, Saʿid b. ʿOṯmān b. ʿAffān to the governorship of Khorasan (56-58/675-77). This near family monopoly on governing positions in Khorasan was accepted by the Muslims.

FACTIONALIZATION AND ASSIMILATION (64-96/683-714)

The second *fetna* (64-73/683-92), as the rebellion of ʿAbd-Allāh Ebn Zobayr has been called, marked the end of Sofyānid Omayyad political rule. It intensified major religious unrest in Iraq. The Kharijites grew stronger and repeatedly attacked Baṣra. Iraq became embroiled in political as well as sectarian wars. As a result, distant Khorasan became a place of political and religious refuge for many Muslims.

When the caliph Moʿāwia II b. Yazid died in 64/683, Omayyad authority throughout Khorasan broke down and individual tribes seized control of the different districts. Tribal warfare ensued with the Qays and Tamim against the Rabiʿa and the Azd. Inter-tribal feuds became common between the Tamim and the Bakr b. Wa'il. Omayyad authority in Khorasan was in tatters.

The Marwanid Omayyad restoration. Ḥajjāj b. Yusof became governor for Iraq in 75/694 and gained authority over Khorasan in 697. Ḥajjāj appointed Mohallab b. Abi Ṣofra over Khorasan. In 699, Mohallab crossed the Oxus and campaigned against Keš, which he made his base of operations for two years. His strategy was to pacify eastern (upper) Ṭoḵārestān (Keš, Ḵottal and Čaḡāniān) as well as western (lower) Ṭoḵārestān, which had never been completely subdued.

Qotayba b. Moslem and the conquest of Sogdia. Qotayba b. Moslem (d. 96/715) became governor over both Khorasan and Sistān in 86/705. Qotayba was forced to subdue rebellion in Sogdia and Ṭoḵārestān instigated by the Arab rebel Musa b. ʻAbd-Allah, who had established an enclave in Termeḏ (72-85/691-704). His father, ʻAbd-Allah b. Ḵāzem, was governor of Khorasan (64-72/683-91) and had the support of the non-Arab rulers of Sogdia.

With the help of the Hepthalite ruler, the Nēzak (see NĒZAK and HEPTHALITES) Qotayba succeeded in concluding agreements in Sogdia and pacifying Ṭoḵārestān. When the Nēzak rebelled and enlisted all of the rulers of Ṭoḵārestān from Bādḡis to Kabul to join him, Qotayba was hard pressed but eventually executed the Nēzak and many of the *moluk al-tawāʾef* of Ṭoḵārestān (Ḵalifa, *Taʾrik*, p. 190; Ebn al-Aṯir, IV, p. 114; Ṭabari, II, pp. 1207-8, 1221-23, tr. XXIII, pp. 154-55, 168-70). Qotayba subsequently pacified the Ratbil in Sistān, subdued Ḵᵛārazm, and captured Samarqand (on his campaigns, see Stark, 2018). He successfully employed a policy of making peace and then impressing local militias into service.

The death of Hajjāj in 95/713, followed a year later by the death of the caliph al-Walid b. ʿAbd-al-Malek caused Qotayba to fear an end of his ten-year posting (Ṭabari, II, p. 1267, tr. XXIII, p. 216; Ebn Aʿṯam, VII, p. 249; Ebn al-Aṯir, IV, p. 132). In 96/714-15, Qotayba incited his army to rebel, but they refused and killed him (ca. August 715). The tribal leaders of Khorasan deferred to Moḍar pre-eminence, but Qotayba's downfall was accomplished by consensus among the Moḍar, the Rabiʿa-Yaman, and the *mawāli* (clients; see ʿARAB iii; CONVERSION ii; IRAN

Table 2
GOVERNORS DURING THE PERIOD OF FACTIONALIZATION AND EXPANSION (64-96/683-714)

Caliphs	Governors of Iraq	Governors of Khorasan
Moʿāwia II b. Yazid (64/683)	ʿObayd-Allāh b. Ziād (56-67/675-86)	ʿAbd-Allāh b. Ḵāzem[1] (64-72/683-91)
ʿAbd-al-Malek (65-86/685-705)		Boḵayr b. Wešāḥ[2] (72-74/691-93)
	Ḥajjāj b. Yusof (75-95/694-713)	Omayya b. ʿAbd-Allāh[3] (74-78/693-97
		Mohallab b. Abi Ṣofra[4] (78-82/697-701)
		Yazid b. Mohallab[5] (82-85/701-4)
		Mofażżal b. Mohallab[6] (85-86/704-5)
al-Walid I (86-96/705-15)		Qotayba b. Moslem[7] (86-96/705-14)

Notes: (1) Almost all of the major sources agree that ʿAbd-Allāh b. Ḵāzem gained his second governorship (64-72/683-91) by having Salm b. Ziād relinquish his authority to him (Ṭabari, II, p. 489, tr., XX, p. 72; Ebn Aʿṯam, V, p. 311; Ebn al-Aṯir, III, p. 31, IV, pp. 20-21; Yaʿqubi, II, p. 252; and Balāḏori, *Fotuḥ*, tr., p. 404). ʿAbd-Allāh b. Ḵāzem then pledged allegiance to Ebn Zobayr.

(2) Boḵayr b. Wešāḥ's dates are firm (Ṭabari, II, pp. 834, 859, tr., XXI, p. 212, and XXII, p. 7; Ebn Aʿṯam, V, p. 312, VI, p. 289; Ebn al-Aṯir, IV, pp. 21, 30). Yaʿqubi documents that Boḵayr beheaded ʿAbd-Allāh b. Ḵāzem (II, p. 271) and Balāḏori affirms Boḵayr's appointment by ʿAbd-al-Malek (*Fotuḥ*, tr. p. 405).

(3) Omayya b. ʿAbd-Allāh's dates are firm (Ṭabari tr., XXII, pp. 7, 178; Ebn Aʿṯam, VI, p. 288, VII, p. 120; Ebn al-Aṯir, IV, pp. 30, 71; Yaʿqubi, II, p. 271; Balāḏori, *Fotuḥ*, tr., p. 406; and Ḵalifa, dismissal, p. 187).

(4) Mohallab b. Abi Ṣofra and two of his sons ruled after Omayya (Ṭabari, II, pp. 1033, 1084, tr., XXII, p. 178, XXIII, p. 32; Ebn Aʿṯam, VII, pp. 78, 120; Ebn al-Aṯir, IV, pp. 71, 83; Yaʿqubi, II, pp. 272, 276; Balāḏori, *Fotuḥ*, tr., p. 407, and Ḵalifa, pp. 185, 187).

(5) Yazid b. Mohallab (Ṭabari, II, p. 1085, 1140, tr., XXIII, pp. 33, 85; Ebn Aʿṯam, VII, pp. 196, 204; Ebn al-Aṯir, IV, pp. 83, 96; Yaʿqubi, appointed, II, p. 276; Balāḏori, appointed by Ḥajjāj b. Yusof, *Fotuḥ*, tr. p. 407; and Ḵalifa, appointed, p. 187).

(6) Ṭabari (II, pp. 1141, 1178, tr., XXIII, pp. 86, 126) and Ebn al-Aṯir (IV, pp. 83, 96) confirm his dates. Yaʿqubi affirms his appointment date (II, p. 276) and Balāḏori, his appointment by Ḥajjāj b. Yusof (*Fotuḥ*, tr., p. 407).

(7) Qotayba b. Moslem's dates are well documented (Ṭabari, II, pp. 1178, 1296, tr. XXIII, p. 126, XXIV, p. 20; Ebn Aʿṯam, appointed, VII, p. 204; Ebn al-Aṯir, IV, pp. 105, 138; Yaʿqubi, appointed, II, p. 276; Ḵalifa, pp. 187, 200), but Balāḏori commences his governorship in 85/704 (*Fotuḥ*, tr. p. 407).

ii[2]). The passing of these three men marked a turning point in Omayyad governance.

ESTRANGEMENT, DIVISION, AND ARBITRATION (97-128/715-45)

Under Qotayba's leadership, the *mawāli* found status, power, and prestige. Men such as Ḥayyān Nabaṭi and his son Moqātel rose to prominence. Ḥayyān's status as the commander of the *mawāli* forces gave him the same status as a chief in the *qabāʾel*-system; but within Muslim society, owing to his non-Arab origin, his advancement could only truly be achieved under the auspices and umbrella of the *ašrāf al-Eslām*. The presence and service of the *mawāli* as part of Muslim authority eclipsed the authority of the non-Muslim *moluk al-ṭawāʾef* and affected the eventual transfer of all local power to Muslim officials (see Ṭabari, II, pp. 1290-91, 1299, 1328-31, tr., XXIV, pp. 13-15, 23, 53-55; Balāḏori, *Fotuḥ*, p. 337, tr. p. 42).

During the caliphate of ʿOmar b. ʿAbd-al-ʿAziz (ʿOmar II; r. 99-101/717-20), there was a focus on reforms and recognizing equality among Muslims regardless of their ethnic origins. A delegation from Khorasan informed him that the *mawāli* participating in campaigns in Khorasan did not receive *ʿaṭāʾ* or *rezq* (salary and maintenance pay) and that converts to Islam still paid the *jezya* (q.v.). ʿOmar II abolished the *jezya* for new converts and triggered a wave of new converts (Ṭabari, II, p. 1354, tr., XXIV, p. 83; Ebn al-Aṯir, IV, p. 158). These mass conversions broke the pattern of controlled conversion, and many administrators believed that these new Muslims had only converted in order to escape the *jezya*. The reforms were short-lived and the *jezya* was re-imposed on many of the "new converts," causing many of them to renounce Islam (see Ṭabari, II, p. 1510, tr., XXV, p. 48).

Samarqand, conversion, and the Murjiʾites. Throughout the Omayyad period governorship was a source of private enrichment. Both the Muslim tax collectors (*ʿommāl*) and the non-Muslim rulers in Sogdia were often corrupt. While lining their own pockets, they were pressured to maintain or increase tax revenues. Exemption from paying the *jezya* for converts to Islam reduced revenues, so these officials continually contended that new conversions were a contrived means to escape taxes. As a result, converts to Islam were forced to pay the *jezya*.

Mass conversions to Islam prompted Jarrāḥ b. ʿAbd-Allāh Ḥakami (gov. 99-100/717-18) to impose a circumcision test as proof of conversion. ʿOmar II stopped this (Ṭabari, II, p. 1354, tr. XIV, p. 83; Madelung, p. 16). Most probably, many converted for economic reasons. However, Ašras b. ʿAbd-Allāh Solami (gov. 109-11/727-30) sponsored a conversion campaign initiated by a *mawlā*, Abu'l-Ṣaydāʿ Ṣāleḥ b. Ṭarif, who converted many by promising them that they would pay no *jezya*, only *ḵarāj* (Ṭabari, II, 1507-10, tr. XXV, pp. 46-48; Ṭabari, II, 1507-10, tr. XXV, pp. 46-48). But, again, when revenues dropped drastically, circumcision tests were re-imposed, and converts were required to recite a *sura* from the Qurʾan (see Ṭabari, II, p. 1508, tr. XXV, p. 47).

Pressure to produce revenues no doubt triggered conversion tests in an effort to detect fraud, but additionally non-Muslim rulers did not wish to see their subjects convert, since that diminished their standing in the community. Another factor that is impossible to gauge is the brand of Islam that was being preached by Abu'l-Ṣaydāʾ. Was his message one approved by the authorities or was it a type of Murjiʾism, where all one needed was to have faith in one's heart with no need for actions or outward displays of religious practice? This question is raised because of the large concentration of Murjiʾite believers in Balḵ and Sogdia. We know that the famous poet-warrior Ṯābit Qoṭnah was a Murjiʾite. He and Abu'l-Ṣaydāʾ actively supported some seven thousand new converts who refused to pay the *jezya* again when it was re-imposed on them. Abu'l-Ṣaydāʾ and Ṯābit withdrew with this group, but they were both imprisoned for a while and Persian elites were humiliated in the streets and forced to pay the *ḵarāj*, while common converts were forced to pay the *jezya* (Ṭabari, II, p. 1508, tr., XXV, p. 47).

Five years later, in 734, Ḥāreṯ b. Sorayj Tamimi rebelled against ʿĀṣem b. ʿAbd-Allāh Helāli (gov. 116-17/734-36). His men consisted of converts and both Yamanis and Tamimis. He advocated for the end of illegal taxes on Muslims, insisted on providing proper pensions for them and called for fairness and justice. He was charismatic and championed the *mawāli* and converts of Sogdia, along with his religious spokesman, Jahm b. Ṣafwān (q.v.; d. 128/746), who founded the Jahmiya. Ḥāreṯ found refuge with the Ḵāqān in Ṭoḵārestān, the Eḵšid of Sogdia, the Yabḡu, the Sabal of Ḵottal, the Eḵšid of Šāš, and the Türgesh. Ḥāreṯ's Murjiʾite version of Islam, like that of the Kharijites, accepted all Muslims as equals. Independent of Omayyad authority, he spread his form of Islam in Khorasan (on Ḥāreṯ and the Murjiʾites, see Wellhausen, pp. 464-72, 485-88; Gibb, pp. 76-85; Madelung, 1982, 1988; Blankinship, pp. 176-84; Agha, 1997).

The Muslim presence in Sogdia completely disrupted the economy and stripped the population of its wealth. Until the governorship of Naṣr b. Sayyār (gov. 120-131/738-48), Omayyad governance had only extracted wealth. It had been corrupted and inconsistent in its policies of tax collection and conversion. Only when peace and commerce were restored could Sogdia begin to accept a new order. Naṣr b. Sayyār, as mentioned before, implemented reforms and was able to win back Sogdian trust. During his governorship, he launched diplomatic missions to China, which successfully established cordial Omayyad-Chinese relations (Beckwith, pp. 124-25). His missions to China became so regular that, in 741, when Inäl Tudun Külüg, the viceroy of Šāš, requested Chinese assistance against the Muslims, the emperor refused it.

An anti-Omayyad movement had begun around 720. Its propaganda concentrated on the population of Khorasan, and finally, in 746, the Abbasid Revolution under the leadership of Abu Moslem Khorāsāni began there. It quickly gained success in Khorasan, toppled Omayyad authority there, and spread westward into Persia and Iraq. Continued victories propelled the movement into Syria and in 750, the Omayyads were defeated and the Abbasid dynasty was established. Abu Moslem Khorāsāni retained control

Table 3

THE ERA OF MISGOVERNANCE—SYRIANS AND KUFANS (97-128/715-745)

Caliphs	Governors of Iraq	Governors of Khorasan
Solaymān		Wakiʿ b. Abi Sud Tamimi[1]
(96-99/715-17)		97/716 (9 mo.)
	Yazid b. Mohallab	Yazid b. Mohallab[2]
	(97-99/715-17)	(98-99/716-17)
ʿOmar II b. ʿAbd-al-ʿAziz		Jarrāḥ b. ʿAbd-Allāh[3]
(99-101/717-20)		(99-100/717-18)
		ʿAbd-al-Raḥmān Noʿaym and ʿAbd-al-Raḥmān
		b. ʿAbd-Allāh[4]
		(100-101/718-19)
Yazid b. ʿAbd-al-Malek	Maslama b. ʿAbd-al-Malek	Saʿid b. ʿAbd-al-ʿAziz[5]
(101-105/720-24)	(101-2/719-21)	(102-103/719-21)
	ʿOmar b. Hobayra	Saʿid b. ʿAmr Ḥarašī[6]
	(103-5/721-23)	(103-104/721-22)
Hešām		Moslem b. Saʿid b. Aslam[7]
(105-25/723-42)		(104-5/722-23)
	Ḵāled b. ʿAbd-Allāh Qasri	Asad b. ʿAbd-Allāh Qasri[8]
	(ca. 105-120/723-38)	(106-9/725-27)
		Ašras b. ʿAbd-Allāh Solami[9]
		(109-11/727-29)
		Jonayd b. ʿAbd-al-Raḥmān[10]
		(111-16/729-34)
		ʿĀṣem b. ʿAbd-Allāh b. Yazid[11]
		(116-17/734-35)
		Asad b. ʿAbd-Allāh Qasri[12]
		(117-20/735-38)
	Yusof b. ʿOmar Ṯaqafi	Naṣr b. Sayyār[13]
	(120-26/738-43)	(120-31/738-48)

Notes: (1) Wakiʿ b. Abi Sud Tamimi was appointed by the Caliph Solaymān after killing Qotayba. He ruled between 9 and 10 months only (Ṭabari, II, pp. 1311-12, tr., XXIV, p. 36; Ebn Aʿṯam, VII, p. 278; Ebn al-Aṯir, IV, p. 145; Yaʿqubi, II, p. 296; Balāḏori, *Fotuḥ*, tr., p. 413); Ḵalifa, appointed 96?, p. 203).

(2) Yazid b. al-Mohallab's dates are well documented (Ṭabari, II, pp. 1306, 1310, 1346, tr., XXIV, pp. 30, 34, XXIIV, p. 75; Ebn Aʿṯam, VII, p. 278; Ebn al-Aṯir, IV, p. 144; Yaʿqubi, II, 296; Balāḏori, appointed by Solaymān, *Fotuḥ*, tr., p. 414).

(3) Jarrāḥ b. ʿAbd-Allāh (Ṭabari, II, 1347, 1352-53, tr., XXIV, p. 75, XXIV, p. 82; Ebn Aʿṯam, VII, p. 320; Ebn al-Aṯir, IV, p. 157; Yaʿqubi, II, p. 302; Balāḏori, *Fotuḥ*, tr., p. 415; Ḵalifa, p. 206 gives a dismissal date of 101/719).

(4) ʿAbd-al-Raḥmān Noʿaym and ʿAbd-al-Raḥmān b. ʿAbd-Allāh divided the administration with the former in charge of the military and prayer and the latter in charge of the *ḵarāj*. Sources have them in office for 1.5 years (Ṭabari, II, 1354-55, 1356-57, tr., XXIV, pp. 84, 86-87; Ebn al-Aṯir, IV, p. 157; Yaʿqubi, II, p. 302; Balāḏori, *Fotuḥ*, tr., p. 415; and Ḵalifa, p. 206, gives an accession date of 101/719).

(5) Saʿid b. ʿAbd al-ʿAziz (Ṭabari, II, 1417-18, 1436, tr., XXIV, pp. 149-50, 166; Ebn al-Aṯir, IV, pp. 177, 183; Yaʿqubi, II, pp. 311, 312; Balāḏori, *Fotuḥ*, tr., p. 416; Ḵalifa, p. 210).

(6) Saʿid b. ʿAmr Harašī (Ṭabari, II, 1436, 1453, tr., XXIV, pp. 166, 183; Ebn Aʿṯam, VIII, pp. 26, 27-28; Ebn al-Aṯir, IV, pp. 183, 188; Balāḏori, *Fotuḥ*, tr., p.416; Ḵalifa, pp. 210, 214; he is not mentioned by Yaʿqubi).

(7) Moslem b. Saʿid b. Aslam (Ṭabari, II, 1458, 1462, tr., XXIV, pp. 187, 193; Ebn Aʿṯam, VIII, p. 28; Ebn al-Aṯir, IV, pp. 188, 195 [gives date as 106]; Yaʿqubi, II, p. 312; Balāḏori, appointed by ʿOmar b. Hubayrah, *Fotuḥ*, tr., p. 416; Ḵalifa, pp. 214, 216 [gives date as 106]).

(8) Asad b. ʿAbd-Allāh Qasri (Ebn Aʿṯam, VIII, pp. 35, 99; Ebn al-Aṯir, IV, pp. 195, 200; Yaʿqubi, II, p. 319; Balāḏori, *Fotuḥ*, tr., p. 417 says he was appointed by his brother Ḵāled b. ʿAbd-Allāh Qasri; Ḵalifa, pp. 216, 233 [gives date as 108]).

(9) Ašras b. ʿAbd-Allāh Solami (Ṭabari, II, pp. 1506, 1527, tr., XXV, pp. 44, 65; Ebn Aʿṯam, VIII, p. 99; Ebn al-Aṯir, IV, pp. 200, 206; Balaḏori, appointed by Hešām, *Fotuḥ*, tr., p. 417; Ḵalifa, p. 233 [gives appointment as 108 and dismissal as 113]; he is not mentioned by Yaʿqubi).

(10) Jonayd b. ʿAbd-al-Raḥmān (Ṭabari, II, pp. 1527, 1565, tr., XXV, pp. 65, 103; Ebn Aʿṯam, VIII, p. 99; Ebn al-Aṯir, IV, pp. 206, 217; Yaʿqubi [earlier]; and Balāḏori, appointed in 112, *Fotuḥ*, tr., p. 418; Ḵalifa, p. 233 [gives appointment as 113 and dismissal as 115]).

(11) ʿĀṣem b. ʿAbd-Allāh b. Yazid (Ṭabari, II, p. 1564, tr., XXV, pp. 102, 111; Ebn Aʿṯam, VIII, p. 106; Ebn al-Aṯir, IV, pp. 217, 219; Balāḏori, appointed by Hešām, *Fotuḥ*, tr. p. 418; Ḵalifa, (pp. 233, 234 [gives appointment and dismissal as 115]; not mentioned by Yaʿqubi).

(12) Asad b. ʿAbd-Allāh Qasri (Ṭabari, II, pp. 1581-82, tr., XXV, p. 119; Ebn Aʿṯam, VIII, p. 106, and VIII, p. 107 mentions his death; Ebn al-Aṯir, IV, pp. 219, 234; Ḵalifa, pp. 224, 233, gives appointment as 115; his appointment is not mentioned by Yaʿqubi.

(13) Sources are generally in agreement for the dates of Naṣr b. Sayyār's governorship (although Ṭabari, II, p. 1638, tr. XXV, p. 170 has the official appointment arriving in Rajab 121/June 739.

of Khorasan and reestablished Muslim control over Transoxiana. However, in 755, he was assassinated, and the Abbasid caliph appointed his own governor of Khorasan.

Bibliography: Saleh Said Agha, "A Viewpoint of the Murji'i in the Umayyad Period: Evolution through Application," *Journal of Islamic Studies* 8/1, 1997, pp. 1-42. Idem, "The Arab Population in Ḫurāsān during the Umayyad Period: Some Demographic Computations," *Arabica* 46/2, 1999, pp. 211-29. Idem, *The Revolution which Toppled the Umayyads: Neither Arab nor ʿAbbāsid*, Leiden and Boston, 2003. Ṣāleḥ Aḥmad ʿAli, *Estiṭān al-ʿarab fi Ḵorāsān*, n.p., n.d. Khalil Athamina, "Tax Reforms in Early Islamic Khurāsān: A Reassessment," *Der Islam* 65, 1988, pp. 272-281. Idem, "Aʿrāb and Muhājirūn in the Environment of Amṣār," *Studia Islamica* 66, 1987, pp. 5-25. Ḥosayn ʿAṭwān, *al-Šeʿr fi Ḵorāsān: Men al-fatḥ elā nehāyat al-ʿaṣr al-Omawi*, Beirut, 1989. Aḥmad b. Yaḥyā Balāḏori, *Ansāb al-ašrāf*, ed. Sohayl Zakkār and Riyāż Zerekli, 13 vols., Beirut, 1996. Idem, *Ketāb fotuḥ al-boldān*, ed. M. J. de Goeje, Leiden, 1866; tr. Francis Clark Murgotten as, *The Origins of the Islamic State* II, New York, 1924. Larissa S. Baratova, "Turkic Khaghanate in Middle Asia (VI-VIII Centuries A.D.)," in Hasan Güzel, ed., *The Turks* I: *Early Ages*, Ankara, 2014, pp. 357-63. W. Barthold, *An Historical Geography of Iran*, tr. Svat Soucek and ed. C. E. Bosworth, Princeton, 1984. Idem, *Turkestan Down to the Mongol Invasion*, 3rd ed., London, 1968. Christopher I. Beckwith, *The Tibetan Empire in Central Asia : A History of the Struggle for Great Power among Tibetans, Turks, Arabs, and Chinese during the Early Middle Ages*, Princeton, 1987. Khalid Yahya Blankinship, *The End of the Jihâd State: The Reign of Hishām Ibn ʿAbd Al-Malik and the Collapse of the Umayyads*, Albany, 1994. Clifford Edmund Bosworth, *Sīstān Under the Arabs: From the Islamic Conquest to the Rise of the Ṣaffārids (30-250/651-864)*, Rome, 1968.

Audrey Burton, "Itineraires commerciaux et militaires entre Boukhara et l'Inde," *Cahier d'Asie Centrale* 1-2, 1996, pp. 13-32. Edouard Chavannes, *Documents sur les Tou-Kiue (Turcs) occidentaux, recueillis et commentés, suivi de notes additionnelles*, Paris, 1942. Arthur Christensen, *L'Iran sous les Sassanides*, Copenhagen, 1944, repr. Osnabrück, 1971. M. Cook, "Activism and Quietism in Islam: The Case of the Early Murjiʾa," in Alexander S. Cudsi and E. Hillal Dessouki, eds., *Islam and Power*, London, 1981, pp. 15-23. Patricia Crone, "A Note on Muqātil b. Ḥayyān and Muqātil b. Sulaymān," *Der Islam* 74, 1997, pp. 238-49. Idem, "Al-Muhallab b. Abī Ṣufra," in *Encyclopaedia of Islam: New Edition* VII, Leiden, 1993, p. 357. Elton L. Daniel, *The Political and Social History of Khurasan Under Abbasid Rule, 747-820*, Minneapolis, 1979. Touraj Daryaee, *Sasanian Iran (224-651 CE) : Portrait of a Late Antique Empire*, Costa Mesa, Calif., 2008. Daniel Clement Dennett, *Conversion and the Poll Tax in Early Islam*, Cambridge, Mass., 1950. ʿAbd al-ʿAziz Duri, "Notes on Taxation in Early Islam," *Journal of the Economic and Social History of the Orient* 17/2, 1974, pp. 136-44. Aḥmad Ebn Aʿṯam Kufi, *Ketāb al-fotuḥ*, 8 vols., Ḥaydarābād (Deccan), 1968-75. ʿEzz-al-Din Ebn al-Aṯir, *al-Kāmil fi'l-taʾriḵ*, 9 vols., Beirut, 1997. Idem, *Osd al-ḡāba fi maʿrefat al-ṣaḥāba*, Cairo, 1964. ʿAli b. Aḥmad Ebn Ḥazm, *Jamharat ansāb al-ʿarab*, ed. ʿAbd-al-Salām Moḥammad Hārun, Cairo, 1962. Abu'l-ʿAbbās Aḥmad b. Moḥammad Ebn Ḵallekān, *Wafayāt al-aʿyān wa-anbaʾ abnāʾ al-zamān*, ed. Yusof ʿAli Ṭawil et al., 6 vols., Beirut, 1998. Emil Esin, "Tarkhan Nīzak or Tarkhan Tirek?," *Journal of the American Oriental Society* 98, 1977, pp. 323-32. Richard Nelson Frye, "The Turks in Khurasan and Transoxiana at the Time of the Arab Conquest," *The Moslem World* 35, 1945, pp. 308-15. Idem, "Bukhārā," in *Encyclopaedia of Islam: New Edition* I, Leiden, 1986, pp. 1293-96. ʿAbd-al-Ḥayy b. Zaḥḥāk Gardizi, *Zayn al-aḵbār*, ed. ʿAbd-al-Ḥayy Ḥabibi, Tehran, 1968. H. A. R. Gibb, *The Arab Conquests in Central Asia*, London, 1923, repr. New York 1970. Idem, "The Fiscal Rescript of ʿUmar II," *Arabica* 2, 1955, pp. 1-16. Frantz Grenet, "Regional Interaction in Central Asia and Northwestern India in the Kidarite and Hephthalite Periods," in Nicholas Sims-Williams, ed., *Indo-Iranian Languages and Peoples*, Proceedings of the British Academy 116, Oxford, 2002, pp. 203-24. Idem, "Nēzak," in *Encyclopædia Iranica*, online version, 2002. Franz Grenet and Étienne de la Vaissière, "The Last Days of Panjikent," *Silk Road Art and Archaeology*, 2002, pp. 155-96.

Moḥammad b. ʿAbd-Allāh Ḥākem Nišāburi, *Tāriḵ-e Nišābur*, ed. Moḥammad-Reżā Šafiʿi Kadkani, Tehrān, 1996. J. Harmatta and B. A. Litvinsky, "Tokharistan and Gandhara Under Western Turk Rule (650-750)," in B. A. Litvinsky et al., eds., *History of Civilizations in Central Asia* III, Paris, 1996, pp. 358-93. Robert Haug, *The Eastern Frontier: Limits of Empire in Late Antique and Early Medieval Central Asia*, London and New York, 2019. Donald Routledge Hill, *The Termination of Hostilities in the Early Arab Conquests, A.D. 634-656*, London, 1971. A. H. Jalilov, "The Arab Conquest of Transoxania," in B. A. Litvinsky et al., eds., *History of Civilizations in Central Asia* III, Paris, 1996, pp. 456-65. Ḵalifa b. Ḵayyāṭ, *Ketāb al-ṭabaqāt*, ed. Sohayl Zakkār, Damascus, 1966. Idem, *Taʾriḵ*, ed. Moṣṭafā Najib Fawwāz and Ḥekmat Kešli Fawwāz, Beirut, 1995. Étienne de la Vaissière, *Sogdian Traders: A History*, Leiden and Boston, 2005. Idem, ed., *Islamisation de l'Asie centrale: Processus locaux d'acculturation du VIIe au XIe siècle*, Cahiers de Studia Iranica 39, Paris, 2008. Idem, "Early Medieval Central Asian Population Estimates," *Journal of the Economic and Social History of the Orient* 60, 2017, pp. 788-817. Idem, "The ʿAbbāsid Revolution in Marw: New Data," *Der Islam* 95/1, 2018, pp. 110–46. Wilferd Madelung, "The Early Murjiʾa in Khurāsān and Transoxania and the Spread of Hanafism," *Der Islam* 59, 1982, pp. 332-39. Idem, "The Murji'a and Sunnite Traditionalism," in idem, *Religious Trends in Early Islamic Iran*, Albany, 1988, pp. 13-25. Roy Andrew Miller, tr. and annot., *Accounts of Western Nations in the History of the Northern Chou Dynasty [Chou Shu 50. 10b-17b]*, Chinese Dynastic Histories Translations 6, Berkeley,

1959. Michael G. Morony, *Iraq After the Muslim Conquest,* Princeton, N. J., 1984. Idem, "Mulūk al-Ṭawāʾif (A.) 1. In Pre-Islamic Persia," in *Encyclopaedia of Islam: New Edition* VII, Leiden, 1993, pp. 551-52.

Saʿid Nafisi, *Tāriḵ-e ejtemāʿi-e Irān az enqerāż-e Sāsāniān tā enqerāż-e Omawiān*, Tehran, 1964. Parvaneh Pourshariati, *Decline and Fall of the Sasanian Empire: The Sasanian-Parthian Confederacy and the Arab Conquest of Iran*, London and New York, 2008. Wadād Qadi, "Madḵal elā derāsat ʿohud al-ṣolh zamān al-fotuḥ," *al-Ejtehād* 1/1, 1988, pp. 43-113. M. Rekaya, "Ḳārinids," in *Encyclopaedia of Islam: New Edition* IV, Leiden, 1978, pp. 644-47. Khodadad Rezakhani, *ReOrienting the Sasanians: East Iran in Late Antiquity*, Edinburgh, 2017. Abu Saʿd ʿAbd-al-Karim b. Moḥammad Tamimi Samʿāni, *Ketāb-al-ansāb*, ed. ʿAbd-al-Raḥmān Yamāni, 13 vols., Hyderabad, 1962-82. Muḥammad Shaban, *Islamic History: A New Interpretation*, Cambridge, 1971. Søren Stark, "Mercenaries and City Rulers: Early Turks in Pre-Muslim Mawarannahr," in L. M. Popova, C. W. Hartley, and A. T. Smith, eds., *Social Orders and Social Landscapes*, Newcastle, 2007, pp. 307-33. Idem, "The Arab Conquest of Bukhārā: Reconsidering Qutayba b. Muslim's Campaigns 87-90 H/706-709 CE," *Der Islam* 95, 2018, pp. 367-400. Boris Y. Stavisky, "Once More about the Peculiarities of the Sogdian Civilization of the 4th-10th Centuries," in Matteo Compareti et al., eds, *Ērān ud Anērān: Webfestschrift Marshak*, Transoxiana Webfestschrift Series 1, 2003, available at www.transoxiana.org/Eran/Articles/Stavisky.html (accessed 10 October 2019). Moḥammad b. Jarir Ṭabari, *Tāriḵ al-rosol wa'l-moluk*, eds. M. J. de Goeje et al., 15 vols., Leiden, 1879-1901, tr. as *The History of al-Ṭabari*, gen. ed. Ehsan Yarshater, 40 vols., Albany, N.Y., 1985-2007 (translators vary). *Tārikẓ-e Sistān*, ed. Moḥammad-Taqi Bahār, Tehran, 1935. Tsʾen Chung-Mien, tr. Penelope A. Herbert in "The Tʾang System of Bureaucratic Titles and Grades," *Tʾang Studies* 5, 1987, pp. 25-31. Julius Wellhausen, *The Arab Kingdom and Its Fall*, tr. Margaret Weir, Calcutta, 1927, repr. Beirut, 1963. Aḥmad b. Abi Yaʿqub Yaʿqubi, *Tārikh*, 2 vols., Beirut; tr. and ed. Matthew S. Gordon et al. as, *The Works of Ibn Wāḍiḥ al-Yaʿqubi: An English translation*, 3 vols., Leiden, 2017. Šehāb-al-Din Abu ʿAbd-Allāh Yāqut b. ʿAbd-Allāh Ḥamawi, *Moʿjam al-boldān*, 5 vols., Beirut, 1955-57.

(MARK LUCE)

v. HISTORY IN THE ʿABBASID PERIOD

The revolution that overthrew Omayyad rule and led to the establishment of the ʿAbbasid caliphate was incubated in Khorasan, and it marked a major watershed in the history of that province, just as it would in the larger Islamic world. Under the Omayyads, the overriding historical dynamic of Khorasan had been that of a frontier contact zone (or "shatterzone" in the terminology of one recent work; Haug, p. 26), with the provincial administration and armies primarily engaged in defending against nomadic invasions from the north and subduing numerous non-Islamic local rulers, often backed by Chinese power, along the eastern marchlands. After the revolution, the historical narrative reflected a political dynamic between center and periphery, with an increasingly unified array of Islamized local elites resisting the voracious demands of a centralizing caliphal bureaucracy and achieving greater and greater degrees of political autonomy in what was becoming more of an Islamic commonwealth than an ʿAbbasid empire.

THE ʿABBASID REVOLUTION AND RISE OF ABU MOSLEM

The conditions for the first stage of the ʿAbbasid revolution resulted from the "third civil war" (Wellhausen, pp. 370-96) that erupted following the death of the Omayyad caliph Hešām in 125/743 and the assassination of his successor Walid II in 126/744. As the struggle for power in Syria and Iraq raged, Khorasan was largely left to its own devices, and the Omayyad establishment there was fractured by internecine strife among the Arab elites.

Hešām had appointed Naṣr b. Sayyār Layṯi Kenāni as governor in 120/737-38 (Ṭabari, II, pp. 1660-62). Naṣr, then more than seventy-years old, had experience in the military and fiscal affairs of Khorasan going back to the time of Qotayba b. Moslem (d. 96/715). As governor, he resumed raids across the Oxus (Āmu Daryā, q.v.) and, in 121/738, introduced a series of fiscal reforms that ostensibly aimed at relieving tax burdens on Arabs and non-Arab converts under the protection of Arab tribes (the *mawāli*), but avoiding deficits by more rigorously imposing tribute, the land tax (*ḵarāj*), and the demeaning poll tax (*jezya*, q.v.) on the "polytheists" (*mošrekin*), who may well have included many nominal converts not affiliated like the *mawāli* with Arab tribes (see Ṭabari, II, pp. 1688-89; Dennett, pp. 110-13). He also unabashedly gave preference to his own tribal bloc, the Możar, and was said to have appointed over a four-year span only Możaris to office (Ṭabari, II, pp. 1664-65). The main intent of Naṣr's reforms seems to have been to create an expanded and tightly controlled Arab administration in Khorasan, disentangling it from the administration of Iraq and reporting directly to the caliph.

Although Khorasan is said to have prospered under Naṣr's governorship (Ṭabari, II, p. 1665), opposition to him grew despite, or more likely because of, the policies he had introduced. One source of opposition would naturally be from the partisans of the house of ʿAli b. Abi Ṭāleb (q.v.), who were not inclined to support Omayyad rule under any circumstances. They, as well as less dedicated sympathizers, were outraged by Naṣr's treatment of Yaḥyā b. Zayd, ʿAli's great-grandson. The young Yaḥyā had fled to Khorasan after the failure of the revolt in Kufa against Hešām led by his father, Zayd b. ʿAli b. Ḥosayn (d. 122/740). Yaḥyā went into hiding first in Saraḵs and then in Balḵ (q.v.), but Naṣr, under pressure from the governor of Iraq, Yusof b. ʿOmar, had his agents hunt Yaḥyā down and ordered him to return to Iraq and face certain death at the hands of Yusof b. ʿOmar. After Yaḥyā attempted to stay in Khorasan, Naṣr's forces attacked and killed him and put his decapitated corpse on display in Jowzjān (q.v.) in 125/743 (on these events, see Ṭabari, II, 1667-88, 1698-1716, 1770-74; Balāḏori, II, pp. 520-46; Eṣfahāni, pp. 152-58).

After Hešām's death, there were intrigues by other rivals to replace Naṣr as governor, but he evaded them until his governorship was affirmed by the caliph Yazid III in 126/744 (Ṭabari, II, p. 1855). Naṣr arrested the most likely of the candidates who had tried to replace him, Jodayʿ b. ʿAli Kermāni, a leader of the Azd tribes and protégé of the former governor and Naṣr's nemesis, Asad b. ʿAbd-Allāh Qaṣri (d. 120/737-38). Kermani quickly escaped and raised an army of supporters who took up camp near Marv and prepared to fight Naṣr (Ṭabari, II, 1858-66). Naṣr then persuaded Yazid III to grant an amnesty to Ḥāreṯ b. Sorayj, a perennial religio-political rebel (who at one time had even allied with the Türgesh against the Omayyads), in the hope of winning him as an ally against Kermāni (Ṭabari, II, 1867-69). Instead, Ḥāreṯ returned from Samarqand and also took up a position near Marv; he rallied his own supporters; denounced tyranny, oppression, and corruption; preached for governance in accord with the Qurʾan and the Sunna; and, after refusing to recognize the accession of Marwān II (r. 127-32/744-50) as caliph, cooperated with Kermāni against Naṣr (Ṭabari, II, 1888-90). The latter retreated to Nishapur in 128/746. As Naṣr had perhaps anticipated, it was less than a month before Ḥāreṯ and Kermāni had a falling out; in their fight, Ḥāreṯ was killed in Rajab 128/April 746 and his decapitated corpse crucified at Marv (Ṭabari, II, 1932-33). Naṣr then resumed his efforts to dislodge Kermāni from Marv, returning to the city and encamping near Kermāni's position in 129/747. Throughout all of this, Naṣr had warned his adversaries of the dangers that would result from the Arab establishment being divided against itself and appealed for unity. He was soon proven correct by the arrival on the scene of a new and quite unexpected contender in the person of Abu Moslem Ḵorāsāni (q.v.), who raised the black banners of revolt in a village outside Marv in Ramażān or Šawwāl 129/June 747.

Abu Moslem's declaration of revolt marked the second stage of the ʿAbbasid revolution, but one that is shrouded, like Abu Moslem himself, in a cloud of mystery. In general, the traditional sources would have us believe that the revolution was the fruit of a conspiracy carefully cultivated over nearly thirty years by a tightly organized, covert, sectarian faction known as the Hāšhemiya. In what was for a while the official version of how the sect got its name, the Hāšemiya were propagandizing for rule by a member of the Prophet Moḥammad's clan of Hāšem, specifically Moḥammad b. ʿAli, the grandson of the Prophet's paternal uncle ʿAbbās, and were directed by him as leader of the ʿAbbasid family from their place of exile in Ḥomayma (a village south of the Dead Sea). An alternative explanation was that the Hāšemiya represented an extremist offshoot of the Kaysāniya (q.v.) propagandizing mostly in Kufa (q.v.) but with little effect, on behalf of Abu Hāšem ʿAbd-Allāh b. Moḥammad b. al-Ḥanafiya (a descendant of the third son of ʿAli b. Abi Ṭāleb by a woman of the Banu Ḥanifa). The childless Abu Hāšem, persecuted by the Omayyads, took refuge in Ḥomayma with Moḥammad b. ʿAli and, near death in 98/716-17, turned over his claim to the caliphate, his esoteric knowledge, and his organization to Moḥammad b. ʿAli (for details and sources, see Daniel, 1979, pp. 26-29; Sharon, 1983, pp. 121-40; Agha, 2003, pp. 4-6).

After a period of mostly ineffective organizing in Kufa, Moḥammad b. ʿAli was persuaded by one of the recruits, Bokayr b. Māhān (q.v.; d. 128/745-46), to shift the focus of the mission (*daʿwa* 'call'; see DAʿI) to Khorasan. He sent Bokayr to begin organizing there in or around the year 100/718-19 (103/722 is a more credible date; Ṭabari, II, p. 1988, and it may have been even later). Bokayr established a network of clandestine revolutionary cells led by twelve *naqib*s 'chiefs' and seventy *daʿi*s 'missionaries' (an unusually detailed account of these and other elements of the revolutionary apparatus may be found in *Aḵbār*, pp. 213-23). So far as can be told, the propaganda of the *daʿi*s used a vague call for rule based on the Qurʾan, the Sunna, and veneration of the family of the Prophet Moḥammad (see AHL-E BAYT), with the objective of bringing about the reign of a Chosen One (*al-reżā*) from among his relatives (slogans expressing such sentiments appeared later on in the oath of allegiance used by Abu Moslem, in speeches to the troops, and on coinage; Ṭabari, ii, p. 1989; *Aḵbār*, pp. 323-24). As for the identity of the sect's leader, the missioners were admonished not to reveal his name publicly. This was typical of many post-Kaysāniya movements, and perhaps a necessary precaution as Shiʿite revolts to that date had shown that those on behalf of a declared candidate were doomed to fail. However, the call for *al-reżā*, while not naming him, was also perhaps more than just a defensive tactic—it was likely rooted in the belief that the Chosen One would be manifested at the proper time through a process of consensus (*šurā*) rather than inheritance (*waṣiya*) and would reign more than rule (see Crone, 1989; Agha, 2003, pp. 101-6).

The initial efforts to recruit partisans in Khorasan was rather inept, as the governor Asad b. ʿAbd-Allāh identified and arrested a number of the propagandists in 107/725 (Ṭabari, II, pp. 1501-3). After that, the revolutionary cells were directed for three years by an illiterate Kufan, Kaṯir b. Saʿd. Among those attracted to the movement was one ʿAmmār (or ʿOmāra) b. Yazid (or Yazdād), better known by the name he gave himself (or was called), Ḵedāš. Reportedly a Christian convert from Kufa then living near Marv, Ḵedāš proved himself a skillful and charismatic preacher: Instead of simply being recruited, Ḵedāš ousted Kaṯir and not only commandeered the movement but transformed it, substituting the esoteric, perhaps neo-Mazdakite, teachings of the *din al-Ḵorramiyya* (Ṭabari, II, pp. 1503, 1588; Balāḏori, III, pp. 116-17; Ebn al-Aṯir, V, pp. 196-97; see ḴORRAMIS) for those of Moḥammad b. ʿAli and the Hāšemiya. The probability is that Ḵedāš dominated the *daʿwa* from the time Kaṯir returned to Kufa (ca. 111/729) until he was arrested, tortured, and killed on orders from

Asad b. ʿAbd-Allāh in 118/736-37. Whatever Ḵedāš was preaching must have been effective, as that is also a period in which the movement reportedly gained many followers, and even Bokayr b. Māhān is said to have recognized Ḵedāš as chief *daʿi* (Ṭabari, II, p. 1588-89). Moḥammad b. ʿAli, however, denounced Ḵedāš and remained estranged from the Hāšemiya of Khorasan until 120/738, when Solaymān b. Kaṯir Ḵozāʿi restored relations and was recognized by Moḥammad b. ʿAli as the leader of the Khorasani *daʿwa* (Ṭabari, II, 1639-40).

Moḥammad b. ʿAli died in 125/743 and was succeeded as imam of the Hāšemiya by his son Ebrāhim. Bokayr b. Māhān visited Khorasan to convey this news to the leaders of the *daʿwa*, some of whom later met with Ebrāhim during the *ḥajj* and accepted his authority. On the return from Khorasan, Bokayr was arrested and briefly jailed in Kufa until ransomed by the head of the Kufan Hāšemiya, Abu Salama Ḵallāl. It was in the Kufan jail that Bokayr and Abu Salama supposedly met the young Abu Moslem, then the servant of another of the prisoners, brought him into the movement, and took him to Ebrāhim in Ḥomayma, where he became a *mawlā* of the family. Ebrahim and Bokayr began dispatching Abu Moslem on missions to Khorasan, and in 128/745-46 (apud Ṭabari, II, p. 1937) ordered him to take over the leadership of the *daʿwa* there. The astonished veteran missioners resisted and wanted to know "from what egg has this nameless upstart hatched or from what nest has he fallen?" (*Aḵbār*, p. 269). Nonetheless, they eventually accepted Ebrāhim's instructions, and it was under the leadership of Abu Moslem that the overt revolt was prepared and launched.

Abu Moslem's execution of the revolt can only be described as brilliant strategically and tactically, coupled with some strokes of luck. With the major Arab armies occupied with each other in Marv, Abu Moslem was free to send out envoys to rally partisans all over Khorasan (Ṭabari, II, p. 1962) and pick off the isolated garrisons one by one. It is fairly clear that Nasr's supporters were either expelled or fled from Marv al-ruḏ, Herat, Āmol, Nasā, Abiward, Balḵ, and Ṭālaqān. Many of the uprisings in those places appear to have involved exceptional mass violence and massacres (see, e.g., *Aḵbār*, p. 284; Theophanes, pp. 654-55, tr. p. 114; Ḵalifa, p. 413; Dinawari, p., 361; Ebn ʿAbd Rabbeh, VI, pp. 477-79; Daniel, 1979, pp. 51-54; Agha, 2000, pp. 344-45; idem, 2003, pp. 75-86). The scattered pro-Omayyad forces—a motley coalition said to include members of all three of the tribal groups at odds with each other in Marv as well as *mawāli* and local Iranian rulers from the districts of Ṭoḵārestān—regrouped at Termeḏ, but they were decisively routed by Abu Moslem's general, Abu Dāwud Ḵāled b. Ebrāhim Šaybāni. Crucially, the ʿAbbasid envoys and propagandists circulating throughout the countryside were free to direct new recruits, often described as "slaves," to Abu Moslem's encampment. Dinavari (p. 361) describes a flood of supporters coming on horses, donkeys, and on foot from all over greater Khorasan to join Abu Moslem, all dressed in black and armed with blackened staves called *kāfer-kubāt* 'infidel bashers' (on the significance of which, see Crone, 2000, pp. 180-83). Naṣr attempted to dislodge Abu Moslem in mid-Šawwāl 129/late-June 747, but underestimated his opponent's strength and failed.

As Abu Moslem's army grew, he moved to a new fortified camp near the village of Māḵwān in Ḏu'l-Qaʿda 129/July 747. The situation in Marv was relatively simple: No one side could prevail alone but had to find allies. The conflict thus became mostly one of propaganda in which Naṣr could appeal to Arab unity, but in which Abu Moslem held almost all the trump cards. First of all, he was able to capitalize on the pro-ʿAlid sentiments in Khorasan that had been inflamed by the killing of Yaḥyā b. Zayd. Yaḥyā was related on his mother's side to Moḥammad b. al-Ḥanafiya, so Abu Moslem and the Hāšemiya were able to use vengeance for Yaḥyā as a rallying cry for their revolt. Second, as has often been noted, the Hāšemiya propaganda was remarkably similar to that of Ḥāreṯ b. Sorayj, from the use of the black banners to its religious appeal to its willingness to join with non-Arabs. After Ḥāreṯ's death, some of his followers (including his son) appear to have joined Naṣr, but it is likely many more went over to Abu Moslem. Whatever effect Naṣr's appeal for Arab unity was beginning to have, it abruptly ended when, in the course of truce negotiations, Naṣr stood by while Ḥāreṯ's son attacked and killed Jodayʿ Kermāni and crucified his corpse next to a fish (an insulting symbol for his tribe). Astonishingly, Naṣr continued to believe Arabism would somehow win over the Kermāni faction, but his efforts to forge a truce quickly failed. Abu Moslem was able to bring Kermāni's forces firmly into his alliance; he flattered Kermāni's son by calling him "amir," but when Abu Moslem asked for his orders ʿAli b. Jodayʿ prudently responded to just keep doing what he had been doing (Ṭabari, II, 1976). ʿAli b. Jodayʿ also helped persuade a Kharijite rebel, Šaybān b. Salama, who had turned up at Marv, to withdraw to Saraḵs, where he was eventually killed by Abu Moslem's followers (Ṭabari, II, 1995-97; *Aḵbār*, pp. 309-10). In one last, desperate gambit, Naṣr tried to make a deal with Abu Moslem against ʿAli b. Jodayʿ, but this was bluntly rejected (Ṭabari, II, p. 1986).

By Rabiʿ I 130/November 747, Naṣr was holed up in Marv, with turmoil in the hinterland, his hope for an Arab coalition in tatters, no prospects of aid from Syria or Iraq, Abu Moslem's forces steadily growing, ʿAli b. Jodayʿ's faction occupying part of the inner city, and ʿAbbasid propagandists active there. Fighting between two parties—exactly which ones is not clear—broke out, probably in Rabiʿ II 130/December 747. Abu Moslem then ceremoniously entered the capital on 9 Jomāda 130/27 January 748 (according to Ṭabari, II, p. 1987), without resistance, posing as a peacemaker, taking up residence at the government palace, accepting the oath of allegiance from the people, and executing Naṣr's most important officials.

Naṣr fled the next day to one of the suburbs and then, after having been warned of Abu Moslem's intention to kill him, on with his Możari supporters to Nishapur. He was pursued by a revolutionary army under the command of Qaḥṭaba b. Šabib Ṭāʾi, assisted (or watched) by two of

Abu Moslem's trusted agents, Ḵāled b. Barmak (see BARMAKIDS) and Abu'l-Jahm b. ʿAṭiya. Qaḥṭaba encamped at Abivard for the winter, and then defeated a detachment of Naṣr's troops at Ṭus, forcing Naṣr to retreat from Nishapur to Qumes in Šaʿbān 130/May 748. Many of his remaining followers then abandoned him and went to join the Omayyad governor of Jorjān, Nobāta b. Ḥanẓala, who had brought Syrian reinforcements there in such large numbers that the Khorasanis were intimidated when they encountered them (Ḏu'l-Qaʿda 130/July 748). The speech Qaḥṭaba gave to encourage the "men of Khorasan" (Ṭabari, II, pp. 2004-6) is of particular interest because, if genuine, it can only be understood as being addressed to an army made up predominately of non-Arab Muslims, who were being given an opportunity not only for vengeance on those who "had burned the House of God" but on the "lowliest nation" (*aḏall omma*), which had defeated their ancestors, seized their land and women, enslaved their children, and then ruled oppressively. This may explain the exceptional violence reported about this battle, in which Nobāta and ten thousand of his troops were killed and thousands more of the surviving garrison massacred after an attempted rebellion.

After that disaster, Naṣr left Qumes for Ḵowār near Ray to await the arrival of another Omayyad army, this one under the leadership of ʿĀmer b. Żobāra Morri. Qaḥṭaba got there first, and Naṣr then fled toward Hamadan, dying along the way at Sāwa (Rabiʿ II 131/December 748). Ebn Żobāra was gathering his "army of armies" near Isfahan and was attacked by Qaḥṭaba's forces at Jābalq in Rajab 131/March 749. The Omayyads were defeated, Ebn Żobāra killed, and vast spoils were taken from his army's camp. The Battle of Jābalq essentially completed and secured the ʿAbbasid victory in the East. Qaḥṭaba remained for a month in the area of Isfahan, where Abu Moslem sent reinforcements totaling 15,000, all said to have been recruited from the villages of Khorasan (*Aḵbār*, p. 351). Qaḥṭaba then advanced to Nehāvand (q.v.); after a siege, the Syrian troops were given safe passage to retreat, but those who had come from Khorasan with Naṣr were massacred (Ṭabari, III, pp. 6-9).

From Nehāvand, Qaḥṭaba moved on to Qermāsin, Ḥolwān, and Ḵāneqin. His objective was Kufa and linking up with the *daʿwa* organization there, but there were two more obstacles: The army of the governor of Iraq, Yazid b. ʿOmar b. Hobayra, and the army of the caliph, Marwān II. The latter delayed in the Jazira and never posed much of a threat, while Ebn Hobayra took up a defensive position near the famous old battlefield of Jalulāʾ (q.v.). After much maneuvering, Qaḥṭaba crossed the Euphrates and launched a successful surprise attack on Ebn Hobayra in Moḥarram 132/August 749, and Kufa was occupied by the ʿAbbasid forces two days later. Qaḥṭaba himself, however, had mysteriously—or suspiciously—disappeared during the fighting, and his body was found later; he had apparently drowned while crossing the Euphrates. He was succeeded as commander by his son Ḥasan. The victorious ʿAbbasid forces waited in Kufa for Abu Salama, Bokayr b. Māhān's successor as the leader of the Kufan *daʿwa* and now styled the *amir* or *wazir āl Moḥammad*, to reveal to them the as yet unknown identity of the Chosen One.

However, Qaḥṭaba was not alone in his untimely demise: The reputed Imam Ebrāhim b. Moḥammad b. ʿAli had been arrested by agents of Marwān II. He was held in confinement in Ḥarrān, where he died the very same month as Qaḥṭaba. Other members of the ʿAbbasid family had taken refuge in Kufa by Ṣafar 132/September 749, and sources claim that one of them, Abu'l-ʿAbbās (the future caliph al-Saffāḥ), had been designated as successor in Ebrāhim's testament. Yet it was only in Rabiʿ I 132/late October 749, after news that the Imam was in Kufa was leaked to the Khorasanis, who had been clamoring to pay allegiance to the Chosen One and were on the verge of mutiny, that Abu Salama finally brought Abu'l-ʿAbbās out of hiding and had him proclaimed as caliph. (On Qaḥṭaba's campaign and this last stage of the revolution, see Sharon, 1990, pp. 179-256; on the machinations in Kufa, see in particular Agha, 2003, pp. 120-35, who views Abu Moslem as the mastermind pulling the strings of what amounted to an ʿAbbasid coup.)

This much abbreviated account of the revolt in Khorasan necessarily glosses over many variations, inconsistencies, and other problems in the sources. There is likely some core of truth behind the narrative, given how embarrassing some of its elements, which must have been too well known to suppress, were for the ʿAbbasid caliphs, but there is also much that needs to be questioned. It has to be remembered that the information in the traditional sources has been filtered through two lenses: The shifting basis on which the ʿAbbasids tried to legitimize their rule, and the tendency in most sources to view events from the perspective of the center rather than the periphery. When that is taken into account, the story on the whole seems contrived to make the reign of the ʿAbbasids seem preordained, their authority uncontested, and their probity untarnished, in particular by exaggerating the degree of ʿAbbasid control over the Hāšemi *daʿwa*, by diminishing and demeaning the role of other actors, and by obscuring the actual nature of the revolt. As a result, there is much that is open to interpretation or that strains credulity. To what extent did the ʿAbbasid family really control or direct the *daʿwa*? Did the ʿAbbasids revolutionize and liberate Khorasan, or did Khorasan lift the ʿAbbasids from obscurity to the caliphate? What exactly did Ḵedāš preach and to which audience? Is it plausible that an unknown and inexperienced young man was plucked from a dungeon in Kufa, plopped down in the political maelstrom of Khorasan, and then proceeded to outmaneuver all contenders and demolish the edifice of Omayyad power in Khorasan in barely six months?

Among modern historians, the notion of a decades long, centrally directed, carefully controlled ʿAbbasid revolutionary conspiracy in Khorasan has been steadily eroded (Shacklady, p. 108; Sharon, 1983, pp. 227-29; Agha, 2003). The presence of a *daʿwa* organization with loose ties to a Kufan offshoot of the Kaysāniya is possible or even probable, but did its inner circles have an actual commitment to a member of the ʿAbbasid family?

The whole point of the idea of *al-reżā* was that a candidate from among the family of the Prophet would emerge and be selected by consensus (*šurā*) after the movement succeeded. It is quite possible that the missioners did not reveal the identity of their Chosen One, not to protect him, but because they had no idea or firm commitment about whom that might be. Moshe Sharon argues that the clandestine organization was small and pro-ʿAlid, and the Hāšhemiya did not become ʿAbbasid before 125/743 (Sharon, 1983, p. 229). Said Saleh Agha goes even further and suggests that it was not until Abu Moslem settled on Ebrāhim as imam and then only nominally, as Abu Moslem was using Ebrāhim for his own purposes rather than the other way around (Agha, 2003, pp. 4-5). Indeed, one could well say the movement was not definitively ʿAbbasid until Abu Salama produced the refugee al-Saffāḥ as imam.

If the movement was open as to leadership, then it is likely that it was equally malleable when it came to its ideology, which has been extensively sanitized in the sources. In that case, Ḵedāš appears not as a heretical outlier but as a core figure of the *daʿwa* and a precursor to the success of Abu Moslem himself. It is not entirely clear whether Ḵedāš was converted and brought into the *daʿwa* by Hāšemi circles in Kufa, or recruited into the organization after his move to Marv, or insinuated himself into it with a view of taking it over. However, there is little reason to doubt that he was the de facto leader of the movement for nearly a decade, that he breathed life into it by winning over large numbers of new supporters (and veteran members of the *daʿwa* organization as well), and that he did so by preaching something very different from the earlier, vague, quasi-Shiʿite propaganda. It is likely that this very success is what brought him to the attention of the authorities and led to his execution on the orders of the governor (Balāḏori's unique claim, III, p. 117, that he was attacked and killed by ʿAbbasid loyalists is a transparent effort to bolster the notion of Moḥammad b. ʿAli's orthodoxy and authority over the *daʿwa*).

The authorities apparently saw Ḵedāš as a Shiʿite because of what he had said about Abu Bakr and ʿOmar (Ṭabari, II, p. 1589; Sharon, 1983, p. 172 also views him as "a loyal follower of the House of ʿAlī"; this assessment is rejected by Crone, 2012, pp. 495-97). The laconic account in Ṭabari of Ḵedāš's substituting the *din al-Ḵorramiya*, specifically the sharing of women, for the teachings of the ʿAbbasid imam is fleshed out by Ebn al-Aṯir (V, p. 196): There was no strict requirement for fasting, ritual prayer, or pilgrimage, all of which could be fulfilled through devotion to the imam. This was further justified on the principle of Qurʾan 5:96, "There is no shame on those who believe and do good deeds" (in that case, because of past dietary practices). As for the sharing of women, Patricia Crone (2012, p. 83) has made the important point that Ḵedāš was not promoting it so much as making an exception or dispensation for it (using the juristic term *raḵḵaṣa*, to grant a concession because of exigent circumstances), essentially reaching a pragmatic accommodation with a local, "nativist" religion (other tenets of which are elucidated in Crone, 2012, pp. 279-438). In all of this, Ḵedāš was setting a low threshold for what constituted conversion to Islam—a very different standard from the nearly contemporary demand by the governor Ašras b. ʿAbd-Allāh Solami in 110/728-29 that, to be counted as a Muslim and avoid the poll tax, it was necessary to be circumcised, perform the obligatory rituals, and recite a chapter of the Qurʾan (Ṭabari, II, p. 1508).

The Ḵedāš phenomenon is strikingly similar to the accusation in a letter of the Omayyad secretary ʿAbd-al-Ḥamid b. Yaḥyā, dated to 128/745-46, that an "evil one" in Khorasan had agitated an upstart rabble (*nābeta*) of people of obscure origin, the lower classes, and "slaves" (*ariqqāʾ*) who "laid claims to Islam while remaining ignorant of it"—not surprisingly, since they had just recently been worshipping fires and idols (Qadi, pp. 32-34). The letter does not name the "evil one," who presumably was Abu Moslem, and it indeed seems that Abu Moslem was able to swell the ranks of his army rapidly by making a special effort to proselytize the masses and "slaves" (*ʿabid*), asking simply if they were Muslims before accepting them (*Aḵbār*, pp. 280-81). It is well known that he deliberately obscured his own background by identifying himself only in terms of religion, Islam, and place, Khorasan. He applied the same egalitarian standards to all those enrolled in the pay register of his army, recording only personal names and home villages. Other distinctions such as ethnicity were swept away by fusing the cause of vengeance on the ruling Omayyad Arabs for their persecution of the family of the Prophet with a much broader general resentment of Omayyad oppression and the promise of a vague Islamic utopia for all.

The extent to which the ʿAbbasid *daʿwa* in Khorasan should thus also be seen as a successful effort at mass conversion to Islam has important implications for the hotly debated question of the social basis for the revolution. If the ʿAbbasid movement was above all an Islamic one, and thus its followers were Muslims, then where did they come from? It has been suggested that significant conversion of the Khorasani population to Islam occurred only after the ʿAbbasid revolution, in which case most of the supporters of the *daʿwa* in Khorasan must have been primarily Arabs (Bulliet, 1979, p. 43). If "conversion" meant meeting the kind of tests imposed by Ašras, the proposition would likely be true, but certainly not in terms of "conversion" according to the standards used by Ḵedāš or Abu Moslem. That there was a large pool of aggrieved, non-Arab, people who considered themselves oppressed Muslims and were ripe for recruitment by the *daʿwa* is suggested by the report that in 121/738-39 Naṣr b. Sayyār's tax collector re-imposed the poll tax on 80,000 "polytheists" who had been exempted from it (Ṭabari, II, p. 1689), presumably by claiming to be Muslims.

Naṣr b. Sayyār, along with at least some of his contemporaries, saw his opponents as neither Arab tribesmen nor their *mawāli* but as "Magians and louts" (*Aḵbār*, p. 324), whose religion was not that of the Prophet or the Qurʾan but simply "the destruction of the Arabs" (Balāḏori, III, p. 132). This was propaganda to be sure, but how much truth was behind it? Nineteenth-century Orientalists such as G.

van Vloten, followed by more than a few Iranian nationalist historians, in much the same fashion as Naṣr, saw
the revolution as an uprising of Iranians in the guise of
Shiᶜism to take revenge on the Arabs, a view moderated in
the more rigorous study by Julius Wellhausen as one that
"did not originate with the Iranian nation, but with a sect
of a fairly circumscribed locality from which the Arabs
were not excluded" (p. 535); in other words, that it was
primarily a movement of the *mawāli* of Kufa and Marv,
Iranians by nationality and shopkeepers and artisans by
trade (p. 514), attempting to overthrow "not the Arabs *per
se*, but the *ruling* Arabs" (p. 535), and that the majority of
Abu Moslem's followers "consisted of Iranian peasants
and of the Mawali of the villages of Marw" (p. 532) along
with some Arabs connected to them by religion. Since
then, as noted by Étienne de la Vaissière (2018, p. 110)
the pendulum of scholarly opinion "has moved toward
the idea of a mainly Arab revolution, only to go back
in the opposite direction in more recent works" (for the
"Arab" case, see Shaban, 1970; Sharon, 1983, 1990; Elad,
2000, and for the "Iranian" or mass uprising case, Daniel, 1979, 1996; Zakeri, 1995; Agha, 2003). The variation
in interpretations is hardly surprising given the tenden-
tious nature of the sources, where so much is uncertain
and almost any statement can be taken as fact by one
historian and dismissed as fiction by another. However,
some empirical data is being brought to bear on these
debates. There is a veritable bonanza of prosopographi-
cal information to be found in the sources, especially the
anonymous *Aḵbār al-ᶜAbbas*, and this has been exhaus-
tively studied by Saleh Abbas Agha (2003, pp. 223-379,
esp. p. 316). As he notes, the rank and file of the movement remain anonymous, but of the known membership
in Khorasan the upper echelons seem to be split more or
less equally between Arabs and *mawāli*, while the lower
ranks are composed overwhelmingly of new converts (62
percent) and *mawāli*. Using archaeological findings and
other sources, de la Vaissière (2018) makes an important
distinction between early phases of the movement, when
significant Arab participation was possible and perhaps
likely, and the overt revolutionary phase, which must have
had the extensive support of Iranian converts or those "on
the verge of converting" (p. 144).

ABU MOSLEM AND KHORASAN

When Qaḥṭaba b. Šabib reached Ray in the winter of
131/748, Abu Moslem moved his capital from Marv to
Nishapur and was already minting coins that year calling
himself the *amir āl Moḥammad* (Guest, p. 555; Ṭabari, III,
p. 60 uses the title *amin* rather than *amir*). Whatever the
truth about Abu Moslem's background and initial role in
the *daᶜwa* organization might be, there can be no doubt he
took this title seriously and moved quickly, relentlessly,
and effectively to consolidate authority over Khorasan in
his hands. Indeed, as the situation in Khorasan stabilized,
he was able to extend his rule to other areas including Yazd
(Aḥmad Kāteb, pp. 59-60; Bafqi, pp. 37-38) , Fārs (where
he executed Abu Salama's appointees and ousted a governor sent by the ᶜAbbasid caliph; Ṭabari, III, pp. 71-72), and

Sistān (*Tāriḵ-e Sistān*, tr., pp. 106-9), and he concluded
an alliance with the Eṣbahbaḏ of Ṭabarestān (*Aḵbār*, p.
333; Ebn al-Aṯir, V, p. 397). He was also able to initiate a
number of campaigns that brought areas beyond the Oxus
firmly under his control. There is also evidence of revital-
ization in the many construction projects carried out by
him or at his direction in Nishapur, Marv, and Samarqand,
including government buildings, mosques, and markets
as well as the city wall of Samarqand (Ḥākem Nišāburi,
pp. 217-18; Herzfeld, p. 172; Haug, p. 157; Karev, 2015,
pp. 113-14), all indicating he was in control of the area's
finances and using the resources for its development.

Abu Moslem still had to deal with two other aspiring
revolutionaries, both of whom had fled to Khorasan from
Iraq after failed efforts there. One was the Kharijite Šaybān
b. Salama, who had arrived at Marv about the same time as
Abu Moslem had declared his revolt. For a while, Šaybān
cooperated with Jodayᶜ Kermāni against Naṣr b. Sayyār,
but then he withdrew to Saraḵs to wait out the conflict.
In Šaᶜbān 130/April 748, after Šaybān arrested and killed
negotiators sent by Abu Moslem, he was attacked and
killed by one of Abu Moslem's commanders (Ṭabari, II,
1996-97; *Aḵbār*, p. 321).

A serious problem for Abu Moslem was the arrival in
Khorasan of ᶜAbd-Allāh b. Moᶜāwiya, the great-grandson
of ᶜAli b. Abi Ṭāleb's brother Jaᶜfar. After a failed revolt in
Kufa in 127/744, he had moved to Fārs and established an
ephemeral government there. Defeated by the Omayyad
general Ebn Żobāra in 129/746-47, he then made his way
to Khorasan. One might think ᶜAbd-Allāh would have been
well-received by Abu Moslem: He was another reputed
legatee of Abu Hāšem, his ideology was virtually identical to that of the Hāšemiya, he used the same slogans,
and, curiously enough, at least three senior members of the
ᶜAbbasid family had served in his administration in Fārs.
When he turned up in Herat, he told Abu Moslem's agent
that he was there because he had heard the revolutionaries were calling for *al-reżā min āl Moḥammad*. However,
the agent reported him to Abu Moslem, who ordered his
arrest and then, it seems, had him smothered, probably in
131/748-49 (Balāḏori, II, p. 66; Ebn al-Aṯir, V, pp. 372-
73). While Abu Moslem had not hesitated to champion the
cause of the martyred Yaḥyā b. Zayd, the appearance of a
credible living candidate to be the Chosen One at a critical
moment in the overt revolution was a threat that had to be
handled quickly and discretely.

Toward the end of 131/June 749 or shortly thereafter, Abu Moslem turned on his erstwhile allies, ᶜAli and
ᶜOṯmān, the sons of Jodayᶜ Kermāni. ᶜOṯmān was promised
the governorship of Ḵottal (q.v.), but he was ambushed and
killed on the way. Abu Moslem had feigned deference to
ᶜAli after the fall of Marv, and the latter accompanied him
to Nishapur. Once there, ᶜAli and his closest supporters
were lured to a meeting on the pretext of receiving hon-
ors and government appointments, but instead they were
all murdered (Ṭabari, II, pp. 1999-2000; Ebn al-Aṯir, V, p.
385; Balāḏori, III, p. 131).

There had been stiff resistance among the older generation of the *daᶜwa* leadership to Abu Moslem, and a purge

of them soon began. First to be executed was Lāhez b. Qorayẓ, accused of alerting Naṣr b. Sayyār to the plot to kill him (Ṭabari, II, p. 1995). In 132/749-50, Abu Moslem either plotted or acquiesced in a plan to murder the chief of the Kufan *daʿwa*, Abu Salama, and sent one of his agents to carry out the assassination. During the subsequent visit by a delegation sent to Khorasan by al-Saffāḥ, including his brother Abu Jaʿfar, Abu Moslem beheaded Solaymān b. Kaṯir for "plotting treachery to the Imam" (Ṭabari, III, pp. 60-61). We are not given any convincing explanation of what the nature of the conspiracy might have been, but it is telling that, after witnessing this, Abu Jaʿfar warned al-Saffāḥ that Abu Moslem "does what he pleases," and the title of caliph would be meaningless as long as Abu Moslem was alive (Ṭabari, III, p. 61).

It was probably early in his tenure in Nishapur that Abu Moslem had to deal with two other very different types of religious opposition. One was a revolt by a breakaway neo-Ḵedāšite faction of the *daʿwa* known as the Ḵālediya after its leader Abu Ḵāled. The group claimed that after the death of the Imam Ebrāhim the office had reverted to the family of ʿAli b. Abi Ṭāleb. Abu Moslem attacked them and forced them to flee and go into hiding across the Oxus. The group continued to be active until 141/758-59, when Abu Ḵaled was captured and killed (*Aḵbār*, pp. 403-4).

The other problem for Abu Moslem in this period was the agitation surrounding a Zoroastrian "false prophet," Behāfarid (q.v.). This event was hardly mentioned in the Arabic historical sources, but it figures in heresiographies and Persian sources (e.g., Ebn al-Nadim, p. 407, tr. Dodge, II, p. 822; Baḡdādi, pp. 354-55, tr. pp. 220-21; Šahrastāni, I, p. 283; Biruni, pp. 210-11, tr., pp. 193-94; Gardizi, pp. 119-20; Ḵᵛāfi, pp. 280-81). Behāfarid was a native of Zuzan in the district of Ḵᵛāf (Ebn al-Nadim says a village near Nishapur) who had spent seven years in China, presumably as a merchant. On his return, he supposedly staged a fake death and resurrection, wearing a green silk shirt he had acquired in China, to dupe peasants into thinking he had returned from heaven. He produced a holy book in Persian instructing his followers to have daily prayers facing the sun, not to drink wine or eat carrion, not to engage in close-kinship marriages or have large dowries, and to pay a seventh of their property and income for the upkeep of roads and bridges. It is not clear whether his movement constituted an actual revolt, but he must have tapped into enough local support to be seen as a threat to the social order. Zoroastrian priestly officials, the *mubaḏ*s and *herbaḏ*s, complained to Abu Moslem that Behāfarid was corrupting both Zoroastrianism and Islam. Abu Moslem, who seems to have been on good terms with the Zoroastrian elite in Nishapur, sent a force to attack Behāfarid and his followers. They fled to the mountains of Bādḡis, but Behāfarid was captured, brought to Nishapur, and executed. Behāfarid has been seen as the leader of a "Mithraic revolt" (Pourshariati, p. 451) or as a Zoroastrian reformer adapting to an Islamic environment (Crone, 2012, pp. 149-51). However, the influence of Islam on his teachings and practices, as well as his claim to be a monotheist, is obvious; indeed, there is a report that he had been converted to Islam by missioners of the ʿAbbasid *daʿwa* (Ebn al-Nadim, p. 407, tr., p. 822). After his execution, his body was displayed at the main mosque of Nishapur (recently constructed by Abu Moslem). The heresiographer Baḡdādi acknowledged that Behāfarid's teachings were "superior" to those of the "original Magians" but still outside the pale of acceptability because they originated after the rise of Islam (tr., p. 221). In a sense, Behāfarid, much like Ḵedāš, could be viewed as attempting to accommodate local beliefs and practices with Islam and thus posed a rival threat Abu Moslem could not ignore.

The last major threat to Abu Moslem's domination of Khorasan was in 132 or 133/750 with the outbreak of a revolt in Bukhara led by Šarik b. Šayḵ Mahri. Šarik was apparently one of many people who had joined the *daʿwa* to support the nebulous call for *al-reżā* but was now disenchanted by the installation of an ʿAbbasid, rather than an ʿAlid, caliph as well as the bloody purges that followed the revolution (Ṭabari, III, p. 74; Gardizi, p. 120; Naršaḵi, tr., pp. 62-65). He rallied a large number of followers from Ḵᵛārazm and Transoxiana, most likely drawn from the Arabs who had earlier been supporters of Kermāni and Ebn al-Kermāni. Abu Moslem gathered his forces at Āmol on the Oxus and sent a detachment under Ziād b. Ṣāleḥ to attack Šarik, but there was a stalemate until the local ruler, Qotayba b. Ṭoḡšāda the Boḵār-ḵodā, sided with Ziād and ordered the non-Arab population to put on ʿAbbasid black and besiege Šarik. Šarik was captured on a foraging mission and killed, and Bukhara was captured after a violent battle.

After the fall of Bukhara, Abu Moslem's forces were able to subjugate or pacify other areas across the Oxus, including Ḵottal, Farḡāna, Šāš (Čāč), and Keš (qq.v). In these areas, many of the local rulers were hostile to Abu Moslem, and a coalition of them appealed to T'ang China for help. A large Chinese force was sent to assist the Eḵšid (q.v.), the Sogdian ruler of Farḡāna, against the king of Šāš, and Abu Moslem retaliated by sending Ziād, his governor in Samarqand, to attack the Chinese and their allies; the main battle took place at Aṭlaḵ (Ṭarāz or Talas) in July 751 and ended in the complete rout of the Chinese coalition. Rarely mentioned by the Muslim historians (an exception is Ebn al-Aṯir, V, p. 449), the battle was of decisive importance in breaking Chinese influence in the region and beginning the process of the integration of Transoxiana into Khorasan (see Barthold, pp. 195-96; Gibb, pp. 97-98; Karev, 2002, pp. 11-16; Haug, pp. 154-58). In its aftermath, a number of the local rulers were executed or they and their families deported; even Qotayba b. Ṭoḡšāda, who had rendered critical assistance in the war with Šarik b. Šayḵ, was executed on a charge of apostasy (Naršaḵi, tr. p. 10). The reasons for this are not clear, but it may be that Abu Moslem was signaling a new policy under which these areas were no longer regarded as autonomous frontier principalities but dependencies of Khorasan, and the local rulers could no longer be compromised by pro-Chinese or un-Islamic loyalties (see discussion in Karev, 2012, pp. 20-21).

Following up on these successes in Central Asia, according to a unique account (Maqdesi, VI, p. 74, tr. p. 75), Abu Moslem was planning to invade China itself, and his activities in Transoxiana were certainly compatible with preparations for such an enterprise. If so, his plans were upset by the tensions that had been building up with the ʿAbbasids in Iraq for some time: the Abu Salama affair; Abu Jaʿfar's visit to Khorasan; the execution of Solaymān b. Kaṯir; disagreement over dealing with the surrender of the Omayyad governor Ebn Hobayra; disputes over the appointment of governors in western Persia and Sind. In 135/752-53, Ziād b. Ṣāleḥ declared a revolt against Abu Moslem, using the same slogan as had Šarik b. Šayḵ (Balāḏori, III, 168-69; Ṭabari, III, pp. 81-82). It is possible that he simply became overly ambitious following his victories in Central Asia, but there are numerous indications that he was inspired to revolt because of intrigues by the ʿAbbasid ruling family in Iraq, who were more than fearful of Abu Moslem. It seems the caliph al-Saffāḥ had secretly sent a letter to Ziād offering him the governorship of Khorasan and encouraging him to kill Abu Moslem if he found an opportunity (Ṭabari, III, 82). On advancing to Āmol, Abu Moslem was informed that the man who had carried the caliphal letter to Ziād, Sibāʾ b. Noʿmān (another former supporter of Jodayʿ Kermāni) was in his entourage; Sibāʾ was flogged and beheaded. Ziād's commanders defected almost at once to Abu Moslem, and Ziād fled to the *dehqān* (q.v.) of a town near Samarqand, but the *dehqān* killed him and sent his head to Abu Moslem, which he, in turn, made an insolent point of sending on to al-Saffāḥ. Abu Moslem subsequently discovered correspondence by ʿIsā b. Māhān (a notorious ʿAbbasid agent) trying to stir up discord between two of Abu Moslem's key commanders. ʿIsā was left to the mercy of the army, and several of the officers put him in a sack and clubbed him to death (Ṭabari, III, pp. 83-84).

In 136/753-54, Abu Moslem requested permission to visit the caliph Abu'l-ʿAbbās al-Saffāḥ at his court at Anbār in Iraq, ostensibly to obtain the caliph's consent to perform the *ḥajj*. Whether his objective was simply to clear the atmosphere of distrust that had developed, or the arena of his ambitions was being expanded (perhaps aiming very high indeed; see Agha, 2003, p. 71) can only be a matter of speculation. His preparations were as usual meticulous: He entrusted the governorship of Khorasan to one of his most loyal commanders, Abu Dawud Ḵāled b. Ebrāhim; stationed troops along the road from Nishapur to Ray (where he also established his treasury); and marched to Anbār with as many men as the caliph would agree to let him bring. The subsequent events outside Khorasan need not be discussed in detail here. In brief, Abu Moslem hoped to add to his prestige by leading the *ḥajj*, but al-Saffāḥ claimed to have already promised that to his brother, and Abu Moslem's fiercest enemy, Abu Jaʿfar al-Manṣur. Al-Saffāḥ died unexpectedly, at the age of thirty-three, while Abu Jaʿfar and Abu Moslem were on the pilgrimage. Abu Jaʿfar had already been plotting to kill Abu Moslem (Ṭabari, III, pp. 85-86) but now had to turn his attention to securing his own accession to the caliphate, as his claim was contested almost at once by his powerful uncle, ʿAbd-Allāh b. ʿAli, commander of the forces that had defeated the Omayyads in Syria. Abu Moslem is also said to have tried to advance another and presumably more pliable candidate, al-Manṣur's cousin ʿIsā b. Musā, who declined (Ṭabari, III, p. 100). Al-Manṣur thus needed Abu Moslem to thwart ʿAbd-Allāh b. ʿAli, while Abu Moslem needed to try to appease al-Manṣur. The uneasy alliance lasted only until ʿAbd-Allāh was defeated and placed under house arrest in Jomādā II 137/November 754, as Abu Moslem and al-Manṣur immediately started quarreling over the division of the spoils. Abu Moslem's close advisors urged him to return to Khorasan, where he would have a loyal army and could do as he pleased, while al-Manṣur sought to keep him away by offering the governorship of Syria and Egypt, by flattery, and finally by threats. At the same, the caliph made overtures to Ḵāled b. Ebrāhim, offering him the governorship of Khorasan for help in persuading (or preventing) Abu Moslem from returning to the province. In the end, whether out of over-confidence or by being trapped by the mythos of loyalty to the Chosen One that he himself had helped create, Abu Moslem ultimately decided to present himself for an audience with al-Manṣur and was promptly assassinated ca. 24 Šaʿban 137/12 February 755 (Ṭabari, III, p. 115).

An anticipated revolt of the Khorasanis in the ʿAbbasid army in response to Abu Moslem's murder did not materialize, thanks to the combined effects of confusion, fear, isolation, and bribery; only some of the disgruntled soldiers eventually had to be expelled (Ṭabari, III, p. 117). There were, however, repercussions in Khorasan. The first of several rebellions to avenge Abu Moslem was led by Sonbāḏ, who either had been left in charge of Abu Moslem's treasury in Ray or took this occasion to seize it. There are numerous conflicting accounts of exactly who Sonbāḏ was, where he came from, and how he initiated his revolt. He is often described as a native of the Nishapur area, perhaps even a high-ranking official (Yaʿqubi, *Taʾriḵ*, II, p. 441; Maqdesi, VI, p. 82; Balʿami, II, p. 1093; Neẓām-al-Molk, tr. p. 279); one late source claims his incitement there of violence against the Arab and Iranian elites won the approval of Abu Moslem, who persuaded him to convert and to join the *daʿwa* (*Tāriḵ-e alfi*, ff. 247b-248a). At the time of Abu Moslem's murder, he was either stationed in Ḥolwān and rebelled after he had been detained on his way back to Khorasan (Balāḏori, III, p. 246), or he was still in Nishapur, where he was encouraged by refugees from Abu Moslem's army to avenge his death (Yaʿqubi, II, p. 442). Most of his followers actually seem to have come from the Jebāl, and it was at Ray that Sonbāḏ apostasized, laid claim to the title Firuz Eṣbahbad, and attacked the Muslim population (Ṭabari, III, p. 119). Al-Manṣur sent an army under Jahwar b. Marrār ʿEjli against him; Sonbāḏ was routed and fled to Ṭabarestān, where he was murdered (Daniel, 1979, pp. 126-30; Crone, 2012, pp. 32-40). After massacring the local Zoroastrian population, Jahwar refused to turn over Abu Moslem's treasury or the spoils to the caliph and then rebelled, supported by a mostly Iranian army, but was eventually defeated, imprisoned, and killed (Ṭabari, III, p. 122).

ABBASID ADMINISTRATION OF KHORASAN

As birthplace of the ʿAbbasid Revolution, Khorasan now came into even greater prominence within the Islamic ecumene. It was from the province's association with the ʿAbbasids that hadiths or traditions came into circulation like the one attributed to the Prophet: "Khorasan is God's quiver; when He becomes angry with a people, he launches at them the Khorasanis" (cited in Herzfeld, pp. 107, 120). As an indicator of feelings of stability and permanence among the Muslims there, one may note the mention of Islamic buildings being constructed in Khorasan, with Abu Moslem's government headquarters (*dār-al-emāra*), mosque, and market at Marv, and his mosque with wooden columns at Nishapur (Herzfeld, p. 172; Ḥākem Nišāburi, pp. 217-18). This new prominence of the region also brought large numbers of Khorasanis, Arabs, and Persian *mawāli* westwards to the new center of the caliphate, Iraq, and its eventual seat there at Baghdad, and the province necessarily basked in ʿAbbasid favor at this time. In a sermon (*ḵoṭba*) delivered at Hāšemiya, the forerunner of al-Manṣur's new capital Baghdad, this second caliph eulogized them as "O people of Khorasan, you are our party (*šiʿa*), our helpers (*anṣār*), and the supporters of our cause (*daʿwa*)" (Masʿudi, VI, p. 203). Among the Khorasanian families who came westwards at this time was the originally Buddhist family of the Barmakids (q.v.) of Balḵ. Ḵāled b. Barmak had joined the ʿAbbasid *daʿwa* and was rewarded by the first caliph of the new line, Abu'l-ʿAbbās Saffāḥ, with the control of military finances, thus inaugurating the family's meteoric but short-lived rise to power and glory at the ʿAbbasid court (Sourdel, I, pp. 129-81; Mottahedeh, pp. 68-71). Many of the caliphs' Khorasani guards and civilian officials, called the *abnāʾ al-dawla* (see ABNĀʾ), settled at Baghdad in the quarter of Ḥarbiya to the north of the city. The *abnāʾ al-dawla* continued to be the mainstay of the caliphate until al-Maʾmun (q.v.; r. 198-218/813-33) and then his brother and successor al-Moʿtaṣem (r. 218-27/833-42) started to recruit contingents of Iranian free troops from Central Asia, the Šākeriya (< Pers. *čākar*, q.v.), and Turkish slave troops (*ḡelmān, mamālik*) purchased in Transoxiana, alongside the older military units of the remnants of the original Arab *moqātela* and the Khorasani *abnāʾ al-dawla* (Crone, 1980, pp. 158 ff.).

In Khorasan itself, however, ʿAbbasid rule was hardly unperturbed. Various groups were disillusioned with the outcome of a revolution that inevitably fell far short of the apocalyptic, messianic, or millenarian expectations it had aroused; or frustrated by the installation of an ʿAbbasid caliphate rather than a Fāṭemid/Ṭālebid one; or alienated by the assassination of Abu Moslem (or at least using his death as an excuse to rebel). Beyond that, there were basic realities the revolution had not changed or that returned with al-Manṣur's policies: Khorasan was again a province of the caliphate in the west, and it was usually in the hands of Arab governors designated by the caliph. Those governors not infrequently provoked revolts or became rebellious themselves. A system continued under which some cities and towns were governed by appointees of the central government, while others and remote districts were dominated by local magnates (either the indigeneous ones or replacements drawn from the *daʿwa* leadership, but now mostly Islamicized). Relations between the central government, backed the *abnāʿ*, and the local elites, the *wojuh* or *moluk Ḵorāsān*, were perennially uneasy.

When Abu Moslem went to Iraq, he had left Khorasan in the hands of Abu Dāwud Ḵāled b. Ebrāhim, who seems to have been an Abu Moslem loyalist, although it is possible that he switched his alliance to al-Manṣur. According to Ṭabari (III, p. 107), after Abu Dāwud had been offered the governorship of Khorasan by al-Manṣur, he admonished Abu Moslem not to oppose al-Manṣur and to return to Khorasan only with the caliph's permission. However, Balāḏori (III, pp. 226-27) indicates that Abu Dāwud was outraged by Abu Moslem's murder and reviled the caliph. This was reported to al-Manṣur, who intrigued with the chief of Abu Dāwud's bodyguard, Abu ʿEṣām, to bring about his death. Other sources indicate that a disturbance of some kind against Abu Dāwud was stirred up in the army at Marv, and during the commotion Abu Dāwud died by falling accidentally, or perhaps not so accidentally, from a parapet (Ṭabari, III, p. 128; Balāḏori, III, p. 227; Maqdisi, tr., VI, p. 83). Gardizi, however, states (p. 123) that Abu Dāwud was killed in 140/757 by the *sapid-jāmagān* 'wearers of white' (a group known in other contexts as religious extremists seeking vengeance for Abu Moslem).

Shortly after Abu Dāwud's death, al-Manṣur appointed ʿAbd-al-Jabbār b. ʿAbd-al-Raḥmān Azdi (q.v.), an early member of the *daʿwa* organization and a prominent officer in the revolutionary army, as governor. The sources give a bewildering and contradictory array of accounts of ʿAbd-al-Jabbār's policies in Khorasan (see Moscati, 1947; Daniel, 1979, pp. 159-62; Crone, pp. 108-10), but they generally involve purges of opponents under the guise of rooting out ʿAlid sympathizers (although he was himself accused of being a Shiʿite), the imposition of heavy taxes, tyrannical behavior, and perhaps some tribal vendettas. To begin with, ʿAbd-al-Jabbār may well have been following, albeit overzealously, the instructions of the caliph to impose centralized control over the province and eliminate ʿAlid partisans, but when a litany of complaints from the local elites (or slanders by his political opponents at the caliphal court) caused al-Manṣur to recall him, ʿAbd-al-Jabbār resisted and ultimately rebelled openly. According to the most detailed sources (Balāḏori, III, pp. 227-30; Gardizi, pp. 123-24), he allied with the "wearers of white" (Ar. *mobayyeża* or Pers. *sapid-jāmagān*) and seems to have promoted their sectarian leader, Barāz-banda, as a kind of counter-caliph who called himself "Ebrāhim al-Hāšemi." Barāz was apparently a disciple of Esḥāq "the Turk" (see ESḤĀQ TORK), who had been sent by Abu Moslem to proselytize among the Turks and who, after Abu Moslem's assassination, taught that Abu Moslem was not dead but in concealment until he would return to re-establish the true religion. As suggested by Patricia Crone (2012, p. 110), ʿAbd-al-Jabbār may thus have been attempting to forge an anti-ʿAbbasid coalition of ʿAlid and Abu Moslem supporters in Khorasan. It that context, it is worth noting that a good many of those purged by ᶜAbd-al-Jabbār came from one of the most pro-ᶜAbbasid tribal groups in Khorasan, the Ḵozāᶜa (who would supply a significant number of later governors of the province). The threat was serious enough for al-Manṣur to designate his son, Moḥammad al-Mahdi, as viceroy for the eastern provinces, based in Ray; al-Mahdi assembled an army to attack ᶜAbd-al-Jabbār. Barāz/Ebrāhim was killed in the fighting, and ᶜAbd-al-Jabbār was defeated and captured in Rabiᶜ I 142/July 759 (Gardizi, p. 124). He was sent to al-Manṣur, who had him executed in a particularly brutal manner (Yaᶜqubi, *Taʾriḵ*, II, p. 446; Ṭabari, III, p. 135).

Al-Mahdi remained at Ray as the overlord of Khorasan until 144/761-62, when he returned to Iraq (Ṭabari, III, p. 143). His tenure there and the struggle with ᶜAbd-al-Jabbār was important in that it gave the future caliph an opportunity to cultivate ties with reliable members of the Khorasani army and to recruit his own retinue of Khorasani supporters, who would be settled in the Roṣafa quarter of Baghdad. After the experience with ᶜAbd-al-Jabbār, al-Manṣur and al-Mahdi were also more cautious, or fortunate, in their selection of governors for Khorasan and faced no such insubordination from them. However, ᶜAbbasid relations with the Khorasani elites continued to be vexed by issues such as the struggle against the Ḥasanid brothers, Moḥammad and Ebrāhim b. ᶜAbd-Allāh, who clearly had many sympathizers in Khorasan (see, e.g., Ṭabari, III, p. 183), and the removal of al-Manṣur's nephew, ᶜIsā b. Musā, from a previously agreed upon line of succession, first by al-Manṣur in 147/764-65 in favor of al-Mahdi and again in 158/774-75 by al-Mahdi in favor of his son Musā al-Hādi. The Khorasani *abnāʾ* in Iraq disliked ᶜIsā b. Musā and clamored for the change in succession (Yaᶜqubi, *Taʾriḵ*, II, p. 457), but ᶜIsa b. Musā had been closely associated with Abu Moslem and remained popular with the pro-Abu Moslem groups and other factions in Khorasan itself (Amabe, p. 90). At least three Khorasani notables had to be arrested and brought from Khorasan in chains in 153/770 because of their support for ᶜIsā b. Musā (Ṭabari, III, p. 371).

The controversies surrounding the deposition of ᶜIsā b. Musā and accession of al-Mahdi were at least a factor in two major revolts that broke out in Khorasan, although both revolts also reflected broader patterns of dissent going back to Sonbāḏ and Behāfarid. The first was the revolt of Ostāḏsis in the rural district of Bāḏḡis, north of Herat and near an important silver mine. People from the area had become at least nominal Muslims during the time al-Mahdi was in Khorasan (Gardizi, p. 125), and Ostāḏsis may have converted during the governorship of Abu ᶜAwn ᶜAbd-al-Malek b. Yazid (ca. 143-46/760-64), with whom he was on friendly terms. Yaᶜqubi (*Taʾriḵ*, II, p. 457) indicates the revolt began after the deposition of ᶜIsā b. Musā, when Ostāḏsis refused to pay allegiance to al-Mahdi. Gardizi (p. 125) says it began after a raid on Kabul in which men from Bāḏḡis had participated, apparently in a dispute over the division of the spoils. Ṭabari (III, pp. 354-58) dates the revolt to 150/767-68, but that probably reflects a later phase of the revolt rather than its beginnings. Again according to Ṭabari, the revolt reached huge proportions, drawing in other areas and dissidents and conquering "most of Khorasan," as Ostāḏsis and his army of 300,000 followers defeated one ᶜAbbasid commander after another. As in other cases, Ostāḏsis is said to have added a religious dimension to the revolt by claiming prophecy and promulgating the doctrines of the Behāfaridiyya; this despite the reports of conversion to Islam and the presence of a *qāżi* in his army. Ostāḏsis was defeated by Ḵāzem b. Ḵozayma in 150/767-68; he, his family, and remaining followers took refuge in a mountain fortress until persuaded by Abu ᶜAwn to surrender. Most of the rebels were released; Ostāḏsis was put in chains and perhaps sent to Baghdad to be executed (Yaᶜqubi, *Taʾriḵ*, II, pp. 457-58), though this is not certain (Gardizi, p. 125, says Abu ᶜAwn honored the promise of protection and Ostāḏsis was not harmed).

Just as the revolt of Ostāḏsis had broken out not long after the first deposition of ᶜIsā b. Musā, the revolt of Yusof b. Ebrāhim Barm began not long after the second deposition. Little is known about Yusof, but the revolt is explicitly described as a rejection of al-Mahdi and his policies (Ṭabari, III, p. 470) and a call for government based on the principle of commanding good (*al-amr be'l-maᶜruf*, see AMR BE MAᶜRUF; Yaᶜqubi, *Taʾriḵ*, II, p. 478); in which case, Jahšiāri's description of him (p. 278) as a *kāfer* 'infidel' is hard to accept. The revolt seems to have originated in the area of Jowzjān and spread to Bušanj (Fušanj, q.v.), Ṭālaqān, and Marv al-ruḏ. Yusof was defeated in 160/776-77 after many of his followers defected; he was sent to Roṣāfa, where he was executed in much the same manner as ᶜAbd-al-Jabbār had been (for details, see Daniel, pp. 166-67; Amabe, p. 92; Crone, 2012, pp. 157-59).

By far the most important of the anti-Abbasid revolts to break out in Khorasan during this period was that of the "veiled prophet," Hāšem b. Ḥakim (or Hāšem-e Ḥakim) Moqannaᶜ (q.v.). The revolt followed a pattern similar to preceding ones of a recruit to the ᶜAbbasid revolution later breaking with it and organizing a local resistance supposedly tinged with an esoteric religious ideology. Said, perhaps incorrectly, to be a native of Balḵ residing in a village near Marv (Maqdesi, VI, p. 97, tr. p. 96; Naršaḵi, p. 90, tr. p.66), he supported the *daᶜwa* and became an officer (*sarhang*) in Abu Moslem's army, secretary (*dabir*) to Abu Dāwud, and then the minister (*wazir*) for ᶜAbd-al-Jabbār. After the fall of ᶜAbd-al-Jabbār, he either went into hiding or was arrested and imprisoned for a while in Baghdad. When he appeared again in Marv, he began organizing a *daᶜwa* of his own that proved particularly successful, thanks to the missionary activities of his father-in-law, ᶜAbd-Allāh b. ᶜAmr, in the districts of Sogdia. The governor Ḥomayd b. Qaḥṭaba ordered Hāšem's arrest, but he managed to escape across the Oxus to strongholds in the area of Keš (q.v.), probably around 157/773-74. There, he was supported by numerous *dehqāns*, the *sapid-jāmagān* (probably anti-ᶜAbbasid, pro-Abu Moslem villagers), Turks, and even the king of Bukhara, Bonyāt b. Ṭoḡšāda.

The sources record an array of fantastic religious teachings as well as tricks used by Hāšem to gather followers:

He claimed to be a prophet and then a god; he taught a doctrine of metempsychosis (*tanāsoḵ*), i.e., the transmission of a divine spirit through ʿAli and Abu Moslem to himself; he created the illusion of a false moon rising at his command from a well in Naḵšab; he wore a veil or mask to shield his followers from the radiance of his face; etc. They depict him as both a lowly tradesman (a fuller) and a skilled engineer, magician, and necromancer; they claim he used his veil as a means of disguising his physical deformities; and they describe his fortress as a luxurious retreat where he could pass the time drinking wine and enjoying his large harem made up of the most beautiful daughters of the *dehqān*s. Such accusations may be evidence more of the hysteria caused by the perceived threat posed by Moqannaʿ and his movement, especially among major Arab landholders such as the sons of Naṣr b. Sayyār in Samarqand, than historical realities (although many scholars take them at face value, and Crone, 2012, pp. 132-33, finds aspects of Maitreya Buddhism in them). In fact, there is a coin minted in the name of "Hāšem, the *waliy* of Abu Moslem" (the meaning of *waliy*—successor, avenger, devotee?—is suggestive but ambiguous in this context) calling only for "faithfulness and justice" (*amara Allāh be'l-wafāʾ wa'l-ʿadl*), a moderate, and quite Islamic, slogan not very dissimilar to those used by Yusof Barm, ʿAbd-al-Jabbār, Šarik b. Šayḵ, Abu Moslem, Ḥāreṯ b. Sorayj, and others (on the coin, see Kochnev).

What is certain is that Moqannaʿ was able to direct a kind of guerilla warfare that kept the ʿAbbasid establishment in the greater part of Sogdia paralyzed and terrorized for years. The local resistance to Moqannaʿ having largely failed, the appeals of the populace to al-Mahdi finally persuaded him (ca. 159/775-76) to designate Jebraʾil b. Yaḥyā as governor of Samarqand, beginning the first of several campaigns against Moqannaʿ and the *sapid-jāmagān*. The latter were gradually driven back from Bukhara and Samarqand, and Moqannaʿ was besieged by Saʿid Ḥaraši in his last fortress at Sanām near Keš in 163/783-84 (or perhaps a little later). Large numbers of the defenders surrendered after being reduced to the point of starvation, and when the outer wall of the fortress fell, Moqannaʿ had his remaining family and followers drink poison and then committed suicide, supposedly throwing himself into an oven that had been heated sufficiently to incinerate his remains (on Moqannaʿ, with references to sources, see Daniel, 1979, pp. 137-47; Crone and Jafari Jazi; Crone, 2012, pp. 106-13, 128-35).

The revolt of Moqannaʿ can be seen as the last significant effort by the radical wing of the *daʿwa* movement in Khorasan to delegitimize the ʿAbbasid caliphate after the assassination of Abu Moslem and to resist the counter-revolution initiated by al-Manṣur. However, a struggle continued in Khorasan over the policies of taxation and centralization backed by the caliphs and the *abnāʾ*, but opposed by the new elites in Khorasan itself. There can be little doubt about the expanding burden of taxation and the efficiency of its extraction under the ʿAbbasids, as attested in contemporary Arabic documents that have been uncovered at Mt. Mugh (Khan, 2007b, pp. 203-9). Accounts of the administration during this period typically describe "bad" governors imposing burdensome taxes and acting oppressively until the complaints of the populace lead to the appointment a "good" governor who reduces the taxes and addresses local concerns. For example, Mosayyab b. Zohayr (ca. 163-66/780-82) taxed ruthlessly (probably to fund the war with Moqannaʿ) until a popular outcry forced his recall and the appointment of Fażl b. Solaymān Ṭusi, who abolished a number of the taxes and began public work projects. Ḡeṭrif b. ʿAṭāʾ, maternal uncle of Hārun al-Rašid (q.v.; r. 170-93/786-809), issued a new coinage for Bukhara that had to be used for paying taxes, effectively raising the tax rate by 600 percent (Naršaḵi, pp. 50-51, tr. pp. 36-37); interfered in the local politics in Farḡāna; and stirred up discontent in other areas of Khorasan. He was replaced by Fażl b. Yaḥyā Barmaki, a model of the "good" governor," who returned to policies intended to appease the local population (for various listings of the governors of Khorasan, see Table 1).

The crisis came with Hārun al-Rašid's appointment in 180/796 of ʿAli b. ʿIsā b. Māhān (q.v.), whose father had been executed by Abu Dāwud for opposing Abu Moslem and was himself a notorious champion of the *abnāʾ*, enemy of ʿIsā b. Musā, and opponent of the Barmakids. Even allowing for a degree of exaggeration in the sources, the avarice, corruption, and tyranny driving ʿAli b. ʿIsā's exploitation of Khorasan were appalling. Not only did he extort huge sums in revenue and antagonize the most prominent of the local elites (Ṭabari, III, pp. 713-14), but he also proved rather ineffective in dealing with the unrest it caused, such as the incursion into Khorasan by the Sistāni Kharijite Ḥamza b. Āḏarak (q.v.) in 182/798 and numerous other rebellions. In 183/799, reports about ʿAli b. ʿIsā's misgovernance caused Hārun al-Rašid to summon him to court for interrogation, but ʿAli secured his return to Khorasan by showering the caliph with lavish gifts and pointing out how much he had increased the revenue from Khorasan in comparison to his predecessors (Ṭabari, III, pp. 648-49; note, too, the extended account in Bayhaqi, pp. 533-42). By 189/804-5, ʿAli b. ʿIsā had again exasperated the Khorasani magnates and brought ruin to the province (Ṭabari, III, p. 703; Bayhaqi, p. 536).

A group of Khorasani notables pleaded for a new governor to be appointed, but it was not until some of them hinted that ʿAli b. ʿIsā might use his wealth to revolt that al-Rašid took action. He moved to Ray, where ʿAli b. ʿIsā came to shower the caliph and his family and officials with rare and valuable gifts. Reassured, al-Rašid confirmed ʿAli b. ʿIsā in his post and returned him to Khorasan. ʿAli b. ʿIsā's subsequent attempt to punish a wayward officer in the Samarqand garrison, Rāfiʿ b. Layṯ (probably the grandson of Naṣr b. Sayyār), became the spark that ignited a new blaze of revolt. Rafiʿ escaped from jail and was hailed by the people of Samarqand as their leader. He repulsed an attack by ʿAli b. ʿIsā, and ʿAli b. ʿIsa's son was killed by the people of Nasaf with the help of the local ruler of Šāš in 191/807 (Ṭabari, III, p. 712). Rafiʿ's revolt rapidly spread throughout Transoxiana and beyond; according to Yaʿqubi (*Taʾriḵ*, II, p. 528), it prevailed not only in Samarqand but

Table 1

ʿABBASID GOVERNORS OF KHORASAN AS GIVEN IN VARIOUS SOURCES

Ḥamza[1]	Yaʿqubi[2]	Gardizi[3]
Abu Moslem Nāqel-al-Dawla (Rabiʿ I 130-Šaʿbān 137/Nov. 747-Jan. 755)	Abu Moslem (130-36/747-54)	Abu Moslem Ḵorāsāni
Abu Dāwud Ḵāled b. Ebrāhim (Šawwāl 137-Rabiʿ I 140/Mar. 755-July 757)	Abu Dāwud Ḵāled b. Ebrāhim Ḏohli	Abu Dāwud Ḵāled b. Ebrāhim Ḏohli (Ramażān 137-Rabiʿ I 140/Feb. 755-Aug. 757)
Abu ʿEṣām b. Solaym (for 13 months)		
ʿAbd-al-Jabbār b. ʿAbd-al-Raḥmān (Rabiʿ II 142/Aug. 759)	ʿAbd-al-Jabbār b. ʿAbd-al-Raḥmān Azdi (148/765 [sic])	ʿAbd-al-Jabbār b. ʿAbd-al-Raḥmān (to Rabiʿ I 142/July 759)
Ḥāzem b. Ḥozayma [sic] (Rabiʿ I 143/June 760)	al-Mahdi > Ḵāzem b. Ḵozayma Tamimi	al-Mahdi > Ḵāzem b. Ḵozayma
Abu ʿAwn ʿAbd-al-Malek b. Yazid (146/763 for six years)		Abu ʿAwn ʿAbd-al-Malek b. Yazid (143-49/760-66)
Abu Mālek Osayd b. ʿAbd-Allāh Ḵozāʿi Ramażān 149-Ḏu'l-Ḥejja 150/Oct. 766-Dec. 767	Osayd b. ʿAbd-Allāh Ḵozāʿi	Osayd b. ʿAbd-Allāh (Ramażān 149-150/Oct. 766-67)
Ḥāzem b. Ḥozayma	Ḥomayd b. Qaḥṭaba Ṭāʾi	ʿAbda b. Qadid (151/768, for 7 months)
Ḥomayd b. Qaḥṭaba (Šaʿbān 151-Šaʿbān 159/ Aug. 768-May 776)	Abu ʿAwn ʿAbd-al-Malek b. Yazid	Ḥomayd b. Qaḥṭaba (Šaʿbān 151-159/Aug. 768-776)
ʿAbd-Allāh [b.] Ḥomayd (for 6 months)	Ḥomayd b. Qaḥṭaba	ʿAbd-Allāh b. Ḥomayd (to end of 159/Oct. 776)
		Abu ʿAwn (second governorship; Ṣafar 160/ Dec. 776)
Abu ʿAwn (second governorship; Ṣafar 160/ Nov. 776)		
Moʿāḏ b. Moslem (Rabiʿ II 161/Jan. 778)	Moʿāḏ b. Moslem Razi	Moʿāḏ b. Moslem (Rabiʿ II 161/Jan. 778)
Zohayr b. Mosayyab Żabbi (Jomādā II 163/ Feb. 780)	Mosayyab b. Zohayr Żabbi	Mosayyab b. Zohayr (Jomādā I 166/Dec. 782)
Abu'l-ʿAbbās Fażl b. Solaymān Ṭusi (Moḥarram 166/August 782)	Fażl b. Solaymān Ṭusi	Abu'l-ʿAbbās Fażl b. Solaymān Ṭusi (Moḥarram 167/Aug. 783 to accession of Hārun al-Rašid [170/786])
Jaʿfar b. Moḥammad Ḵozāʿi (Ḏu'l-Ḥejja 170-Ramażān 173/May 787-Jan. 790)	Jaʿfar b. Moḥammad b. Ašʿaṯ Ḵozāʿi	Jaʿfar b. Moḥammad b. Ašʿaṯ
	ʿAbbās b. Jaʿfar b. Moḥammad b. Ašʿaṯ	ʿAbbās b. Jaʿfar (3 years, to 175/792)
Ḥasan b. Qaḥṭaba (Šawwāl 173/Feb. 790)		
Ḡeṭrif b. ʿAṭāʾ (Ramażān 175/Jan. 792)	Ḡeṭrif b. ʿAṭāʾ	Ḡeṭrif b. ʿAṭāʾ Kendi (175/792)
Ḥamza b. Mālek Ḵozāʿi (Moḥarram 177/ April 793)	Ḥamza b. Mālek b. Hayṯam Ḵozāʿi	
Fażl b. Yaḥyā b. Ḵāled (Ramażān 177/ Dec. 793)	Fażl b. Yaḥyā b. Ḵāled b. Barmak	Fażl b. Yaḥyā Barmaki (Ramażān 177/Dec. 793 or Jan. 794)
Manṣur b. Yazid b. Manṣur (Ḏu'l-Ḥejja 179/ Feb. 796)		Manṣur b. Yazid > Saʿid b. Manṣur (Ḏu'l-Qaʿda 179/Feb. 796)
Jaʿfar b. Yaḥyā b. Ḵāled		
ʿAli b. ʿIsā b. Māhān (Jomādā II 180/Aug. 796)	ʿAli b. ʿIsā b. Māhān	ʿAli b. ʿIsā b. Māhān (Moḥarram 180/ Mar. 796)
Harṯama b. Aʿyan (Rabiʿ II 192/Feb. 808)	Harṯama b. Aʿyan	Harṯama b. Aʿyan (191/807)
al-Maʾmun (Jomāda I 193/Feb. 809)	al-Maʾmun	al-Maʾmun
Fażl b. Sahl (Rajab 196/Mar. 812)		
Rajāʾ b. Żaḥḥāk	Rajāʾ b. Żaḥḥak	
Ḡassān b. ʿAbbād (203/818 for 2 years)	Ḡassān b. ʿAbbād (204-5/819-20)	Ḡassān b. ʿAbbād (Rajab 204/Dec. 819 or Jan. 820)
Ṭāher b. Ḥosayn (Ramażān 205-206/Feb. 821-822)	Ṭāher b. Ḥosayn b. Moṣʿab Bušanji	Ṭāher b. Ḥosayn (Šawwāl 205/Mar. 821)

[1]Ḥamza Eṣfahāni, *Taʾriḵ sani moluk al-arż wa'l-anbiāʾ*, ed. Yusof Yaʿqub Maskuni, Beirut, 1961, pp. 161-68. Inaugural dates are usually based on arrival in Marv. [2]Aḥmad b. Abi Yaʿqub Yaʿqubi, *Ketāb al-boldān*, ed. M. J. De Goeje, Leiden, 1892, pp. 302-7. [3]Abu Saʿid ʿAbd-al-Ḥayy Gardizi, *Zayn al-aḵbār*, ed. ʿAbd-al-Ḥayy Ḥabibi, Tehran, 1968, pp. 119-35. Note: These governor lists are likely based to varying degrees on the lost *Taʾriḵ wolāt Ḵorāsān* by Abu ʿAli Ḥosayn Sallāmi (fl. 4th/10th century); see the hypothetical reconstruction in Kāẓembayki, ed., pp. 121-34. Another early source, Ḵalifa b. Ḵayyāṭ (d. 240/854), *Taʾriḵ*, pp. 413, 432, 441, 446, 462-63, provides lists of administrators under the last year of a caliph's reign. See also Zambaur, pp. 47-48.

in Bukhara, Šāš, Farḡāna, Ḵojand, Osrušāna, Ṣaḡāniān, Balḵ and Ṭoḵarestān, Ḵottal, and other districts, and it received support from Tibetans and Ḵarloḵ (Qarluq) and Oḡuz Turks (see also Beckwith, pp. 158-59).

As the rebellion threated the whole of Khorasan, Hārun al-Rašid's chief of the post (i.e., spy), the eunuch Ḥammawayh, informed him that the movement was not aimed at the ʿAbbasid caliphate but purely at ʿAli b. ʿIsā's malfeasance with the goal of bringing about his removal from office (Ṭabari, III, p. 718). Al-Rašid then decided to dismiss ʿAli b. ʿIsa and replace him with Harṯama b. Aʿyan; the purported texts of the letters he wrote ordering punishment for ʿAli b. ʿIsa and instructing Harṯama to appease the Khorasanis are preserved in Ṭabari's history, as are Harṯama's letters describing his actions and the caliph's response (III, pp. 716-18, 724-30). Harṯama went to Khorasan under the pretext of helping ʿAli b. ʿIsā fight Rafiʿ; caught by surprise, ʿAli b. ʿIsā was then presented with the caliph's letter of dismissal, arrested, publicly rebuked, sent to Baghdad to be imprisoned, and his fortune confiscated. Harṯama tried to persuade Rafiʿ's allies in Sogdia and Ṭoḵarestān to withdraw their support, but without much success, and Rafiʿ himself rejected an offer of pardon (suggesting that the rebellion now involved more than just opposition to ʿAli b. ʿIsā).

Meanwhile, Hārun al-Rašid had set out for Khorasan in 192/808 to deal in person with the multiple problems there, reaching Jorjān in Ṣafar 193/November-December 808 and taking possession of the property confiscated from ʿAli b. ʿIsā. Hārun then moved to Ṭus and sent his son ʿAbd-Allāh al-Maʾmun and a number of army commanders on to Marv. About the same time, Harṯama launched a new military campaign that retook Bukhara; Rafiʿ's brother, Bašir, was captured there and sent to Hārun in Ṭus; Hārun denied him clemency and had him hacked to pieces (Ṭabari, III, pp. 733-35). Hārun himself died shortly thereafter in a village near Ṭus, where he was buried.

Already in 186/802, Hārun had instituted an administrative reorganization and succession agreement often called the Meccan Protocols (because the relevant documents were posted in the Kaaba). Under its terms, Hārun would be succeeded as caliph by his son Moḥammad al-Amin. Al-Amin's older half-brother, ʿAbd-Allāh al-Maʾmun (q.v.), would be next in line for the succession and was designated in the meanwhile as the autonomous viceroy over the eastern provinces, from Ray and Hamadan to the further reaches of Khorasan and its dependencies. The agreement was unworkable from the start, and al-Amin and al-Maʾmun, guided by their respective mentors, Fażl b. Rabiʿ and Fażl b. Sahl b. Zādānfarruḵ (q.v.), sought to undo it. It was no doubt to guarantee that al-Maʾmun assumed the position promised him that Fażl b. Sahl arranged for him to accompany Hārun to Ṭus and thence, along with the chief army officers, to Marv. For his part, al-Amin covertly sent instructions for the *abnāʾ* and Jaziran troops accompanying al-Maʾmun to fight Rafiʿ b. Layṯ to return to Baghdad if Hārun died, and most of them complied. He also returned ʿAli b. ʿIsā b. Māhān to office, made changes to the succession agreement in favor of his son Musā, demanded territorial and financial concessions, and finally, in 195/810, abrogated and burned the texts of the Meccan Protocols and demanded al-Maʾmun return to Baghdad. ʿAli b. ʿIsā was again appointed governor of Khorasan and set out with an army to dislodge al-Maʾmun by force.

The young al-Maʾmun felt threatened on all sides (Ṭabari, III, p. 815), but he was in a stronger position in Khorasan than it might appear: Hārun al-Rašid, on his deathbed, had summoned the *wojuh* of Khorasan and the army to pledge allegiance to al-Maʾmun and they readily agreed, calling him "our nephew and the [descendant] of the Prophet's uncle" (Azdi, p. 318). Indeed, al-Maʾmun had personal connections to the province. Fażl b. Sahl reminded al-Maʾmun that he was "among [his] maternal uncles" (Ṭabari, III, p. 773)—apparent confirmation of the report that al-Maʾmun's mother Marājel was the daughter of Ostāḏsis (see Madelung, 2002), as well as Gardizi's identification (p. 133) of Ḡāleb b. Ostāḏsis, one of his officers, as his maternal uncle. Beyond that, al-Maʾmun followed policies designed to appeal to religious scholars as well as Shiʿite groups (calling himself Imam, dispensing justice, praising the Sunnah), Arab tribal leaders, "military commanders, kings, and descendants of kings" (Ṭabari, III, p. 774). There is no doubt that many of the Khorasani magnates, such as Ḥosayn b. Moṣʿab of Bušanj, who had been abused and threatened by ʿAli b. ʿIsā and forced to take refuge in Mecca with Hārun al-Rašid, regarded al-Maʾmun as one of their own and supported him wholeheartedly, especially after the jarring insult of ʿAli b. ʿIsā's return to power. Others were won over by al-Maʾmun's judicious policies and reduction of taxes. Apparently among them was Rafiʿ b. Layṯ, who heard reports about al-Maʾmun's good behavior and accepted an amnesty arranged by Harṯama and Asad b. Sāmānḵodā (q.v.) (Ṭabari, III, p. 777; Naršaḵi, pp. 104-5, tr. p. 76). On the advice of his vizier Fażl b. Sahl, al-Maʾmun was also able to stabilize and pacify the frontier districts of Central Asia (Beckwith, pp. 158-59). Al-Maʾmun also had the advantage of being able to block the roads from Iraq to Khorasan while maintaining a network of informants at al-Amin's court, among them the son of ʿIsā b. Musā.

As ʿAli b. Isā advanced toward Ray, al-Maʾmun sent a relatively small force led by Ṭāher b. Ḥosayn to oppose him. Ṭāher was the son of Ḥosayn b. Moṣʿab and was no doubt eager to fight ʿAli b. ʿIsā, as were other Khorasani notables with scores to settle, such as ʿAli b. Hešām b. Farr-Ḵosrow, son of another of ʿAli b ʿIsā's victims. Beyond that, Ṭāher's forces were made up of what appears to have been a personal retinue of Turks, Khwarazmians, and Bukharans he had probably recruited during the campaigns against Rafiʿ b. Layṯ. The crucial battle took place outside Ray in 195/811. ʿAli b. ʿIsā, who had seriously underestimated Ṭāher's resolve, was defeated and killed. The announcement of the victory, along with ʿAli's head, was sent to Khorasan, where the news was met with relief and jubilation, and al-Maʾmun was hailed as caliph (Ṭabari, III, p. 825). This marked the beginning of a fierce civil war leading to the siege of Baghdad and the death of Moḥammad al-Amin, while attempting to surrender to Harṯama, at the hands of Ṭāher's troops in Moḥarram 198/September 813.

Al-Maʾmun remained at Marv, now effectively the capital of the ʿAbbasid caliphate, until 202/818. Fażl b. Sahl was given authority over the east, with the title of Ḏu'l-Reʾāsatayn (holder of the dual offices of military and administrative command). Fażl reversed policy for the frontier principalities, conducting campaigns against the Kābol-šāh, who surrendered and became a Muslim (the tribute he sent is described in Azraqi, pp. 225-26); Otrārbanda, ruler of Fārāb; the Ḵarloḵ Turks; and the Tibetans (Beckwith, p. 160). However, Fażl's achievements were overshadowed by developments in Baghdad and the west, where Fażl's far less competent brother Ḥasan faced increasing difficulties, including an ostensibly pro-ʿAlid revolt led by the renegade Abu'l-Sarāyā on behalf of Moḥammad b. Ebrāhim, known as Ebn Ṭabāṭabā (see Kennedy, pp. 207-11). Despite these problems, Ḥasan b. Sahl kept Ṭāher b. Ḥosayn isolated and marginalized by sending him off to fight rebels in Syria, but Harṯama b. Aʿyan slipped back to Marv in Ḏu'l-Qaʿda 200/June 816 to warn al-Maʾmun of the problems brewing in Iraq and to persuade him to return to Baghdad. Fażl b. Sahl was able to convince al-Maʾmun that Harṯama was stirring up discord for his own purposes; Harṯama was then imprisoned and murdered in jail (Ṭabari, III, pp. 996-98; Yaʿqubi, *Taʾriḵ*, II, p. 546).

The resurgence of the ʿAlids must have factored into one of the most controversial policies initiated by al-Maʾmun in Khorasan: the designation in 201/817 of ʿAli b. Musā al-Kāẓem as his successor, reaching back into the early ideology of the *daʿwa* to give him the title of al-Reżā (see Tor, 2001; Madelung, 1981; Buyukkara). The architect of this policy was assumed, perhaps unjustly, to be Fażl b. Sahl, who, along with his brother Ḥasan, was hated in Iraq as much as ʿAli b. ʿIsā had been in Khorasan. The news of this change led senior members of the ʿAbbasid family to proclaim Ebrāhim, son of al-Mahdi, as a counter-caliph in Baghdad. Fażl continued to keep al-Maʾmun in the dark about affairs in Iraq, but ʿAli al-Reżā managed to alert him to the seriousness of the situation (Ṭabari, III, p. 1025). In 202/817-18, al-Maʾmun decided to take matters into his own hands and travel back to Baghdad. At Saraḵs in Šaʿbān 202/February 818, Fażl b. Sahl was attacked and killed by some of al-Maʾmun's followers; al-Maʾmun had them executed and their heads sent to Ḥasan b. Sahl, presumably as a preemptive measure to avoid alarming him. Then, ca. Ṣafar 203/September 818, while al-Maʾmun was visiting the grave of his father, Hārun al-Rašid, near Ṭus, ʿAli al-Reżā died unexpectedly and was buried next to Hārun, with al-Maʾmun himself presiding over the service (Ṭabari, III, 1030; Yaʿqubi, *Taʾriḵ*, II, pp. 550-51). Once again, the caliph's involvement and objectives are a matter of dispute, but al-Reżā's death was certainly used to try to pave the way for the caliph's return to Baghdad. Al-Maʾmun finally reached the city in Ṣafar 204/August 819, where he was received by the ʿAbbasid family, army officers, and Ṭāher b. Ḥosayn.

According to Yaʿqubi (*Taʾriḵ*, II, p. 550), al-Maʾmun had left the administration of Khorasan in the hands of Rajāʾ b. Abi'l-Żaḥḥāk, a relative of Ḥasan b. Sahl, who proved to be a weak administrator. He was then replaced by Ḡassān b. ʿAbbād, a paternal cousin of Fażl b. Sahl (Ṭabari, III, p. 1043). Yaʿqubi praises his competence and says he won over the local princes (*Taʾriḵ*, II, p. 550); other sources suggest Ḡassān was not particularly effective either (Ṭabari, III, p. 1042-43), but this may have been part of an effort to discredit him. Ṭāher b. Ḥosayn, who had become extremely powerful and influential in Iraq, had designs on the office, and Aḥmad b. Abi Ḵāled, now al-Maʾmun's chief advisor, recommended Ṭāher be sent to Khorasan to prevent a possible Turkish rebellion. The appointment of Ṭāher in 205/821 would usher in a significant new chapter of Khorasani history.

Bibliography: Sources. Moḥammad b. ʿObayd-Allāh Abu'l-Maʿāli, *Bayān al-adyān*, ed. ʿAbbās Eqbāl, Tehran, 1933. Aḥmad Kāteb, *Tāriḵ-e jadid-e Yazd*, Yazd, 1939. *Aḵbār al-dawla al-ʿabbāsiya wa fihi aḵbār al-ʿAbbas wa waladihi*, ed. ʿAbd-al-ʿAziz Duri and ʿAbd-al-Jabbār Moṭṭalebi, Beirut, 1971. Abu Zakariyā Yazid b. Moḥammad Azdi, *Taʾriḵ al-Mawṣel*, ed. ʿAli Ḥabiba, Cairo, 1967. Abu Walid Moḥammad b. ʿAbd-Allāh Azraqi, *Aḵbār Makka*, ed. Rošdi Malḥas, Mecca, 1965. Moḥammad Mofid Mostawfi Bafqi, *Jāmeʿ-e mofidi*, ed. Iraj Afšār, Tehran, 1964. ʿAbd-al-Qāher b. Ṭāher Baḡdādi, *al-Farq bayna'l-feraq*, ed. M. ʿAbd-al-Ḥamid, Cairo, 1964, part tr. A. S. Halkin, as *Moslem Schisms and Sects*, Tel Aviv, 1935. Aḥmad b. Yaḥyā Balāḏori, *Ansāb al-ašrāf* II, ed. Wilferd Madelung, Berlin and Beirut, 2003. Idem, *Ansāb al-ašrāf* III: *al-ʿAbbās b. ʿAbd-al-Moṭṭaleb wa waladoh*, ed. ʿAbd-al-ʿAziz Duri, Beirut, 1978. Abu ʿAli Moḥammad Balʿami, *Tāriḵ-nāma-ye Ṭabari gardānida-ye mansub ba Balʿami*, ed. Moḥammad Rowšan, 3 vols., Tehran, 1987. Abu'l-Fażl Moḥammad Bayhaqi, *Tāriḵ-e Bayhaqi*, ed. ʿAli-Akbar Fayyāż, Mashhad, 1971; tr. C. Edmund Bosworth with full revision by Mohsen Ashtiany, as *The History of Beyhaqi: The History of Sultan Masʿud of Ghazna, 1030-1041*, 3 vols., Boston, 2011. Abu'l-Rayḥān Moḥammad Biruni, *al-Āṯār al-bāqiya ʿan al-qorun al-ḵāliya*, ed. E. Sachau, Leipzig, 1878, tr. E. Sachau, as *The Chronology of Ancient Nations*, London, 1879. Abu Ḥanifa Dinavari, *al-Aḵbār al-ṭewāl*, ed. A. ʿĀmer, Cairo, 1960. Abu ʿOmar Aḥmad Ebn ʿAbd Rabbeh, *Ketāb al-ʿeqd al-farid*, ed. Aḥmad Amin et al., 7 vols., Cairo, 1940-53. ʿEzz-al-Din Ebn al-Aṯir, *Ketāb al-kāmel fi'l-taʾriḵ*, ed. C. J. Tornberg, 13 vols., Beirut, 1965. Abu'l-Faraj Moḥammad Ebn al-Nadim, *Ketāb al Fehrest*, ed. Reżā Tajaddod, Tehran, 1971, tr. Bayard Dodge, as *The Fihrist*, 2 vols., New York, 1970.

Abu Saʿid ʿAbd-al-Ḥayy Gardizi, *Zayn al-aḵbār*, ed. ʿAbd-al-Ḥayy Ḥabibi, Tehran, 1968. Abu ʿAbd-Allāh Ḥākem Nišāburi, *Tāriḵ-e Nišābur*, tr. Moḥammad b. Ḥosayn Nišāburi, ed. Moḥammad-Reżā Šafiʿi-Kadkani, Tehran, 1996. Ḥamza Eṣfahāni, *Taʾriḵ sani moluk al-arż wa'l-anbiāʾ*, ed. Yosof Yaʿqub Maskuni, Beirut, 1961. *Ḥodud al-ʿālam men al-mašreq ela'l-maḡreb*, ed.

Manučehr Sotuda, Tehran, 1962; tr. with commentary Vladimir Minorsky, as *Hudūd al-ʿĀlam: The Regions of the World*, London, 1970. Abū ʿAbd-Allāh Moḥammad Jahšīārī, *Ketāb al-wozarāʾ wa'l-kottāb*, Cairo, 1938. Majd-al-Din Ḵᵛāfi, *Rawżat al-ḵold*, ed. M. Farruḵ, Tehran, 1967. Moṭahhar b. Ṭāher Maqdesi, *Ketāb al-badʾ wa'l-taʾriḵ*, ed. and tr. M. Cl. Huart, as *Le livre de la création et de l'histoire*, 6 vols., Paris, 1899-1919. Abu'l-Ḥasan ʿAli Masʿudi, *Moruj al-ḏahab wa maʿāden al-jawhar*, ed. and tr. Charles Barbier de Meynard and Abel Pavet de Courteille, as *Les prairies d'or*, 9 vols., Paris, 1861-1917. Abu ʿAbd-Allāh Moḥammad b. Aḥmad Moqaddasi, *Aḥsan al-taqāsim fi maʿrefat al-aqālim*, ed. M. J. de Goeje, Leiden, 1877.

Abu Bakr Moḥammad Naršaḵi, *Tāriḵ-e Boḵārā*, tr. Abu Naṣr Aḥmad Qobāvi, ed. Moḥammad-Taqi Modarres Rażawi, Tehran, 1972; tr. R. N. Frye, as *The History of Bukhara*, Cambridge, Mass. 1954. Neẓām-al-Molk, *Siāsat-nāma*, ed. H. Darke, 2nd ed., Tehran, 1985. Moḥammad b. ʿAbd-al-Karim Šahrastāni, *Ketāb al- melal wa'l-neḥal*, 3 vols., Cairo, 1968. Abu Manṣur ʿAbd-al-Malek Ṯaʿālebi, *Laṭāʾef al-maʿāref*, ed. Ebrāhim Ebyāri and Ḥasan Kāmel Ṣayrafi, Cairo, 1960; tr. C. E. Bosworth, as *The Book of Curious and Entertaining Information*, Edinburgh, 1968. Idem, *Yatimat al-dahr fi maḥāsen ahl al-ʿaṣr*, ed. M. M. ʿAbd-al-Ḥamid, 4 vols., Cairo, 1956-58. Moḥammad b. Jarir Ṭabari, *Taʾriḵ al-rosol wa'l-moluk*, ed. M. J. De Goeje et al., 3 vols. in 15, repr. Leiden, 1964; tr. by various scholars as *The History of al-Ṭabari*, 40 vols., Albany, N.Y., 1985-2007. *Tāriḵ-e alfi*, MS British Library, London, Add. 16681. *Taʾriḵ al-ḵolafāʾ*, facs. ed. P. A. Gryaznevich, as *Istoriya khalifov anonimnogo avtora XI veka*, Moscow, 1967. *Tāriḵ-e Sistān*, ed. Moḥammad-Taqi Malek-al-Šoʿarāʾ Bahār, Tehran, 1935; tr. Milton Gold, as *The Tārikh-e Sistān*, Rome, 1976. Theophanes the Confessor, *Chronographia* I, ed. Johannes Classen, Bonn, 1839, part. tr. Harry Turtledove, as *The Chronicle of Theophanes*, Philadelphia, 1982. Aḥmad b. Abi Yaʿqub Yaʿqubi, *Ketāb al-boldān*, ed. M. J. De Goeje, Leiden, 1892; tr. Gaston Wiet, as *Les pays*, Cairo, 1937. Idem, *Taʾriḵ al-Yaʿqubi*, ed. M. Th. Houtsma, as *Historiae*, 2 vols., Leiden, 1883. Ẓahir-al-Din ʿAli Bayhaqi (Ebn Fondoq), *Tāriḵ-e Bayhaq*, ed. Aḥmad Bahmanyār, Tehran, 1938.

Studies. Saleh Said Agha, "A Viewpoint of the Murjiʾa in the Umayyad Period: Evolution through Application," *Journal of Islamic Studies*, 1997, pp. 1-42. Idem, "The Arab Population in Ḫurāsān during the Umayyad Period: Some Demographic Computations," *Arabica* 46, 1999, pp. 211-229. Idem, "Abu Muslim's Conquest of Khurāsān: Preliminaries and Strategy in a Confusing Passage of the *Akhbār al-dawla al-ʿAbbāsiyya*," *JAOS* 120, 2000, pp. 333-47. Idem, "Did Qaḥṭabah b. Shabib al-Ṭāʾī Hail from Kūfah?," *Studia Islamica* 92, 2001, pp. 187-93. Idem, *The Revolution which Toppled the Umayyads: Neither Arab nor ʿAbbāsid*, Leiden, 2003. Fukuzo Amabe, *The Emergence of the ʿAbbāsid Autocracy: The ʿAbbāsid Army, Khurāsān and Adharbayjān*, Kyoto, 1995. Sean W. Antony, "Chiliastic Ideology and Nativist Rebellion in the Early ʿAbbāsid Period: Sunbādh and *Jāmāsp-Nāmah*," *JAOS* 132, 2012, pp. 641-55. V. Vladimirovich Barthold, *Turkestan Down to the Mongol Invasion*, London, 1968. Christopher I. Beckwith, *The Tibetan Empire in Central Asia*, Princeton, 1987. Clifford Edmund Bosworth, *Sīstān under the Arabs: From the Islamic Conquest to the Rise of the Ṣaffārids (30-250/651-864)*, Rome, 1968. Idem, "The Ṭāhirids and Arabic Culture," *Journal of Semitic Studies* 14, 1969, pp. 45-79. Idem, "The Ṭāhirids and Ṣaffārids," in Richard N. Frye, ed., *The Cambridge History of Iran* IV: *From the Arab Invasion to the Saljuqs*, Cambridge, 1975, pp. 90-135. Richard W. Bulliet, *The Patricians of Nishapur: A Study in Medieval Islamic Social History*, Cambridge, Mass., 1972. Idem, *Conversion to Islam in the Medieval Period: An Essay in Quantitative History*, Cambridge, Mass. 1979. M. Ali Buyukkara, "Al-Maʾmūn's Choice of ʿAli al-Riḍā as His Heir," *Islamic Studies* 41, 2002, pp. 445-46. Patricia Crone, *Slaves on Horses: The Evolution of the Islamic Polity*, Cambridge, 1980. Idem, "On the Meaning of the ʿAbbāsid Call to al-Riḍā," in C. E. Bosworth et al., eds., *The Islamic World: Essays in Honor of Bernard Lewis*, Princeton, 1989, pp. 95-111. Idem, "Were the Qays and Yemen of the Umayyad Period Political Parties?," *Der Islam* 71, 1994, pp. 1-57. Idem, "The ʿAbbāsid Abnāʾ and Sasanid Cavalrymen," *JRAS* 8, 1998, pp. 1-19. Idem, "The Significance of Wooden Weapons in al-Mukhtār's Revolt and the ʿAbbāsid Revolution," in I. R. Netton, ed., *Studies in Honour of Clifford Edmund Bosworth* I, Leiden, 2000, pp. 174-85. Idem, "Abū Tammām on the Mubayyiḍa," in Omar Ali-de-Unzaga, ed., *Fortresses of the Intellect: Ismaili and other Islamic Studies in Honour of Farhad Daftary*, London, 2011, pp. 167-88. Idem, *The Nativist Prophets of Early Islamic Iran: Rural Revolt and Local Zoroastrianism*, Cambridge, 2012. Patricia Crone and M. Jafari Jazi, "The Muqannaʿ Narrative in the *Tārikhnāma*," *BSOAS* 73, 2010, pp. 157-77, 381-413.

Farhad Daftary, *The Ismāʿīlīs: Their History and Doctrines*, Cambridge, 1990. Elton L. Daniel, *The Political and Social History* of *Khurasan under ʿAbbasid Rule 747-820*, Minneapolis and Chicago, 1979. Idem, "The Anonymous 'History of the ʿAbbasid Family' and Its Place in Islamic Historiography," *IJMES* 14, 1982, pp. 419-34. Idem, "The 'Ahl-al-Taqādum' and the Problem of the Constituency of the ʿAbbasid Revolution in the Merv Oasis," *Journal of Islamic Studies* 7, 1996, pp. 150-79. Idem, "Arabs, Persians, and the Advent of the ʿAbbasids Reconsidered," *JAOS* 117, 1997, pp. 54-48. Daniel C. Dennett, *Conversion and the Poll Tax in Early Islam*, Cambridge, Mass., 1950. D. Dunlop, "A New Source of Information on the Battle of Talas or Atlakh," *Ural-Altaische Jahrbücher* 36, 1964, pp. 326-30. Amikam Elad, "Aspects of the Transition from the Umayyad to the ʿAbbasid Caliphate," *Jerusalem Studies in Arabic and Islam* 19, 1995, pp. 89-132. Idem, "The Ethnic Composition of the ʿAbbāsid Revolution: A Reevaluation of some Recent Research," *Jerusalem Studies in Arabic and Islam* 24, 2000, pp. 246-326. Richard N. Frye, "The Role of Abū Muslim in the ʿAbbāsid Revolt," *Muslim World*

37, 1947, pp. 28-38. Idem, "Development of Persian Literature under the Samanids and Qarakhanids," in *Yád-náme-ye Jan Rypka: Collection of Articles on Persian and Tajik Literature,* Prague, 1967, pp. 69-73. Idem, "The Sāmānids," in idem, ed., *The Cambridge History of Iran IV: From the Arab Invasion to the Saljuqs,* Cambridge, 1975, pp. 136-61. H. A. R. Gibb, *The Arab Conquests in Central Asia,* London, 1923. Rhuvon Guest, "A Coin of Abū Muslim," *JRAS* 3, 1932, pp. 555-56. Robert Haug, *The Eastern Frontier: Limits of Empire in Late Antique and Early Medieval Central Asia,* London and New York, 2019. Minoru Inaba, "Between Zābulistān and Gūzgān: A Study on the Early Islamic History of Afghanistan," *Journal of Inner Asian Art and Archaeology* 7, 2016, pp. 209-25.

Yury Karev, "La politique d'Abū Muslim dans le Māwarāʾannahr: Nouvelles données textuelles et archeeologiques," *Der Islam* 79, 2002, pp. 1-46. Idem, *Samarqand et le Sughd à l'époque ʿabbāsside: Histoire politique et sociale,* Paris, 2015. Moḥammad ʿAli Kāẓembayki, ed., *Aḵbār wolāt Ḵorāsān le'l-Sallāmi,* Tehran, 2011 (useful collection of quotations in other works from this lost history of Khorasan). Hugh Kennedy, *The Early ʿAbbasid Caliphate: A Political History,* London, 1981. Geoffrey Khan, *Arabic Documents from Early Islamic Khurasan,* London, 2007a. Idem, "Newly Discovered Arabic Documents from Early ʿAbbasid Khurasan," in Petra Sijpesteijn et. al, eds., *From al-Andalus to Khurasan,* Leiden, 2007b, pp. 201-15. Boris Kochnev, "Les monnaies de Muqannaʿ," *Studia Iranica* 30, 2001, pp. 143-50. Étienne de la Vaissière, *Sogdian Traders: A History,* Leiden and Boston, 2005. Idem, *Samarcande et Samarra: Élites d'Asie centrale dans l'empire abbasside,* Paris, 2007. Idem, ed., *Islamisation de l'Asie Centrale: Processus locaux d'acculturation du VIIe au XIe siècle,* Paris, 2008. Idem, "The ʿAbbasid Revolution in Marw: New Data," *Der Islam* 95, 2018, pp. 110-46. A. K. S. Lambton, *Landlord and Peasant in Persia: A Study of Land Tenure and Land Revenue Administration,* London 1953. Jacob Lassner, *The Shaping of ʿAbbāsid Rule,* Princeton, 1980. Idem, "Abū Muslim al-Khurāsāni: The Emergence of a Secret Agent from Khurāsān, Irāq, or was it Iṣfahān?," *JAOS* 104, 1984, pp. 165-75. Idem, "Abū Muslim, Son of Salīṭ: A Skeleton in the ʿAbbasid Closet?," in Moshe Sharon, ed., *Studies in Islamic History and Civilization in Honour of Professor David Ayalon,* Jerusalem and Leiden, 1986a, pp. 91-104. Idem, *Islamic Revolution and Historical Memory: An Inquiry into the Art of ʿAbbāsid Apologetics,* New Haven, 1986b.

Wilferd Madelung, "New Documents Concerning al-Maʾmūn, al-Faḍl b. Sahl and ʿAlī al-Riḍā," in Wadad al-Qadi, ed., *Studia Arabica et Islamica: Festschrift for Iḥsān ʿAbbās,* Beirut, 1981, pp. 333-46. Idem, "The Early Murjiʾa in Khurāsān and Transoxiana and the Spread of Hanafism," *Der Islam* 59, 1982, pp. 32-39. Idem, "Was the Caliph al-Maʾmun a Grandson of the Sectarian Leader Ustādhsis?," in S. Leder et al., eds., *Studies in Arabic and Islam,* Leuven, 2002, pp. 485-90. Josef Marquart/Markwart, *Ērānšahr nach der Geographie des Ps. Moses*

Xorenacʿi, Abhandlungen der Königlichen Gesellschaft der Wissenschaften zu Göttingen, phil.-hist. Kl., N. F. 3/2, 1901. Irène Mélikoff, *Abū Muslim: Le "Porte-Hache" du Khorassan dans la tradition épique turco-iranienne,* Paris, 1962. George C. Miles, *Numismatic History of Ray,* New York, 1938. Sabatino Moscati, "La Revolta di ʿAbd al-Ğabbār contro il califfo al-Manṣūr," *Rendiconti Reale Accademia dei Lincei* ser. 8/2, 1947, pp. 613-15. Idem, "Studi su Abū Muslim," *Rendiconti Lincei* ser. 8/4, 1949-50, pp. 323-35, 474-95, ser. 8/5, 1950-51, pp. 89-105. Roy Mottahedeh, "The ʿAbbāsid Caliphate in Iran," in Richard N. Frye, ed., *The Cambridge History of Iran IV: From the Arab Invasion to the Saljuqs,* Cambridge, 1975, pp. 57-89. Tilman Nagel, *Untersuchungen zur Entstehung des ʿAbbasidischen Kalifates,* Bonn, 1972. A. C. S. Peacock, "Khurasani Historiography and Identity in the Light of the Fragments of the *Akhbār Wulāt Khurāsān* and the *Tārīkh-i Harāt,*" in A. C. S. Peacock and D. G. Tor, eds., *Medieval Central Asia and the Persianate World: Iranian Tradition and Islamic Civilisation,* London and New York, 2015, pp. 143-60. Parvaneh Pourshariati, "Local Histories of Khurāsān and the Pattern of Arab Settlement," *Studia Iranica* 27, 1998, pp. 41-82. Idem, *Decline and Fall of the Sasanian Empire: The Sasanian-Parthian Confederacy and the Arab Conquest of Iran,* London and New York, 2008. Wadad al-Qadi, "The Earliest 'Nābita' and the Paradigmatic 'Nawābit'," *Studia Islamica* 78, 1993, pp. 27-61.

Gholam Hossein Sadighi, *Les mouvements religieux iraniens au IIe et au IIIe siècle de l'hégire,* Paris, 1938. M. A. Shaban, *The ʿAbbāsid Revolution,* Cambridge, 1970. Idem, "Khurāsān at the Time of the Arab Conquest," in Clifford Edmund Bosworth, ed., *Iran and Islam: In Memory of the Late Vladimir Minorsky,* Edinburgh, 1971, pp. 479-90. H. Shacklady, "The ʿAbbasid Movement in Khurāsān," *Occasional Papers of the School of ʿAbbasid Studies* 1, 1986, pp. 98-112. Moshe Sharon, *Black Banners from the East: The Establishment of the ʿAbbāsid State,* Jerusalem, 1983. Idem, *Revolt: The Social and Military Aspects of the ʿAbbasid Revolution,* Jerusalem, 1990. Dominique Sourdel, *Le vizirat ʿabbāside de 749 à 936 (132 à 324 de l'Hégire),* 2 vols., Damascus, 1959-60. Deborah Gerber Tor, "An Historiographical Re-examination of the Appointment and Death of ʿAlī al-Riḍā," *Der Islam* 78, 2001, pp. 103-28. Idem, *Violent Order: Religious Warfare, Chivalry, and the ʿAyyar Phenomenon in the Medieval Islamic World,* Würzburg, 2007. Faruq Umar, *The ʿAbbāsid Caliphate 132/750-170/786,* Baghdad, 1969. Julius Wellhausen, *Das arabische Reich und sein Sturz,* Berlin, 1902; tr. Margaret Graham Weir, as *The Arab Kingdom and its Fall,* Calcutta, 1927. Ḡolām Ḥosayn Yusofi, *Abu Moslem: sardār-e Ḵorāsān,* Tehran, 1966. ʿAbd al-Ḥusayn Zarrīnkūb, "The Arab Conquest of Iran and Its Aftermath," in Richard N. Frye, ed., *The Cambridge History of Iran IV: From the Arab Invasion to the Saljuqs,* Cambridge, 1975, pp. 1-56.

(EIr.)

vi. History in the Taherid and Samanid Periods

In the Taherid and Samanid periods, Khorasan became virtually synonymous with the Mašreq or "Islamic East," stretching from Ray far into Central Asia. It enjoyed a bourgeoning economy built on agriculture and trade, and it participated in a brilliant efflorescence of Islamic scholarship while simultaneously constructing a distinct Perso-Islamic, and laying the foundations for a subsequent Turko-Persian, culture throughout the region. As the author of the 4th/10th-century geographical treatise *Ḥodud al-ʿālam* put it (tr., p. 102), Khorasan was "a vast country with much wealth and abundant amenities," as well as a salubrious climate, healthy people, its own king (*padšāy*), and a frontier protected by march lords (*moluk-e aṭrāf*). The anonymous Persian author's near contemporary, the Arab geographer Moḥammad b. Aḥmad Moqaddasi, who visited the region, likewise praised Khorasan in this period for its climate and its natural resources as well as the strength, piety, virtue, wisdom, and industry of its people (p. 294).

The Taherids

The Taherids, based initially in Pušang/Bušanj (see FUŠANJ), came to prominence during the period of the *daʿwa* in Khorasan and faithfully served the ʿAbbasid cause there for some fifty years, before founding their own autonomous and hereditary provincial dynasty. An ancestor of the family, likely of Iranian ethnicity, had reputedly accompanied one of the Arab armies invading Khorasan, converted to Islam, and become a client (*mawlā*) of the tribe of Ḵozāʿa (on the conflicting traditions about this, see Kaabi, 1983, I, pp. 62-64). Abu Manṣur Ṭalḥa b. Zorayq (or Rozayq) b. Asad is well-attested as a *naqib* 'chief' of the *daʿwa* organization; living at that time in a village near Marv, he later held an administrative or military office in Herat (sources given in Agha, pp. 372-73, no. 351). His brother, Moṣʿab, was a lower-ranking member of the organization and was later an official in nearby Bušanj, where he was succeeded by his son Ḥosayn b. Moṣʿab (a notable in the time of Hārun al-Rašid and enemy of ʿAli b. ʿIsā b. Māhān).

Ṭāher b. Ḥosayn, later known by the honorific title Ḏu'l-Yaminayn ("The Ambidextrous") because of his military prowess, rose to prominence during the wars with Rafiʿ b. Layṯ and the civil wars between al-Amin and al-Maʾmun (q.v.), defeating ʿAli b. ʿIsā b. Māhān, participating in the siege of Baghdad, and engineering the death of the defeated al-Amin (on these events, see KHORASAN v.). He shrewdly bided his time during the administration of Ḥasan b. Sahl, building up a power base and a fortune in Iraq. When al-Maʿmun was returning to Baghdad in Ṣafar 204/August 819, he was accompanied by Ṭāher from Nahrawān to Roṣāfa, and Ṭāher was given authority over the Jazira, all of Baghdad, and the Sawād and made commander of the security force (*ṣāḥeb al-šorṭa*), a position members of the family would hold for almost a century, acquiring further fame and riches in the capital. By this time, Ṭāher had turned sharply against Ḥasan b. Sahl and his policies, and it was Ṭāher who was said to have persuaded al-Maʾmun to abandon the wearing of green garments and return to the traditional ʿAbbasid black (Ṭabari, III, pp. 1037-38).

Al-Maʾmun appointed Ṭāher governor of Khorasan, "from the City of Peace to the most distant districts of the East," in late Ḏu'l-Qaʿda 205/May 821 (Ṭabari, III, p. 1043). Ṭāher had barely had time to make some administrative appointments (Ebn Abi Ṭāher Ṭayfur, pp. 58-60; *Tāriḵ-e Sistān*, p. 177) before he died unexpectedly in his sleep at the age of 48 in 208/822. There are wildly different explanations for why Ṭāher was made governor of Khorasan, as well as conspiracy theories about his untimely demise. In both cases, the issue hinges on whether Ṭāher and al-Maʾmun were still on good terms or whether there had been a rift between them. The official rationale for the appointment seems to have been that there were disturbances in Khorasan that the acting governor, Ḡassān b. ʿAbbād, could not handle; moreover, Ḡassān was a paternal cousin of Fażl b. Sahl and an appointee of Ḥasan b. Sahl, so his removal was needed as part of the post-Sahlid housecleaning (Ṭabari, III, 1043). However, there are also claims that Ṭāher tricked al-Maʾmun into making the appointment with the help of his friend, the vizier Aḥmad b. Abi Ḵāled Aḥwal, since he had learned that the caliph resented him because of his involvement in killing al-Amin and was being encouraged by al-Amin's mother to seek revenge (Ṭabari, III, p. 1042; Masʿudi, VI, pp. 485-87). It is also possible that al-Maʾmun was anxious to get an overly powerful general away from Baghdad, and Ṭāher was reluctant to go: He was certainly in no hurry to leave for Khorasan, taking about a year to prepare, but that may have been to make the arrangements for his son ʿAbd-Allāh b. Ṭāher (q.v.) to take over his interests in Baghdad and the Jazira. As for his death, his son and uncles indicated it was after a high fever, and Ṭāher had a premonition of it as his last words were *dar marg niz mardi wāyaḏ* 'one must be manly even in the face of death' (Ṭabari, III, p. 1063). However, it was also noted that he died shortly after failing or "forgetting" to mention the caliph's name in his Friday sermon, which was an indication of independence from the caliphate in Baghdad. Aḥmad b. Abi Ḵāled had vouched to al-Maʾmun for Ṭāher's behavior and had made arrangements to eliminate him should he act otherwise (Ṭabari, III, p. 1064; Ebn al-Aṯir, VI, pp. 381-83). It is also a fact that Ṭāher had begun to omit al-Maʾmun's name from coins struck at his mints (Bosworth, 1975, p. 95).

Yet no such suspicions perturbed relations of the caliph with other members of the family either in Iraq or Khorasan. Both al-Maʾmun and Aḥmad b. Abi Ḵāled agreed that the obvious choice as Ṭāher's successor should be his son Ṭalḥa, just as Ṭāher is said to have wanted (Gardizi, p. 135). This may have been in the expectation that Ṭalḥa's older brother in Iraq, ʿAbd-Allāh, would keep him in line. It is equally likely that it was a considered decision that the goal of stability in Khorasan while al-Maʾmun dealt with manifold problems developing in the West would be in the interest of all and best met by keeping a Taherid as governor. Any threat the young Talḥa might have posed

Table 1
THE TAHERIDS OF KHORASAN

Dates	Governor
205-7/821-22	Ṭāher b. Ḥosayn Ḏu'l-Yaminayn
207-13/822-28	Ṭalḥa b. Ṭāher
213-30/828-45	ʿAbd-Allāh b. Ṭāher
230-48/845-62	Ṭāher (II) b. ʿAbd-Allāh
248-59/862-73	Moḥammad b. Ṭāher (II)

Source: C. E. Bosworth, *The Islamic Dynasties*, Islamic Surveys 5, Edinburgh, 1967, p. 99.

was further diminished by returning Aḥmad b. Abi Ḵāled to Khorasan to assist in another offensive into Ošrusana (Ṭabari, III, pp. 1065-66; Ebn al-Aṯir, VI, p. 382). Talḥa's tenure was mostly occupied in dealing with the continuing threat from the Kharijites and Ḥamza b. Āḏarak (q.v.). Both Talḥa and Ḥamza died in 213/828.

The third Taherid governor, ʿAbd-Allāh b. Ṭāher, ruled for seventeen years (213-30/828-45). Marv ceased to be the administrative capital of Khorasan, and the Taherids established themselves at Nishapur, which experienced a period of prosperity and florescence under them and their successors, the Samanids (Barthold, 1984, pp. 96-98). ʿAbd-Allāh was himself highly cultured and a lover of literature and of music and singing, and he gathered around himself a distinguished circle of Arabic poets and litterateurs, with such visiting luminaries as the poet Abu Tammām and the genealogist and historian Zobayr b. Bakkār (see Bosworth, 1969, pp. 58-67). He assembled a team of experts who compiled a *Ketāb al-qoni* as an authoritative guide to the law and practice of irrigation and water rights; the Ghaznavid historian ʿAbd-al-Ḥayy Gardizi (q.v) states that this was still in use in Khorasan during his own time, that is, two centuries later (Gardizi, p. 137; cf. Barthold, p. 213). Whereas Khorasan had been a distant province of the caliphate in earlier times, its importance being primarily military and strategic (Herzfeld, pp. 119-20), its agricultural prosperity now increased. According to Yaʿqubi (*Boldān*, p. 308), the land-tax (*ḵarāj*) of Khorasan amounted to 40 million dirhams a year under the Taherids. It benefited from the commercial transit traffic bringing the products of Transoxiana and the Inner Asian steppes to the caliphal heartlands. Leather products, weapons, honey, furs, and various luxury items were imported, and a *spécialité du pays* is mentioned for the Nishapur district, namely *noql* or edible earth, praised by the great physician Moḥammad b. Zakariyā Rāzi (d. ca. 313/925) and so prized that it was exported as far as Egypt and the Maghrib (Ṯaʿālebi, pp. 131-32). Above all, there was the transit trade across Khorasan in Turkish slaves from the steppes from the early 3rd/9th century, increasingly becoming a component of the caliphal and other armies in the central and eastern Islamic lands. Slaves normally formed a substantial part of the annual tribute forwarded to Samarra and Baghdad by the Taherids and then as presents by their successors the Samanids (see Barthold, pp. 235-38, on all this traffic in imports in Samanid times, this information being substantially valid for the preceding Taherid period; see also Bosworth, 1975; la Vaissière, 2005, pp. 291-302).

As governors in Khorasan, the Taherids were strong upholders of Sunni orthodoxy against various heterodox and sectarian movements and outbreaks of religio-social protest, which were racking Khorasan and Transoxiana at this time. They campaigned against the veteran Kharijite Ḥamza b. Āḏarak in Khorasan and against Māzyār b. Qāren in the Caspian provinces and the Zaydi Shiʿite Hasanids there. It is not therefore surprising that the sources regard with great favor the orthodox and obedient Taherids as servants of the caliphs when they were at the height of their power (Bosworth, 1975, pp. 105-6). They also preserved a certain independence of action but always regarded themselves as faithful servants of the caliphs, acknowledging the ʿAbbasids in the sermons and on coins. All in all, the ʿAbbasid-Taherid relationship was a symbiotic partnership and "the most successful solution the Abbasids ever found to the problem of governing the province" (Kennedy, p. 166).

Taherid power in Khorasan seems to have loosened with later governors of the line. There may have been a certain feeling in Sunni orthodox circles that the later Taherids were failing to cope with threats from the Kharijites and the ʿAlids of the Caspian provinces, a feeling that facilitated the overthrowing of the Taherids in Khorasan by the Saffarid Yaʿqub b. Layṯ (q.v.), who in 259/873 captured Nishapur from Moḥammad b. Ṭāher II (*Tāriḵ-e Sistān*, pp. 219-23; Ebn al-Aṯir, VII, pp. 261-64; Bosworth, 1994, pp. 109-21; Tor, pp. 118-22, 134-53). Yaʿqub then became embroiled in ventures in the Caspian provinces and then in western Persia and Iraq, and speedily lost control of Khorasan (*Tāriḵ-e Sistān*, pp. 223 ff.; Ebn al-Aṯir, VII, pp. 268-69, 276-77, 290-92; Bosworth, 1994, pp. 123-26). For some two decades, the province was a battleground for contending military leaders, some, such as Aḥmad Ḵojestāni (q.v.), claiming to represent the former Taherid interest there (Ebn al-Aṯir, VII, pp. 296-97); others merely seeking their own aggrandizement, until in 283/896 Yaʿqub's brother and successor ʿAmr established his control over the province. This restored Saffarid power in Khorasan was, however, short-lived. In 287/900, the Samanid Amir Esmāʿil b. Aḥmad (q.v.) defeated ʿAmr in battle, so that the province then entered upon a century of Samanid domination, as an integral part of their empire centered on the Transoxianan cities of Bukhara and Samarqand (*Tāriḵ-e Sistān*, p. 234-35, 254-56; Naršaḵi, pp. 119-25; Ṭabari, III, pp. 2194-95; Ebn al-Aṯir, VII, pp. 500-503; Bosworth, 1994, pp. 217 35).

THE SAMANIDS

The eponym of the Samanids was Sāmān-ḵodā, usually understood as meaning the landlord (*dehqān*, q.v.) of the town of Sāmān. Sāmān has been claimed to have been located near Samarqand, Termeḏ, or Balḵ. Naršaḵi, for example, indicates that Sāmān-ḵoda hailed from Balḵ and built the village or estate of Sāmān there (Naršaḵi, tr., p. 59), but Menhāj-e Serāj Juzjāni (I, p. 201) identifies him as the chief (*ra'is*) of the district of Sāmān near Samarqand. The question is of some interest in terms of the ethnic origins of the Samanids. The later Samanids claimed, and probably believed, they were descended from Bahrām Čōbin (q.v.) and the Parthian Mihranid family (an idea accepted even by the usually sceptical Biruni, p. 39, tr., p. 48; see also Bosworth, 1973, pp. 58-59). Samarqand and the Zarafšān basin suggest a Sogdian background or even Turkish ancestry, while Balḵ and Ṭoḵarestān raise the possibility of Iranian, Hephthalite or other connections (Kamoliddin, pp. 79-114, has argued for a Buddhist-Manichean background and descent from the *yabḡu* Jabbā Khan; Togan, p. 283; see also Treadwell, 1991, pp. 64-71).

Another factor that speaks strongly in favor of a connection to Balḵ, is the widely reported account of Sāmān-ḵodā's friendship with the Omayyad governor Asad b. ʿAbd-Allāh Qaṣri (d. 120/737-38). According to Naršaḵi (tr., p. 59), Sāmān-ḵodā fled, for unspecified reasons, from Balḵ to Marv, where Asad treated him honorably and returned him to Balḵ. Sāmān converted to Islam at the hands of Asad and named his son after him. Naršaḵi's account is certainly plausible, since Asad is known to have held the governorship of Khorasan on two occasions (106-9/724-28 and 117-20/735-37), and, in both cases, he campaigned extensively in areas around Balḵ; Asad also died in Balḵ (Daniel, 2009).

The grandsons of Sāmān-ḵodā—Nuḥ, Aḥmad, Yaḥyā, and Elyās—joined the forces of Harṯama b. Aʿyan after he was sent by Hārun al-Rašid to put down the rebellion of Rafiʿ b. Layṯ. They were subsequently instrumental in arranging a negotiated end to the conflict. Their assistance had been specially requested by al-Maʾmun, and he was so pleased with the results that, as caliph, he instructed his governor in Khorasan, Ḡassān b. ʿAbbād, in 202/817 or 204/819, to reward them with districts to govern. Nuḥ was given Samarqand; Elyās, Herat; Yaḥyā, Šāš (Čāč); and Aḥmad, Farḡāna (Ebn al-Aṯir, VII, p. 279; Gardizi, p. 146; Juzjāni, I, p. 203; Mirḵᵛānd, pp. 1-2). Ṭāher b. Ḥosayn confirmed the appointments when he became governor of Khorasan, and sent a robe of honor to Nuḥ (Manini, I, p. 348) and the offices continued to be held during the governorships of Ṭalḥa and ʿAbd-Allāh b. Ṭāher. Ṭalḥa even visited Samarqand in 212/827-28 (Treadwell, p. 78).

The family of Abu'l-Fażl Elyās b. Asad appears to have acted more often as Taherid officers than as administrators of Herat. Ṭalḥa b. Ṭāher sent Elyās to Sistān in Ṣafar 208/July 823 to fight the Kharijites, but he was there only until Jomādā I 208/October 823. He is named, somewhat surprisingly, as a governor of Alexandria under ʿAbd-Allāh b. Ṭāher in 212/827 (Kendi, p. 184). During the governorship of ʿAbd-Allāh b. Ṭāher in Khorasan, Elyās and some cadet members of the Samanid family were again sent to Sistān, ca. 216/831 and then again between 222/837 and 225/840 (*Tāriḵ-e Sistān*, pp. 177-78, 182-83, 187-89). Elyās died in Herat in 241/855 (Samʿāni, VII, p. 26). His son Ebrāhim was the commander (*sepahsālār*) of the Taherid army fighting the Saffarid Yaʿqub b. Layṯ. He was defeated and pushed out of Herat and Bušanj in 253/867; he advised Moḥammad b. Ṭāher that Yaʿqub could not be defeated and recommended a policy of appeasement; and, after the fall of Nishapur in 259/873, he went with other army officers to seek clemency from the victorious Yaʿqub. He was given a robe of honor and sent to Sistān, so with that the Herat branch of the Samanids came to an end (*Tāriḵ-e Sistān*, pp. 208, 225).

It was in Transoxiana that the Samanids flourished greatly, helped latterly by the confused state of post-Taherid Khorasan under a succession of ambitious military leaders culminating in ʿAmr b. Layṯ (q.v.).

In 225/840, Nuḥ b. Asad assisted ʿAbd-Allāh in arresting the son of Afšin (q.v.; a former ruler of Ošrusana, q.v., in the service of the caliph al-Moʿtaṣem, then out of favor and on trial for treason; see Ṭabari, III, p. 1307). Nuḥ also sent an expedition against the town of Asfijāb (q.v.) in the middle Syr Darya valley and built defenses there against marauders from the Turkish steppes (Balāḏori, p. 422; Samʿāni, VII, p. 26; Ebn al-Aṯir, VI, p. 509). Asfijāb remained as a separate, dependent province of what became the Samanid empire, with its local Turkish ruler still enjoying a freedom, unique in the Samanid lands, from tax liabilities (Ebn Ḥawqal, II, p. 510; tr. Kramers, II, p. 488). After the death of Nuḥ b. Asad in 227/841-42, the governor of Khorasan ʿAbd-Allāh b. Ṭāher (q.v.) appointed the remaining two brothers in Transoxiana, Yaḥyā and Aḥmad, over Samarqand and Sogdiana; on the death of the former in 241/855, Šāš reverted to Aḥmad also. Aḥmad thus emerged as the commanding figure in the family, and all subsequent rulers of the dynasty descended from him. Yaḥyā had not apparently struck even a local copper coinage at Samarqand, whereas *folus* of Aḥmad begin there in 244/858-59. Aḥmad's son Naṣr (I) (r. 250-79/864-92) extended his power from his capital Samarqand westwards to Bukhara, which was later, under Naṣr's brother Esmāʿil b. Aḥmad (q.v.), to become the permanent capital of the Samanids. The ʿAbbasid caliph al-Moʿtamed (r. 256-79/870-92) formally invested Naṣr with the governorship of Transoxiana in 261/875 (Ṭabari, III, p. 1889), in opposition to the claims of the Saffarid Yaʿqub b. Layṯ who was at that point striking at the heartland of the caliphate in central Iraq. It was only around this time that direct caliphal interest in Transoxiana could no longer be sustained. The caliph al-Moʿtaṣem (r. 218-27/833-42) had, with some reluctance, contributed two million dirhams toward the digging of an irrigation canal in the province of Šāš (Ṭabari, III, p. 1326), and, up to the time of Naṣr b. Aḥmad, the ʿAbbasids still drew revenue from their crown demesnes in Transoxiana (see Barthold, pp. 95, 99, 212). Naṣr had begun to mint dirhams of a mixed ʿAbbasid-Samanid type from the 240s/860s onwards, and then at the formal accession of Esmāʿil b. Aḥmad (279/892), the regular minting of Samanid dirhams and dinars began, with acknowledgement of the ʿAbbasids as suzerains (Miles, p. 374).

Naṣr sent his brother Esmāʿil to take over Bukhara from a certain Ḥosayn b. Moḥammad Ḵawāreji (or Ḵᵛārazmi?), apparently an adherent of the Saffarids, and in summer 260/874 Esmāʿil entered the city and delivered the Friday sermon (*ḵoṭba*) for Naṣr instead of for Yaʿqub b. Layṯ. The brothers quarreled, however, leading to a military conflict that ended in the capture of Naṣr by Esmāʿil (autumn 275/888); Esmāʿil wisely retained his brother as the official ruler in Samarqand until Naṣr's death in 279/892, while himself remaining at Bukhara and eventually making it his capital (Naršaḵi, pp. 94-101; tr. pp. 79-86; Barthold, pp. 222-23).

Naṣr had appointed Esmāʿil as his heir, so that the latter succeeded unchallenged as amir (q.v.) of Transoxiana and Farḡāna. Esmāʿil (I)'s reign (279-95/892-907) marks the formal constituting of the Samanid state as a powerful force in the Islamic east, especially as his victory over the Saffarid ʿAmr b. Layṯ in 287/900, though technically an act of rebellion against the caliph's appointee over Khorasan and Transoxiana, in practice brought him recognition by al-Moʿtażed (r. 279-89/892-902) and what must have been approbation as governor of both those provinces (Ṭabari, III, p. 2195). This was essentially a confirmation of the fact that the ʿAbbasids, their direct authority now confined to Iraq and western Persia, could no longer exert any power over the east. Even so, right to the end, the Samanids usually paid due respect to the caliphs, placing their names in the *koṭba* and on the coinage (*sekka*), and claiming for themselves no higher title than that of amir; presents were sent to Baghdad, although there is no evidence that any taxation or tribute was ever forwarded. Hence, Amir Esmāʿil may be regarded as the real founder of the Samanid state and certainly as the ablest of his dynasty. The historical and literary sources praise him as such, and speak of his wisdom and just rule, awarding him the honorific titles of *amir-e ʿādel* 'The Just Amir' and *amir-e māżi* 'The Late Amir'. He may also now consciously have endeavoured to raise himself, as amir now of a united principality, to a level above the families of nobles and landowners, from which class his own family had earlier risen. They probably still regarded the Samanids as socially not much more than *primi inter pares*. According to Naršaḵi (p. 96; tr. Frye, p. 82), when Esmāʿil was still the theoretical subordinate of his brother Naṣr, he had already taken steps to reduce the power of the Bukharan leaders (*mehtarān*) because they had not sufficiently shown him the respect (*haybat*) due to a ruler.

The amirate was at this time young and vigorous, and under Esmāʿil its borders expanded in all directions and the northern frontier defended against the pressure of the nomads. In 280/893, Esmāʿil led a major expedition that captured Talas (Ṭarāz) from the Qarluq Turks (possibly led by Oğulčak Kadïr Khan, son of the Ilak-khan Bilge Kül Kadïr Khan; Golden, p. 352-57), capturing a great booty of slaves and beasts. He extended Samanid suzerainty over the Afšin, local rulers of Ošrusana, south of the middle Syr Darya; over the Khwarazmshahs (see CHORASMIA ii); and, as coins seem to indicate, over petty princes of the upper Oxus lands such as the Abu Dāwudids or Banijurids (on them, see Bosworth, 1996, p. 174) of Ḵottal and Toḵārestān, and the Farigunids of Guzgān (see ĀL-E FARIḠUN). Expansion westwards into the Caspian provinces and northern Persia was a special concern of Esmāʿil, who in 288/901 personally led armies into Gorgān (q.v.) and Ṭabarestān against the ʿAlid Moḥammad b. Zayd, restored the supremacy of the Sunna there, and compensated those who had suffered losses under the Zaydis (Madelung, 1975, p. 208). Samanid authority was likewise extended over Ray, with the caliph al-Moktafi (r. 289-95/902-8) at the beginning of 290/902 investing Esmāʿil as governor of Ray and Qazvin (Ṭabari, III, pp. 2220-21; Miles, 1938, pp. 132-33), the westernmost outposts of Samanid power, although these regions soon slipped away from Samanid hands. Esmāʿil died in 295/907 (see also ESMĀʿIL B. AḤMAD B. ASAD SĀMĀNI).

Esmāʿil was succeeded by his son Aḥmad (II) (r. 295-301/907-14). Despite the brevity of his reign, he nevertheless managed to bring Sistān temporarily under Samanid rule. After the defeat of ʿAmr, various short-reigned Saffarid princes held power in Sistān and southern Persia, but Aḥmad then intervened there, dispatching two expeditions in 298/911 and 300/912-13 under the amir's cousin, Abu Ṣāleḥ Manṣur b. Esḥāq b. Aḥmad (q.v.), who functioned ineffectively as governor in Sistān for a while (see SAFFARIDS). More pressing for Ahmad were measures to retrieve the position in the west. In Ray, a Samanid governor, Moḥammad b. ʿAli Ṣoʿluk, was probably in place by 298/910-11, and he remained there into the succeeding reign of Naṣr b. Aḥmad (Miles, 1938, pp. 135-36). In the Caspian provinces, however, the Zaydi Ḥasan b. ʿAli Oṭruš made firm his authority in Deylam (see DEYLAMITES) and Gilān (q.v.) and then extended eastwards into Ṭabarestān, which was under his control by Amir Aḥmad's death (Madelung, 1975, pp. 208-9); measures against him could only be undertaken in the next reign. Aḥmad's reign was cut short when his military slaves (*ḡolāms*) assassinated him at Farabr near Bukhara in 301/914, allegedly because he was showing excessive favor to the ulema and other religious dignitaries and because he attempted to restore Arabic as the language of the divans; obviously, Persian had by then established itself as the working language of these government departments (see Naršaḵi, pp. 110-11; tr. pp. 94-95; Gardizi, pp. 148-50; Barthold, p. 240). Aḥmad's murder earned him the posthumous title of *amir-e šahid* 'The Martyred Amir.' As noted above, his father had already become known as "The Just, or, the Late Amir," and this practice of giving honorifics (*laqab*s) after death was to become general amongst the Samanids, though some of the amirs also acquired regnal titles in their own lifetimes and used them on coinage, such as Nuḥ (I) b. Naṣr's one of *al-malek al-moʾayyad* 'The [Divinely] Supported King', and Nuḥ (II) b. Manṣur (I)'s one of *al-malek al-manṣur* 'The Victorious King' (see Bosworth, 1962, pp. 214-15).

The long reign which followed, that of Naṣr (II) b. Aḥmad (II), called *amir-e saʿid* 'The Fortunate Amir' (301-31/914-43), in many ways marks the zenith of Samanid power and glory, although the amir himself was no charismatic war leader or outstanding administrator. But he was fortunate to be served by highly competent officials, often from families with long traditions of service in the bureaucracy, who were appointed at least in part because of the medieval Islamic belief that such competence was a hereditary trait of such families. Hence, Naṣr was fortunate in having capable viziers such as Abu ʿAbd-Allāh

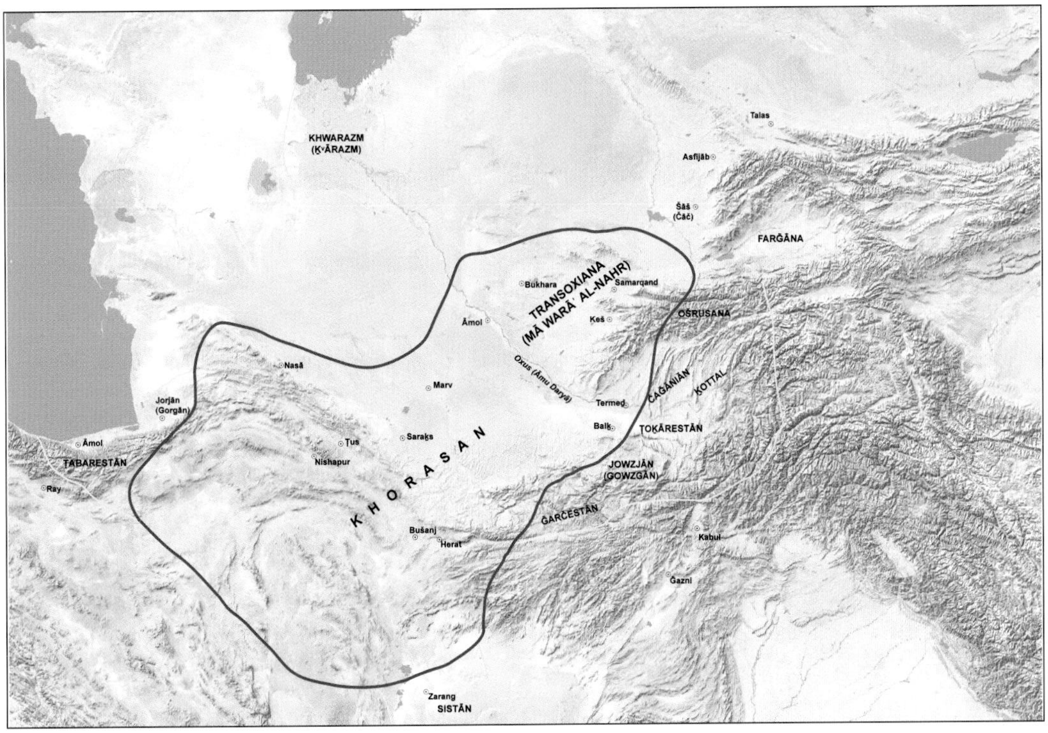

Figure 1. The Samanid Realm: Core territories (blue border); areas under local rulers, contested, or tributary (yellow border). After R. N. Frye, ed., *Cambridge History of Iran* IV, Cambridge, 1975, p. 139. (Map background data from US National Park Service World Physical Map.)

Jayhāni and his son Abu ʿAli Moḥammad, and Abu'l-Fażl Balʿami (q.v.), all famed as much for their own scholarship and patronage of learned and literary men as for their administrative skills. Thus, the first Jayhāni was vizier ca. 302-10/914-22 but was also the author of a geography, a *Ketāb al-masālek wa'l-mamālek,* which Moqaddasi (pp. 3-4) praises for its topographical and astronomical information, amongst much else; he saw a manuscript of it, in seven volumes, in the library of the Buyid Amir ʿAżod-al-Dawla (q.v., r. 338-72/949-83), but it is now known only from citations. Jayhāni apparently incorporated information personally gathered on his travels plus that gained from merchants and travelers to the land of the Turks and to India (Barthold, pp. 12-13).

The young amir faced a series of revolts on his accession, which only the skills of his vizier Jayhāni and military commanders such as Ḥamuya b. ʿAli enabled him to survive. These revolts were raised by discontented members of the Samanid family who felt that their adulthood gave them a greater claim to the throne than that of the eight-year-old boy. Thus, Naṣr's great-uncle Esḥāq b. Aḥmad came out immediately at Samarqand, aided by his two sons Elyās and Manṣur. The latter, the ex-governor of Sistān, raised his standard at Nishapur, and after his death there, the revolt was carried on by one of his military commanders; Elyās fled to Farḡāna after the suppression of the Samarqand outbreak and thence to Šāš and the Turks. Several years passed during which Naṣr's authority was unchallenged, but ca. 317/929 there was a further serious rebellion, this time in the capital Bukhara, involving three of Naṣr's own brothers (Gardizi, pp. 152-53); the suppression of this marks the opening of the ascendancy in Khorasan during the middle decades of the 4th/10th century of the Moḥtāj or Čaḡāni family, to whose head, Abu ʿAli Aḥmad, the amir entrusted the governorship of western Khorasan (see ĀL-E MOḤTAJ).

Through all these vicissitudes, a vigorous external Samanid policy was carried on. This involved, amongst other things, attempting to extend Samanid power into the rich and strategically important region of northern Persia with its main city, Ray. Moḥammad b. ʿAli Ṣoʿluk held Ray as a Samanid vassal intermittently till his death in 316/928, but thereafter the Samanid hold was increasingly challenged by various Deylami and Jili soldiers of fortune such as Asfār b. Širuya, Mākān b. Kāki and the Ziarid brothers Mardāvij and Vošmgir, all of whom at times held the city of Ray until 329/940, when Abu ʿAli Čāḡāni was sent with a strong force that defeated the allied forces of Mākān and Vošmgir. Samanid coins were then once again issued from the Ray/Moḥammadiya mint, but not for long. The strongest and most lasting of the Deylami adventurers, the three Buyid brothers, were now consolidating their power in western and central Persia (see BUYIDS). Rokn-al-Dawla Ḥasan b. Buya (r. 335-66/947-77) had definitively taken over Ray, making it the center of what became the northern Buyid amirate of Ray and Jebāl. Only sporadically thereafter did the Samanids control Ray.

Thus, the rise of the Buyids meant that the Samanids were in the long run unable to retain Ray and northern Persia. Their successes in the Caspian provinces were also intermittent, for the region became a battleground for various Deylami contenders, including the Buyids, the Zaydi Shiʿite Imams, and the Samanids themselves. Abu ʿAli Čāḡāni secured those provinces for Amir Naṣr, forcing Vošmgir to become the Samanids' vassal. The latter in fact gave military aid to Vošmgir against the Buyids, and control over the region oscillated between the various parties involved, punctuated by a general peace in 344/955 between Rokn-al-Dawla and the Samanid ʿAbd-al-Malek (I) b. Nuḥ (I), which did not however last. Vošmgir was once more driven out by the Buyids, and, after his death in 356/967, there was a division in the Ziarid family between his sons, with the Samanids at the outset favoring Qābus and the Buyids favouring Abu Manṣur Bisotun b. Vošmgir (q.v.; r. 356-67/967-78), who married ʿAżod-al-Dawla's daughter. Qābus eventually succeeded as ruler in the Caspian provinces on his brother's death, but offended the powerful ʿAżod-al-Dawla two years later, in 369/980, and fled to a seventeen-year exile in Samanid Khorasan. Samanid forces under the generals Tāš and Fāʾeq (q.v.) were sent with the aim of restoring Qābus to his domains but were defeated. The Samanid amirate was by now in increasing internal difficulties, and henceforth the amirs could not exert any influence beyond western Khorasan (Madelung, pp. 211-15; Busse, p. 290).

The closing years of the reign of Naṣr b. Aḥmad saw efforts by Ismaʿili agents (who apparently worked independently of the Fatimid movement in the lands further west) to spread their *daʿwa* (see DĀʿI). Evidence for this radical Shiʿite movement rests on sources that are non-historical (Ebn al-Nadim's *Fehrest* [q.v.], Ṯaʿālebi's *Ādāb al-moluk*, and Neẓām-al-Molk's *Siyāsat-nāma*), but everything points to the historicity of Ismaʿilism as a significant current of thought, philosophical rather than messianic in nature, in Samanid Khorasan and Transoxiana. The Ismaʿili *dāʿis* or propagandists made converts at the highest levels of Samanid court society, culminating in their securing the adhesion of the amir himself, and recruited adherents amongst others of the elite such as army commanders, *dehqāns*, divan secretaries, and urban headmen. This provoked a reaction among the Sunni ulema and their allies, the Turkish commanders of the army. The details are confused, but there was certainly a general massacre of the Ismailis and their adherents in Khorasan and Transoxiana. If the amir was not forced to abdicate in favour of his son Nuḥ (I), he did apparently live out the rest of his life as a secluded ascetic and invalid, dying in 331/943, possibly still as an Ismaʿili sympathizer. It is clear that much of the achievement of his reign can be laid at the door of Naṣr's viziers and military commanders rather than at that of the amir himself (Naršaḵi, pp. 111-12; tr. 95-96; Gardizi, pp. 150-54; Barthold, pp. 240-44; Stern, pp. 77-80; Frye, 1975, pp. 141-42; 1997, pp. 52-56; Daftary, pp. 120-23; Crone and Treadwell, pp. 37-48, 52-56, 61-67; see also for more details, NAṢR [I] B. AHMAD [I] B. ESMĀʿIL).

Naṣr's reign in many ways marks the apogee of Samanid power and splendor. As already noted, Naṣr and other Samanid rulers enjoyed over a long period the services of notable viziers, several of them from families with traditions of vizieral service such as the Jayhānis, Balʿamis and ʿOtbis; many of these made their mark as much in the academic and literary world as in the realm of administration and military leadership. Under their direction, what must have been a corps of skilled secretaries (Ar. *kottāb,* Per. *dabirān;* see DABIR ii.) and officials raised the bureaucracy in Bukhara to a high level of specialized functioning and complex administrative techniques. Naršaḵi, the historian of Bukhara, enumerates ten divans (see DIVĀN ii.) of the Samanid central administration housed in what he calls the *sarāy-e ʿommāl*, "officials' building," near the portal of the ruler's palace and the government headquarters complex built by the Amir in the Rigestān of Bukhara. All this could not have evolved *ex nihilo* but must have been based on the ʿAbbasid divans in Baghdad, mediated through the example of the Taherid ones in Nishapur. The Samanid official Abu ʿAbd-Allāh Ḵᵛārazmi has a chapter on *ketāba*, or chancery practice, in his encyclopaedia of the sciences, *Mafātiḥ al-ʿolum* (ca. 977), that deals with administrative and financial techniques, documents, registers, methods of correspondence, etc., that clearly stemmed largely from ʿAbbasid models, but it also includes specific references to practices specific to the eastern Iranian lands, such as that of the *divān al-māʾ*, or office concerned with the maintenance of the irrigation systems and the division of waters in the Marv oasis in Khorasan and the valley of the Zarafšān river in Sogd (see IRRIGATION); and the section on weights and measures used by government surveyors and taxation assessors refers in part to practice in the Samanid provinces of Khorasan and Toḵārestān on the upper Oxus and to the adjacent province, theoretically subject to the Samanids, of Khwarazm (see Bosworth 1969a, pp. 115, 147-54).

It was this bureaucracy, and its subordinate organs in the provinces, that collected taxes from the rich agricultural oases of Sogdiana, Farḡāna, and Khorasan, together with customs duties and transit duties *(mokus)* levied on trade entering the Islamic lands from Inner Asia and beyond, a trade that had been in existence since pre-Islamic times and in which the Sogdians of Transoxiana had played a leading role. These last comprised luxury goods, such as furs, Chinese silks, and even Chinese porcelain, but above all, Turkish slaves, Transoxiana being one of the principal entry points for this traffic. The geographers describe how dues were levied on slave imports at the Oxus crossings. Authors such as Ebn Ḥawqal (q.v.) and Moqaddasi, who travelled within the Samanid lands in the third quarter of the 10th century CE, lavish praise on the amirs as just and enlightened rulers, in whose lands taxation was light, with provisions and everything for ease of life plentiful and at hand (see Barthold, pp. 234-40; Bosworth, 1963, pp. 27-33; Negmatov, pp. 84-85). This direct taxation was supplemented by the tribute and presents that the amirs, in their heyday, were able to require as overlords from local rulers in such regions as the upper Oxus lands and northern parts of modern Afghanistan such as the princes of Čaḡāniān, Ḵottal, Gowzgān (Jowzjān, q.v.), and Garčestān (q.v.); the regions such as the middle Syr Darya basin, including from the *dehqān*s of Ošrusana (q.v.) and Ilāq; and the ancient kingdom of Khwarazm (see CHORASMIA). In all these cases, the Samanid amirs preferred to leave these local structures of power in place rather than to incorporate them within what would have become an extended, and hence unwieldy, empire.

The power and authority of the amirs rested, of course, on the armed forces at their disposal, needed both to maintain the ruler in power against other members of the Samanid family who coveted the throne and to guard the northern frontiers against pressure from the Turks in the outer steppe and to carry out the amirs' "forward policy" in the Caspian coastlands region and northern Persia. The first troops of the Samanids stemmed from the free Iranian population of Transoxiana, the *dehqān* (q.v.) class. At the time when the Samanids, themselves probably *dehqān*s, were first emerging as governors in Transoxiana and the upper Oxus region, this class of landowners was also providing high-level commanders for the ʿAbbasid armies in the central lands of the caliphate, seen in the careers of the Afšin (q.v.) Ḵayḏar from the ruling family in Ošrusana and of various members of the Sajid family from this same period. The *dehqān*s of the Samanid lands functioned as commanders for the amirs' armies and brought with them levies of their local tenantry and peasantry to swell the rank-and-file.

There was an ever-present need to maintain forces along the lengthy frontiers of the amirate against the Turks, not only from the obvious motive of state security but also because waging war (*jehād* or *ḡazā*) against non-Muslims was a religious duty for Muslims in such regions. Hence, there was a stimulus for the formation of bands of ghazis or volunteer fighters for the faith who manned the *rebāṭ*s or frontier posts in provinces such as Asfijāb and other districts along the Syr Darya valley. The *rebāṭ*s of Asfijāb, numbered, according to Moqaddasi (p. 273), 1,700; they were manned substantially by volunteers from Naḵšab, Bukhara, and Samarqand (Barthold, pp. 175-76; Bosworth, 1963, pp. 31-32). The degree of state control of such enthusiasts probably varied; contingents of volunteers from Bukhara, under their own commander and with their own banners, are mentioned as parading alongside regular troops (Bosworth, 1969b, pp. 20-21). Such warriors must have been usually self-financed and have borne their own weapons and equipment unless helped by funds from such pious endowments as the *rebāṭ*s; and a similar lack of central control must have been the case with the bands of *ʿayyār*s (q.v.) mentioned as elements in the urban societies of Bukhara and Samarqand (Bosworth, 1969b, p. 21; Paul, pp. 14-20).

Neither of these two elements, the troops raised and led by local landowners, the *dehqān*s, and the religiously-motivated volunteers, owed any direct, unbreakable loyalty to the Samanid state as such, and the latter were in any case only of use against pagans outside the Abode of Islam, and their usefulness and their activities seem to have decreased as the Turks of the steppes gradually accepted Islam (Paul, pp. 23-24). Troops from these sources were, however, supplemented by Turkish slave soldiers *(ḡelmān, mamālek)* from an early date, certainly from the time of Esmāʿil b. Aḥmad onwards, since the Turk Simjur Davāti, founder of a line destined to play a leading role in later Samanid military and public affairs (see SIMJURIDS), is described as his *mawlā* (here in the sense of slave; see *Tāriḵ-e Sistān*, p. 293; tr. Gold, p. 237). These could be purchased from slave markets on the fringes of the outer steppes or captured in raids, such as that of Esmāʿil to Talas (see above). We know that Sebüktegin, subsequently the founder of the Ghaznavid dynasty, purchased in the first place by the Samanid general Alptigin (q.v.) for his personal following, came from Barsḵān on the shores of the Issiq Köl, in the region of Semirečye, now within the Kyrgyz Republic. Over the course of time, the amirs came to depend increasingly on these Turkish troops. From the higher ranks of these were recruited important offices of state and court such as the *amir-e ḥaras,* commander of the police and internal security guard (see Barthold, pp. 227-28 [who, however, attached too much importance to the romanticized and embroidered account of the training of Turkish *ḡolām*s in Neẓām-al-Molk's *Siyāsat-nāma*]; Bosworth, 1969b, pp. 9-11; Frye, 1975, pp. 149-51; BARDA AND BARDA-DĀRI iii.).

However, at the side of those soldiers who were undoubtedly of servile origin, the amirs were from an early date served also by personal retainers who are variously called in the sources *mawāli* or *čākarān* (see ČĀKAR) and who were apparently free vassals. The exact significance of the terminology here is uncertain, but it may be that the status of *čākar* had its roots in pre-Islamic Iranian and Turkish Central Asia (as maintained by Beckwith, pp. 32-40). Esmāʿil b. Aḥmad seems to have been especially concerned to build up around himself a body of reliable guards and retainers, as part of the policy of elevating himself above the landowning classes of Transoxiana from which his family had sprung and of reducing dependence on the provincial magnates (see Paul, pp. 27-30; la Vaissère, 2005b).

It was the leading army commanders who filled some of the most important offices in the Samanid state after that of the amir himself and his vizier, such as the command-in-chief *(sepahsālāri)* of the army and the governorship of the rich province of Khorasan. In the halcyon years of the amirate, the army of Khorasan was used for expansion westward into northern Persia and southward into Sistān. In the later decades of the 10th century CE, holders of this governorship, whether from native Iranian local potentates and landowners like the Čaḡānis and Abu Manṣur b. ʿAbd-al-Razzāq (q.v.), or from the Turkish slave soldiery such as the Simjuris, Tāš, Alptigin, and Fāʾeq, increasingly used their power and resources to further their own ambitions, to interfere in the workings of the central administration, and to make and unmake amirs. A precedent for this last had been set as early as 301/914 when Aḥmad (II) b. Esmāʿil had been murdered by his own *ḡolāms*; by the later part of the 10th century CE, a governor of Khorasan such as Abu ʿAli Moḥammad Simjuri arrogated to himself the style, titulature, and powers of an independent sovereign.

Whereas volunteers tended to live off the land and were lured on by the prospects of plunder, and locally raised Iranian troops could disperse after a campaign back to their estates and villages, the cost of maintaining a standing, professional army, whether of free retainers or of Turkish *ḡolāms*, was formidable. These last had to be paid with cash allowances every quarter *(bistgāni*, q.v.), and were liable to become mutinous or to refuse to go out on campaign if these payments fell into arrears. The commitment of paying the army had to be a first charge on the revenues collected from the Samanid lands, but in the course of the 4th/10th century, the state became increasingly unable to find enough money for this. External conquests no longer brought in fresh revenue so that the amirs resorted to the expedients of levying new and unusual taxes (Barthold, pp. 339, 246-47), whilst the leading army commanders quarreled over the allocation of provincial governorships, from which they could raise taxation to pay their troops; the result was almost continuous crisis in the Samanid state from the mid-10th century onwards (Paul, pp. 30-32).

Barthold noted that, with the reign of Nuḥ (I) b. Naṣr (II), posthumously called *amir-e ḥamid* 'The Praiseworthy Amir' (r. 331-43/943-54), there were distinct signs of the weakening of the dynasty. With the anti-Ismaʿili reaction and exaltation of the orthodox Sunni ulema, the vizierate passed to a religious scholar *(faqih),* Abu'l-Fażl Moḥammad Solami, more noted for his piety than his administrative talents. The army had to be used to quell a revolt against Samanid overlordship in Khwarazm and against the Turks on the northern borders, but when the people of Nishapur complained of the governor Abu ʿAli Čāḡāni's oppression in Khorasan, and Nuḥ tried to replace him with the Turkish general Ebrāhim b. Simjur, there was a financial crisis when the army refused to move until it received its pay arrears, compelling the administration to increase taxation. Even so, the army would not march, and Abu ʿAli was able temporarily to place on the throne in Bukhara a Samanid prince and uncle of Amir Nuḥ, Ebrāhim b. Aḥmad (II). Although Nuḥ retrieved his position, Abu ʿAli was still powerful and had the backing of the local princes of his native upper Oxus region, so that peace had to be made, with Abu ʿAli recovering his governorship, only to lose it when the amir felt strong enough to revoke his appointment (Naršaḵi, pp. 113-15; tr. pp. 97-98; Gardizi, pp. 154-59; Barthold, pp. 246-49; Frye, 1975, p. 151).

On Nuḥ's death, his eldest son ʿAbd-al-Malek (I), called *amir-e rašid* "The Rightly-Guided Amir" (r. 343-50/954-61), succeeded. He confirmed the deposition of Abu ʿAli and appointed Moḥammad b. ʿOzayr as his vizier. Despite securing help from the Buyids, Abu ʿAli was unable to maintain himself in Khorasan, and died of plague in 344/955. A succession of governors in Khorasan ensued, until the commander Alptigin achieved this post in 350/961, placing his own nominee, Abu ʿAli Moḥammad b. Moḥammad Balʿami (see AMIRAK BALʿAMI), in the vizierate. The great military leaders were clearly now getting the upper hand in the state, and this was to be the pattern for the remaining four decades or so of Samanid rule (Naršaḵi, p. 115; tr. p. 98; Gardizi, pp. 159-60; Barthold, pp. 249-50). It also seems that, on the evidence of Neẓām-al-Molk, toward the end of ʿAbd-al-Malek's reign, there was a recrudescence of Ismaʿili activity, or possibly Ḵorrami (q.v.) disturbances, in such provincial regions of the Samanid empire as the upper Oxus lands and Farḡāna (Crone and Treadwell, pp. 48-50).

The country fell into chaos when ʿAbd-al-Malek died in 961 in an accident. Naršaḵi (p. 115, tr. p. 98) says that "the army became turbulent and rebelled; everyone coveted the kingdom, and civil strife appeared." Alptigin and Balʿami tried to place ʿAbd-al-Malek's young son Naṣr on the throne, doubtless seeing in him a willing tool for their own interests, but their putsch failed, and the late amir's next brother was placed on the throne as Manṣur (I) b. Nuḥ (I) (r. 350-65/961-76), called *amir-e sadid* 'The Upright Amir.' Alptigin was in disgrace and forced to withdraw to Ghazna, but his son and successor, Abu Esḥāq Ebrāhim, could only retain his position there against the returning, dispossessed, former local ruler by seeking help from Bukhara in 354/965, after which the line of Turkish commanders in Ghazna continued to acknowledge the Samanid amirs as their suzerain and to place their names on the coinage almost till the final demise of the Samanid dynasty. From his base in Khorasan, the Samanid governor Moḥammad b. Ebrāhim b. Simjur was able to support the Ziarid ruler Vošmgir against threats from Rokn-al-Dawla in 356/967, and when Vošmgir died, his son Bisotun was compelled to pay tribute to Bukhara. The effective policies of the Samanid governors in Nishapur led to a peace agreement with the Buyids in 361/971-72 by the terms of which, Rokn-al-Dawla agreed to pay an annual tribute to the Samanid amirs, but four years later, Manṣur died, and it is unclear how long the Buyids had continued to pay these substantial sums (Naršaḵi, pp. 115-16; tr. pp. 98-99; Gardizi, pp. 161-64; Barthold, pp. 250-52; see for a more detailed consideration of this reign, MANSUR [I] B. NUḤ [I]).

The reign of Nuḥ (II) b. Manṣur (I), who was called *amir-e rażi* 'The Well-Pleasing Amir', was the last substantial one for a Samanid amir (365-87/976-97). It witnessed the disintegration of the amirate under the double pressure of the Samanids' own ambitious commanders internally, and the advent of the Turkish Qara-khanids (see ILAK-KHANS) from outside the empire. With, yet again, only a youth on the throne, executive power was at the outset in the hands of a vizier, Abu'l-Ḥosayn ʿAbd-Allāh ʿOtbi (see ʿOTBI), whose authority was, however, contested by the amir's Turkish military commanders. ʿOtbi was successful in removing Moḥammad b. Ebrāhim Simjuri from the governorship of Khorasan in favor of his own nominee, Tāš. The peace treaty with Rokn-al-Dawla lapsed at some unspecified point, hence war was resumed against the Buyids, now headed by the formidable ʿAżod-al-Dawla; but it went badly for the Samanids, with ʿOtbi being murdered shortly afterwards with the connivance of Moḥammad b. Ebrāhim b. Simjuri and Fāʾeq Ḵāṣṣa (q.v.). The ensuing years witnessed a power struggle between the Simjuris, Fāʾeq, Begtuzun (q.v.) and other ambitious generals. The territory controlled by Nuḥ shrank, and, inevitably, the tax basis with which he hoped to pay his troops.

Thus, at least in the territories across the Oxus, there was a growing power vacuum, and within this there appeared in 382/992 a new factor, that of the Qara-khanids, a Turkish steppe confederation nomadizing beyond the Syr Darya whose nucleus was probably made up of the Qarluq tribe. Abu ʿAli Moḥammad b. Moḥammad Simjuri intrigued with Buğrā Khan Hārun (q.v.) to partition the Samanid dominions, the Khan to have Transoxiana and Abu ʿAli to have Khorasan. Nuḥ was driven from his capital Bukhara by the Turks, but given a respite by the khan's illness and death. Now faced with a coalition of Abu ʿAli and Fāʾeq, Nuḥ could only call upon Sebüktegin and his son Maḥmud, who defeated the rebel commanders. When a fresh Qara-khanid incursion took place in 386/996, the amir's impotence was such that Sebüktegin and Maḥmud ended by making an agreement with the new Qara-khanid leader, Arslan Ilig Naṣr, that would have left Nuḥ with the Zarafšān valley only, with all the Syr Darya basin ceded to the Qara-khanids; shortly after this, in 387/997, Nuḥ died (Naršaḵi, p. 117, tr. pp. 99-100; Manini, I, pp. 163-255; Gardizi, pp. 167-69; Barthold, pp. 252-54, 257-64; Frye, 1975, pp. 156-58; see also NUḤ (II) B. MANṢUR (I)).

The remaining, short-reigned amirs could only struggle hopelessly against the approaching demise of their dynasty. Nuḥ's son Manṣur (II) (r. 387-89/997-99) followed his father. Much of the power in his shrunken realm was exercised by Fāʾeq, and it was Fāʾeq and Begtuzun who deposed Manṣur after two years, raising to the throne his younger brother ʿAbd-al-Malek (II) (r. 389-90/999-1000). Maḥmud b. Sebüktegin was now ruling Khorasan as its independent ruler, and when Fāʾeq died, the Arslan Ilig Naṣr occupied Bukhara unopposed, carried off ʿAbd-al-Malek and other Samanid princes, and thus ended the Samanid dynasty. The later amirs had failed to retain the support of their subjects, and an appeal to the state-salaried *ḵaṭibs* or preachers in Bukhara to rouse the populace for resistance, when the Qara-khanids appeared for a second time, fell on deaf ears (see Bosworth, 1963, p. 34). The former amir's brother Esmāʿil, called *al-montaṣer* 'The Victorious', succeeded in escaping from Qara-khanid captivity and over the five years 390-95/1000-1005 attempted a revanche and the restoration of his house, procuring the help of the Oghuz Turks, achieving some victories and even reoccupying Bukhara at one point; but in the end he was overwhelmed by Arslan Ilig Naṣr's superior forces, and amid what seems to have been a general apathy of the subject population, the rule of the Samanids came to its definitive end (Gardizi, pp. 171-73; Manini, I, pp. 268-347; Barthold, pp. 264-70; Nazim, pp. 42-47; Frye, 1975, pp. 157-60; see also MANṢUR (II) B. NUḤ (II)).

Throughout the Samanid period, Khorasan enjoyed a great cultural and intellectual efflorescence, building on foundations laid in the Taherid period. It continued to be a great center for orthodox Sunni legal and Quranic studies; four of the six compilers of the canonical collections of Hadith, either stemmed from or had connections with the eastern Islamic lands (Mottahedeh, pp. 66-70). The theological pietistic Sunni movement, the Karrāmiya (q.v.) was initiated in Khorasan with its intellectual center at Nishapur; several towns, such as Nishapur and Bayhaq, had within them Shiʿite communities, with important families of Sayyeds; and Khorasanian ascetics and mystics (e.g., Abu Saʿid Abi'l-Ḵayr, Bāyazid Besṭāmi, qq.v.) played significant roles in the development of Sufism (Madelung, 1988, pp. 39-46; Chabbi). The desire to perpetuate the fame and learning of notable scholars and theologians was a strong factor in the genre of local histories, which flourished in Khorasan from this time onwards, seen in those known to have been composed in centers such as Nishapur, Bayhaq, Herat, and Balḵ, several of which are extant or whose material is contained in later works (Barthold, pp. 13 ff.; Browne, I, pp. 416 ff; Ṣafā, passim; Pourshariati; and the special issue of *Iranian Studies,* 32/1-2, 2000, devoted to local historiography of the mediaeval period). Virtually all this scholarship was written in Arabic; several local histories were later translated into Persian. There is a large representation of Khorasanian poets and stylists writing in Arabic from the Samanid and early Ghaznavid periods in *Yatimat al-dahr,* the literary-biographical anthology by the Nishapuri author Abu Manṣur Ṯaʿālebi (d. 426/1038), and in its continuations by ʿAli b. Ḥasan Bāḵarzi (q.v.; likewise from the Nishapur region, d. 467/1074) and ʿEmād-al-Din Moḥammad Kāteb Eṣfahāni (q.v.; d. 597/1201).

Samanid Khorasan also played a significant role in the rise of New Persian language and literature, a reflection of the Samanids' patronage of the pioneer poets in New Persian, Daqiqi (q.v.) and Rudaki, at their court and that court's part in the commissioning of epitomized translations of Ṭabari's *Taʾriḵ* and *Tafsir* (Lazard; Daniel, 2008; Peacock). Above all, the origins of Ferdowsi's version of the national epic, the *Šāh-nāma,* lie in Khorasan, where in 346/947 the local governor of Ṭus, the *dehqān* Abu Manṣur Moḥammad b. ʿAbd-al-Razzāq (q.v.; d. 350/961), commissioned translations of the Pahlavi text of the royal epic, *Xwadāy-nāmag*, into New Persian (Browne, I, pp. 445 ff.; Minorsky, pp. 159-79; Rypka, pp. 133 ff.; Ṣafā, I, pp. 206-7, 163-76, 610-20).

Descendants of the Samanid house continued to reside in the Zarafšān basin and to enjoy respect for their ancient name, but a decisive break in the history of Central Asia had been made. Henceforth, regions north of the Oxus which had for millennia been bastions of Indo-Iranian population and language, and ruled by monarchs from this ethnic and linguistic background, were to pass under the control of an alien power from the steppes, that of the Inner Asian Turks. The process of Turkification may have begun on the fringes of Transoxiana and of Khwarazm with the influx during Samanid times of Turkish auxiliaries along the frontiers, but it then speeded up so that (whilst New Persian has remained a language of culture in Central Asia almost up to the present day, and in the cities at least is still used by many speakers as a second or third language after Turkish and Russian) only reduced areas of monoglot Iranian speakers now survive, most notably in the modern Republic of Tajikistan and in pockets of the upper Zarafšān valley in Uzbekistan.

See also SAMANIDS, TAHERIDS.

Bibliography: Sources. Abu'l-ʿAbbās Aḥmad b. Yaḥyā b. Jāber Balāḏori, *Ketāb fotuḥ al-boldān*, ed. M. J. de Goeje, Leiden, 1866. Abu'l-Fażl Moḥammad Bayhaqi, *Tāriḵ-e Bayhaqi*, ed. ʿAli-Akbar Fayyāż, Mashhad, 1971; tr. C. E. Bosworth with full revision by Mohsen Ashtiany, as *The History of Beyhaqi: The History of Sultan Masʿud of Ghazna, 1030-1041*, 3 vols., Boston, 2011. Abu Rayḥān Biruni, *Ketāb al-āṯār al-bāqia ʿan al-qorun al-ḵālia*, ed. Eduard Sachau, Leipzig, 1878, tr. idem, as *The Chronology of Ancient Nations*, London, 1879. Ebn Abi Ṭāher Ṭayfur, *Ketāb Baḡdād*, Beirut, 1968. Ebn al-Aṯir, *Ketāb al-kāmel fi'l-taʾriḵ*, ed. C. J. Tornberg, 13 vols., Beirut, 1965. Abu'l-Qāsem b. Ḥawqal Naṣibi, *Ketāb ṣurat al-arż*, ed. J. H. Kramers, Leiden, 1938; tr. J. H. Kramers and Gaston Wiet, as *La configuration de la terre*, 2 vols., Paris and Beirut, 1964. Abu Saʿid ʿAbd-al-Ḥayy Gardizi, *Zayn al-aḵbār*, ed. ʿAbd-al-Ḥayy Ḥabibi, Tehran, 1968. *Ḥodud al-ʿālam men al-mašreq ela'l-maḡreb*, ed. Manučehr Sotuda, Tehran, 1962; tr. with commentary Vladimir Minorsky, as *Hudūd al-ʿĀlam: The Regions of the World*, 2nd ed., London, 1970. Moḥammad b. ʿAbdus Jahšiāri, *Ketāb al-wozarāʾ*, ed. M. Saqqa, Cairo, 1938. Menhāj-e Serāj Juzjāni, *Ṭabaqāt-e nāṣeri*, ed. ʿAbd-al-Ḥayy Ḥabibi, 2nd ed., 2 vols., Kabul, 1963-64. Shaikh Aḥmad b. ʿAli Manini, *Šarḥ al-Yamini al-mosammā be'l-Fatḥ al-wahbi ʿalā Taʾriḵ Abi Naṣr al-ʿOtbi*, 2 vols. in one, Cairo, 1869. Abu'l-Ḥasan ʿAli Masʿudi, *Moruj al-ḏahab wa maʿāden al-jawhar*, ed. and tr. Charles Barbier de Meynard and Abel Pavet de Courteille, as *Les prairies d'or*, 9 vols., Paris, 1861-1917. Mir Moḥammad b. Sayyed Borhān-al-Din Ḵᵛāvandšāh Mirḵᵛānd, *Rawżat al-ṣafā*, part ed. and tr. M. Defrémery, as *Histoire des Samanides*, Paris, 1845. Abu ʿAbd-Allāh Moḥammad Moqaddasi, *Aḥsan al-taqāsim fi maʿrefat al-aqālim*, ed. M. J. de Goeje, Leiden, 1877. Ḥamd-Allāh Mostawfi, *Tāriḵ-e gozida*, ed. ʿAbd-al-Ḥosayn Navāʾi, Tehran, 1960. Abu Bakr Jaʿfar Naršaḵi, *Tārik-e Boḵārā*, ed. M.-T. Modarres Rażawi, 2nd ed., Tehran, 1972; tr. R. N. Frye, as *The History of Bukhara*, Cambridge, Mass., 1954. Abu Saʿd ʿAbd-al-Karim b. Moḥammad Tamimi Samʿāni, *Ketāb-al-ansāb*, ed. ʿAbd-al-Raḥmān Yamāni, 13 vols., Hyderabad, 1962-82. ʿAbd-al-Malek b. Moḥammad Ṯaʿālebi, *Laṭāʾef al-maʿāref*, tr. C. E. Bosworth, as *The Book of Curious and Entertaining Information*, Edinburgh, 1968. Moḥammad b. Jarir Ṭabari, *Ketāb taʾriḵ al-rosol wa'l-moluk*, eds. M. J. de Goeje et al., 3 vols. in 15, Leiden, 1879-1901. *Tāriḵ-e Sistān*, ed. M.-T. Bahār, Tehran, 1935; tr. Milton Gold, as *The Tārikh-e Sistān*, Rome, 1976. Aḥmad b. Abi Yaʿqub Yaʿqubi, *Ketāb al-boldān*, ed. M. J. De Goeje, Leiden, 1892. Idem, *Taʾriḵ al-Yaʿqubi*, ed. M. Th. Houtsma, as *Historiae*, 2 vols., Leiden, 1883.

Studies. Saleh Said Agha, *The Revolution which Toppled the Umayyads: Neither Arab nor ʿAbbāsid*, Leiden, 2003. V. V. Barthold, *Turkestan Down to the Mongol Invasion*, 3rd ed., London, 1969, pp. 209-70. C. I. Beckwith, "Aspects of the Early History of the Central-Asian Guard Corps in Islam," *Archivum Eurasiae Medii Ævi* 4, 1984, pp. 29-43. C. E. Bosworth, "The Rise of the Karramiyya in Khorasan," *Muslim World* 50, 1960, pp. 6-14. Idem, "The Titulature of the Early Ghaznavids," *Oriens* 15, 1962, pp. 21-33. Idem, *The Ghaznavids: Their Empire in Afghanistan and Eastern Iran 994-1040*, Edinburgh, 1963. Idem, "Abū ʿAbdallāh al-Khwārazmī on the Technical Terms of the Secretary's Art: A Contribution to the Administrative History of Mediaeval Islam," *JESHO* 12, 1969a, pp. 113-64. Idem, "An Alleged Embassy from the Emperor of China to the Amir Nasr b. Ahmad: A Contribution to Samanid Military History," in *Yād-nāma-ye irāni-ye Minorsky*, ed. M. Minovi and I. Afšār, Tehran, 1969b, pp. 1-13. Idem, "An Early Arabic Mirror for Princes: Ṭāhir Dhū l-Yamīnain's Epistle to his Son ʿAbdallāh," *JNES* 29, 1970, pp. 25-41. Idem, "The Heritage of Rulership in Early Islamic Iran and the Search for Dynastic Connections with the Past," *Iran*, 11, 1973, pp. 58-59. Idem, "The Ṭāhirids and Ṣaffārids," in R. N. Frye, ed., *The Cambridge History of Iran* IV: *From the Arab Invasion to the Saljuqs*, Cambridge, 1975, pp. 90-135. Idem, *The History of the Saffarids of Sistan and the Maliks of Nimruz*, Columbia Lectures on Iranian Studies 8, Costa Mesa, Calif. and New York, 1994. Idem, *The New Islamic Dynasties*, Edinburgh, 1996, pp. 170-71. E. G. Browne, *A Literary History of Persia*, 4 vols., London, 1902-24. H. Busse, "Iran under the Būyids," in R. N. Frye, ed., *The Cambridge History of Iran* IV, Cambridge, 1975, pp. 250-304. Jacqueline Chabbi, "Remarques sur le dévoloppement historique des mouvements ascétiques et mystiques au Khurasan: IIIe/IXe siècle-IVe/Xe siècle," *Studia Islamica* 46, 1977, pp. 5-72. Patricia Crone and Luke Treadwell, "A New Text on Ismailism at the Samanid Court," in Chase F. Robinson, ed., *Texts, Documents and Artefacts: Islamic Studies in Honour of D. S. Richards*, Leiden and Boston, 2002, pp. 37-67.

Farhad Daftary, *The Ismāʿīlīs: Their History and Doctrines*, Cambridge, 1990, pp. 120-23. Elton L. Daniel, "The Sāmānid 'Translations' of al-Ṭabari," in Hugh Kennedy, ed., *Al-Ṭabarī: A Medieval Muslim Historian and His Work*, Princeton, 2008, pp. 263-98. Idem, "Asad b. ʿAbdallāh," in Kate Fleet, et al., eds., *Encyclopaedia of Islam Three*, Leiden, 2009, s.v. R. N. Frye, "The Sāmānids," in R. N. Frye, ed., *The Cambridge History of Iran* IV: *From the Arab Invasion to the Saljuqs*, Cambridge, 1975, pp. 136-61. Idem, *Bukhara, the Medieval Achievement*, repr. Costa Mesa, Calif., 1997. P. B. Golden, "The Karakhanids and Early Islam," in Denis Sinor, ed., *The Cambridge History of Early Inner Asia*, Cambridge, 1990, pp. 343-70. Idem, *An Introduction to the History of the Turkic Peoples*, Wiesbaden, 1992. Ernst Herzfeld, "Khorasan: Denkmalsgeographische Studien zur Kulturgeschichte des Islam in Iran," *Der Islam* 11, 1921, pp. 107-74. Robert Hillenbrand, "Content versus Context in Samanid Epigraphic Pottery," in A. C. S. Peacock and D. G. Tor, eds., *Medieval Central Asia and the Persianate World: Iranian Tradition and Islamic Civilisation*, London, 2015, pp. 56-107. Mongi Kaabi, "Les origins ṭāhirides dans le daʿwa ʿabbāside," *Arabica* 19, 1972, pp. 145-64. Idem, *Les Ṭāhirides*, 2 vols., Paris, 1983. Shamsiddin Kamoliddin, *The Samanids: The First Islamic Local Dynasty in Central Asia*, Saarbrücken, 2011. Moḥammad b. Yusof Kendi, *Wolāt Meṣr*, ed. Rhuvon Guest as, *The Governors and Judges of Egypt*, Gibb Memorial Series 19, Leiden and London, 1912. Hugh Kennedy, *The Early ʿAbbasid Caliphate: A Political History*, London, 1981. Étienne de la Vaissière, *Sogdian Traders: A History*, Leiden, 2005a. Idem, "Châkars d'Asie centrale," *Stud. Ir.* 34, 2005b, pp. 139-49. Gilbert Lazard, *La langue des plus anciens monuments de la prose persane*, Paris, 1963. T. Levicki, "Le commerce des sâmânides avec l'Europe orientale et centrale à la lumière des trésors de monnaies coufigues," in D. K. Kouymjan, ed., *Near Eastern Numismatics, Iconography, Epigraphy and History: Studies in Honor of George C. Miles*, Beirut, 1974, pp. 219-33. Wilferd Madelung, "Minor Dynasties of Northern Iran," in R. N. Frye, ed., *The Cambridge History of Iran* IV, Cambridge, 1975, pp. 198-249. Idem, "Sufism and the Karramiyya," in idem, *Religious Trends in Early Islamic Iran*, New York, 1988, pp. 39-53. G. C. Miles, *Numismatic History of Rayy*, New York, 1938, pp. 135-54. Idem, "Numismatics," in R. N. Frye, ed., *The Cambridge History of Iran* IV, Cambridge, 1975, pp. 364-77. V. Minorsky, "The Older Preface to the Shāh-nāmeh," in *Studi Orientalistici in Onore de Giorgio Levi Della Vida* II, Rome 1956, pp. 159-79. Roy Mottahedeh, "The Transmission of Learning: The Role of the Islamic Northeast," in Nicole Grandin and Marc Gaborieau, eds., *Madrasa: La transmission du savoir dans le monde musulman*, Paris, 1997, pp. 63-72.

Saʿid Nafisi, *Tāriḵ-e ḵāndān-e ṭāheri*, Tehran, 1335 Š./1956. M. Nazim, *The Life and Times of Sultan Maḥmud of Ghazna*, Cambridge, 1931, pp. 28-32, 42-47, 180-83. N. N. Negmatov, "The Samanid State," in M. S. Asimov and C. E. Bosworth, eds., *History of Civilizations of Central Asia. IV. The Age of Achievement: A.D. 750 to the End of the Fifteenth Century. Part 1: The Historical, Social and Economic Setting*, Paris, 1998, pp. 77-94. E. E. Oliver, "The Decline of the Sámánís and the Rise of the Ghaznavís in Máwará-un-Nahr and Part of Khurasan (With Some Unpublished Coins)," *J(R)ASB* 55, 1886, pp. 91-106, 120. Jürgen Paul, *The State and the Military: The Samanid Case*, Papers on Inner Asia 26, Bloomington, Ind., 1994. A. C. S. Peacock, *Mediaeval Islamic Historiography and Political Legitimacy: Balʿamī's Tārīkhnāma*, New York, 2007. Parvaneh Pourshariati, "Local Histories of Khurāsān and the Pattern of Arab Settlement," *Studia Iranica* 27, 1998, pp. 41-82. Jan Rypka et al., *History of Iranian Literature*, ed. Karl Jahn, Dordrecht, 1968. Ḏabiḥ-Allāh Ṣafā (Zabihollah Safa), *Tāriḵ-e adabiyāt dar Irān* I, rev. ed., Tehran, 1956. Dominique Sourdel, "Les circonstances de la mort de Ṭāher Ier au Ḫurāsān en 207/822," *Arabica* 5, 1958, pp. 66-69. S. M. Stern, "The Early Ismāʿīlī Missionaries in North-West Persia and in Khurāsān and Transoxania," *BSOAS* 23, 1960, pp. 77-81, 82-83. Z. V. Togan, "The Topography of Balkh down to the Middle of the Seventeenth Century," *Central Asiatic Journal* 14, 1970, pp. 277-88. W. L. Treadwell, "The Political History of the Sāmānid State," Ph.D. diss., Oxford University, 1991. Idem, "A Unique Portrait Medallion from Bukhara Dated 969 AD," *The Ashmolean* 36, 1999, p. 9-10. Idem, "Ibn Zafir al-Azdi's Account of the Murder of Ahmad ibn Ismaʿil al-Samani and the Succession of his Son Nasr," in Carole Hillenbrand, ed., *Studies in Honour of Clifford Edmund Bosworth* II: *The Sultan's Turret*, Leiden, 2000, pp. 397-419. Idem, "Shāhānshāh and al-Malik al-Muʾayyad: The Legitimation of Power in Sāmāni and Būyid Iran," in F. Daftary and J. W. Meri, eds., *Culture and Memory in Medieval Islam: Essays in Honor of Wilferd Madelung*, London, 2003, pp. 318-37. Idem, "The Account of the Samanid Dynasty in Ibn Zāfir al-Azdi's *Akhbār al-duwal al-munqaṭiʿa*," *Iran* 43, 2005, pp. 135-73.

(†C. Edmund Bosworth and *EIr*.)

vii. History from the Ghaznavids to the Mongol conquest

The era extending from the late 3rd/10th century to the second decade of the 7th/13th witnessed both the zenith of Khorasan's blossoming as the center of Sunni Muslim culture and power and its subsequent eclipse. Khorasan had already assumed a growing prominence in the unitary caliphate from the time of the ʿAbbāsid Revolution beginning in 130/late 747, which had been based militarily upon a Khorasanian army. This importance had also been expressed politically in the dominance of Khorasanian figures such as the Barmakid and Taherid (qq.v) families of administrators, culminating in the brief functioning of Marv as the capital of the caliphate itself during al-Maʾmun's early reign; and, culturally and religiously, in the prominence of figures of Khorasanian origin, especially in both the proto-Sunni and the ascetic (*zohd*) movements, ranging from Aḥmad b. Ḥanbal (d. 241/855; see HANBALITE MAḎHAB) to ʿAbd-Allāh b. al-Mobārak (118-81/736-97; q.v.) and Bešr Ḥāfi (d. 841).

Once the caliphate began fragmenting politically around 235/850, Greater Khorasan (which comprised not only Khorasan proper, but also the Transoxianan lands of Central Asia that had traditionally been assigned to its governorship) had become, under the Saffarid (q.v.) and Samanid dynasties, in most respects the center of Islamic civilization: it was the seat of the most powerful polities in the central Islamic lands east of the Mediterranean, and also the cultural, religious, and intellectual center of the Sunni Muslim world, producing many of the major works of classical Islamic civilization. This primacy continued under the Ghaznavids (q.v.), under whom the political center shifted once more into cis-Oxanian Khorasan proper, and reached its apogee under the Saljuqs, under whom Khorasan's flourishing continued until the province was physically laid waste in the late 540s-early 550s/1150s by rampaging Oghuz Turkmen nomads during the Saljuq downfall; thereafter, from the 1150s until the Mongol invasions under Čengiz (Chenggis) Khan (q.v.) in 1220, Khorasan reverted to a more peripheral role, functioning largely as the devastated bone of contention between the rival powers that lay on opposite edges of the province: the Central-Asian based Khwarazmshahs (q.v.) to the northwest and the India-centered Ghurid (q.v.) dynasty in the southeast.

KHORASAN DURING THE GHAZNAVID PERIOD

The Ghaznavids were notable in that this was the first major dynasty in the central and eastern Islamic lands to have been founded by a Turkic slave soldier (*ḡolām*; see BARDA AND BARDA-DĀRI) who formally assumed rulership. In 350/961 one of the most prominent Samanid *ḡolām* army commanders, Alptigin (q.v.), staged a failed palace coup. As a result, he fled into exile in Ghazna (see ḠAZNI), in the south-easternmost marcher area on the Samanid borders, where he established an emirate after having wrested the town from the brother-in-law of the Hendušāhi Kābolšāh, the ruler of the culturally Indian realm that constituted at the time the main power standing in the way of Islamic expansion into the Indian world. He also in 351/962 defeated a Samanid army sent against him, although the Ghaznavids technically recognized Samanid overlordship, and ruled as their amirs (q.v.).

Following Alptigin's death, which occurred by 352/963, he was succeeded first by his son and, after the latter's death without heirs in 355/966, by a succession of two of his slave commanders (*ḡolāmān*). Finally, in 366/977, the *ḡolām* army magnates chose from amongst themselves the commander Sebüktegin (d. 387/997; q.v.), Alptigin's son-in-law, as amir; he and his progeny would continue to rule over Khorasan until the Seljuqs wrested the province from them in 431/1040; and, after that date, from Ghazna eastwards into India, as Seljuq vassals until the Ghurids finally conquered Ghazna in 545/1150-51, first driving the dynasty out of Khorasan entirely; and subsequently, in 582/1186, conquering Lahore and ending Ghaznavid rule completely.

Throughout Sebüktegin's reign, until 389/999, when his son Maḥmud was well established as the ruler in Ghazna, the Ghaznavids acknowledged Samanid overlordship and technically governed as their representatives. Sebüktegin, however, laid the moral foundations for autonomous dynastic legitimacy by following an outstandingly *ḡāzi* policy, continued by his successors, in which the resources and manpower of Khorasan were directed toward jihad (see ISLAM IN IRAN xi. JIHAD IN ISLAM). Under the three Ghaznavid amirs who ruled Khorasan—Sebüktegin, Maḥmud (r. 388-421/998-1030; q.v.), and Masʿud (r. 421-32/1030-41)—the region became the center of a *ḡāzi* polity, dedicated to expanding the borders of the *Dār al-Eslām* (see DĀR AL-HARB), especially toward the east and south. This was a notable accomplishment, since the frontier of Islam in India had essentially remained static since the time of the original Muslim conquest establishing the provincial foothold of Sind; the Ghaznavids, harnessing the resources of Khorasan, were to break this barrier and extend the borders of Islam well into the Gangetic plain.

During the early decades of Ghaznavid rule under Sebüktegin and throughout at least the early years of Maḥmud's rule, Khorasan benefitted from this expansionist *ḡāzi* focus, due to its territorial enlargement and the enormous wealth—including vast numbers of slaves and copious amounts of precious metals—that flowed into it from the conquests: among the lands added to Khorasan by Sebüktegin and placed under Muslim rule, were Zābolestān and the Kabul (q.v.) valley in eastern Afghanistan, and Qoṣdār (Khuzdar) in northern Baluchistan. It was this holy warrior prestige that Sebüktegin and his sons acquired that allowed Maḥmud b. Sebüktegin, in precisely the same manner as the holy war founder of autonomous Samanid power, Eṣmāʿil b. Aḥmad (r. 260-79/874-92; q.v.), had originally established that dynasty's legitimacy, officially to put an end to the pretense of acknowledging Samanid overlordship in 389/999, when the Samanid lands were divided between the Ghaznavids in Cis-Oxiana and the Qara-khanids (see ILAK-KHANIDS) in Transoxiana.

Maḥmud of Ghazna is known as one of the outstanding *ḡāzi*s of history; he not only continued his father's campaigns to the east and south, on a much larger scale, but his reign was one of unremitting expansionist warfare against non-Muslim polities in India, the remaining non-Islamized areas of Afghanistan, and the western Himalayan regions. One of his conquests, hitherto un-Islamized Ḡur (q.v.), Maḥmud subjected to a systematic campaign of Islamization after its conquest, building mosques and sending Muslim clerics there to instruct the populace in the new religion, thus laying the foundation for the eventual domination of Khorasan, and the entire Muslim East, by the Šansabāni (Ghurid) dynasty in the latter part of the 12th century.

Increasingly, however, as Maḥmud focused on his unremitting war effort and directed all his polity's resources toward that end, Khorasan was not just neglected, but exploited and mulcted. This trend was only exacerbated under the rule of Maḥmud's son and successor, Masʿud, whose "heart was occupied with India [Hendustān]" (Rāvandi, p. 95), and therefore spent almost all his time in the Indian part of his realm, neglecting Khorasan and its affairs. This neglect in turn enabled Turkmens, under the leadership of the Saljuq dynasty, who had been permitted to cross the Oxus from Central Asia, first to begin plundering and then to establish their rule in Khorasan throughout the 420s/1030s; by the time Masʿud bestirred himself to address the crisis in Khorasan in person, in 431/1040, it was too late; he and his army were soundly defeated, ejected from all of Khorasan apart from Ghazna and its immediate surroundings, and Khorasan became a component land of the newly constituted Great Saljuq empire.

KHORASAN DURING THE SALJUQ PERIOD (431-552/1040-1157)

During the Saljuq period, Khorasan, once the conquests were over, throve in every respect, apart from a brief period during the early part of the civil strife that followed upon the sudden death of Malekšāh (q.v.) in 485/1092. During the early decades of Saljuq rule, when the capital of the empire was located in the ʿErāqayn (the "two Iraqs" of ʿErāq-e ʿAjam[i], q.v., and ʿErāq-e ʿArab; viz., much of today's western Iran and the province of Iraq proper), the Saljuq polity was run largely by Khorasani viziers (Bowen), culminating with the decades-long dominance of the realm by the greatest of all Islamic viziers, Neẓām-al-Molk (q.v.); although Saljuq rule allowed a large measure of Khorasani local autonomy and self-government (Klausner, pp. 9-22).

With the death of Malekšāh and Neẓām-al-Molk in 485/1092, Khorasan was troubled both by the outbreak of civil war among Malekšāh's minor sons and the deceased sultan's brothers, who were jockeying for power; and also by the great Nezāri Ismaʿili uprising (see ISMAʿILISM iii. ISMAʿILI HISTORY). For the first four years of this chaotic interlude, from 485/1092 until 490/1097, the dominant Saljuq figure in Khorasan was Malekšāh's brother, Arslān Arḡun, who headed the Turkmen element whose influence in Khorasan was constantly growing, in a process that has been described as the "re-nomadisation" (Paul, 2011, p. 111) of the country. Although this steady rise of the Turkmen component received a check with Arslān Arḡun's murder by one of his mistreated ḡolāmān (Bondāri, p. 258), this Turkmen setback was to prove only temporary.

The zenith of Khorasan's political, economic, and cultural flourishing transpired during the long reign of Sultan Sanjar (q.v.), who ruled Khorasan and the entire East from 490/1097 until his downfall in 548/1153; first as "King of the East," then, from 511/1118, as Supreme Sultan, at which time he moved the capital of the empire to Marv, thereby making Khorasan the heart of the Saljuq empire. According to Ẓahir-al-Din Nišāpuri (d. ca. 580/1184), "the Khorasan region in his [Sanjar's] era became the [coveted] destination of all the people of the world, and the native soil of the sciences, the fountain of literary attainments, and the mine of knowledge" (p. 56); Sanjar himself is described as "the mightiest monarch whom [God] ever made king" (Ḥosayni, p. 92) whose wealth and power provided decades of peace and prosperity for the empire as a whole, but above all for Khorasan. Partly, this was due to Khorasan's domination of adjacent lands; not only did Sanjar's overlordship extend westward over the lands that had formerly constituted the center of the empire, but also over the Qara-khanid lands in Transoxiana until 536/1141 and over the Ghaznavid lands in India.

Culturally, the flowering of classical Persian literature that had begun under the Samanids reached its apogee during the Ghaznavid and Saljuq eras (see SALJUQS V. SALJUQID LITERATURE). This period includes the magnificent literary productions of poets such as Ferdowsi (q.v.), Manučehri

Dāmḡāni, Faḵr-al-Din Gorgāni (q.v.), and Awḥad-al-Din Anwari (q.v.); the belletristic and historical writings of Abu Naṣr ʿOtbi (q.v.), ʿAbd-al-Ḥayy Gardizi (q.v.), and the consummate historian Abu'l-Fażl Bayhaqi (q.v.); political writings on rulership by Neẓām al-Molk, Kaykāvus b. Eskandar (q.v.), and Emām-al-Ḥaramayn Jovayni (q.v.); and the great religious and Sufi texts, in both Persian and Arabic, of luminaries such as Abu ʿAbd-al-Raḥmān Solami, Abu Noʿaym al-Esfāhāni (q.v.; who studied in Nishapur), ʿAbd-Allāh Anṣāri (q.v.), Abu'l-Ḥasan ʿAli Hojviri (q.v.), and Abu Ḥāmed Moḥammad Ḡazāli (q.v.).

This Khorasani golden age was brought to an end by nomadic power. The very fact of Sanjar's succession to the Great Sultanate after his brother provides an important indication that the power of the Turkmen element in both Khorasan and the Saljuq polity was steadily increasing throughout Saljuq rule, especially from the late 11th century onwards. For prior to 511/1118, in the succession struggles that invariably ensued upon the death of a Great Sultan between a camp espousing Perso-Islamic succession norms of father to son and a Turkmen camp espousing the traditional nomadic seniorate succession to an older male, usually a brother or uncle of the previous ruler, the Perso-Islamic camp had always won the struggle. In 511/1118, however, the Turkmen camp was finally powerful enough to emerge triumphant: Sanjar, the brother rather than the son of the previous Great Sultan, acceded, and his removal of the imperial capital, not merely to Khorasan, but to Marv rather than Nishapur, on the very edge of the steppes, is yet another indication of growing Turkmen presence and influence.

The first nomadic threat from the Turkic steppe to Khorasan's flourishing came in 536/1141, when the non-Muslim Qarā Ḵeṭāy (q.v.) invaders from China, probably allied with disaffected nomads in Transoxiana, met and defeated Sanjar's Khorasani army at the battle of Qaṭvān, wresting the province of Transoxiana not just from Khorasani rule, but from Islamic rule entirely. This stinging defeat, which undermined Sanjar's aura of invincibility, led to a brief two-year period of instability in Khorasan, in which various actors, mainly nomad-supported, attempted to wrest control of several regions of the province. By 538/1143, however, this turbulence had ended, and Sanjar had re-established rule in Khorasan after several military campaigns. Thereafter, Cis-Oxanian Khorasan proper remained the flourishing, dominant power of the Islamic world east of the Mediterranean up until 548/1153; and the armies of Khorasan, over the course of the succeeding decade, conducted successful campaigns against the only other powers of the eastern Islamic world, both of whom were rebellious Saljuq vassals: the ḵᵛārazmšāh, the ambitious hereditary governor of Ḵᵛārazm (see ĀL-E AFRIḠ; CHORASMIA ii. IN ISLAMIC TIMES), who was a grandson of the ḡolām first appointed to the position by the Saljuqs in the 11th century; and the Ghurid dynasty of the Šansabāni family, against whom Sanjar conducted a highly successful military campaign in 547/1152.

The extinguishing of Khorasan's prosperity and preeminence came abruptly in 548/1153, when Sanjar, having lost control over his magnates due to the increasing infirmity accompanying senescence (Bondāri, p. 276; Ḥosayni, p. 123), was defeated and taken prisoner near Balḵ (q.v.) by an army composed of Oghuz (see ḠOZZ) Turkmens newly arrived from the steppes (Ebn al-Aṯir, XI, p. 176), in which durance he was held until his escape in 551/1156, dying in the spring of 552/1157. After Sanjar was taken captive by the Oghuz, Khorasan splintered politically. Although some of the Oghuz leaders did take over rule in several of the towns that they left standing—for instance, Ghazna, which they ruled for over a decade—the Oghuz tribesmen on the whole seem to have spent the bulk of their time over the succeeding years on what the sources describe as a systematic campaign of pillage and destruction.

The Oghuz Turkmens in fact ravaged the province on a vast and unprecedented scale; not only did they virtually destroy entire cities, such as Marv and Nishapur, killing tens of thousands of people, but they also targeted the religious clerics, the Khorasani intelligentsia, who were perceived as part and parcel of the Saljuq governing apparatus (Tor, 2016, p. 401). Anwari's famous elegiac poem, the so-called "Tears of Khorasan," was written in reaction, as a desperate plea to solicit outside help (Anwari, pp. 201-5). At the same time, Sanjar's disloyal magnates were quick to carve out fiefdoms for themselves, the strongest of these being Sanjar's *ḡolām* Moʾayyed Ay-Aba (q.v.; d. 569/1174). The general anarchy and confusion in the province during Sanjar's captivity also provided an opportunity for the Ismaʿilis to take the offensive; in 549/1154 Khorasan was attacked by a force of 7,000 *bāṭeniya* (q.v.) from Kuhestān; they were repelled by several erstwhile Saljuq amirs but in 551/1156 succeeded in sacking Ṭabas and capturing a number of Saljuq officials. This political turmoil was to persist in Khorasan for several decades, compounding the effects of the original Oghuz devastation of the province.

FROM THE END OF SALJUQ RULE TO THE MONGOL INVASIONS

After the death of Sanjar in 552/1157, there was no longer any unified governing authority in Khorasan for several decades, and the province lost not only its central political and cultural standing, but its political agency and unity. Khorasan was riven by various contending forces, both inside and outside, including the continuing activities of the Oghuz tribesmen; and, from having been an imperial center, it became a zone of contention to be fought over, mainly by the two neighboring powers of the Khwarazmian and Ghurid dynasties. During the last quarter of the 6th/12th century, with the capture of Herat in 571/1175-76, the Ghurids gained the upper hand in the struggle, and succeeded by the end of the 6th/12th century in imposing their rule over much of Khorasan, which once again, albeit briefly, and never fully unified, became the center of a powerful polity, located in present-day Ḡōr province in Afghanistan. This success was, however, not only partial, but also short-lived—Ghurid control over the Balḵ area, for instance, lasted only a mere eight years (Bosworth, 2015, p. 216); by 601/1204 the Khwarazmshahs had definitively defeated the Ghurid sultan in battle, and taken over Khorasan, making it an appendage to their growing steppe-based empire. The Ghurid Empire itself fell apart shortly thereafter; only its Indian dominions were to emerge reconstituted, under the Ghurids' former *ḡolāms*, as the Delhi sultanate (q.v.). Khorasan was by the early 7th/13th century, at the close of this period, in a ruinous state, after many decades of both pillaging and all-out warfare, not only on the regional level, but also among numerous rival local forces and strongmen. The country remained a subordinate province under the Khwarazmshahs for only a decade and a half, until the empire of the Khwarazmshahs was in turn swept away in the cataclysmic Mongol invasions under Čengiz Khan, beginning in 616/1219.

Bibliography: Awḥad-al-Din ʿAli b. Moḥammad Anwari, *Divān-e Anwari*, ed. M.-T. Modarres Reżawi, Tehran, 1959. Abu'l-Fażl Bayhaqi, *Tāriḵ-e masʿudi: Maʿruf beh Tāriḵ-e Bayhaqi*, ed. Saʿid Nafisi, Tehran, 3 vols., Tehran, 1940-53. Nāser-al-Din ʿAbd-Allāh b. ʿOmar Bayżāwi, *Neẓām al-tawārikh*, ed. B. M. Karimi, Tehran, 1934. W. Barthold, *Turkestan Down to the Mongol Invasion*, tr. T. Minorsky and ed. C. E. Bosworth, 3rd ed., Taipei, 1968. Michal Biran, *The Empire of the Qara Khitai in Eurasian History: Between China and the Islamic World*, Cambridge, 2005. Fatḥ b. ʿAli b. Moḥammad Bondāri, *Zobdat al-noṣra wa noḵbat al-ʿoṣra*, ed. Th. Houtsma, Leiden, 1889. C. E. Bosworth, "G͟hazna," *EI²*, [1965a], II, pp.1048-50. Idem, "G͟hūrids," *EI²*, [1965b], II, pp. 1099-1104. Idem, "Maḥmūd of Ghazna in Contemporary Eyes and in Later Persian Literature," *Iran* 4, 1966, pp. 85-92. Idem, "The Political and Dynastic History of the Iranian World (A.D. 1000-1217), in J. A. Boyle, ed., *The Cambridge History of Iran* V: *The Saljuq and Mongol Periods*, Cambridge, 1968, pp. 1-202. Idem, *The Ghaznavids: Their Empire in Afghanistan and Eastern Iran 994-1040,* 2nd ed., Beirut, 1973. Idem, "The Early Ghaznavids," in R. N. Frye, ed., *The Cambridge History of Iran* IV: *The Period from the Arab Invasion to the Saljuqs*, Cambridge, 1975, pp. 162-97. Idem, "The Ghurids in Khurasan," in A. C .S. Peacock and D. G. Tor, eds., *Medieval Central Asia and the Persianate World: Iranian Tradition and Islamic Civilisation*, London, 2016, pp. 210-21. Harold Bowen, "Notes on Some Early Seljuq Viziers," *BSOAS* 20, 1957, pp. 105-10.

ʿEzz-al-Din Ebn al-Aṯir, *al-Kāmel fi'l-taʾriḵ*, ed. C. J. Tornberg, Beirut, 1979. Abu'l-Ḥasan Ẓahir-al-Din ʿAli b. Zayd Bayhaqi Ebn Fondoq, *Tāriḵ-e Bayhaq*, ed. A. Bahmanyār, Tehran, 1942. Abu'l-Faraj ʿAbd-al-Raḥmān Ebn al-Jawzi, *al-Montaẓam fi taʾriḵ al-omam wa'l-moluk*, ed. M. ʿA. ʿAṭā, Beirut, 1992. Moʿin-al-Din Moḥammad Zamči Esfezāri, *Rawżat al-jannāt fi awṣāf madinat Herāt*, ed. Sayyed Moḥammad Kāẓem Emām, Tehran, 1959. ʿAbd-al-Ḥayy b. Żaḥḥāq Gardizi, *Tāriḵ-e Gardizi*, ed. ʿAbd-al-Ḥayy Ḥabibi, Tehran, 1944. Peter Golden, *Central Asia in World History*, Oxford, 2011. Wael B. Hallaq, "Caliphs, Jurists and the Saljuqs in the Political Thought of Juwayni," *The Muslim World* 74/1, 1984, pp. 26-41. Ṣadr-al-Din Ḥosayni, *Aḵbār al-dawla al-saljuqiya*, ed. M. Iqbāl, Beirut, 1984. Minoru Inaba,

"A Venture on the Frontier: Alptegin's Conquest of Ghazna and its Sequel," in A.C.S. Peacock and D.G. Tor, eds., *Medieval Central Asia and the Persianate World: Iranian Tradition and Islamic Civilisation*, London, 2016, pp. 108-28. Peter Jackson, *The Mongols and the Islamic World: From Conquest to Conversion,* New Haven, 2017. Menhāj-e Serāj Jowzjāni, *Ṭabaqāt-e nāṣeri yā Tāriḵ-e Irān va Eslām*, ed. ʿAbd al-Ḥayy Ḥabibi, 2 vols., Tehran, 1963-64. Ḡiāṯ-al-Din b. Homām-al-Din Ḵᵛāndamir, *Dastur al-wozarāʾ*, ed. Saʿid Nafisi, Tehran, 1938. Carla Klausner, *The Seljuk Vezirate: A Study of Civil Administration 1055-1194*, Cambridge, Mass., 1973. Mehmed Altay Köymen, *Büyük Selçuklu Imparatorluğu Tarihi* V, Ankara, 1991. Julie Meisami, *Persian Historiography to the End of the Twelfth Century,* Edinburgh, 1999. Moḥammad b. Borhān-al-Din Ḵᵛāvandšāh Mirḵᵛānd, *Tāriḵ-e rawżat al-ṣafā*, 8 vols., Tehran, 1960. Ḥamd-Allāh Mostawfi Qazvini, *Tāriḵ-e gozida*, ed. ʿAbd-al-Ḥosayn Navāʾi, Tehran, 1983. Ẓahir-al-Din Nišāpuri, *Saljuq-nāma*, ed. A. H. Morton, Warminster, U.K., 2004. Abu Naṣr Moḥammad b. ʿAbd al-Jabbār ʿOtbi, *al-Yamini: fi šarḥ aḵbār al-solṭān Yamin-al-Dawla wa Amin-al-Milla Maḥmūd al-Ḡaznavi*, ed. Ihsan Z. Ṯāmeri, Beirut, 2004.

J. Paul, "Arslān Arghūn–Nomadic Revival?," in Christian Lange and Songul Mecit, eds., *The Seljuqs: Politics, Society, and Culture*, Edinburgh, 2011, pp. 99-116. Idem, "Sanjar and Atsız," in J. Paul, ed., *Nomad Aristocrats in a World of Empires*, Wiesbaden, 2013, pp. 81-130. Idem, "Alptegin in the *Siyāsat-nāma,*" *Afghanistan* 1, 2018, pp. 122-140. A. C. S. Peacock, *The Great Seljuq Empire*, Edinburgh, 2015. Rašid-al-Din Fażl-Allāh, *Jāmeʿ al-tawāriḵ*, ed. Aḥmad Āteš, Tehran, n.d. Moḥammad b. ʿAli Rāvandi, *Rāḥat al-ṣodur wa āyāt al-sorur dar tāriḵ-e āl-e Saljuq*, ed. M. Iqbāl, repr. Tehran, 1333/1954. Neẓāmi ʿArużi Samarqandi, *Čahār maqāla*, ed. M. Moʿin, Tehran, 1955. Abu'l-Moẓaffar Sebṭ b. al-Jawzi, *Merʾāt al-zamān fi taʾriḵ al-aʿyān*, ed. Kāmel Joburi et al., Beirut, 2013. D. G. Tor, "The Islamization of Central Asia in the Sāmānid Era and the Reshaping of the Muslim World," *BSOAS* 72, 2009, pp. 272–99. Idem, "Mamlūk Loyalty: Evidence from the Late Saljūq Period," *Asiatische Studien* 65/3, 2011, pp. 767-96. Idem, "The Importance of Khurāsān and Transoxiana in the Classical Islamic World," in A.C.S. Peacock and D. G. Tor, eds., *Medieval Central Asia and the Persianate World: Iranian Tradition and Islamic Civilisation*, London, 2015, pp. 1-12. Idem, "The Political Revival of the ʿAbbāsid Caliphate: Al-Muqtafī and the Seljuqs," *Journal of the American Oriental Society* 137/2, 2017, pp. 301-14. Idem, "The Eclipse of Khurasan in the Twelfth Century," *BSOAS* 81/2, 2018, pp. 251-76. Andre Wink, *al-Hind: The Making of the Islamic World* II: *The Slave Kings and the Islamic Conquest 11th-13th Centuries*, Leiden, 2002. Moḥammad b. Moḥammad b. Neẓām Ḥosayn Yazdi, *al-ʿOrāża fi'l-ḥekāya al-Saljuqiya*, ed. Maryam Mir Šamsi, Tehran, 1968.

(D. G. Tor)

viii. History from the Mongol Conquest to the Timurids. See Supplement.

ix. History in the Timurid Period. See Supplement.

x. History in the Safavid and Afsharid Periods

Khorasan changed hands several times between the Safavids and the Uzbeks during the 16th century. Eventually, it was under Shah ʿAbbās I (q.v.) that the province was fully integrated into the Safavid system of the "guarded domains" (*mamālek-e maḥrusa*). Under the Safavids, major urban centers in Khorasan, including Herat and Mashhad, suffered ravages of war and administrative discontinuity, which in turn brought about successive bouts of famine and plague. The long years of civil war in Iran during the years leading up to Shah ʿAbbās' ascent to the throne gave the Uzbeks opportunity to expand the range of their attacks outside Khorasan, destabilizing Kerman, Yazd, Sistān, Nimruz, and even Kandahar. Forced and coordinated mass migration from eastern Anatolia, the Caucasus, and Azerbaijan in the 16th and 17th centuries had a lasting impact on demographic characteristics of Khorasan as waves of Turkic and Kurdish nomadic and semi-nomadic clans and tribes entered the provinces, where they had been granted pastures and agricultural lands in the valleys and foothills of the Hezār-Masjed and Binālud ranges, forming a bulwark against the incursions of the Uzbeks. Early in the 18th century, when the Safavid dynasty entered its terminal phase, the Uzbeks from the north and the Abdāli (q.v.) Afghans from the east invaded Khorasan, bringing the political order established there by the Safavids to the brink of disintegration.

Upon the death of the last Timurid ruler of Khorasan, Solṭān-Ḥosayn Bāyqarā (q.v.; r. 875-911/1470-1506), on 11 Ḏu'l-ḥejja 911/5 May 1506, two of his sons, Badiʿ al-Zamān and Moẓaffar-Ḥosayn, suspended their fight over the Timurid throne to form a joint front against the Uzbeks. The last decade of Bāyqarā's reign was witness to the consolidation of the power base of the Yadgarids and the Abu'l-Khayrids (q.v.) as paramount clans of the Uzbek tribal confederations of Dašt-e Qepčāq and Transoxiana (Dickson, 1963, pp. 209-10). Led by Abu'l-Fotuḥ Moḥammad Khan Šībāni (Šaybāni), the Abu'l-Khayrid Uzbeks posed an immediate threat to Khorasan. At the close of the 15th century, they descended on Balḵ, Šaborḡān, and the Morḡāb valley shortly after their capture of Samarqand and Bukhara from the Timurid and Toḡloq/Timurid princes of Central Asia. The pillage and destruction wrought by the Uzbeks in Balḵ, the easternmost fortress town in Khorasan, which had been made the appanage of Badiʿ-al-Zamān Mirzā toward the end of the reign of Solṭān-Ḥosayn Bāyqarā, are reported to have been notably gruesome, raising alarm for inner cities of the province to abandon the path of resistance and surrender (Rāqem Samarqandi, p. 83). The scarcity of foodstuff and fodder in the winter of 1507 on the one hand, and the resurfacing of internal feuds among Solṭān-Ḥosayn Bāyqarā's sons on the other, led to a major breakup in the Timurid army camped outside Herat (Ḵ^vāndamir, IV, pp. 372-73; Mir Moḥammad Maʿṣum, p. 101). It was under these circumstances that Herat fell to the Uzbeks on 8 Moḥarram 913/20 May 1507, just over a year after Solṭān-Ḥosayn Bāyqarā's death; a week later, on 15 Moḥarram/27 May, the Friday prayer sermon was officially preached at the congregational mosque in Herat in Šibāni's name. Shortly thereafter, the Uzbeks easily quelled a series of pro-Timurid uprisings in Mashhad, Abivard, Nishapur, and Sabzavār (Ḵᵛāndamir, IV, pp. 367-81; Bābor, I, pp. 127-47; Doḡlāt, pp. 121-23, tr., pp. 97-98; Qaṭaḡān, pp. 124-25; Mir Moḥammad Maʿṣum, pp. 99-102; Roemer, pp. 124-25; Mukminova, pp. 34-35; Hajianpur, pp. 157-58).

Šibāni Khan is argued to have had a strong support base in Herat (Szuppe, 1992, p. 161). Yet the fact is that, soon after his victories in Khorasan, the Uzbek ruler introduced draconian fiscal policies that in the short run incited widespread disaffection with the Uzbeks in Khorasan (Semenov, p. 65; Tumanovich, p. 98). What is more, Šibāni Khan's distrust of the dominantly pro-Timurid urban elites in Herat led him, in less than three years after his annexation of Khorasan, to plan for moving the center of his khanate out of the city. The new capital, to be called Yādgār-e Ḵāni, had been planned to be built on the ruins of Ṭus, a bastion of Sunni Islam in eastern Iran under the Saljuqids, located some 20 miles northwest of Mashhad. During a visit to Mashhad in Ṣafar 915/June 1509, Šibāni stopped over in Ṭus to pay tributes to Sunni worthies buried there, including the prominent jurist Abu Ḥāmed Ḡazāli (q.v.; Ḵonji Eṣfahāni, 1976, pp. 348-51). It was there that he appointed a local Sunni bureaucrat as chief judge of Yādgār-e Ḵāni with powers to adjudicate all over Transoxiana and Khorasan. The appointment letter (*nešān*) issued and sealed by Šibāni contains references to his plans to relocate several hundred households from among the Turkish, Persian, and Arab nomads of Khorasan and Transoxiana to Yādgār-e Ḵāni upon the completion of the city's walls and ramparts in 1511 (Šarifi Nasafi, fols. 134a-136b; Ghereghlou, 2016; Elias, p. 777).

Underlying Šibāni Khan's westward territorial expansionism was his quest for the revival of Sunnism in Iran and Central Asia. The mistreatment of Sunni Muslims in Safavid Iran made him even more eager to pursue a policy of all-out war with the Safavids, drawing on his mentor Fażl-Allāh Ḵonji Eṣfahāni's (d. 1521) radical interpretations of the doctrine of jihad. A notable Sunni jurist and Hadith (q.v.) expert who had barely escaped after Shah Esmāʿil's (q.v.; r. 1501-24) annexation of ʿErāq-e ʿAjam (q.v.) in the late fall of 1503, Ḵonji considered the Safavids and their supporters in Iran as no more than "apostates and idolaters" whose extermination was mandatory upon any devoted Muslim ruler (Ḵonji Eṣfahāni, 1983, p. 398; Ḵonji Eṣfahāni, fol. 226b). To the Uzbeks, the Safavids were occupiers of the land of Islam, blocking the access of Central Asian Muslims to the holy cities of Hejaz. In one of his diplomatic dispatches to Shah Esmāʿil, the Uzbek Šibāni Khan vows to secure the free passage of Sunni pilgrims to the Hejaz via Khorasan and ʿErāq-e ʿAjam, a plan that entailed the undoing of Safavid rule in Iran (*Majmuʿa makātib*, fols. 250a-251b). The same issue resurfaces in the correspondence of later generations of Uzbek rulers, including ʿObayd-Allāh Khan's (d. 1540) who, in one of his letters to Shah Ṭahmāsp (q.v.; r. 1524-76) accused the Safavids of blocking the road to Mecca and Medina for Central Asian Muslims (Ivoḡli, fols. 108a-109b). Late in the 16th century, in a letter to the Ottoman Sultan Morād II (r. 1574-95), the Uzbek khan ʿAbd-al-Moʾmen (d. 1598) deemed it his duty to "uproot the thorn bushes hindering the access of Sunni Muslims to Mecca" (Ḵuzāni Eṣfahāni, III, pp. 64-65; McChesney, 2003, pp. 145-46). The early Safavids, in their turn, denied such charges, accusing the Uzbeks of "spreading false statements and outrageous lies" regarding the conditions of Sunni Muslims in Safavid Iran (Navāʾi, 1989, pp. 81-88; Doḡlāt, pp. 198-99, tr., pp. 155–56; Ḵᵛāndamir, IV, p. 504; Budāq Monši, p. 87; Rāqem Samarqandi, p. 92; Dickson, 1958, pp. 42-46). The Safavids' claims were more of territorial nature reflecting the core values of the eastern policy of the Aq Quyunlu (q.v.) Uzun Ḥasan, who took advantage of the power struggles that rocked the Timurid sultanate in the latter part of the 15th century to meddle in the internal affairs of Khorasan and the neighboring province of Astarābād. During the closing decade of his reign, the Aq Quyunlu ruler backed the Šāhroḵid prince Yādgār Moḥammad Mirzā (d. 1470) during the civil war that broke out following the death of Abu Saʿid Mirzā (d. 1469), with the objective of installing him as his vassal in eastern Iran (Ṭehrāni Eṣfahāni, pp. 513-14; Navāʾi, 1962, pp. 320-23; Moʾayyad Ṯābeti, pp. 384-87; Woods, 1990, p. 46; idem, 1999, pp. 112-13).

Shah Esmāʿil began meddling in the internal affairs of Khorasan and Astarābād even before Bāyqarā's death. Already in Ḏu'l-ḥejja 909/May-June 1504, he had charged one of his military deputies with installing the Timurid prince Moẓaffar-Ḥosayn Mirzā as head of a vassal appanage in Astarābād, a move that excited Bāyqarā's ire, for he had just appointed his other son Moḥammad-Ḥosayn Mirzā as governor of Astarābād (Ḥayāti Tabrizi, pp. 312-15). Bāyqarā then sent a terse letter of protest to the Safavid ruler, reprimanding him for his uninvited meddling in the internal affairs of the Timurid sultanate (Marvārid, fol. 30b, tr., p. 121). It was in reaction to this letter that Shah Esmāʿil attacked Ṭabas in Ramażān 910/February 1505, shortly after his conquest of Yazd with assistance from the Arab nomads of Ḵur (q.v.). It is reported that the Safavids sacked villages outside Ṭabas and put to the sword several hundred farmers and pastoralists (Ḵᵛāndamir, IV, p. 480; Amini Heravi, pp. 242-43; Ḥayāti Tabrizi, pp. 327-29). When the Uzbeks took Herat, the provinces of Kerman and Sistān became the targets of their occasional raids. In Kerman, they pillaged Govāšir, Ḵabiṣ (present-day Šahdād), Rāvar, and Zangiābād in 1506-7 (Amini Heravi, p. 325; Waziri Kermāni, pp. 264-65; Aubin, 1988, p. 27). In spring 1506, a close relative of Šibāni Khan led a raid against Uq (present-day Qalʿa-ye Kāh), a rural town outside Farāh, forcing Malek Maḥmud, the ruler of Sistān, to escape along with his clan to Bam and Narmāšir (Sistāni, p. 139). In winter 1508, the Uzbeks invaded Astarābād and Dāmḡān, driving the Timurid prince Badiʿ-al-Zamān Mirzā from the province. He ultimately escaped to ʿErāq-e ʿAjam, where he put himself under the protection of Shah Esmāʿil (Qaṭaḡān, pp. 102-3).

The Battle of Maḥmudi, which was fought on 28-30 Šaʿbān 916/30 November-2 December 1510 outside Ṭāherābād, a small village some 20 miles south of Marv, sealed the fate of Moḥammad Khan Šibāni, who was cornered by the Safavid troops and suffocated in a cavalry melee. The Safavid invasion of Khorasan, taking place out of season late in fall, was a complete surprise for the Uzbeks. It is reported that, upon Shah Esmāʿil's arrival in Ray (q.v.), the Uzbek governor of Dāmḡān Aḥmad-Solṭān, who had married Šibāni Khan's daughter or sister, and Ḵᵛāja Aḥmad Qonqrāt, who led the Uzbek forces in Astarābād, vacated their posts and fled to Transoxiana, leaving Khorasan undefended to Safavid penetration (Ḵᵛāndamir, IV, pp. 509-14; Amini Heravi, pp. 339-45; Rumlu, pp. 1050-54; Doḡlāt, pp. 199-200, tr., pp. 156-57; Qaṭaḡān, pp. 104-12; Ḵāki Širāzi, fol. 593a; Sarwar, pp. 61-62; Tumanovich, p. 100; Savory, pp. 78-80). Subsequently, Shah Esmāʿil entered Herat and within a few weeks of his victory assigned all cities and major rural towns in Khorasan to his military deputies, who ran their land assignments as *toyul* or military fief and within the temporal scope of one fiscal year produced more than 150 *tümen*s for the Safavid central treasury. The amount generated by *toyul*-holders posted to Khorasan made up more than 20 percent of the tax yield of all *toyul* land enfeoffments in the provinces Azerbaijan, ʿErāq-e ʿAjam, Diyarbakir, Iraq, Kurdistan, Fārs, and Kerman between fiscal years 913-19/1508-13 (Ghereghlou, 2015, pp. 94, 98). Early in spring 917/1511, Shah Esmāʿil mounted a punitive campaign against the Uzbek forces in Maymana and Fāryāb. During the peace negotiations that ensued following this military campaign, the Uzbeks agreed to recognize the Oxus as the natural border separating the Safavid domain in Khorasan from Transoxiana. Shortly afterwards, the Safavid ruler appointed Bayrām Beg Qarāmānlu, a tribal military commander from Ṭāleš, as governor of Balḵ, Andḵoy, Šaborḡān, Čičaktow, Maymana, Fāryāb, Morḡāb, and Ḡarčestān (Ḵᵛāndamir, IV, p. 519; Ebn Ḵᵛāndamir, p. 73).

On 15 Rajab 917/8 October 1511, Shah Esmāʿil made the Timurid prince Ẓahir-al-Din Moḥammad Bābor (q.v.) governor-general of Khorasan. At that time, major urban centers in the province were faced with depopulation and food shortage. Dated circa 1511, two missives from Safavid bureaucrats in Khorasan point to the difficulties Shah Esmāʿil's deputies were experiencing in collecting annual taxes from their military fiefs in Khorasan on the eve of Bābor's rise to power as governor-general of the province (Evrâk 12212; Evrâk 8316; Fekete, p. 270; Aubin, 1988, p. 31). These reports are borne out by two 16th-century Persian chroniclers, who discuss in some detail the unfolding turmoil in Khorasan during the opening years of the 1510s (Ḡaffāri Qazvini, p. 278; Novidi Širāzi, pp. 55-56). During his tenure, which lasted only eight months until Rabiʿ I 918/May-June 1512, Bābor managed to score a series of military victories against the Uzbeks in Ḵatlān (Ḵottalā), Baqlān, and Qondoz, thanks mainly to the active support of the Timurid prince Mirzā Solṭān-Ovays (Ḵᵛāndamir, IV, pp. 523-24). Late in the spring of 918/1512, however, the Uzbeks recaptured Samarqand, forcing him to escape to the south, first to Qondoz and then to Kabul (Doḡlāt, pp. 208, 217, tr., pp. 163, 170; Dale, pp. 188-200; Budāq Monši, pp. 91-92). Bābor's downfall coincided with the Yādgārid/Aminaki Ṣufiān Khan's (r. ca. 1511-35) rise to power and his subsequent capture of Khiva (Urganj), the city he later made the administrative capital of the Khanate of Ḵᵛārazm, which encompassed vast swathes of land located between Su-boyu, the strip of agricultural lands along the western bank of the Oxus, and Tāḡ-boyu, southern foothills of the Küren-Dāḡ and Köpet-Dāḡ ranges in northeastern Khorasan (Bartol'd, 1963-77, II/1, pp. 596-97; idem, 1956-62, III, pp. 135-36). Under Shah Esmāʿil, the ruler of Kandahar, Šojāʿ Beg, who later had to escape to Sind valley, where he founded the Arghunid dynasty, was one of the few claimants to power in eastern Iran who defied Safavid superiority. In summer 1513, he fled from Eḵtiār-al-Din Castle in Herat, where he had been detained by the Safavids, and managed to take refuge for a while in Kandahar. The Safavid forces, led by Šāhroḵ Beg Afšār, then attacked Šojāʿ Beg, but it came to naught (Ḵᵛāndamir, IV, p. 541; Ḵuzāni Eṣfahāni, I, fols. 217a–b; Ḵāki Širāzi, fol. 597a; Aubin, 1984, p. 21).

Under Shah Esmāʿil, the Sunni population of Khorasan were subjected to various forms of maltreatment, from indiscriminate violence to forced migration. On the eve of the Safavid ruler's arrival in Herat, the prayer sermons (*ḵoṭba*) were delivered in the name of the Shiʿite imams at the city's congregational mosque. There followed a violent crackdown on the Sunni population of Herat as soon as a few Sunni notables dared to protest the elimination of the names of the Sunni caliphs from the *ḵoṭba*. The Safavid royal guards (*qurči*s) then massacred several dozen Sunni protesters and set aflame the main entrance to ʿAbd-al-Raḥmān Jāmi's mausoleum, the city's main Sunni shrine (Vāṣefi Heravi, II, pp. 247-51; Moin). In Marv, the Safavid ruler is reported to have ordered the mass execution of Sunni denizens of the city following the Battle of Maḥmudi (Amini Heravi, pp. 347, 349; Doḡlāt, p. 200, tr. p. 156). Shortly thereafter, Shah Esmāʿil sent three embassies to Khiva, Urganj, and Hazār-Asb in Ḵᵛārazm in an attempt to form an alliance with the Uzbek Ilbārs Khan (r. 910-30/1503-24). When the shah's request was rejected firmly by Ilbārs, in 1505, one of the Safavid envoys to Ḵᵛārazm declared a Yesevi Sufi *sayyed* called Ḥosām al-Dīn ruler of Ḵᵛārazm. In the battle that ensued following this incident, Ilbārs defeated the pro-Safavid Ḥosām al-Dīn and for the rest of his reign kept the province safe from the Safavid invasion (Munes and Āgahi, pp. 105-107). During his stay in Herat, Shah Esmāʿil personally executed the Naqšbandi mystic and Ḥanafi religious dignitary (*šayḵ-al-eslām*) of Khorasan Sayf-al-Din Aḥmad Taftāzāni (Doḡlāt, pp. 200-201, tr., p. 157; Rumlu,

p. 1057). Shortly thereafter, the first Safavid governor of Herat and Shah Esmāʿil's brother-in-law, Eḵtiār-al-Molk Ḥosayn Beg Šāmlu, had recourse to a carrot-and-stick policy in his dealings with the Sunni population of the city, providing a handful of Sunni notables with employment opportunity in local bureaucracy while forcing groups of their coreligionists to leave Khorasan for Transoxiana (Vaṣefi Heravi, I, pp. 17-18). Under Ḥosayn Beg Šāmlu, all public lands confiscated by the state (ḵāleṣa) sector during the centralizing reforms of the 1490s were liberalized, empowering the Safavid authorities in Herat to incentivize these lands for winning over the support of local notables across Khorasan (Amini Heravi, p. 358).

The Uzbek recapture of Samarqand in the spring of 918/1512 and Bābor's withdrawal from Khorasan shortly thereafter prompted Shah Esmāʿil to assign his grand vizier Najm-al-Din Yār-Aḥmad Ḵuzāni with leading the Safavid forces during a major military campaign against Samarqand in close collaboration with the military governor of Astarābād Dēv-ʿAli Beg Rumlu. The Safavid army crossed the Oxus at Termeḏ late in Rajab 918/early October 1512 and descended on Qarši (Nasaf) and Bukhara. The decisive battle was fought in Ḡojdovān (q.v.), a village some 25 miles northeast of Bukhara, during which Yār-Aḥmad Ḵuzāni was arrested alive and beheaded in the battlefield. The Uzbeks then descended on Khorasan advancing westward as far as Esfarāyen (q.v.). They laid a successful siege to Herat and captured the city by the end of Moḥarram 919/March 1513. Contingents of the Uzbek forces, led by Moḥammad Timur-Solṭān and ʿObayd-Allāh Khan, engaged in offensive operations against Mashhad and captured the city shortly after the fall of Herat, at the end of a harsh winter that had already ushered in a season of famine and pestilence in Khorasan and Transoxiana. In Herat, groups of pro-Safavid elements were rounded up and put to the sword (Ḵᵛāndamir, IV, pp. 530-34; Amini Heravi, pp. 379-99; Vāṣefi Heravi, I, pp. 62-72; Qaṭaḡān, pp. 128-32; Rumlu, pp. 1065-068; Ebn Ḵᵛāndamir, pp. 81–84; Sayfi Qazvini, p. 284). The emergence of Abu'l-Qāsem Baḵši, an ex-Timurid army clerk, as leader of an anti-Safavid movement in Pušang (Bušang, Fušang; present-day Zendajān), a rural town outside Herat, contextualized Moḥammad Timur-Solṭān's merciless suppression of local backers of the Safavids in Herat. Later in 1512, when the Safavids recaptured Herat, Piri Beg Qājār went after Abu'l-Qāsem and his supporters in rural suburbs of Herat and executed many of them. Shortly afterwards, Zaynal Khan Šāmlu was made governor-general of Khorasan (Ḵᵛāndamir, IV, pp. 536-38; Qaṭaḡān, pp. 136-38; Szuppe, 1992, pp. 149-50).

Three years later, in early 1516, Shah Esmāʿil made Khorasan an appanage for his eldest son, Ṭahmāsp Mirzā, charging Amir Khan Mawṣellu, the former governor of Qāʾen and a close relative of Ṭahmāsp Mirzā's mother Tājlu Ḵānom Mawṣellu (d. 1539), with supervising him as guardian (lala) and governor-general of Khorasan (Ḵᵛāndamir, IV, p. 553; Ebn Ḵᵛāndamir, p. 89; Sayfi Qazvini, p. 287; Ḡaffāri Qazvini, p. 278; Ḥosayni ʿErāqi, pp. 64, 71; Ḵāki Širāzi, fol. 598a). In Rabiʿ I 922/April 1516,

Majd-al-Din Moḥammad Kermāni was made vizier of Khorasan and Mir Ḡiāṯ-al-Din Moḥammad Heravi took over as ṣadr, or minister for religious affairs and endowments. Less than two years later, early in 1518, Kermāni was replaced by Ḵᵛāja Moẓaffar Bitikči, an influential scribe and landed notable from Astarābād. Shortly thereafter, Amir Khan Mawṣellu made his own brother, Ebrāhim Beg, his deputy (wakil) in Khorasan. During the early years of Amir Khan's tenure, factional feuds among the Safavid administrators in Herat had become so violent and destabilizing that Shah Esmāʿil decided to intervene and to reinstate, on Rabiʿ I 924/March-April 1518, the beleaguered ṣadr Mir Ḡiāṯ-al-Din Moḥammad b. Yusof Heravi. Yet Heravi's enemies in Herat, led by Amir Khan Mawṣellu, stepped up their opposition and he was ultimately assassinated on 7 Rajab 927/13 June 1521 at the hands of one of Amir Khan's adjutants for his rumored pro-Timurid leanings (Ḵᵛāndamir, IV, pp. 554, 575-76, 583-84; Sayfi Qazvini, p. 288; Ḡaffāri Qazvini, pp. 279-80; Ebn Ḵᵛāndamir, pp. 107-10; Ḥosayni ʿErāqi, pp. 75-76). Heravi's murder took place on the eve of the Uzbek invasion of Khorasan. Shortly before this incident, Amir Khan had the tongue of a prominent Herat-based Kobrawi (see KOBRAWIYYA) mystic and poet called Āgahi cut (Ḵāki Širāzi, fol. 599a). Late in the spring of 1521, famine broke out in Herat, forcing the Uzbek ʿObayd-Allāh Khan and his armies to cut short their presence in Khorasan and withdraw to Transoxiana by the end of Jomādā II 927/June 1521 (Ḵᵛāndamir, IV, pp. 579-81; Ḥosayni ʿErāqi, pp. 70-71; Novidi Širāzi, p. 58). This incident marked the end of Amir Khan Mawṣellu's tenure as governor-general of Khorasan.

On 25 Ḏu'l-Qaʿda 927/6 November 1521, Shah Esmāʿil appointed Durmeš Khan Šāmlu (q.v.; d. 1525), his nephew and the military governor of Astarābād, as guardian (lala) of his second son Sām Mirzā (d. 1568) and governor-general of Khorasan (Ḵᵛāndamir, IV, p. 588; Ebn Ḵᵛāndamir, pp. 112-13; Sayfi Qazvini, p. 288; Ḥosayni ʿErāqi, pp. 75-76; Ḵāki Širāzi, fol. 599a). In an unpublished letter, which is dated Ḏu'l-Ḥejja 927/November-December 1521 and is addressed to his military deputies in Khorasan, Shah Esmāʿil instructed them to collaborate closely with Durmeš Khan in his efforts to restore peace and prosperity in Khorasan (Ḥosayni Širāzi, f. 318a). Upon his arrival in Herat, Durmeš Khan appointed Aḥmad Beg Ṣufi-Oḡlu Ālplu Afšār military governor of Farāh, the administrative capital of Sistān. Furthermore, he made Zaynal Khan Šāmlu, one of his close relatives, governor of Astarābād. He also ordered his military underlings in Khorasan to recognize Bābor's annexation of Kabul and Kandahar, which at that time had been given to Bābor's son, Moḥammad Kāmrān Mirzā. Gubernatorial posts in Mashhad, Nishapur, Sabzavār, and Esfarāyen were filled by a trio of Durmeš Khan's close allies. On 3 Ramażān 928/6 August 1522, the underage prince Sām Mirzā arrived in Herat and was put under the tutelage of Durmeš Khan (Ḵᵛāndamir, IV, pp. 590-92; Ebn Ḵᵛāndamir, pp. 111-14, 116; Novidi Širāzi, p. 58). Durmeš Khan's free hand in posting his relatives and cronies to Astarābād and Sistān can be taken to imply the administrative integration of these two provinces into Khorasan. Under Durmeš Khan and his vizier, Ḵᵛāja Ḥabib-Allāh Sāvaji (d. 932/1526), Khorasan became administratively centralized, excessive taxing practices introduced under Amir Khan Mawṣellu were discontinued; abandoned agricultural lands were irrigated and re-cultivated; dilapidated educational and Sufi institutions were repaired and revived; religious endowments to be used for feeding the poor were reestablished; and pro-Safavid notables of the province were offered tax exemptions (Ebn Ḵᵛāndamir, pp. 116-18; Szuppe, 1992, pp. 93-96).

The political instability that engulfed Safavid Iran during the opening years of the reign of Shah Ṭahmāsp enabled the Uzbeks to attack Herat and plunder its neighboring rural towns (Ebn Ḵᵛāndamir, pp. 128-33; Rumlu, pp. 1138-40). They eventually annexed vast swathes of land in eastern Khorasan forcing the Safavids out of Termeḏ, Šaborḡān, Balḵ, and Farāh (Bacqué-Grammont, p. 430). Shortly thereafter, they recaptured Mashhad, Nišāpur, Sabzavār, Esfarāyen, Dāmḡān, and Semnān, bringing all Khorasan under their control. In due course, Astarābād also fell to the Uzbeks (Ḥosayni ʿErāqi, pp. 84-89, 91-92, 94; Ṣafawi, pp. 582-83; Monši, p. 93; Novidi Širāzi, p. 62; Dickson, 1958, pp. 88-92). Durmeš Khan passed away following the Uzbek invasion of Herat in 1526. He was replaced by his younger brother Ḥosayn Khan Šāmlu as governor-general of Khorasan. Within a few weeks of Ḥosayn Khan's rise to power in Herat, his underlings assassinated Ḥabib-Allāh Sāvaji and promoted Aḥmad Beg Nur-e Kamāl Eṣfahāni, a bureaucrat in service of Ḥosayn Khan, to vizier of Khorasan (Ebn Ḵᵛāndamir, pp. 135-37; Ṣafawi, p. 578; Ḡaffāri Qazvini, p. 283; Novidi Širāzi, p. 62; Ḵuzāni Eṣfahāni, II, ff. 23a-24a). Shortly after Shah Ṭahmāsp's ascent to the throne, the Timurid ruler of Kabul and Kandahar, Bābor achieved a series of major conquests in India, a feat that prepared the way for him to build an empire outside Khorasan, leading the Timurids to quit the struggle for supremacy in eastern Iran (Bābor, pp. 324ff, Engl. tr., I, 445ff; Ebn Ḵᵛāndamir, pp. 137-39; Dale, pp. 320-54; Dickson, 1958, pp. 47-50). Following his territorial gains in inner Khorasan and Astarābād, ʿObayd-Allāh Khan, who at the time held office as governor of Bokhara and ranked among the most influential military commanders of the Abu'l-Khayrid ruler of Transoxiana, Güçgünci Khan (r. 1512-30), attacked Herat, triggering a bout of famine that was soon to spread to other parts of the province. The Uzbeks then laid a successful siege on Mashhad and by the end of 933/1527 managed to bring Astarābād and Dāmḡān under their control (Ebn Ḵᵛāndamir, p. 144; Qaṭaḡān, pp. 140-41; Ḥosayni Qomi, pp. 171-72; Ḥosayni ʿErāqi, p. 96; Ḵuzāni Eṣfahāni, II, ff. 24b-25a; Dickson, 1958, pp. 54-63).

The Safavids were intent on regaining supremacy in eastern Iran in the short run, but the campaign to repel the Uzbeks from Khorasan was delayed as the result of infighting between various factions of Shah Ṭahmāsp's army in Azerbaijan and ʿErāq-e ʿAjam. In the spring of 1528, the Safavid vanguard forces proceeded to Sāvoj-bolāḡ, some 50 miles to the west of Ray, and it was on 21 Šaʿbān 934/21 May 1528 outside the mountainous fortress town of Firuzkuh that Zaynal Khan Šāmlu, the former governor of Astarābād, engaged the Uzbek forces, an encounter that cost Zaynal Khan and a handful of high-ranking Safavid military commanders their lives (Ebn Ḵᵛāndamir, pp. 142-43; Ḥosayni ʿErāqi, p. 98; Ḥosayni Qomi, p. 173; Ḡaffāri Qazvini, p. 284; Novidi Širāzi, p. 64; Ḵuzāni Eṣfahāni, II, ff. 32a-b; Ḵāki Širāzi, f. 601b; Dickson, 1958, pp. 93-108). Late in the summer of 1528, Shah Ṭahmāsp led his army into Khorasan forcing the Uzbeks to end their siege of Herat, which lasted for seven months and caused the outbreak of famine in Khorasan. ʿObayd-Allāh Khan and his military deputies in the province then regrouped for the decisive battle, which was fought on 11 Moḥarram 935/5 October 1528 in Sāruqameš (present-day Zurābād/Ṣāleḥābād), a cluster of rural settlements some 50 miles north of Jām. The Battle of Sāruqameš ended with Ṭahmāsp's hurried withdrawal to ʿErāq-e ʿAjam. In the peace negotiations that ensued following the battle, Ḥusayn Khan Šāmlu, the Safavid governor of Herat, and the Uzbek governor of Bokhara, ʿObayd-Allāh Khan agreed to halt hostilities during the winter (Ebn Ḵᵛāndamir, pp. 146-52; Rumlu, pp. 1172-179; Ḥosayni Qomi, pp. 176-78, 179-89; Ḥosayni ʿErāqi, pp. 101-2; Novidi Širāzi, p. 65; Ḵuzāni Eṣfahāni, II, ff. 30b-32a, 42b-45a; Qaṭaḡān, p. 124).

Between 1528 and 1539, the year in which ʿObayd-Allāh Khan died and his Central Asian khanate plunged into several decades of civil war and administrative instability, the Safavids and the Uzbeks fought five major battles over Khorasan. During the same period, the province was also made an appanage to four Safavid princes—Shah Ṭahmāsp's two brothers, one of his nephews, and his oldest son, Moḥammad Mirzā, who later was crowned as Moḥammad Ḵodābanda. Within a few months of Shah Ṭahmāsp's withdrawal from Khorasan, which took place on 16 Rabiʿ I 937/17 November 1530, however, ʿObayd-Allāh Khan and his military deputies attacked Herat and Mashhad. In Mashhad, where the Uzbeks led by ʿObayd-Allāh Khan defeated overnight an army of about 4,000 Safavid troops, several hundred pro-Safavid civilians were arrested and massacred. At that time, the Safavid garrison in Mashhad was under the command of Aḥmad Beg Afšār, whose hurried escape to Farāh, his permanent military fief in Sistān, which took place on the night of ʿObayd-Allāh Khan's arrival before the wall of Mashhad, enabled the Uzbeks to enter Mashhad with no resistance. Shortly before the fall of Mashhad, ʿObayd-Allāh Khan had negotiated a ceasefire with Ḥusayn Khan Šāmlu, the governor-general of a famine-stricken Herat, agreeing to provide him, the Safavid prince Sām Mirzā, and their entourage safe passage to Sistān. Before making their way to Fārs, the retreating forces from Herat mounted a series of raids against Kij and Makorān (Makrān) (Rumlu, pp. 1180-82; Ḡaffāri Qazvini, p. 285; Ḥosayni Qomi, pp. 190-93; Eskandar Beg, pp. 57-58, tr., pp. 93-95). While Safavid chroniclers have chronicled in detail the fall of Herat to the Uzbeks and subsequent suppression of the pro-Safavid notables of the city, during which "many Shiite Muslims" were either tortured or beheaded in the hands of ʿObayd-Allāh Khān's armies, there is evidence from an eyewitness account that Herat did not fall to the Uzbeks at this time. The Herat-based chronicler Ebn K̲ᵛāndamir tells us that immediately after the Battle of Sāruqameš Shah Ṭahmāsp bestowed Khorasan as an appanage to his younger brother, Bahrām Mirzā (d. 1549), posting him to Herat immediately, where the Safavid prince was to live under the tutelage of Ḡāzi Beg b. Čerkes Ḥasan Tekkelu, who had just been appointed as governor-general of Khorasan. Bahrām Mirzā and Ḡāzi Beg, as Ebn K̲ᵛāndamir points out, heroically resisted and survived the Uzbek siege of Herat, which lasted for about 20 months from the spring of 1530 up until the latter part of October 1532. At the close of this long siege, when the Uzbeks decided to withdraw to Transoxiana, Shah Ṭahmāsp made Khorasan once again an appanage for Sām Mirzā and appointed Āḡzivār Khan Šāmlu as his guardian and governor-general of Herat. On 7 Ṣafar 939/18 September 1532, Shah Ṭahmāsp left Khorasan for ʿErāq-e ʿAjam (Ebn K̲ᵛāndamir, pp. 156, 158-61).

Soon after his rise to power, the Safavid governor of Herat, Āḡzivār Khan Šāmlu, and his close relatives were implicated in an attempt on the life of Shah Ṭahmāsp. It is reported that between the fall of 1532 and the early spring of 1535, the Šāmlu of Herat and their allies led by Āḡzivār Khan were involved in systematic ransacking of public funds and maltreatment of non-collaborating bureaucrats and landed notables. Consequently, within a few months of Shah Ṭahmāsp's departure, local bureaucracy broke down and the city started to suffer from depopulation and ruin. Eventually, on 15 Šaʿbān 941/1 March 1535, Āḡzivār Khan and Sām Mirzā fled to Kandahar, preparing the way for the Uzbeks to re-enter Khorasan and restore their rule on Herat. On 19 D̲u'l-qaʿda 941/1 June 1535, the Uzbeks imposed a crushing defeat on Safavid forces in Herat, massacred almost all remaining pro-Safavid elements in the city, including the renowned chronicler and bureaucrat Ṣadr-al-din Ebrāhim Amini Heravi, and then left to plunder Ḡarjestān. Ṣufiān K̲alifa Rumlu, the Safavid governor of Mashhad, then recaptured Herat, but before long introduced draconian taxes exacerbating the preexisting political chaos and administrative discontinuity. This resulted in the outbreak of a riot by the urban poor, during which the Safavid vizier of Herat, Nur-al-Din Aḥmad Eṣfahāni, was killed. Closely scrutinizing these developments, the Uzbeks laid a siege to Mashhad, forcing Ṣufiān K̲alifa and his military deputies out of Herat. In the battle that broke out on 20 Rajab 942/24 January 1536 in ʿAbdolābād, a small village outside Nišāpur, Ṣufiān K̲alifa was captured alive and beheaded on the battlefield. In Herat, the local population sided with the Uzbeks. It is reported that Amir Abu-Ṭāher b. Ṣadr-al-din Ebrāhim Amini Heravi, who had been assigned with the task of defending Herat against the Uzbeks, gave his backing to ʿObayd-Allāh Khan and agreed to raze the city's walls to the ground, which was done on 27 Ṣafar 943/25 August 1536. It was under these circumstances that the Uzbeks brought Herat under their control (Ebn K̲ᵛāndamir, pp. 162-81; Rumlu, pp. 1236-244; Budāq Monši, pp. 78-80; Ḥosayni ʿErāqi, pp. 134-35, 137-38).

Six months later, late in Šaʿbān 943/Feburary 1537, ʿObayd-Allāh Khan retreated to Bukhara on the eve of Shah Ṭahmāsp's invasion of Khorasan. The Safavid ruler then made Herat an appanage for his oldest son, Moḥammad Mirzā, who entered Herat in early Šawwāl 943/late March 1537 along with his guardian, Moḥammad Khan Šaraf-al-din Oḡli Tekkelu (d. 1557). Less than a week later, Shah Ṭahmāsp arrived in the city and remained there for almost two months. By the end of the spring of 1537, the Safavid forces invaded Kandahar and brought the city under their control. Shah Ṭahmāsp left Khorasan on 9 Rabiʿ I 944/26 August 1537 (Ebn K̲ᵛāndamir, pp. 187-97). Under the new administration, major steps were taken to revive trade and agriculture in Herat and the rural settlements clustered around it. Moḥammad Khan Tekkelu introduced regulations to curb the rising food prices. Several unruly powerbrokers and Sunni malefactors in Herat and K̲ᵛāf were arrested and executed, and from 1538 onwards Moḥammad Khan arranged for Shiite clerics to occupy top-ranking posts in local administration (Ebn K̲ᵛāndamir, pp. 198-202). Under Moḥammad Khan's leadership, the Safavid forces in Khorasan played a decisive role in restoring stability and order in Astarābād, where a group of landed notables from Fenderesk led by Moḥammad Ṣāleḥ Bitikči, a close relative of K̲ᵛāja Moẓaffar Bitikči, had risen in revolt against Shah Ṭahmāsp (Ebn K̲ᵛāndamir, pp. 203-6; Rumlu, pp. 1257-60; Ḥosayni Qomi, pp. 284-85; Reid; Abisaab). The Safavids kept Khorasan under their firm control for the rest of the long reign of Shah Ṭahmāsp.

In the fall of 1548, a contingent of the Uzbek army invaded Sarak̲s, exciting a fast and furious response from the Safavid governor of Herat. The Safavid forces defeated the Uzbek invaders in Pol-e K̲ātun, a small village outside Sarak̲s (Ebn K̲ᵛāndamir, pp. 229-30). On the night of Wednesday 15 Moḥarram 956/23 February 1549, a huge earthquake struck southern Khorasan. Bajestān, a rural town some 280 miles west of Herat, was the epicenter of the earthquake, but the disaster claimed several thousand lives to the south as far as K̲usf and Birjand (Ebn K̲ᵛāndamir, p. 231; Rumlu, p. 1332; Eskandar Beg, p. 117, tr., p. 194). In 1550, the year in which ʿObayd-Allāh Khan's son and successor, ʿAbd-al-ʿaziz Khan died, the Uzbeks, led by Borāq Khan, the new governor of Bukhara, and his military deputies in Samarqand and Tashkent, descended on Herat, laid an unsuccessful siege to the city, and then mounted a series of raids against Farāh, the administrative capital of Sistān. Until 1559-60, the Uzbeks led by ʿAbd-Allāh Khan, the governor of Balk̲, and his military deputies, including ʿAbd-al-Laṭif Khan of Samarqand and Borāq Khan of Tashkent, attacked Khorasan several times, fighting Safavid forces outside Mashhad, Torbat-e Ḥaydari, Sarak̲s, Jām, and Farāh. Consequently, rural life in the war-torn areas of the province came to a halt and thousands of agriculturalists and pastoralists across Khorasan were displaced (Ebn K̲ᵛāndamir, pp. 233-36; Rumlu, pp. 1334-36; Ḥosayni Qomi, pp. 344-45; Eskandar Beg, pp. 93-94, tr., pp. 155-56). In 1555, Shah Ṭahmāsp appointed his son Esmāʿil Mirzā to governor of Herat. Esmāʿil Mirzā departed for Herat on 6 Rabiʿ

II 962/10 March 1555, with orders to put himself under the guardianship of Moḥammad Khan Šaraf-al-Din Oḡli Tekelu (Ḥosayni-Qomi, pp. 379-81; Rumlu, p. 1395; Novidi Širāzi, p. 110). He arrived in Herat on 23 Jomādā I 963/14 April 1556 (Ḥosayni Qomi, p. 384; Jonābadi, pp. 543-44). During the year intervening between his departure from Qazvin and arrival in Herat, he had toured various cities of Khorasan, including Sabzavār, Toršiz, Zāva, Maḥwalāt, Ḵᵛāf, Bāḵarz, and Ḡuriān, deliberately avoiding a visit to the holy shrine of Imam ʿAli b. Musā al-Reżā in Mashhad, the city that had recently been assigned to his paternal cousin, Ebrāhim Mirzā b. Bahrām Mirzā (Ḥosayni-Qomi, p. 385). It is reported that during Esmāʿil Mirzā's short tenure as governor of Herat, many Sunni learned and landed notables, who had fled Khorasan early in the reign of Shah Ṭahmāsp, were exonerated and allowed resettlement in the city. The Safavid prince's pro-Sunni policies in Herat were soon to be exploited by his enemies in Qazvin who used the occasion to persuade Shah Ṭahmāsp to recall him from Khorasan (Kāmi Qazvini, f. 144a). According to Šaraf Khan Bedlisi (II, p. 208), it was the outbreak of a bitter feud between Moḥammad Khan Tekelu and his elder son, Zayn-al-Din ʿAli-Solṭān, a close friend and maternal cousin of Esmāʿil Mirzā, that prompted Ṭahmāsp to recall his son from Khorasan in less than two years. During Esmāʿil Mirzā's stay in Khorasan, Zayn-al-Din ʿAli-Solṭān Tekelu was arrested and tortured to death in Qazvin for complicity in the Safavid prince's disgraceful flings with consenting boys (Ḥosayni Qomi, p. 386; Novidi Širāzi, p. 110; Hinz, p. 35).

In 1558, shortly after the Mughal emperor Homāyun's escape to Iran (see HOMĀYUN PĀDEŠĀH), Safavid forces in Khorasan mounted a military campaign against Kandahar and, amid the chaos that erupted in Mughal India following the Afghan Šir Khan's rebellion, easily annexed the province. Shah Ṭahmāsp's nephew, Solṭān-Ḥosayn Mirzā b. Bahrām Mirzā was then posted to serve as governor-general of Kandahar. Before his departure, Shah Ṭahmāsp married off his eldest daughter, Pariḵān Ḵānom (q.v.), to Solṭān-Ḥosayn Mirzā's younger brother, Badiʿ-al-Zamān Mirzā and appointed him as governor-general of Sistān and assigned his guardianship to Moḥammad Jān Beg Ḏu'l-Qadr, a military commander from Shiraz (Rumlu, p. 1406; Ḥosayni Qomi, pp. 396-97; Eskandar Beg, pp. 90-92, tr., pp. 151-54). A year later, in 1559, a contingent of the Uzbek forces from Ḵᵛārazm led by ʿAli-Solṭān descended on Nišāpur and Esfarāyen, plundering major rural settlements clustered around both fortress towns. The same Uzbeks attacked Mashhad four years later in 1563. It is reported that ʿAli-Solṭān, who had turned Nasā/Nesā into his base, had allied with Šahriār, a powerful landed notable in Ḵabušān who claimed descent from the Sarbedārs (q.v.). Subsequently, in 1564, the Safavid forces attacked Ḵabušān and massacred Šahriār and his clan. Shah Ṭahmāsp then appointed Āyḡut Beg Čāvošlu as governor of Kalidar, a major rural settlement outside Ḵabušān (Ḥosayni Qomi, pp. 435, 442, 447). In the same year, Qazāq Khan Tekkelu, who had inherited the governorship of Herat from his father Moḥammad Khan Tekkelu and reportedly planned an armed rebellion against the Safavids, was arrested on his deathbed by a group of Safavid military commanders in Khorasan led by Shah Ṭahmāsp's nephew and son-in-law, Ebrāhim Mirzā (Ḥosayni Qomi, pp. 448-49; Rumlu, pp. 1436-39). The Uzbeks of Bukhara entered Khorasan in the winter of 1567 and laid a siege to Herat. Yet the Safavid forces in the city endured the siege and eventually repelled the Uzbeks from Khorasan before the end of winter (Ḥosayni Qomi, pp. 457-58).

Under Shah Ṭahmāsp and his immediate successors various Turkic and Kurdish tribes and clans were forced and/or coordinated to settle in Khorasan. Prominent among the Turkic clans that were sent to Khorasan are those affiliated with the Afšārs, which had been granted permanent *toyul* land assignments in Farāh and Abivard, a fortress town some 180 miles north of Mashhad. The Afšār clans posted to Abivard and its rural suburbs on the foothills of the Hazār Masjed mountain range bore the Turkish moniker *qereqlu* (from Turkish *qırıq/kırık* meaning broken off, cut off, detached), that is, clans dismembered from the mother tribe, and were composed mainly of the Eyerlu (also Ajarlu and Abarlu) and Šarvānlu (also Sarvarlu). According to the 16th-century Ottoman land surveys, we know that the Eyerlu Afšārs were originally from eastern Anatolia and a major community of them is reported to have lived, as early as 1530, a nomadic life in the defunct Ḏu'l-Qadr (q.v.) emirate in the areas stretching from Aleppo to Kayseri (*998 Numaralı Muhâsebe*, II, col. 624; Refik, pp. 96-100; Mirniā, II, pp. 25, 29; Mostawfi, p. 412). The earliest known group of the Qereqlu, led by a certain Ḵosrow-Solṭān, is reported to have moved to Khorasan under Ṭahmāsp (Eskandar Beg, p. 140, tr. pp. 222-24). Under Shah ʿAbbās they were joined by another group of the Qereqlu Afšārs from central Anatolia, whose leader, a certain Ebrāhim-Solṭān, is reported to have held office as governor of Saraḵs (Eskandar Beg, p. 1085, tr., p. 1310). A branch of the Ostājlu/Afšār Kurds and Turkmens, headed by a certain Biktāš Khan, had been granted military fiefs in Marv, Nasā, and Abivard under Shah ʿAbbās (Eskandar Beg, p. 1085). In the opening part of the 17th century, groups of Eyerlu and Qereqlu Afšārs lived in Abivard, where they were responsible for thwarting the Uzbeks' threat against major urban centers in inner Khorasan (Eskandar Beg, *Ḏayl*, p. 22; Vāleh Eṣfahāni, p. 26). According to a mid-18th-century chronicler, after his recapture of Azerbaijan in the opening years of the 17th century, Shah ʿAbbās sent 4,500 households of the Afšārs, together with 30,000 households of Kurds from rural and nomadic settlements clustered around Lake Urmia, to Khorasan, where the Afšārs had already been granted land in Abivard and Darragaz, a rural settlement some 30 miles southeast of Abivard. A group of Qājārs from Tabriz were also sent to settle in Marv shortly thereafter (Marvi, I, pp. 4-5; Qoddusi, p. 20; Astarābādi, pp. 26-27, 49). Various clans associated with the Çemişgezek (present-day Dersim) Kurdish nomads of eastern Anatolia, including the Zaʿfarānlu, Qochkānlu, Šādlu (also Saʿdlu), Kāvānlu (also Kayvānlu), and Dudānlu, were also granted lands and pastures in northern Khorasan, mainly in Rādkān, Kalāt, the rural suburbs of Ḵabušān and Abivard, and Esfarāyen (Mirniā, I, pp. 13-14; Eskandar Beg, p. 141, tr., pp. 226-27; Mostawfi, pp. 410-11). Groups of Siāh-Manṣur (or Siāh-Mondur) Kurds, who were originally from Dersim, had been posted as well to Khorasan under the Safavids, where one of them by the name of Emāmqoli Khan held office as governor of Esfarāyen during the reign of Shah ʿAbbās (Eskandar Beg, p. 1086, tr., p. 1313). In the closing years of the 16th century, small groups of the Šāhseven tribal confederacy of Azerbaijan and Qarābāḡ ended up in Khorasan (Oberling, p. 38). Under the early Safavids, several clans of the Šāmlu and the Tekkelu clans settled in Herat, Jām, and Mashhad (Eskandar Beg, p. 140, tr., p. 225). Under Shah ʿAbbās, the Chagatai (also Jaḡatāʾi) Mongols and the Bayāt Turkmens of Khwarazm, including the Jalāyer, Qarabayāt, and Garāyeli (also Qarāʾi) clans, held high-ranking military posts in Kalāt, Nišāpur, Sabzavār, Buzanjerd (present-day Bojnurd, q.v.), and Jargalān (Eskandar Beg, p. 1087, tr., p. 1314; Mostawfi, pp. 412). Later in the reign of Shah ʿAbbās II (r. 1052-77/1642-66), the leader of the Pāzuki tribe, Mortażāqoli Khan Saʿdlu, was instructed by the Safavid ruler to move all Georgian converts in service of the Safavid bureaucracy to Khorasan, where they were to be placed in charge of local Muslim communities (Waḥid Qazvini, p. 757). Under the later Safavids, all nomadic and semi-nomadic tribes and clans of Khorasan were considered part of the Qara-Olus, or the country's taxpayer nomads, paying taxes to the vizier of Qarā Olus, an official in charge of keeping record of the livestock, movements, and tax proceeds of nomads across Safavid Iran (Anṣāri Eṣfahāni, p. 592).

Shortly after Esmāʿil II's (q.v.) ascent to the throne, which occurred in the summer of 984/1576, and following the bloody purges that claimed the lives of almost all male members of the Safavid dynasty, Jalāl Khan, the Uzbek governor of Urganj, invaded Khorasan, where his troops plundered Nasā, Abivard, Jām, and Saraḵs. The decisive battle was fought outside ʿEšqābād, a small village some 25 miles south of Nišāpur, during which the Safavid forces, led by Mortażāqoli Khan Pornāk, the governor (*beglarbeg*) of Mashhad, arrested Jalāl Khan alive and beheaded him on the battlefield. This victory intensified rivalries between Mortażāqoli Beg and the Safavid governor of Herat, ʿAliqoli Beg Šāmlu, preparing the way for the outbreak of civil war in Khorasan (Eskandar Beg, pp. 229-30, tr., pp. 342-44). In 1577, Shah Esmāʿil II removed his elder brother, Moḥammad Mirzā, as nominal governor of Herat and imprisoned him in Fārs. Still, the Šāmlu notables of Herat kept Solṭān-Moḥammad Mirzā's newborn son, ʿAbbās Mirzā, in Heart and, by Shah Esmāʿil II's order, the governor-general of Khorasan, ʿAliqoli Khan Šāmlu, who had recently married Shah Ṭahmāsp's daughter, Zaynab Begum (q.v.), acted as his guardian (Ḥosayni Qomi, pp. 650-51; Eskandar Beg, pp. 243-45, tr., pp. 362-64).

Backed by the Afšārs, Kurds, and his Torkmān (Rumlu and Pornāk) relatives in Mashhad, Jām, Ḵabušān, Esfarāyen, and Nišāpur, the governor of Mashhad, Mortażāqoli Khan Pornāk soon entered a war with the Šāmlu clan and their Ostājlu allies in Herat. In 1580, the Šāmlu forces laid a siege to Mashhad, which lasted for four months, during which a group of local notables, including the chief superintendent of Imam ʿAli al-Reżā's shrine, Mir ʿAbd-al-Karim, were killed and a large part of the city's fortifications was leveled to the ground. It is reported that toward the end of the siege of Mashhad Mortażāqoli Khan Pornāk ordered the confiscation of all gold and silver reserves of the Shiʿite shrine of the city, a move that enabled him to mint new coins to buy the loyalty of his troops. Nišāpur and Sabzavār were also attacked and plundered by the Šāmlu (Eskandar Beg Torkmān, pp. 254-56, Engl. tr., pp. 375-80; Ḥosayni Qomi, pp. 711-13; Jonābadi, pp. 609-17).

Following their victories in Khorasan, late in the summer of 1581, the Šāmlu of Herat and their Ostājlu allies led by Moršedqoli Khan Čāvošlu swore allegiance to ʿAbbās Mirzā in Zāva, a rural settlement some 120 miles south of Nišāpur, as Shah ʿAbbās. The turn of events in Khorasan excited a vigorous response from Azerbaijan. In the spring of 1583, the grand vizier Mirzā Salmān Jāberi, who had planned to enthrone Ḥamza Mirzā , his son-in-law and ʿAbbās Mirzā's older brother, as shah, led the Safavid army from Azerbaijan to Khorasan. During the battle that took place in Ḡuriān, a rural town outside Herat, the Šāmlu and Ostājlu military commanders defeated Mirzā Salmān and beheaded him on the battlefield (Eskandar Beg, pp. 276-78, tr., pp. 375-80, 406-8; Ḥosayni Qomi, pp. 736-47; Jonābadi, pp. 618-21; Afuštaʾi Naṭanzi, pp. 131-35; Savory, 1964).

In the years leading to Shah ʿAbbās' rise to power as ruler of all Iran, Khorasan suffered greatly from political strife and military conflicts between various factions of the Qezelbāš. In the spring of 1589, the Uzbeks led by ʿAbd-Allāh Khan captured Herat after a short siege and massacred several hundred pro-Safavid elements in the city. They then invaded Mashhad and laid a long siege to the city. One year later, in the spring of 1590, while Shah ʿAbbās was busy eliminating his opponents from among the Qezelbāš military commanders, the Uzbek ʿAbd-al-Moʾmen Khan b. ʿAbd-Allāh Khan captured Mashhad and beheaded almost all renowned supporters of the Safavid dynasty there. This new round of territorial conquests eventually brought Khorasan under the firm control of the Uzbeks (Eskandar Beg, pp. 386-89, 411-14, tr. pp. 557-65, 588-91). In 1592, the Safavid forces led by Farhād Beg Qarāmānlu invaded Khorasan and managed to recapture Esfarāyen, an important fortress town some 65 miles north of Sabzavār (Eskandar Beg, pp. 443-45, tr. pp. 617-19). One year later, pro-Safavid forces in Mazinān killed their Uzbek governor and helped the Safavid forces in Esfarāyen bring this major rural settlement, sitting astride the route from Sabzavār to Dāmḡān, under their control (Eskandar Beg, pp. 451-53, tr. pp. 625-28). In 1593, the Uzbeks fought a major battle against the Safavid forces in Tun, a rural town some 85 miles west of Qāʾen, where the invaders were surprised by Safavid auxiliary forces sent to Khorasan from Kerman and had to withdraw to Herat and Mashhad (Eskandar Beg, pp. 455-56, tr. pp. 628-30). In 1593-94, the Uzbeks descended on Toršiz, where they defeated the Safavid forces and annexed Tun and Ṭabas. This victory emboldened the Uzbeks to attack Yazd a year later, where they plundered the dominantly Zoroastrian-populated neighborhoods of the city (Eskandar Beg, pp. 489-90, 525-26, tr. pp. 663-66, 701-2; Ghereghlou, 2017, p. 61). In the spring of 1596, Farhād Khan Qarāmānlu, the incumbent generalissimo (*amir-al-omarāʾ*), led the Safavid army into Khorasan, where they invaded Jājarm and Esfarāyen, forcing ʿAbd-al-Moʾmen Khan to withdraw to Mashhad. Yet the Uzbek forces made a quick comeback and captured Sabzavār, where ʿAbd-al-Moʾmen Khan ordered the massacre of all pro-Safavid elements together with their families (Eskandar Beg, pp. 509-12, tr. pp. 681-89).

Eventually it was in 1598 that Shah ʿAbbās personally mounted his major military campaign against the Uzbeks in Khorasan. The Safavid army captured the province with no significant resistance on the part of ʿAbd-al-Moʾmen Khan and his underlings, who following the death of ʿAbd-Allāh Khan and subsequent outbreak of civil war in Samarqand and Bukhara in the same year, had to withdraw to Balḵ. In Balḵ, ʿAbd-al-Moʾmen Khan was assassinated by his opponents and Din-Moḥammad, a nephew of ʿAbdallāh Khan, ascended to the throne as khan (Eskandar Beg, pp. 556-63, tr. pp. 738-48). The decisive battle was fought in Pol-e Sālār, a small village outside Herat, during which the Uzbeks were defeated and all major urban centers in Khorasan, including Herat, Mashhad, Nišāpur, Sabzavār, Toršiz, Tun, and Ṭabas, were brought under the undisputed control of the Safavid forces (Eskandar Beg, pp. 570-76, tr. pp. 755-63). Shah ʿAbbās returned to Khorasan in 1599 to conduct a series of punitive campaigns in the provinces, including a raid against Abivard, Nasā, and Marv in 1600, where his forces drove out the remaining Uzbeks (Eskandar Beg, pp. 595-605, tr. pp. 783-96). More than two years later, in 1602-3, Shah ʿAbbās attacked Balḵ. The Safavid forces descended on major rural towns, including Bādḡis and Andḵoy, on their way from Herat to Balḵ. The military campaign against Balḵ ended without a significant victory. Yet it was a pre-emptive engagement aimed at destroying the Uzbek support network and thwarting them in their quest for making a quick comeback after Shah ʿAbbās' departure from Herat (Eskandar Beg, pp. 619-30, tr. pp. 809-22).

In 1612, during his visit to Khorasan, Shah ʿAbbās ordered a major expansion project in the Shiʿite shrine of Mashhad. The central courtyard of the shrine was subsequently broadened. A new veranda was also added. Additionally, a boulevard was constructed extending from the shrine's main entrance to the city's western gate (*darvāza-ye Ḵabušān*). All houses and local businesses located along Mashhad's Upper Street (*bālā ḵiābān*), to the south of the shrine, were connected to a newly expanded *qanāt* network, allowing local authorities to build new hostels and bathhouses there. In the same year, Shah ʿAbbās ordered the construction of two local shrines in Khorasan, one in a cemetery called Ḵᵛāja Rabiʿ outside Mashhad and the other outside Nishapur on the site of a popular sanctuary called Qadam-gāh (Bāfqi, pp. 228-29; Afżal-al-Molk Kermāni, p. 252). Shah ʿAbbās then ordered the settlement of several hundred Arab immigrants from Bahrain in Qadam-gāh, charging them with supervising the newly founded shrine (Afżal-al-Molk Kermāni, p. 93). On 27 Moḥarram 1012/7 July 1603, an orphanage and boarding school for the *sayyeds* was established in Mashhad by royal fiat. This institution remained in operation until the end of the reign of Shah ʿAbbās II (1052-77/1642-66) (Jahānpur, pp. 69-78). Funded by the Georgian governor of Shiraz Allāh-Verdi Khan (q.v.; d. 1613), the construction of a new dome together with a decorated veranda and portal was completed in 1612 (Afżal-al-Molk Kermāni, pp. 253-54). In 1613, construction work on a major irrigation canal called *nahr-e šāhi*, designed to bring water to Mashhad from the Gel-Asb springs (*češma-ye gel-asb*, also *češma-ye gilās*) located some 35 miles west of Mashhad in the foothills of the Hazār Masjed range, was finished. In Jomādā I 1023/June-July 1614, Shah ʿAbbās officially endowed to the Shiʿite shrine in Mashhad all the revenues to be collected from the villages, farmlands, and businesses located along this irrigation canal (Rawšani Zaʿfarānlu, pp. 324-25).

Shortly after Shah Ṣafi's ascent to the throne in the winter of 1629, the Uzbeks of Urganj led by Esfandiār Khan invaded Khorasan. Major infightings are reported to have been taken place in the summer of the same year in Abivard, where the Eyerlu and Qereqlu Afšārs, led by the Ostājlu governor of Marv, Bekiš Khan; the Georgian governor of Abivard, Jamšid-Solṭān; and the Circassian governor of Mashhad, Manučehr Khan, killed many Uzbeks in a series of ambushes, forcing Esfandiār Khan out of Khorasan (Vāleh Eṣfahāni, pp. 24-30; Moḥammad Maʿṣum Eṣfahāni, pp. 57-59; Eskandar Beg, *Ḏayl*, pp. 21-22; Vaḥid Qazvini, pp. 225-26). A year later, Shah Ṣafi sent several divisions of his harquebusiers (*tofangčis*) to Khorasan, where Manučehr Khan posted them to Abivard, Nasā, and Marv (Moḥammad Maʿṣum Eṣfahāni, pp. 61-62). In the winter of 1630, Shah Ṣafi was presented with a petition from Ḥasan Khan Šāmlu, the governor of Herat, and his underlings in Khorasan, in which they had complained about a remarkable increase in the number and frequency of Uzbek raids against rural and pastoral settlements in northern Khorasan. Accordingly, the Safavid ruler issued a new order, instructing his military deputies in Khorasan "to kill or die" in their border confrontations with the Uzbek invaders (Moḥammad Maʿṣum Eṣfahāni, pp. 122-23). In the spring of 1632, new auxiliary forces from among the Afšār, Pāzuki, and Silsupur tribes of Kerman and Semnan were posted to Marv and fortress towns of Abivard and Nasā immediately after the news of a new Uzbek invasion of Khorasan reached Isfahan (Eṣfahāni, pp. 132-34). Border clashes with the Uzbeks continued during the remaining years of the reign of Shah Ṣafi (1038-52/1629-42). There is evidence that in most cases Safavid forces in the province were successful in their efforts to ward off the Uzbek advances beyond Marv, Abivard, and northern suburbs of Herat (Moḥammad Maʿṣum Eṣfahāni, 171, 175, 190-92, 259).

In 1674, a devastating earthquake hit Mashhad, causing considerable damages to the Shiite shrine in the city. Two years later, Shah Solaymān I (q.v.) ordered major repairs on the shrine's main dome (*Tārik̲-e Mašhad*, fol. 1a; Basṭāmi, p. 50; Afżal-al-Molk Kermāni, p. 254). Šāh-Verdi Khan, a high-ranking official at the court of Shah Solaymān, is also reported to have financed the construction of a caravanserai, a public bath, and a bazaar in Mashhad (Basṭāmi, p. 50). In 1708-9, the Safavid governor of Tun and Ṭabas, Malek Maḥmud b. Fatḥ-ʿAli Sistāni, whose brother Malek Ḥosayn held office as governor of Kerman, brought much of Khorasan under his control and eventually, in 1723, made Mashhad his capital. His supporters were mainly from among the Arab tribes of southern Khorasan, including the Zanguʾi, Nak̲aʿi, Lālāʾi (also Loʾloʾi), and Bābāʾi (Vāred Ṭehrāni, pp. 118-31; *Tārik̲-e Mašhad*, f. 1a). In 1717, the Uzbek ruler of Urgenj Šir Khan descended on northern Khorasan, plundering Marv, Abivard, Nishapur, K̲abušān, and Sabzevār (Marʿaši, pp. 22-23).

The inaction and negligence on the part of the late Safavid authorities in Isfahan soon excited public outrage in Khorasan. In Sabzavār, a local cleric called Shaikh Bahāʾ-al-Din Estiri, rebelled against the Safavids and, upon the Uzbek Šir Khan's arrival in Khorasan in 1717, led an army of his local supporters to the battlefield. When the Uzbeks withdrew from Khorasan, he traveled to the court of Shah Solṭān-Ḥosayn (q.v.; r. 1105-35/1694-1722) to discuss the seriousness of the situation in Khorasan with the Safavid rulers' bureaucratic underlings, but Shiite clerics in Isfahan accused him of apostasy and armed rebellion against the just ruler (Astarābādi, pp. 6-7). In the meantime, the Abdāli Afghans descended on Mashhad, where they fought a brief battle with the Safavid forces and laid an unsuccessful thirty-five-day siege to the city (*Tārik̲-e Mašhad*, f. 1a). Estiri was ultimately nabbed by the Safavid governor of Khorasan, Ṣafiqoli Khan Torkestānoḡli, also known as *divāna* (lunatic), and put to the sword for his anti-Safavid leanings (Marʿaši, pp. 24-26). Likewise, in Abivard, the local governor of the fortress town, Bābā-ʿAli Beg Köse-Aḥmadlu Afšār and his son-in-law Nāderqoli Qereqlu Afšār organized local centers of resistance against the Uzbeks to repel them from the northern and northwestern suburbs of Mashhad. On the eve of Sistāni's rise to power, two Kurdish military commanders from the Ganjlu Kalāvand clan staged a military coup against the Safavid governor of the city, Esmāʿil Khan Šāmlu, and seized Mashhad, an incident that in the short run brought about political chaos and administrative instability in the province (Mostawfi, *Zubdat*, pp. 175-76). Under Ṣafiqoli Khan Torkestān-oḡli, the Safavid military commanders in Mashhad had to confiscate all gold and silver reserves of the Shiite shrine in the city to mobilize their forces against the Abdāli rebels of Herat. Internal feuds among Ṣafiqoli Khan's Kurdish and Qājār supporters resurfaced shortly before the decisive battle, which was fought in Kāfer-Qalʿa outside Herat, leading to Ṣafiqoli Khan's defeat and death on the battlefield (Marʿaši, pp. 27-28; Astarābādi, p. 8). The plunder of the Shiite shrine in Mashhad was repeated under Malek Maḥmud Sistāni, who spent the remainder of its gold and silver reserves to mint new coins in his own name (Mostawfi, *Zobdat*, p. 180).

In 1721, the Ḡalzāʾi (Ḡalzi, q.v.) Afghans descended on Mashhad but failed to capture the city (*Tārik̲-e Mašhad*, f. 1a). After the fall of Isfahan in the fall of 1722, Nāderqoli Beg Qereqlu Afšār emerged victorious from his clashes with Malek Maḥmud Sistāni. Ṭahmāsp II (r. 1135-45/1722-32) entered Mashhad together with Nāderqoli Beg on 27 Moḥarram 1138/5 October 1725 after a ten-month siege, during which Malek Maḥmud Sistāni vehemently resisted the Safavid ruler and his armies (*Tārik̲-e Mašhad*, f. 1b). Shortly thereafter, Nāderqoli Beg eliminated Fatḥ-ʿAli Khan Qājār, and on 16 Rabiʿ I 1138/22 November 1725 was promoted to head of the royal guards (*qurči-bāši*). He then plotted against his old rival, Malek Maḥmud Sistāni, who had now taken refuge inside the shrine. Ultimately, one of Nāder's allies by the name of Qelič Khan Ganjlu Kalāvand, who held office as the prefect of Mashhad, arrested and executed Malek Maḥmud together with a group of his relatives on 4 Rajab 1139/25 February 1727 (Mostawfi, *Zobdat*, pp. 183-84; *Tārik̲-e Mašhad*, ff. 1a-b).

Under Nāder Shah (r. 1148-60/1736-47) and his immediate successors, Khorasan was no longer threatened by the Uzbeks. Nāder Shah invested huge amounts of money on expanding Imam ʿAli al-Reżā's shrine and its endowments in Khorasan (Basṭāmi, pp. 53-54). A large group of Jews were transplanted from Qazvin and Daylamān to Mashhad early in the reign of Nāder Shah, where he took them under his protection and settled them in a newly built neighborhood outside the city walls (Levi, III, p. 473). During his short reign, Nāder Shah's nephew and successor, ʿAliqoli Khan Qereqlu Afšār, also known as ʿAdel Shah (q.v.), who ascended to the throne on 27 Jomāda II 1160/6 July 1747, also invested in the expansion of the endowments of Imam ʿAli al-Reżā's shrine in Mashhad. ʿĀdel Shah built a sanatorium (*dār al-šefā*) in Mashhad and endowed to the shrine several villages outside the city (Naqdi Kadkani, pp. 87-88). Internal strife under ʿAdel Shah led to his downfall and execution two years later at the hands of Nāder Shah's grandson, Šāhrok̲, who shortly after his victory over ʿĀdel Shah, allied himself with the Qom-based Sayyed Moḥammad Marʿaši Ṣafawi, who claimed descent from Shah Solaymān and at the time had been put in charge of the treasures confiscated by ʿĀdel Shah's younger brother Ebrāhim during his short reign in Azerbaijan and ʿErāq-e ʿAjam, including the Kuh-e Nur (see KOH-I-NOOR) and Daryā-ye Nur (q.v.) diamonds. Šāhrok̲ invited Sayyed Moḥammad to Mashhad, but less than a year after his arrival in Mashhad, he fell into disfavor and even the Afsharid ruler of Khorasan tried to assassinate him. Upon the failure of the assassination plot, all the erstwhile supporters of Šāhrok̲ sided with Sayyed Moḥammad and declared him shah. Sayyed Moḥammad took Mashhad under his control by the end of 1749 and on 5 Ṣafar 1163/14 January 1750, was crowned as the Safavid Shah Solaymān II (Marʿaši Ṣafawi, 90-115; Marʿaši, pp. 97-110; Perry, pp. 4-5). Less than three months later, the sightless Šāhrok̲ was reinstated and Sayyed Moḥammad, now blinded by his opponents, was removed from office. Toward the end of the reign of Šāhrok̲, Aḥmad Shah Dorrāni invaded Mashhad and, in the early summer of 1754, laid a siege to the city, which lasted for nine months, but failed to capture it (Marʿaši Ṣafawi, 90-115; Marʿaši, pp. 112-21). Šāhrok̲ remained in power as governor of Mashhad until 1795, the year in which Āqā Moḥammad Khan Qājār entered the city and put an end to the reign of the Afsharids (Sāravi, pp. 285-88).

Bibliography: Sources: *998 Numaralı Muhâsebe-i Vilâyet-i Diyâr-i Bekr ve 'Arab ve Zü'l-Kâdiriyye Defteri (937/1530)*, Osmanli Arşivleri Daire Başkanlığı 40, ed. Ahmet Özkılınç, 2 vols., Ankara 1998-99. Maḥmud b. Hedāyat-Allāh Afušta'i Naṭanzi, *Noqāwat al-āṯār fi ẕekr al-ak̲yār* [*sic*], ed. Eḥsān Ešrāqi, Tehran, 1971. Ṣadr-al-din Ebrāhim Amini Heravi, *Fotuḥāt-e šāhi*, ed. Moḥammad-Reżā Naṣiri, Tehran, 2004. Moḥammad Rafiʿ Anṣāri Eṣfahāni, "Dastur al-moluk," in *Daftar-e tārik̲* I, ed. Iraj Afšār, Tehran, 2001, pp. 477-651. Mahdi Khan Astarābādi, *Jahāngošā-ye nāderi*, ed. ʿAbd-Allāh Anwār, Tehran, 1962. Ẓahir-al-din Moḥammad Bābor, *Bābor-nāma*, ed. N. Ilminski, as *Babernameh: Djagataice ad fidem codicis petropolitani*, Kazan, 1857; Engl. tr. Annette Susannah Beveridge, as *The Bābur-nāma in English: Memoirs of Babar*, 2 vols., London, 1921-22. Moḥammad Mofid Bāfqi, *Mok̲taṣar-e Mofid*, ed. I. Afšār and M. R. Abu'i-Mahrizi, Tehran, 2011. Nowruz-ʿAli Basṭāmi, *Ferdaws al-tawārik̲*, ed. ʿAli-Reżā Akrami, Tehran, 2011. Šaraf Khan Bedlisi, *Šaraf-nāma*, ed. Vladimir Véliaminof-Zernof, 2 vols., St. Petersburg, 1860-62. Mirzā Moḥammad-Ḥaydar Doğlāt, *Tarikh-i-Rashidi: A History of the Khans of Moghulistan*, ed. and tr. Wheeler M. Thackston, Cambridge, Mass., 1996.

Amir Maḥmud Ebn K̲ᵛāndamir, *Tārik̲-e Šāh Esmāʿil va Šāh Ṭahmāsb Ṣafavi (Ḏayl-e Ḥabib al-siar)*, ed. Moḥammad-ʿAli Jarrāḥi, Tehran, 1991. Moḥammad-Maʿṣum b. K̲ᵛājagi Eṣfahāni, *K̲olāṣat al-siar*, ed. Iraj Afšār, Terhan, 1989. Eskandar Beg Monši Torkmān, *Ḏayl-e tārik̲-e ʿālam-ārā-ye ʿabbāsi*, ed. Aḥmad Sohayli K̲ᵛānsāri, Tehran, 1938. Idem, *Tārik̲-e ʿālam-ārā-yi ʿabbāsi*, ed. Iraj Afšār, Tehran, 1954-56; tr., Roger M. Savory, *History of Shah ʿAbbas the Great*, 3 vols., Boulder, Col., 1978-86. Evrâk 8316, Topkapı Palace Museum Archives, Istanbul, MS Dev-ʿAli Beg Rumlu to grand vizier ʿAbd al-Bāqi Kermāni (undated). Evrâk 12212, Topkapı Palace Museum Archives, Istanbul, MS Amir Khan Mawṣellu to Shah Esmāʿil (undated). Lajos Fekete, *Einführung in die persische Paläographie. 101 persische dokumente*, ed. Gyorgy Hazai, Budapest, 1977 (Persian text and German translation on opposite pages). Aḥmad Ğaffāri Qazvini, *Tārik̲-e jahānārā*, Tehran, 1964. Qāsem Beg Ḥayāti Tabrizi, *A Chronicle of the Early Safavids and the Reign of Shah Ismail*, ed. Kioumars Ghereghlou, New Haven, Conn., 2018. Moḥammad-ʿAli Ḥazin Lāhiji, "Wāqeʿāt-e Irān o Hind," in idem, *Rasā'el-e Ḥazin Lāhiji*, ed. ʿAli Awjabi, Tehran, 1998. K̲oršāh Ḥosayni ʿErāqi, *Tārik̲-e ilči-e Neẓām-Šāh*, ed. Moḥammad-Reżā Naṣiri and Ko'ichi Haneda, Tehran, 2000. Aḥmad Ḥosayni Qomi, *K̲olāṣat al-tavārik̲*, ed. Eḥsān Ešrāqi, 2 vols., Tehran, 2004. Mir Abu'l-Mafāk̲er Ḥosayni Širāzi, *Majmuʿa*, Majles Library, Tehran, MS 8536. Abu'l-Qāsem Beg Ivoğli, *Majmaʿ al-enšā'*, British Library, London, MS Add.7688. Mirzā Beg Jonābadi, *Rawżat al-Ṣafawiyya*, ed. Ğolām-Reżā Ṭabāṭabā'i Majd, Tehran, 1999. Ḥasan Beg K̲āki Širāzi, *Aḥsan al-tawārik̲*, British Library, London, MS Or.1649. Mir ʿAlā'-al-Dawla Kāmi Qazvini, *Nafā'es al-ma'āṯer*, Bayerische Staatsbibliothek, Munich, MS Persien 3. Ğiāṯ-al-Din K̲ᵛāndamir, *Tārik̲-e ḥabib al-siar*, ed. Moḥammad Dabirsiāqi, 4 vols., Tehran, 1954. ʿAli Karimiān, "Bāzk̲ᵛāni-e čand farmān-i Nāder Šāh Afšār," *Ganjina-ye asnād* 7/1-2, 1997, pp. 212-22. G. Ḥ. Afżal-al-Molk Kermāni, *Ẓafar-nāma-yi ʿażodi (Zād-al-mosāfer, 1301 H.Q.)*, ed. M. R. Qaṣṣābiān, Mashhad, 2010. Fażl-Allāh Ruzbehān K̲onji Eṣfahāni, *Ebṭāl-e nahj al-bāṭel*, Majles Library, Tehran, MS 10488. Idem, *Mehmān-nāma-ye Bok̲ārā*, ed. Manučehr Sotuda, Tehran, 1976. Idem, *Soluk al-moluk*, ed. Moḥammad-ʿAli Mowaḥḥed, Tehran, 1983. Fażli Beg K̲uzāni Eṣfahāni, *Afżal al-tawārik̲* I, Cambridge University Library, MS Pote-Eton 278; II, British Library, London, MS Or. 4678; III, ed. Kioumars Ghereghlou as *A Chronicle of the Reign of Shah ʿAbbās*, 2 vols. with continuous pagination, Cambridge, 2015.

Majmuʿa makātib, Majles Library, Tehran, MS 606. Moḥammad-K̲alil Marʿaši, *Majmaʿ al-tawārik̲ dar tārik̲-e enqerāż-e ṣafawiyya wa waqāyeʿ-e baʿd tā sāl-e 1207 hejri qamari*, ed. ʿAbbās Eqbāl, 1949, repr. 1983. Solṭān-Hāšem Mirzā Marʿaši Ṣafawi, *Zabur-e āl-e Dāvud*, ed. ʿAbd-al-Ḥosayn Navā'i, Terhan, 2000. ʿAbd-Allāh Marvārid, *Šaraf-nāma*, İstanbul Üniversitesi Kütüphanesi, MS F87, facsimile ed. and tr., Hans Robert Roemer as *Staatsschreiben der Timuridenzeit: Das Šaraf-nāmä des ʿAbdallāh Marwārīd in Kritischen Auswertung*, Wiesbaden, 1952. Moḥammad Kāẓem Marvi, *Tārik̲-e ʿālam-ārā-ye nāderi*, ed. Moḥammad-Amin Riāḥi, 3 vols., Tehran, 1985. Mir Moḥammad Maʿṣum Behkari (Bakkari), *Tārik̲-e Send*, ed. ʿOmar b. Moḥammad Dā'udputa, Tehran, 2003. ʿAli Mo'ayyad Ṯābeti, *Asnād wa nāmahā-ye tāriki: Az awā'el-e dawrahā-ye eslāmi tā awāk̲er-e ʿahd-e Šāh Esmāʿil Ṣafawi*, Tehran, 1967. Budāq Monši Qazvini, *Javāher al-ak̲bār*, ed. Moḥammad-Reżā Naṣiri and Koi'chi Haneda, Tokyo, 1999. Moḥammad-Ḥosayn Mostawfi, "Tafṣil-e ʿasāker-i firuzi ma'āṯer-e Šāh Solṭān-Ḥosayn Ṣafavi," *FIZ* 20, 1974, pp. 396-421. Moḥammad-Moḥsen Mostawfi, *Zobdat al-tawārik̲*, ed. Behruz Gudarzi, Tehran, 1996. Moḥammad Yusof b. K̲ᵛāja Baqā Monši, *Taḏkera-ye moqimk̲āni: Siar-e tārik̲i, farhangi, wa ejtemāʿi-e Māwarā'-al-nahr dar ʿahd-e Šaybāniān wa Aštark̲āniān*, ed. Ferešta Ṣarrāfān, Tehran, 2001. Šir-Moḥammad Mirāb Munes and Moḥammad-Reżā Mirāb Āgahi, *Ferdaws al-eqbāl: K̲ᵛārazm tārik̲i*, ed. Yuri E. Bregel, Leiden, 1988. Moḥammad Šarif Nasafi, *Safina*,

National Library of Iran, Tehran, MS 1194423. ʿAli-Naqi Naṣiri, *Alqāb wa mawājeb-e dowra-ye salāṭin-e Ṣafawiya*, ed. Yusof Raḥimlu, Mashhad, 1992. ʿAbd-al-Ḥosayn Navāʾi, ed., *Asnād wa mokātebāt-e tāriḵi az Timur tā Šāh Esmāʿil*, Tehran, 1962. Idem, ed., *Šāh Ṭahmāsb Ṣafawi: Majmuʿa-ye asnād wa mokātebāt-e tāriḵi*, Tehran, 1971. Idem, ed., *Šāh ʿAbbās: Majmuʿa-ye asnād wa mokātebāt-e tāriḵi*, Tehran, 1973. Idem, *Šāh Esmāʿil Ṣafavi: Asnād wa mokātebāt-e tāriḵi*, Tehran, 1989. ʿAbdi Beg Novidi Širāzi, *Takmilat al-aḵbār: Tāriḵ-e Ṣafawiya az āḡāz tā 978 hejri qamari*, ed. ʿAbd-al-Ḥosayn Navāʾi, Tehran, 1990.

Moḥammad-Yār b. ʿArab Qaṭaḡān, *Mosaḵḵer al-belād: Tāriḵ-e Šibāniān*, ed. Nādera Jalāli, Tehran, 2006. Mir Sayyed Šarif Rāqem Samarqandi, *Tāriḵ-e Rāqem*, ed. Manučehr Sotuda, Tehran, 2001. Qodrat-Allāh Rawšani Zaʿfarānlu, "Vaqf-nāma-ye āb-e ḵiābān-e Mašhad," *FIZ* 28, 1989, pp. 323-25. Ḥasan Beg Rumlu, *Aḥsan al-tawāriḵ*, ed. ʿAbd-al-Ḥosayn Navāʾi, Tehran, 2004. Shah Ṭahmāsp Ṣafawi, *Taḏkera*, ed. and tr. Paul Horn, as "Die Denkwürdigkeiten des Šâh Ṭahmâsp I von Persien," *ZDMG* 45, 1890, pp. 563-649. [Mirzā Samiʿā], *Tadhkirat al-Mulūk: A Manual of Ṣafavid Administration (circa 1137/1725)*, tr. Vladimir Minorsky, London, 1943. Moḥammad Fatḥ-Allāh Sāravi, *Tāriḵ-e Moḥammadi*, ed. Ḡolām-Reżā Ṭabāṭabāʾi Majd, Tehran, 1993. Yaḥyā b. ʿAbd-al-Laṭif Sayfi Qazvini, *Lubb al-tawārikh*, ed. Mir Hāšem Moḥaddeṯ, Tehran, 2007. Šāh-Ḥosayn Sistāni, *Tāriḵ-e Sistān*, ed. Manučehr Sotuda, Tehran, 1966. *Tāriḵ-e Mašhad*, National Library of Iran, Tehran, MS 16106. Abu Bakr Ṭehrāni Eṣfahāni, *Ketāb-e Diārbakriya*, ed. Necati Lugal and Faruk Sümer, as *Kitāb-i Diyārbakriyya: Ak-Koyunlular Tarihi*, 2 vols. with continuous pagination, Ankara, 1962-64. Moḥammad Yusof Vāleh Eṣfahāni, *Irān dar zamān-i Šāh Ṣafi wa Šāh ʿAbbās-e dovvom (1038-1071): Ḵold-e barin, ḥadiqa-yi šešom wa haftom az rawża-ye haštom*, ed. Moḥammad-Reżā Naṣiri, Tehran, 2001. Moḥammad Ṭāher Waḥid Qazvini, *Tāriḵ-e jahān-ārā-ye ʿabbāsi*, ed. Saʿid Mir-Moḥammad Ṣādeq, Tehran, 2004. Moḥammad-Šafiʿ Wāred Ṭehrāni, *Merʾāt-e vāredāt*, ed. M. Ṣefatgol, Tehran, 2004. Zayn-al-din Maḥmud Vāṣefi Heravi, *Badāyeʿ al-waqāyeʿ*, ed. A. N. Boldyreva, 2 vols., Tehran, 1970. Aḥmad-ʿAli Khan Waziri Kermāni, *Tāriḵ-e Kermān (Sālāriya)*, ed. Moḥammad-Ebrāhim Bāstāni Pārizi, Tehran, 1961.

Studies. Rula J. Abisaab, "Peasant Uprisings in Astarabad: The Siyāh Pūshān (Wearers of Black), the Sayyids, and the Safavid State," *Iranian Studies* 49/3, 2015, pp. 471-92. Jean Aubin, "Šāh Ismāʿil et les notables de l'Iraq persan (Etudes safavides I)," *JESHO* 2/1, 1959, pp. 37-81. Idem, "Révolution chiite et conservatisme: Les soufis de Lâhejân, 1500-1514 (Etudes safavides II)," *Moyen Orient et Océan Indien* 1, 1984, pp. 1-40. Idem, "L'avènement des Safavides reconsidéré (Etudes safavides. III.)," *Moyen Orient et Océan Indien* 5, 1988, pp. 1-130. Jean-Louis Bacqué-Grammont, "Une liste ottomane de princes et d'apanages abu'l-khayrides," *Cahiers du Monde russe et soviétique* 11/3, 1970, pp. 423-53. Vasili V. Barthold, *Sochineniya* (Collected works), 9 vols., Moscow, 1963-77. Idem, *Four Studies on the History of Central Asia*, tr. Vladimir and Tatiana Minorsky, 3 vols., Leiden, 1956-62. Yuri Bregel, *An Historical Atlas of Central Asia*, Leiden, 2003. Stephen F. Dale, *The Garden of the Eight Paradises: Bābur and the Culture of Empire in Central Asia, Afghanistan and India (1483-1530)*, Leiden, 2004. Martin B. Dickson, "Sháh Ṭahmásb and the Úzbeks (The Duel for Khurásán with ʿUbayd Khán, 930-946/1524-1540)," PhD diss., Princeton University, 1958. Idem, "Uzbek Dynastic Theory in the Sixteenth Century," in Bobozdhan G. Gafurov, ed., *Proceedings of the 25th International Congress of Orientalists (Moscow, 9-16 August 1960)*, 4 vols., Moscow, 1963, III, pp. 208-16. N. Elias, "An Apocryphal Inscription in Khorāsān," *JRAS*, January 1896, pp. 767-79. N. Falsafi, "Dāstān-e yak bāda-gosāri dar kāsa-ye sar-e došman," *Soḵan* 4, March 1952, pp. 287-96. Kioumars Ghereghlou, "Cashing in on Land and Privilege for the Welfare of the Shah: Monetisation of *Tiyūl* in Early Safavid Iran and Eastern Anatolia," *AOASH* 68/1, 2015, pp. 87-141. Idem, "Muḥammad Khān Shībānī in Ṭūs (915/1509)," *Manuscripta Orientalia* 22/1, 2016, pp. 55-67. Idem, "On the Margins of Minority Life: Zoroastrians and the State in Safavid Iran," *BSOAS* 80/1, 2017, pp. 45-71. Walther Hinz, "Schah Esmaʿīl II. Ein Beitrag zur Geschichte der Ṣafavīden," *Mitteilungen des Seminars für Orientalische Sprachen an der Friedrich-Wilhelms-Universität zu Berlin* 36, 1933, pp. 19-100. Mahin Hajianpur, "The Shaybanids," in Gavin Hambly, ed., *Central Asia*, London, 1969, pp. 163-74. Fāṭema Jahānpur, *Maktab-ḵāna'hā wa madāres-e qadim-e āstān-e quds-e rażawi*, Mashhad, 2008. Ḥabib Levi, *Tāriḵ-e Yahud-e Iran*, 3 vols., Tehran, 1960.

Robert D. McChesney, "The Conquest of Herat 995-6/1587-8: Sources for the Study of Ṣafavid/Qizilbâsh-Shibânid/Uzbek Relations," in J. Calmard, ed., *Etudes safavides*, Paris, 1993, pp. 69-107. Idem, "The Central Asian Hajj-Pilgrimage in the Time of the Early Modern Empires," in Michel M. Mazzaoui, ed., *Safavid Iran and Her Neighbors*, Salt Lake City, 2003, pp. 129-56. Sayyed ʿAli Mirniā, *Ilāt va ṭavāyef-e Daragaz dar ḵedmat-e mihan*, 2 vols., Mashhad, 1982-83. Azfar Moin, "Shah Ismail Comes to Herat: An Anecdote from Vasefi's 'Amazing Events' (*Badayiʿ al-Vaqayiʿ*)," in Behdad Aghaei and Mohammad Mehdi Khorrami, eds., *Persian Mosaic: Essays on Persian Language, Literature and Film in Honor of M. R. Ghanoonparvar*, Bethesda MD, 2015, pp. 86-101. Roziâ G. Mukminova, "The Shaybanids," in C. Adle and I. Habib, eds., *History of Civilizations of Central Asia* V: *Development in Contrast: From the Sixteenth to the Mid-Nineteenth Century*, Paris, 2003, pp. 33-44. Reżā Naqdi Kadkani, "Mawqufāt-e Nāder Šāh wa ʿAli Šāh Afšār dar Mašhad-e moqaddas," *Waqf mirāṯ-e jāvdān* 77, 2004, pp. 84-93. Pierre Oberling, *The Turkic Peoples of Iranian Azerbaijan*, Washington, D.C., 1961. John R. Perry, *Karim Khan Zand: A History of Iran, 1747-1779*, Chicago, 1979. Moḥammad-Ḥosayn Qoddusi,

Nāder-nāma, Mashhad, 1960. Ahmet Refik [Altinay], *Anadolu'da Türk aşiretleri (966-1200)*, Istanbul, 1930. James J. Reid, "Rebellion and Social Change in Astarabad, 1537-1744," *IJMES* 13/1, 1981, pp. 35-53. Hans R. Roemer, "The Successors of Tīmūr," in Peter Jackson and Laurence Lockhart, eds., *The Cambridge History of Iran* VI: *The Timurid and Safavid Periods*, Cambridge, 1986, pp. 98-146. G. Sarwar, *History of Shāh Ismāʿīl Safawī*, Aligarh, 1939. Roger M. Savory, "The Significance of the Political Murder of Mīrzā Salmān," *Islamic Studies* 3, 1964, pp. 181-90. Idem, "The Consolidation of Ṣafawid Power in Persia," *Der Islam* 41/1, 1965, pp. 71-94. Aleksander A. Semenov, "Shejbani Khan i zavoevanie im imperii Timuridov" ["Šibāni Khan's conquest of the Timurid Empire"], *Materialy po istorii tadjikov i uzbekov Srednej Azii*, Leningrad, 1954, pp. 39-83. Maria Szuppe, *Entre Timourides, Uzbeks et Safavides: Questions d'histoire politique et sociale de Hérat dans la première moitié du XVIe siècle*, Paris, 1992. Nataliya N. Tumanovich, *Gerat v XVI-XVII vekakh*, Moscow, 1989. Thomas Welsford, *Four Types of Loyalty in Early Modern Central Asia: The Tūqāy-Tīmūrid Takeover of Greater Mā Warā al-Nahr, 1598-1605*, Leiden, 2013. John E. Woods, *The Timurid Dynasty*, Indiana University Research Institute for Inner Asian Studies Papers on Inner Asia no. 14, Bloomington, Ind., 1990. Idem, *The Aqquyunlu: Clan, Confederation, Empire*, Salt Lake City, 1999.

(KIOUMARS GHEREGHLOU)

xi. HISTORY IN THE QAJAR AND PAHLAVI PERIODS

This article surveys two centuries of the history of Khorasan, an important province of eastern Iran, from the accession of the first Qajar shah, Āḡā Moḥammad Khan (q.v.), in Ramażān 1210/March 1796 to the fall of the last Pahlavi shah, Moḥammad Reżā, in January 1979. At the beginning of this period, the province of Khorasan comprised a much larger area than it did in the Pahlavi era, as it included, at least nominally, parts of what are now western Afghanistan and southern Turkmenistan and cities such as Herat and Marv (Hedāyat, ed. Kiānfar, XII, pp. 7389-92; see also KHORASAN i. CONCEPT OF KHORASAN).

During the Qajar period, although Khorasan was considered one province geographically and the document of investiture as governor-general was issued in the name of one person, in practice the administration of large parts of it was in the hands of local tribal khans (q.v.). Among the most prominent of these khans, one may mention the Arab Ḵozayma (ʿAlam) family in Birjand, the Qāʾenāt, and southern Khorasan (see ʿALAM KHAN and ʿALAM, MOḤAMMAD); the Zanguʾi in Ṭabas; the Qaraʾi (see KARĀʾI) khans in Torbat Ḥaydariya and parts of eastern Khorasan; the Bayāt (q.v.) in Nishapur and in northern Khorasan; the Zaʿfarānlu in Čenārān and Qučān (formerly Ḵabušān); and the Šādlu khans in Esfarāyen and Bojnurd (for more information, see Ḵāvari Širazi, I, pp. 400-495; Noelle-Karimi, pp. 211-15 and genealogical tables).

During the 130-year rule of the Qajar dynasty, a total of about fifty individuals, many of them Qajar kinsmen, served as governor-generals of the province. Some of these governors were responsible for administering the province during several different tenures (see Fāżeli Birjandi, pp. 42-364). Among the most prominent governors of Khorasan during the Qajar period were ʿAbbās Mirzā Nāyeb-al-Saltanah (q.v.; d. 1833), Moḥammad Mirzā (later Moḥammad Shah, q.v.; r. 1834-48), Allāh-Yār Khan Āṣaf-al-Dawla (on whom, see Noelle-Karimi, pp. 225-30), Solṭān Morād Mirzā Ḥoṣām-al-Salṭana (d. 1883; see Noelle-Karimi, pp. 230-34), Mirzā Ḥosayn Khan Sepahsālār (d. 1881), Kāmrān Mirzā Nāyeb-al-Salṭana (q.v.; d. 1929), Aḥmad Qawām-al-Salṭana (d. 1955; see Šawkat, pp. 75-109), and Jaʿfarqoli Khan Sardār Asʿad Baḵtiāri (d. 1934; see BAḴTIĀRI, s.v. "Jaʿfarqoli Khan"). All of these were eminent Iranian statesmen and politicians of their time, and some went on to take up positions as monarch, vicegerent, prime minister, or cabinet minister.

The province of Khorasan underwent various changes during the Qajar period. Qajar officials faced two major problems in protecting the borders of Khorasan. The first included rebellions by local rulers in areas such as Herat and military attacks by the Khiva and Bukhara khanates on important places such as Marv, as well as occasional Turkmen raids in the north and east of Khorasan. The second problem was the presence, influence, and rivalry of the British and Russian governments in areas adjacent to Khorasan and their persistent meddling in the affairs of Iran within its borders, including Khorasan.

EFFORTS OF ĀḠĀ MOḤAMMAD KHAN AND FATḤ-ʿALI SHAH QĀJĀR TO RULE KHORASAN

According to Reżāqoli Khan Hedāyat (q.v.; 1800-1871), the first Qajar official in Khorasan was Reżā Khan Qājār Qoyunlu, who was appointed by Āḡā Moḥammad Khan in 1200/1785 (Hedāyat, XIII, p. 7299). ʿAbd-al-Razzāq Beg Donboli (q.v.; 1762-1828) also mentions the name of an early official appointed by Āḡā Moḥammad Khan in Khorasan, Ḥosayn Khan Qullar Āḡāsi (Donboli, p. 80). However, until 1210/1795, when Āḡā Moḥammad Khan entered Mashhad and was greeted by Šāhroḵ Afšār (grandson of Nāder Shah, q.v.) and a group of the province's ulema and khans (Sepehr, I, p. 80), Khorasan could not truly be considered part of the Qajar domain. In that year, Āḡā Moḥammad Khan, after severely torturing Šāhroḵ, appropriated the crown jewels that had been bequeathed to him by Nāder Shah (Qazvini, p. 157) and appointed Moḥammad Wali Khan Qājār as the governor-general for Khorasan (Šamim, pp. 27-28). Āḡā Moḥammad Khan, who intended to seize Herat, Balḵ, Marv, and Bukhara from their Afghan and Uzbek rulers, had to abandon his expedition in 1796 to deal with a Russian invasion of the eastern Caucasus (Motavalli Ḥaqiqi, 2004, p. 152). Upon the death of the first Qajar shah, Nāder Mirzā, son of Šāhroḵ, supported by the Afghan rulers from Herat, returned to Mashhad and called himself the sovereign of Khorasan (Anonymous MS, f. 166).

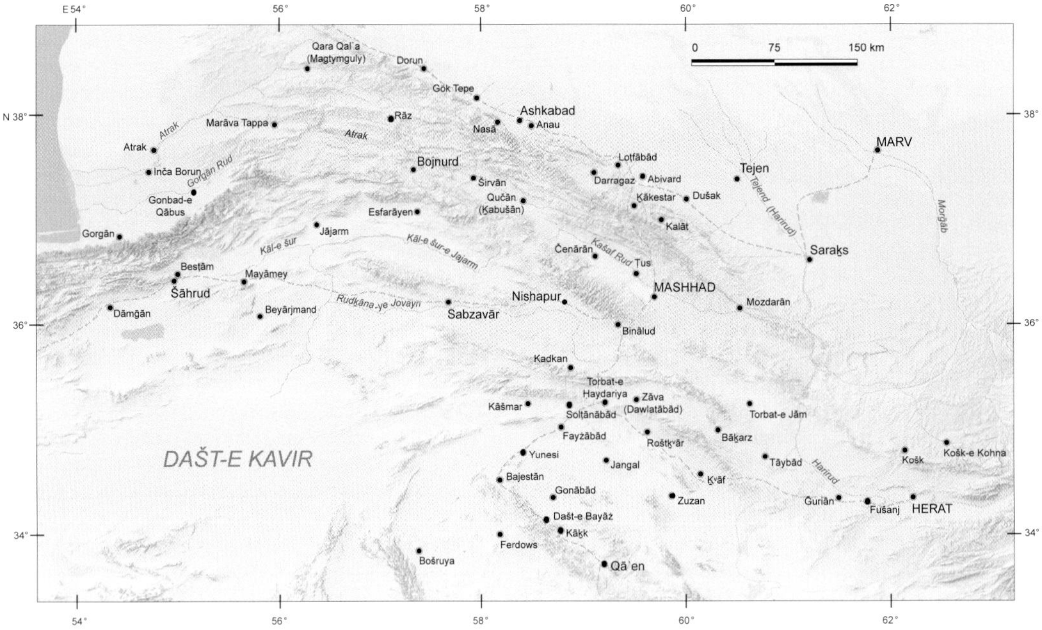

Figure 1. Northern Khorasan and environs in the Qajar to Pahlavi era. (Map prepared with QGIS 3.10 and data from US National Park Service World Physical Map.)

Fatḥ-ʿAli Shah Qājār (q.v.) ascended the throne of Iran in 1212/1797, but, in the early years of his reign, Khorasan was outside the area of his authority. He made unsuccessful attempts to seize Mashhad and Khorasan in 1213/1799 and 1215/1801 (Hedāyat, IX, p. 3353), until finally, in 1218/1803, he was able to enter Mashhad after besieging it for several months.

To protect the eastern and northern borders of Khorasan, Qajar officials undertook a number of measures, including several military campaigns. Ḥosayn Khan Qājār's expedition to Herat in 1222/1807, leading to the surrender of Fēruz-al-Din Mirzā, the governor of that city, was one of these measures (Sepehr, I, p. 164; Ḵāvari Širāzi, pp. 265-66; Nuri, pp. 308 ff.; HERAT vi). Dispersed but continuous attacks by the Turkmens of the Ḵāvarān plain and occasional raids by Uzbek khans on the territory of Khorasan, which sometimes led to the capture of innocent people and looting of their property, as well as revolts by some local Khorasani khans such as Esḥāq Khan Qarāʾi and Reżāqoli Khan Zaʿfarānlu, were among the problems for the people of Khorasan in this historical period. The city of Marv had slipped from Qajar control in 1200/1785, when the Uzbek Manghits (q.v.) killed the governor Bāyrām ʿAli Khan ʿEzz-al-Dinlu Qājār, occupied the city, and destroyed its irrigation system (Skrine and Ross, pp. 206-7), yet it could still be considered an Iranian city. However, in 1223/1808, with the failure of the governor-general of Khorasan, Moḥammad Vali Khan, in his assault on the city, and the subsequent deportation of a thousand families from Marv to Mashhad, the last roots of Iran in the ancient and historic land of Marv were severed (Sayyedi, pp. 282-89). The deteriorating situation in Khorasan forced Fatḥ-ʿAli Shah to send the crown prince, ʿAbbās Mirzā, to the province in 1831 to bring things under control (Hedāyat, ed. Kiānfar, XV, p. 8544). After arriving in Khorasan, ʿAbbās Mirzā was able to suppress all the revolts and to kill, imprison, or subjugate their leaders (Mir Niā, I, pp. 84-87; Noelle-Karimi, pp. 224-25). He then sent his son Moḥammad Mirzā to conquer Herat. The death of ʿAbbās Mirzā in 1833 brought the siege of Herat to an end, and a settlement was reached with Kāmrān Mirzā Sadōzi (Motavalli Ḥaqiqi, 2004, pp. 203-5). The Herat question itself, however, remained unresolved (see HERAT vi).

KHORASAN IN THE ERA OF MOḤAMMAD SHAH AND NĀṢER-AL-DIN SHAH

Moḥammad Mirzā became shah in 1250/1834 and appointed his uncle Allāh-Yār Khan Āṣaf-al-Dawla to govern Khorasan. He besieged Herat in 1253/1837, but the British support for Kāmrān Mirzā Sadōzi, along with the British occupation of Kharg (q.v.) island and the subsequent destabilization of Fārs, caused the siege to be lifted the next year (Šamim, pp. 145-46; Noelle-Karimi, pp. 225-30; Martin, pp. 110-15).

Not long after the setback at Herat, there were disturbances in Mashhad that led in Moḥarram 1255/March 1839 to the conversion, at least outwardly and under duress, of the Jewish community of Mashhad to Islam, an event referred to as Allāhdād 'God's Judgment' (Hedāyat, X, p. 284; Wolff, p. 147; Pirnazar, pp. 115-36; Basch Moreen, p. 242; Nissimi).

In the last years of Moḥammad Shah's reign, Moḥammad-Ḥasan Khan Sālār (d. 1850), the son of Allāh-Yār Āṣaf-al-Dawla, started a revolt in Khorasan, along with a group of khans in the region, against the central government (Bāmdād, I, p. 158; Noelle-Karimi, pp. 228-30) that continued until the early years of the reign of Nāṣer-al-Din Shah (r. 1848-96). The activities of a prominent follower of ʿAli Moḥammad Bāb (q.v.), Mollā Moḥammad-Ḥosayn Bošruʾi (q.v., 1814-49), also led to local disturbances until he was forced to leave Mashhad in 1848 (Sepehr, III, pp. 1010-14; see also KHORASAN XV. THE BABI-BAHAI COMMUNITY IN KHORASAN).

With the accession of Nāṣer-al-Din Shah in 1264/1848, his prime minister, Mirzā Taqi Khan Amir Kabir (q.v.), faced two immediate problems in Khorasan: the revolt of Ḥasan Khan Sālār and the disobedience of the governors of Herat (Noelle-Karimi, pp. 228-30). He first sent Solṭān Morād Mirzā Ḥosām-al-Salṭana to suppress the revolt of Sālār, who surrendered and was executed in 1850, and then he addressed the problem of regaining control of Herat with a plan of his own (Motavalli Ḥaqiqi, 2004, pp. 235-44; Noelle-Karimi, pp. 231-32). A terrible earthquake in 1267/1851 caused death and destruction among the people and various regions of Khorasan such as Mashhad, Qučān, and Torbat Ḥaydariya (Eʿtemād-al-Salṭana, *Montaẓam* III, p. 1717). The rebellion of Mirzā Rafiʿ Khan, based at Furg, a citadel in the Qāʾenāt (described in Forbes and Rawlinson, pp. 22-25), also ended with his defeat and flight to Herat (Ḵurmuji, pp. 118-19).

With the death of Amir Kabir, the officials in Herat became disobedient again. Although Ḥosām-al-Salṭana, the governor-general of Khorasan, conquered Herat in October 1856 (see Noelle-Karimi, pp. 232-34), the British intervention and occupation of southern Iran led to the Persian withdrawal from Herat, the signing of the Treaty of Paris between Iran and Britain, and the separation of Herat from Iran. (Motavalli Ḥaqiqi, 2004, pp. 257-64; Champagne, p. 377; see also ANGLO-PERSIAN WAR [1856-57]).

Occasional attacks by Turkmens of the Ḵāvarān plain was another problem for the people of Khorasan during the Nāṣeri era. Ḥamza Mirzā Hešmat-al-Dawla (d. 1880), the governor-general of Khorasan, tried to suppress the Turkmen in campaigns beginning 1275/1859, but he suffered a severe defeat outside Marv in 1277/1860 (see Rowšani Zaʿfarānlu, pp. 75-144; Noelle-Karimi, p. 234). This defeat was, in fact, the beginning of the end of Iran's claims to dominion over the Ḵāvarān plain. The Akhal (Āḵāl) boundary convention, signed in 1299/1881 between Iran and Russia, effectively ended Iran's historical claims to lands beyond the Tejen river and to cities such as Meyhana, Abivard, Nesā, and Marv (Sayyedi, pp. 378-79; text in Krausse, pp. 360-62).

During his reign, Nāṣer-al-Din Shah traveled to Khorasan twice. The first time was in 1284/1867, and the second time was in 1300/1882. The travel accounts of these two journeys are recognized as among the most important sources for the history of Khorasan in the Nāṣeri era (Qahramān, passim). One of the worst developments for Khorasan during the last three decades of Nāṣer-al-Din Shah's reign was the Great Famine that began 1285/1869 and lasted until 1288/1873. It was so severe that people were reduced to eating grass, animals, and religiously forbidden meats, or even digging up corpses for food (Eʿtemād-al-Salṭana, *Matlaʿ*, II, p. 377; Majd, 2018, pp. 53-68). The Tehran to Mashhad telegraph line was established under the direction of Albert Houtum-Schindler (q.v.; d. 1916) in 1293/1876 (Eʿtemād-al-Salṭana, *Montaẓam*, III, p. 1964). A house-by-house census of Mashhad was conducted by Zayn-al-ʿĀbedin Mirzā Qājār (Qājār, passim) in 1878, and British and Russian consulates were opened in the spring of 1306/1889 (Curzon, I, pp. 170-74, tr., I, pp. 237-40). The cholera epidemic of 1309/1891 spread along the road from Afghanistan to Khorasan and caused the death of an estimated 20,000 people in Khorasan (Riāżi Heravi, pp. 105-6). One might also note the migration of large groups of Shiʿites, Sādāts, and Hazāras (q.v.) from Afghanistan to Khorasan due to the anti-Shiʿite and anti-Hazāra policies of the Afghan *pādšāh* (amir) ʿAbd-al-Raḥmān Khan (r. 1297-1319/1880-1901; Motavalli Ḥaqiqi, 2004, pp. 308-10; see AFGHANISTAN X; HAZĀRA ii). The "Tobacco Rebellion," which began in 1308/1891 against the transfer of the exclusive right to buy and sell tobacco to the Régie, a monopoly owned by a British subject (see Keddie; CONCESSIONS ii), spread to Mashhad, and the people of Khorasan and Mashhad, led by Sheikh Moḥammad-Taqi Bojnurdi, began their protests. Nāṣer-al-Din Shah and the British were forced to yield after a five-day uprising by the people of Mashhad and several other cities in Khorasan, exempting Khorasan from this concession (Motavalli Ḥaqiqi, 2013, I, p. 364; cf. Nouraie, pp. 221-31); the concession itself was cancelled in January 1892.

In the last decade of Nāṣer-al-Din Shah's reign, the situation in Khorasan province became very unstable because of perceptions of tyranny and oppression under governors of Khorasan such as ʿAbd-al-Wahhāb Khan Āṣaf-al-Dawla Širāzi, Moḥammad-Taqi Mirzā Rokn-al-Dawla, and Abu'l-Fatḥ Mirzā Moʾayyed-al-Dawla (q.v.; d. 1330/1912). People in the city of Mashhad often revolted to protest the high prices for bread, meat, and other supplies (Motavalli Ḥaqiqi, 2013, I, pp. 22-26, 45-50). Nāṣer-al-Din Shah Qājār was assassinated in 1313/1896, after reigning for almost 50 years. It was against this background of turmoil and hardship that people in Khorasan, and in other regions of Iran, began to challenge the status quo and the actions of the Qajar government.

KHORASAN IN THE LATE QAJAR PERIOD

In the early years of the reign of Moẓaffar-al-Din Shah (r. 1896-1907), Khorasan continued to face various social crises and uprisings. In those years, the governors of Khorasan seemed to be motivated only by personal greed. Āṣaf-al-Dawla Šāhsavan was one of the governors who was notorious for having his agents beat up their subjects in Khorasan until they were almost dead in order to extort taxes from them. The most infamous episode of his administration occurred in 1905 in Qučān, where the authorities forcibly separated about 300 girls from their families and sold them to the Turkmen for a petty price in lieu of taxes

(Nāẓem-al-Eslām Kermāni, pp. 305-6; Browne, pp. 174-79; Najmabadi). The publication of this news became an incentive for intellectuals and constitutionalists to resist the despotic government (Šarif Kāšāni, IV, p. 851).

Simultaneously with the beginning of public dissatisfaction with the Qajar rule in the last years of the reign of Nāṣer-al-Din Shah Qājār and the first years of Moẓaffar-al-Din Shah's reign, modernization and interest in the achievements of Western civilization began in Khorasan. The creation of new schools, the publication of newspapers, the formation of cultural associations, the organization of various reformist groups among the ulema and merchants, and the emergence of a fledgling group of journalists were the most significant aspects of modernization in Khorasan and Mashhad. Mirzā Ḥasan Rošdiya took the initiative in creating new schools in Mashhad, and others, such as Moḥammad ʿAli Modir, Moḥammad Ḥasan Khan Ṣabā, and Ḥāj Asad-Allāh Fatḥ-Allāh Yusof Ḵāmenaʾi, continued to do so (Motavalli Ḥaqiqi, 2005, p. 129). The establishment of new schools in other cities in Khorasan dates to the post-constitutional years. Birjand, Qučān, Bojnurd, Nishapur, and Torbat-e Ḥaydariya were among the cities that witnessed the launch of new schools a few years after the victory of the Constitutional Revolution (q.v.; Motavalli Ḥaqiqi, 2005, passim). The first newspaper printed in Khorasan, called *Adab* (q.v.), was founded in Tabriz but published in Mashhad from Ramażān 1318/December 1900 to Rajab 1321/October 1903 under the editorship of Adib-al-Mamālek Farāhāni (q.v.; d. 1917). *Adab* was the first Iranian newspaper to employ cartoons to express its views (Ṣadr Hāšemi, I, pp. 82-87). Although Khorasan had initially lagged behind other parts of Iran in press publication due to pressures from Tsarist Russia, after the victory of the constitution, dozens of newspapers were published in Mashhad and other cities of Khorasan, which turned this province into a major hub of journalism in Iran (see Elāhi, passim; KHORASAN xxviii. NEWSPAPERS OF KHORASAN). Simultaneously with the establishment of new schools and the publication of newspapers, the province of Khorasan was also home to important writers and political activists such as Ḥaydar Khan ʿAmu-Oḡli (q.v.; d. 1921), Adib-al-Mamālek Farāhāni, Moḥammad-Taqi Mālek-al-Šoʿarāʾ Bahār (q.v.; d. 1951), Sheikh Aḥmad Bahār, and Sheikh Aḥmad Ruḥ-al-Qodos Torbati, better known as Solṭān-al-ʿOlamāʾ Ḵorāsāni. They were among the first notables to participate in the beginning of the Constitutional Revolution in Mashhad (Motavalli Ḥaqiqi, 2013, I, pp. 82-83). The profound dissatisfaction of the citizenry with the government, along with the efforts and struggles of the activist groups, caused some of the people of Khorasan, albeit a little later on, to join the ranks of the constitutionalists.

At the urging of Khorasan's representatives in the first Majles, the ground was prepared for the dismissal of Āṣaf-al-Dawla Šāhsavan and also the dismissal and trial of ʿAziz-Allāh Khan Šādlu (Sardār Moʿazzaz Bojnurdi), the governor of Bojnurd, on charges of collaborating with the Turkmen in capturing the girls from the Bāškānlu tribe of Qučān (Aʿẓām Qodsi, pp. 175-92). In Mashhad, the Khorasan Provincial Association (Anjoman-e Eyālati-e Ḵorāsān) took over the administration of the city's affairs. In addition to this association, the Saʿādat Charity Association (Anjoman-e ḵayriya-ye saʿādat) was established with the goal of spreading public culture and establishing new schools in Mashhad (M.-T. Bahār, I, p. *yak*). With the death of Moẓaffar-al-Din Shah and the succession of his son Moḥammad-ʿAli Shah, who had no interest in compromise with the constitution and the constitutionalists, the situation in Iran, including Khorasan, underwent various transformations.

The general situation in Khorasan was almost calm between the victory of the constitutionalists and the attack on the Majles in June 1908, but with the shelling of the Majles and the beginning of the "Lesser Despotism" (*estebdād-e ṣaḡir*) in Tehran, the ground was also prepared in Khorasan for the opponents of the constitution. The anti-constitutionalist ulema in Khorasan were led by those such as Sayyed ʿAli Sistāni and Sheikh Mahdi Wāʿez Ḵorāsāni (Motavalli Ḥaqiqi, 2013, I, pp. 88-89). Other prominent opponents of the constitution in Mashhad included figures such as Yusof Khan Herāti, Moḥammad Qušābādi, and Moḥammad Ṭāleb-al-Ḥaqq Yazdi (Kāviāniān, pp. 87-88). Rabble-rousers and brigands, backed by the financial and military support of the Russians, these people were able to create chaos in Mashhad and other parts of Khorasan, trying to pave the way for the return of the deposed Moḥammad-ʿAli Shah to Iran. They made the courtyards of the Rażawi shrine (see ĀSTĀN-E QODS-E RAŻAWI) and the Gowhar-šād mosque (q.v.) the center of their activities. However, the Russians, once it was clear that the effort to restore Moḥammad-ʿAli Shah had failed, took matters into their own hands and withdrew their support for Yusof Khan and his forces and decided to remove them from the Gowhar-šād mosque and the Rażawi shrine. On 29 March 1912, the Russians directed a volley of hundreds of artillery shells and bullets at the Rażawi shrine (Adib Heravi, pp. 211-12; Sykes, II, p. 426; Matthee; Figure 2). In addition to damaging the dome of the Rażawi shrine, and despite Yusof Khan Herāti and his confederates having left the shrine and its surrounding structures, the Russians brutally occupied the courtyard with their cavalry and infantry, killing many innocent pilgrims. Estimates of the number of people who died in this incident vary greatly, from 40 to 800 (Motavalli Ḥaqiqi, 2013, I, pp. 145-47).

The situation in Khorasan on the eve of World War I was tumultuous due to internal mismanagement and foreign interference. Local miscreants in areas such as Zašk and Čenārān also took advantage of these conditions for their own purposes and banditry (Modarres Rażavi, pp. 233-34). With the outbreak of World War I in 1914, despite the declaration of neutrality by Iran, the country, including the province of Khorasan, became an arena for foreign competition and interference. The Russians, who considered Khorasan to be in their sphere of influence, sent additional troops to occupy most of the territory of the province (Motavalli Ḥaqiqi, 2013, I, p. 156).

Foreign intervention and the irresponsibility of the governors of Khorasan in the last years of the First World War caused famine, exorbitant prices for food and goods, and

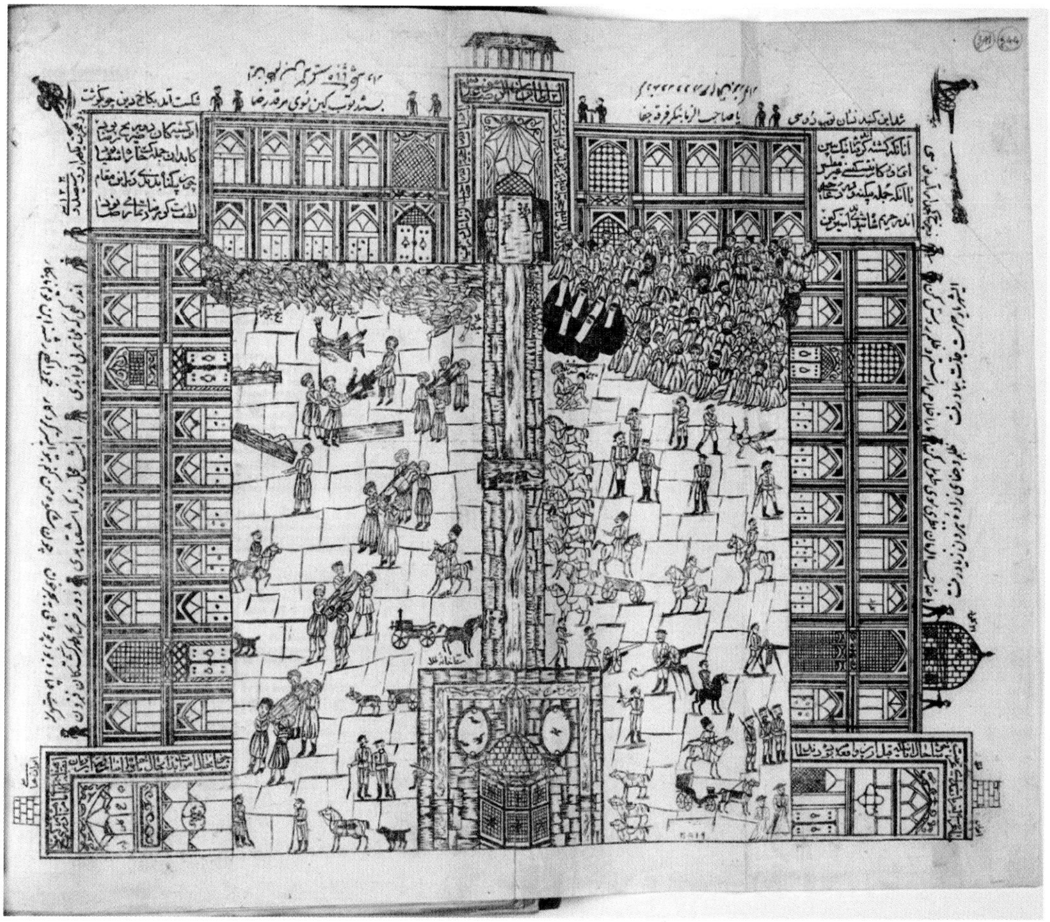

Figure 2. Illustration of the Russian bombardment of the Imam Reżā Shrine in Mashhad, 1912, prepared by a local artist at the request of the British consul in Mashhad, Percy Sykes. The marginal verses read "O Lord of the Time [the Mahdi], Regard Ṭus / The harshness and the oppression of the son of Hārun-al-Rašid is increased. / Release us from the tyranny and oppression of the Russians. | O King [Imam Reżā], the honor of thy ancestor is gone to the wind. / From the crooked ebony revolution of the heavens, / This dome became the target of Russian guns. | O Lord of the Time! Regard this race of tyrants. / They entered the Shrine of the Saint, / they laid guns on the tomb of the Imam Reżā / This tyranny was enough that they all wore long boots [instead of removing them in the shrine]. | The building of Islam cracked in 1330 [1912]. | The place was the refuge of the weak / On that night it became the battle-place of the black-hearted. | Round the grating of the sacred tomb / There were many killed, lying in blood / like fish in a pool / How can I complain of this to Thee, / O Secret of God. / Thou knowest the action of the doers of the bad deeds." Image and translation of text after India Office Records and Private Papers, British Library, File 52/1912 IOR/L/PS/10/209, 343r-344r; available at www.qdl.qa/en/archive/81055/vdc_100029742540.0x00005d. Copyright status unknown.

made life difficult for the Khorasani masses. In addition to inflation and famine, the spread of diseases such as cholera and tuberculosis affected the population in such a way that numerous poor people died of starvation and disease every day (Motavalli Ḥaqiqi, 2013, I, p. 158). Although there is no accurate report on casualties among the people of Khorasan during the period of World War I, it was, according to some estimates, one of the deadliest eras in Iran and in the history of Khorasan in the modern period (Majd, 2008, pp. 59-67, tr. pp. 85-91). The outbreak of the Bolshevik Revolution caused the Russians to withdraw from the territory of Khorasan temporarily, in contrast to the very visible presence the British had amassed in Khorasan (Maḥbub Farimāni and Neʿmati, pp. 346-47).

One of the most important events in the history of Khorasan in the last years of Qajar rule was the uprising of Colonel Moḥammad-Taqi Khan Pesyān (q.v.; 1892-1921; see Cronin, 1997b, p. 693). In September 1920, Pesyān left for Mashhad to assume command of the Khorasan Gendarmerie (q.v.), and, with the cooperation of Qawām-al-

Salṭana, the governor-general of Khorasan, he succeeded in suppressing Khorasani rebels such as Ḵodāverdi Sardār Širvāni, Morsal Khan, and Zabar-dast Khan Darragazi (Mir Niā, I, pp. 296-301). Following the Coup d'Etat of 1299/1921 (q.v.), Sayyed Żiāʾ-al-Din Ṭabāṭabāʾi became prime minister, and Pesyān, acting on the orders of the prime minister, arrested Qawām-al-Salṭana, sent him to Tehran, and took control of Khorasan himself (Motavalli Ḥaqiqi, 2001, pp. 47-56). When Sayyed Żiā's cabinet fell and Qawām-al-Salṭana replaced him as prime minister, Pesyān refused to cooperate with the new government. Finally, after some military conflicts and despite some peace negotations, the Kurdish khans of northern Khorasan, on instructions from Qawām-al-Salṭana and under the direction of Sardar Moʿazzaz of Bojnurd, defeated the Gendarmeries of Širvān, Fāruj, and Qučān and killed Pesyān in the environs of Qučān on 30 Moḥarram 1340/3 October 1921 (Motavalli Ḥaqiqi, 2001, pp. 96-108; see also Šawkat, pp. 75-110 for a reassessment of these events).

Shortly after attaining the position of prime minister of Iran, Reżā Khan Mir Panj, the former minister of war in Sayyed Żiāʾ's "Black Cabinet," sought to hold a referendum on establishing a republic. In Mashhad, groups of people led by Sayyed Ḥasan Meškān Ṭabasi, Sheikh Aḥmad Bahār (see the preface to his *Divān*), and Aḥmad Dehqān supported the declaration of a republic, but smaller groups also expressed their opposition (Motavalli Ḥaqiqi, 2013, I, pp. 194-95). In Khorasan, after the defeat of the plan for establishing a republic and abolishing the monarchy, Jān Moḥammad Khan (q.v.), the military commander of Khorasan; Moḥammad Arjomand, the head of the post; and Morteżā Khan Makri, the military commander of Mashhad, established a committee called Nahżat-e Šarq (Movement of the East) and sent telegrams to Tehran expressing the dissatisfaction of the people of Khorasan with the Qajars and demanding their deposition as rulers of Iran (Arjomand, pp. 67-69). The news of the abolition of the Qajar dynasty and subsequently the rule of Reżā Shah was met with joy by groups of people and ulema of Khorasan, who sent messages of congratulations to Reżā Shah and expressed their support for the changes (Mirzā Ṣāleḥ, p. 569).

KHORASAN IN THE PAHLAVI PERIOD

During the 54-year reign of the Pahlavi dynasty, about 30 people were appointed as governors of Khorasan. Seven of them were appointed during the reign of Reżā Shah (1924-41; see Šaybāni, pp. 6-9), and 23 were appointed during the 38-year reign of Moḥammad Reżā Shah (1941-79; see Fāżeli Birjandi, pp. 13-16).

In the new provincial administrative division of the country created by Reżā Shah in 1937, Khorasan was recognized as the "Ninth Province" (Ostān-e Nohom), with Mashhad as its provincial capital and the seven sub-provinces (*šahrestān*s) of Sabzavār, Gonābād, Bojnurd, Qučān, Birjand, Torbat Ḥaydariya, and Mashhad. In 1950, the sub-provinces of Darragaz, Nishapur, Ferdows, and Kāšmar were formed, so the number of sub-provinces was expanded to eleven. In 1956, Darragaz was annexed to Qučān and the two sub-provinces of Torbat-e Jām and Ṭabas were created. In 1960, Darragaz became a sub-province again, and the sub-provinces of Širvān and Esfarāyen were also created. In 1975, the Bāḵarz district (*baḵš*) became the center of Torbat-e Jām and Tāybād was changed from a district to a sub-province (details from Sāzmān-e modiriyat, s.v. "Moʿarrefi-e ostān").

Although the governors of Khorasan during the Pahlavi period, unlike those of the Qajar period, were not kinsmen of the royal family, many of them were considered to be among the most eminent political and military figures of Iran in their time. They included such notables as Maḥmud Jam (q.v.), Sayyed Ḥasan Taqizāda (q.v.), Major-General Fatḥ-Allāh Pākravān, Rajab-ʿAli Manṣur, Ṣadr al-Ašrāf, Sayyed Jalāl-al-Din Ṭehrāni, General Nāder Bātmānqalič, General Ṣādeq Amir ʿAzizi, and ʿAbd-al-ʿAẓim Valiān. Many of them, before or after being governor of Khorasan, held the rank of prime minister or ministers in various cabinets of Iran. There was an added dimension to their role and prestige as governors of a major province: Many of them, in addition to the duties of their post, would also be entrusted with the administration of the extensive religious-economic resources supporting the shrine around the tomb of Imam Reżā (q.v.), the eighth Imam of the Shiʿites, and held the title of deputy-trustee (*nāyeb al-tawliya*; on this office, see Nouraie, p. 89) of the Āstān-e Qods-e Rażawi.

The revolt of Lahāk Khan Bāvand broke out during the early years of Reżā Shah's reign. Lahāk Khan, at the head of a group of soldiers from the Marāva Tappa garrison, initiated a mutiny in July 1926 (Cronin, 2014, pp. 55-56). He had communist sympathies and, after taking over the Inča Borun guardpost, went on to capture the city of Bojnurd (Motavalli Ḥaqiqi, 2008, p. 180). He then took Širvān and Qučān, but he was defeated by government forces at Qučān and fled to the Soviet Union (Bayāt, pp. 440-41).

In Farvardin 1307/April 1928, Reżā Shah appointed Maḥmud Jam to be governor-general of Khorasan. During his two terms of office (April 1928-January 1929 and August 1929-September 1933), Jam introduced numerous reforms. In May 1929, during the governorship of Ḥasan Taqizāda, the powerful Bāḡān earthquake shook the northern cities of Khorasan, such as Qučān, Širvān, and Bojnurd, causing great loss of life and property (Motavalli Ḥaqiqi, 2013, I, p. 237; Berberian, p. 247). The arrest and execution of two troublemakers, the brothers Ḏu'l-Feqār and Ḡanbar-ʿAli (also known as Zolfo and Qamo), who were robbing travelers on the roads of Khorasan, was another of Taqizāda's achievements in Khorasan (Šākeri, p. 114). In the 1930s, when many Jews from around the world were immigrating to Palestine, numerous Jews from Mashhad also moved there (Yazdāni, pp. 21-27).

In 1934, during the governorship of Faraj-Allāh Bahrāmi (q.v.), the millenary celebration of Ferdowsi (*jašn-e hazāra*) was held, with the goal of promoting Iranian nationalism (see FERDOWSI iv). That same year, Reżā Shah made his fourth trip to Khorasan and dedicated the new monumental tomb (*ārāmgāh*) of Ferdowsi in a ceremony attended by many prominent orientalists (see FERDOWSI iii).

One of the most important events in the modern history of Khorasan, the Gowhar-šād uprising, also regarded as the most significant anti-government movement in the early Pahlavi era, occurred during the governorship of Fatḥ-Allāh Pākravān (1934-41). In the absence of Ayatollah Sayyed Ḥosayn Ṭabāṭabāʾi Qomi, who had traveled to Tehran to protest the shah's new policy requiring men to use the *chapeau* (western-style hats, see CLOTHING xi; KOLĀH-E PAHLAVI) as headgear and was confined there, groups of Mashhad residents and other Khorasanis assembled at the Gowhar-šād Mosque under the influence of speeches by a firebrand religious student, Moḥammad-Taqi Gonābādi, known as Bohlul, and denounced Reżā Shah's secularizing policies. Government forces attacked, killed, and wounded a number of the protesters at the Gowhar-šād Mosque over two days, on the mornings of 20 and 21 Tir 1314/12 and 13 July 1935 (Motavalli Haqiqi, 2013, I, pp. 277-302).

In the first months of his reign, Reżā Shah had appointed Moḥammad-Wali Khan Asadi as the deputy-trustee of the Āstān-e Qods. With a flurry of activity, Asadi had been able to change the face of Mashhad from that of a middling city to that of a relatively large and semi-modern metropolis. His impovements included the construction of the capacious and modern Šāhreżā Hospital and the digging of several *qanāt*s (see KĀRIZ) to supply drinking water to Mashhad, as well as the introduction of administrative reforms for the Āstān-e Qods organization (Moʾtaman, pp. 31, 107, 275) and the development of new schools (Motavalli Ḥaqiqi, 2005, p. 162). The construction of a traffic circle around the shrine, connecting the two main avenues in Mashhad, was another of Asadi's reforms (Šuštari, pp. 226-27). He remained one of the most influential figures in the history of Khorasan until the time of the Gowhar-šād incident. Asadi's disagreement and rivalry with Pākravān, the governor-general of Khorasan, then led Pākravān to take advantage of Asadi's opposition to the *chapeau* policy as a means of discrediting him in the eyes of the shah and putting the blame on him for the uprising at the Gowhar-šād Mosque. This resulted in Asadi's dismissal, trial, and execution in 1935 (Motavalli Ḥaqiqi, 2013, I, p. 276).

After Asadi's execution, Pākravān, in addition to being the governor-general, also became the deputy-trustee of the shrine. During his seven years in Khorasan, he carried out many of the government's directives vigorously and thoroughly on issues such as removing head-coverings from women and developing new schools (Mir Niā, II, p. 142).

With the outbreak of World War II in 1939, although Iran had declared neutrality, Soviet troops moved into Khorasan from the Saraḵs, Darragaz, and Bājgirān fronts on 3 Šahrivar 1320/1941. After brief clashes with Iranian forces and following the declaration of surrender by the Iranian government, the Soviets occupied all of Khorasan, based primarily in cities such as Mashhad and Bojnurd. Soviet forces were present in Khorasan from then until the winter of 1943. The presence of Soviet forces and the conditions of the war caused severe shortages, and famine and high prices in Khorasan made the lives of the people very difficult (Motavalli Ḥaqiqi, 2013, II, p. 39).

The khans of Khorasan, who had been severely repressed during the reign of Reżā Shah, began to revolt after his downfall (Mir Niā, II, p. 192). The rebellions of the khans of the Milānlu tribe in Esfarāyen (Tavaḥḥodi, p. 191) and of Faraj-Allāh Beyg of ʿId-Moḥammad Zuri in Torbat-e Jām were among these revolts (Rāmin-nežād, p. 318). But the biggest revolt during this period was the revolt of Moḥammad Yusof Khan Hazāra, known as Ṣawlat-al-Salṭana. Yusof Khan, who had been the first representative of the people of Mashhad in the Fifth Majles, was exiled from Khorasan during the reign of Reżā Shah and imprisoned for some time on charges of collaborating with Soviet agents (as confirmed by Agabekov, tr., p. 91, Pers. tr., p. 12). After the fall of Reżā Shah, he moved to occupy the eastern regions of Khorasan and rebel against the central government. However, he was eventually killed by agents sent by Rajab-ʿAli Manṣur, the governor-general of Khorasan (Bayāt, passim, and also Mir Niā, II, p. 202).

Another incident that occurred during the Soviet occupation of Khorasan was the uprising of Tuda (communist) officers from the Mashhad garrison in the summer of 1945, led by Major ʿAli-Akbar Eskandāni. He and twenty-five other officers and soldiers of the Tuda armed forces of Khorasan, using several vehicles and military equipment, reached Marāva Tappa and then Gonbad on 25 Mordād 1324/16 August 1945, but they were defeated by gendarmerie forces in Gonbad on 29 Mordād/20 August. Eskandāni was killed, and his remaining supporters fled (Rāmin-nežād, p. 364).

An attack on the Jewish or "New Muslim" inhabitants of Mashhad in the ʿIdgāh neighborhood took place in March 1946. Some Jews were injured and their property looted (Nazarzāda, p. 477). In October 1948, during the governorship of ʿAbbāsqoli Golšāʾiān (q.v.; d. 1990), a severe earthquake centered near Ashgabat in Turkmenistan shook the cities of Mashhad, Darragaz, Qučān, Bojnurd, Širvān, and Bājgirān, causing great damage to the cities and villages of Khorasan, killing or injuring more than a thousand people (Fāżeli Birjandi, p. 449).

The British and also the Americans had various activities in Khorasan in the 1940s and 1950s. The formation of the United Kingdom Commercial Corporation (UKCC) transportation company (Skrine, pp. 150, 197, 200), the publication of a newspaper, and the establishment of a branch of the British-Iranian Cultural Relations Association in Mashhad were among these activities (Elāhi, pp. 173-170). The Americans established their consulate in Mashhad in Ḵordād 1328/July 1949 (Motavalli Ḥaqiqi, 2013, II, p. 97) and also opened offices in Khorasan for Truman's Point Four program. In the 1950s, at the same time people across Iran were calling for the nationalization of the oil industry, so did newspapers, political parties, and many groups of people in Khorasan. The leaders of the nationalization movement in Khorasan were Moḥammad-Taqi Šariʿati, representing educators and intellectuals; Ḥāji ʿAli-Aṣḡar ʿĀbedzādeh, representing the bazaar merchants and craftsmen; and Sheikh Maḥmud Ḍākerzāda Tulāyi, known as Ḥalabi, representing a group of religious clerics (Jalāli, 118-21). With Moḥammad Moṣaddeq's rise to power in 1951, the political parties, press, ulema, and people were divided into two groups. Khorasani notables such as Ayatollah Kalbāsi, took the side of Moṣaddeq's government, while religious scholars such as Mirzā Aḥmad Kafāʾi Ḵorāsāni opposed Moṣaddeq and supported the royalists (Motavalli Ḥaqiqi, 2013, II, pp. 130, 169). After the Coup d'Etat of 1332 Š./1953 (q.v.) and the fall of the Moṣaddeq government, the suppression of members of the Tuda party of Khorasan began (see Baqiʿi, passim; COMMUNISM iii).

In the decades of the 1950s, 60s, and 70s, the Soviet government had little influence in Khorasan. As Russian influence declined, American and British influence in Khorasan increased in various ways (Motavalli Ḥaqiqi, 2013, II, p. 179). During the Coup d'Etat of 1332 Š./1953, many Khorasani newspapers and political parties that opposed the coup were shut down or dissolved. In the period between the Coup d'Etat of 1332 Š.1953 and Bahman 1357/ 1979, a total of fourteen people were named as governor-generals of Khorasan (Motavalli Ḥaqiqi, 2013, p. 210). The Tehran-Mashhad railway, the construction of which had begun in March 1937 but was halted due to the Allied invasion and occupation of Iran in 1941, was completed, and the first train arrived in Mashhad in January 1957 (Saʿidi, p. 90). This railway played a great role in the development of Mashhad, the increase in the number of visitors, and the prosperity of business. The severe Dašt-e Bayāż earthquake in Khorasan struck on 31 August 1968 during the governorship of Bāqer Pirniā. The earthquake was so devastating that it levelled cities such as Ferdows, Gonābād, and Kāḵk, with many deaths and extensive destruction (Fāżeli Birjandi, p. 542; Ambraseys and Tchalenko).

In the 1960s and 1970s, Khorasan also witnessed the opposition of a group of ulema and people against the government. Religious scholars such as Ḥasan Qomi and Moḥammad-Hādi Milāni and clerics such as ʿAbd-al-Karim Hāšemi-nežād, ʿAli Ḵāmenaʾi, ʿAbbās Wāʿeẓ Ṭabasi, and Sheikh ʿAli Ṭehrāni were among the most prominent of these dissidents. Among Khorasan intellectuals, those such as Moḥammad-Taqi Šariʿati and ʿAli Šariʿati were outspoken in their opposition to the government. Among the most prominent governors of Khorasan during this period, Bāqer Pirniā (governor from October 1967 to September 1970) and ʿAbd-al-ʿAẓim Valiān (May 1974 to August 1978) implemented modernization and secularization policies that fueled this discontent in the province; the designation of Valiān as *nāyeb al-tawliya* was especially unpopular (see Motavalli Ḥaqiqi, 2013, II, pp. 383-433; Bill, pp. 187-88).

Bibliography: [Anonymous], "Aḥmad Šāh Dorrāni," tr. Sayyed Ḥosayn Ṣadr al-Maʿāli, MS Ketāb-ḵāna-ye Āstān-e Qods-e Rażawi, Mashhad (dated 1320/1902-3). ʿAli Āḏari, *Qiām-e Kolonel Moḥammad-Taqi Ḵān Pesyān dar Ḵorāsān*, 3rd ed., Tehran, 1965. Ḡolām-Reżā Āḏari Ḵākestar, *Šenāsāʾi va moʿarrefi avvalinhā-ye šahr-e Mašhad*, Mashhad, 2016. Moḥammad Ḥasan Adib Heravi, *al-Ḥadiqa al-rażawiya*, Mashhad, 1946. Grigoriĭ Sergeevich Agabekov, *GPU: Zapiski Chekista*, Berlin, 1930, tr. Henry W. Bunn, as *OGPU: The Russian Secret Terror*, New York, 1931; Pers. tr. Ḥosayn Abu Torābiān, as *Ḵāṭerāt-e Āqa Bekof*, Tehran, 1978. Abbas Amanat and Arash Khazeni, "The Steppe Roads of Central Asia and the Persian Captivity Narrative of Mirza Mahmud Taqi Ashtiyani," in Nile Green, ed., *Writing Travel in Central Asian History*, Bloomington, Indiana, 2014, pp. 113-31. N. N. Ambraseys and J. S. Tchalenko, "The Dasht-e Bayāz (Iran) Earthquake of August 31, 1968: A Field Report," *Bulletin of the Seismological Society of America* 59, 1969, pp. 1751-92. Atepheh Amid, "Night, Space and Urban Design: Case Study of Mashhad, Iran," Ph.D. diss., University of Westminster, U.K., 2013. Mirzā Qahramān Amin-Lašgar, *Ruznāma-ye safar-e Ḵorāsān*, eds. Iraj Afšār and Moḥammad Rasul Daryāgašt, Tehran, 1995. Moḥammad Arjomand, *Šeš sāl dar darbār-e pahlavi*, Tehran, 2006. Mirzā ʿAbd-al-Wahhāb Khan Āṣaf-al-Dawla, *Asnād*, eds., ʿAbd-al-Ḥosayn Navāʾi and Nilufar Kasri, Tehran, 1998. Ḥosayn Aʿẓām Qodsi, *Ḵāterāt-e man yā rowšan šodan-e tāriḵ-e ṣad sāla*, 2 vols., Tehran, 1970. Aḥmad Bahār, *Divān*, ed. Rāšed Bahār, Tehran, 1991. Mehrdād Bahār, ed., *Dar bāra-ye qiām-e žāndārmeri-e Ḵorāsān be rahbari-e Kolonel Moḥammad-Taqi Ḵān Pesyān*, Tehran, 1990. Moḥammad-Taqi Bahār, *Tāriḵ-e moḵtaṣar-e aḥzāb-e siāsi dar Irān*, 2 vols., repr. Tehran, 1992-93. Mahdi Bāmdād, *Šarḥ-e ḥāl-e rejāl-e Irān*, 6 vols., Tehran, 1968-69. Ḡolām-Ḥosayn Baqiʿi, *Angiza: Ḵāṭerāti az dawrān-e faʿʿāliat ḥezb-e tuda*, Tehran, 1994. V. V. Barthold, *An Historical Geography of Iran*, tr. Svat Soucek, Princeton, 1984. Vera Basch Moreen, "The Jews in Iran," in Abdelwahab Meddeb and Benjamin Stora, eds., *A History of Jewish-Muslim Relations: From the Origins to the Present Day*, Princeton, 2013, pp. 239-47. Kāva Bayāt, *Ṣawlat-al-Salṭana Hazāra va šureš-e Ḵorāsān dar zamestān 1320 šamsi*, Tehran, 1991. Idem, *Qiām-e nāfarjām: Šureš-e Lahāk Ḵān Sālār Jang*, Tehran, 1996. Kāva Bayāt, ed., *Enqelāb-e Ḵorāsān: Majmuʿa-ye asnād wa madārek-e sāl-e 1300 šamsi*, Tehran, 1991. Manuel Berberian, *Earthquakes and Coseismic Surface Faulting on the Iranian Plateau*, Oxford and Amsterdam, 2014. James Bill, *The Eagle and the Lion*, New Haven, 1988. E. G. Browne, *The Press and Poetry of Modern Persia*, Cambridge, 1914, pp. 174-79 ("Ballad of the Girls of Qúchán").

David Charles Champagne, "The Afghan-Iranian Conflict over Herat Province and European Intervention 1796-1863: A Reinterpretation," Ph.D. diss., The University of Texas at Austin, 1981. Arthur Conolly, *Journey to the North of India, Overland from England, through Russia, Persia, and Affghaunistaun*. 2 vols., London, 1834. Stephanie Cronin, *The Army and the Creation of the Pahlavi State in Iran 1910-1926*, London, 1997a. Idem, "An Experiment in Revolutionary Nationalism: The Rebellion of Colonel Muhammad Taqi Khan Pasyan in Mashhad, April-October 1921," *Middle Eastern Studies* 33/4, 1997b, pp. 693-750. Idem, "The Provincial Cities in Revolt (i): Colonel Pasyan and the Mashhad Rebellion, April-October 1921," in idem, *Sol-*

diers, Shahs and Subalterns in Iran: Opposition, Protest and Revolt, 1921-1941, Basingstoke, 2010, pp. 44-100. Idem, "Riza Shah and the Paradoxes of Military Modernization in Iran, 1921-41," in idem, ed., *The Making of Modern Iran: State and Society under Riza Shah, 1921-1941*, London, 2014, pp. 37-64. George N. Curzon, Persia and the Persian Question, 2 vols., London, 1892, tr. Ḡolām-ʿAli Vaḥid Māzandarāni, as *Irān va qażia-ye Irān*, Tehran, 2001. ʿAbd-al-Razzāq Donboli, *Maʾāṯer-e solṭāniya (az ru-ye nosḵa-ye muzeh-ye Baritāniā)*, ed. Firuz Manṣuri, Tehran, 2004. Moḥammad Eḥtešām Kāviāniān, *Šams al-šamus yā tāriḵ-e Āstān-e qods*, Mashhad, 1976. Ḥosayn Elāhi, *Ruznāma va ruznāma-negāri dar Ḵorāsān az āḡāz tā šahrivar 1320*, Mashhad, 2000. Idem, *Aḥzāb va sāzmānhā-ye siāsi va ʿamalkard-e ānhā dar Ḵorāsān 1320 tā 1332*, Mashhad, 2003. Maḥmud-Taqi ʿEmād-al-Daftar Āštiāni, *ʿEbrat-nāma: ḵāṭerāti az dawrān-e pas az janghā-ye Herāt va Marv*, ed. Ḥosayn ʿEmādi Āštiāni, Tehran, 2003. Moḥammad Ḥasan Khan Ṣaniʿ-al-Dawla Eʿtemād-al-Salṭana, *Maṭlaʿ al-šāms*, Tehran, 1983. Idem, *Tāriḵ-e montaẓam-e nāṣeri*, ed. M. Reżwāni, 3 vols, Tehran, 1988. Mohammad H. Faghfoory, "The Impact of Modernization on the Ulama in Iran, 1925-1941," *Iranian Studies*, 26/3-4, 1993, pp. 277-312. Elāha Maḥbub Farimāni and Behzād Neʿmati, *Asnād-e ḥożur-e dawlathā-ye bigāna dar šarq-e Irān*, Mashhad, 2003. Fatema Soudavar Farmanfarmaian, "James Baillie Fraser in Mashhad or the Pilgrimage of a Nineteenth-Century Scotsman to the Shrine of the Imām Riḍā," *Iran* 34, 1996, pp. 101-15. Idem, "An Iranian Perspective of J. B. Fraser's Trip to Khorasan in the 1820s," *Iranian Studies* 44/2, 2011, pp. 217-42.

Maḥmud Fāżeli Birjandi, *Tārikčaʾi-e farmān-ravāyān-e Ḵorāsān az āḡāz-e Qājār tā pāyān-e Pahlavi*, Tehran, 2019. Frederick Forbes and W. Rawlinson, "Route from Turbat Haïderí, in Khorásán, to the River Herí Rúd, on the Borders of Sístán" *The Journal of the Royal Geographical Society of London* 14, 1844, pp. 145-92. Reżāqoli Khan Hedāyat, *Tāriḵ-e rawżat al-ṣafā-ye nāṣeri*, ed. Jamšid Kiānfar, 10 vols. in 15, Tehran, 2001. Ḡolām-Reżā Jalāli, *Taqvim-e tāriḵ-e Ḵorāsān az mašruṭa tā enqelāb-e eslāmi*, Tehran, 1377/1998-99. Fażl-Allāh b. ʿAbd-al-Nabi Ḵāvari Širāzi, *Tāriḵ-e Ḏu'l-Qarnayn*, Tehran, 2001. Nikki R. Keddie, *Religion and Rebellion in Iran: The Tobacco Protest of 1891-92*, London, 1966. Alexis Krausse, *Russia in Asia*, New York, 1899. Moḥammad Jaʿfar Ḵurmuji, *Ḥaqāʾeq al-aḵbār-e nāṣeri*, Tehran, 1984. Mohammad Gholi Majd, *The Great Famine and Genocide in Persia, 1917-1919*, Lanham, Md., 2003, tr. Moḥammad Karimi, as *Qaḥṭi-e bozorg*, Tehran, 2008. Idem, *A Victorian Holocaust: Iran in the Great Famine of 1869-1873*, Lanham, MD, 2018. Ḥosayn Makki, *Tārikh-e bist sāla-ye Irān* VI: *Estemrār-e diktātori-e Reżā Šah Pahlavi*, Tehran, 1983, pp. 252-57. Vanessa Martin, "Social Networks and Border Conflicts: The First Herat War 1838-1841," in Roxane Farmanfarmaian, ed., *War and Peace in Qajar Persia*, London and New York, 2008, pp. 110-22. Rudi Matthee, "Infidel Aggression: The Russian Assault on the Holy Shrine of Imam Reza, Mashhad, 1912," in idem and Elena Andreeva, eds., *Russians in Iran: Diplomacy and Power in the Qajar Era and Beyond*, London, 2018, pp. 136-72. Sayyed ʿAli Mir Niā, *Waqāyeʿ-e ḵāvar-e Irān dar dawra-ye Qājār*, Mashhad, 1988. Ḡolām-Ḥosayn Mirzā Ṣāleḥ, *Forupāši-e Qājār va bar āmadan-e Pahlavi*, Tehran, 2008 (compilation of consular documents). Moḥammad-Taqi Modarres Rażavi, *Sāl-šomār-e vaqāyeʿ-e Mašhad dar qarnhā-ye panjom tā sizdahom*, ed. Iraj Afšār, Tehran, 1999. ʿAli Moʾtaman, *Rāhnemā yā Tāriḵ va tawṣif-e darbār-e velāyatmadār-e Rażavi*, Tehran, 1969. Yusof Motavalli Ḥaqiqi, *Az Tabriz tā Mašhad: pežuheši pirāmun-e zendagi va qiām-e Kolonel Moḥammad-Taqi Ḵān Pesyān*, Mashhad, 2001. Idem, *Afḡānestān va Irān: Pežuheši pirāmun-e ravābeṭ-e siāsi va čālešhā-ye marzi az Aḥmad Šāh Dorrāni ta Aḥmad Šāh Qājār*, Mashhad, 2004. Idem, *Tāriḵča-ye āmuzeš va parvareš-e novin-e Ḵorāsān az āḡāz tā enqelāb-e eslāmi*, Mashhad, 2005. Idem, *Ḵorāsān-e šomāli: Pežuheši pirāmun-e tāriḵ-e taḥavollāt-e siāsi-e šahrhā-e Ḵorāsān-e šomāli az āḡāz tā enqelāb-e eslāmi*, Mashhad, 2008. Idem, *Tāriḵ-e moʿāṣer-e Mašhad: Pežuheši-e pirāmun-e tāriḵ-e taḥavvolāt-e siāsi-ejtemāʿi-e Mašhad az enqelāb-e mašruṭa tā enqelāb-e eslāmi*, Mashhad, 2013.

Afsaneh Najmabadi, *The Story of the Daughters of Quchan: Gender and National Memory in Iranian History*, Syracuse, 1998. Moḥammad Naẓarzāda, "Maḥallahā-ye qadimi-e šahr-e Mašhad: Maḥalla-ye ʿIdgāh," in Markaz-e asnād-e Āstān-e qods-e rażavi, *Daftar-e asnād*, vols. II-III. Moḥammad Nāẓem-al-Eslām Kermāni, *Tāriḵ-e bidāri-e Irāniān*, ed. ʿAli-Akbar Saʿidi Sirjāni, 4th printing, 5 vols. in 2, Tehran, 1983. Hilda Nissimi, "Memory, Community, and the Mashhadi Jews during the Underground Period," *Jewish Social Studies*, n.s. 9/3, 2003, pp. 76-106. Christine Noelle-Karimi, *The Pearl in Its Midst: Herat and the Mapping of Khurasan (15th-19th Centuries)*, Vienna, 2014. Morteza Nouraei, "Mashhad between 1890 and 1914: A Socio-historical Study," Ph.D. diss., University of Manchester, 2000. Moḥammad Taqi Khan Nuri, *Ašraf al-tawāriḵ* I: *Vaqāyeʿ-e marbuṭ ba dawra-ye ḥokumat-e Moḥammad Vali Mirzā dar Ḵorāsān, sālhā-ye 1218-1331*, ed. Susan Aṣili, Tehran, 2007. Jaleh Pirnazar, "The Anusim of Mashhad," in H. Sarshar, *Esther's Children*, Philadelphia, 2002, pp. 115-36. Abu'l-Ḥasan Qazvini, *Fawāʾed al-ṣafaviya*, ed. Maryam Mir Aḥmadi, Tehran, 1988. Rāmin Rāmin-nežād, *Tāriḵ-e laškar-e Ḵorāsān*, Mashhad, 2012. Moḥammad-Yusof Riāżi Heravi, *ʿAyn al-waqāyeʿ*, ed. M. Āṣaf Fekrat, Tehran, 1993. Qodrat-Allāh Rowšani Zaʿfarānlu, *Seh safarnāma (Herāt, Marv, Mašhad)*, Tehran, 1968. Moḥammad Ṣadr Hāšemi, *Tāriḵ-e jarāyed va majallāt-e Irān*, 2nd ed., 4 vols., Isfahan, 1984-85. Ebrāhim Ṣafāʾi, *Asnād-e now-yāfta*, Tehran, 1970. Idem, *Yak ṣad sanad-e tāriḵi*, Tehran, 1974. Ramażān-ʿAbbās Saʿidi, "Joḡrāfiā-ye šahr-e Mašhad," *Majalla-ye Dāneškada-ye adabiāt-e Dānešgāh-e Mašhad* 2-3, 1965. ʿAli Šākeri, *Atrak-nāma: Tāriḵ-e jāmeʿ-e Qučān*, Tehran, 1986. ʿAli-Aṣḡar Šamim, *Irān dar dawra-ye salṭanat-e Qājār*, Tehran, 1964.

Moḥammad-Mehdi Šarif Kāšāni, *Wāqeʿāt-e ettefāqiya [dar] ruzgār*, ed. Manṣura Etteḥādiya (Neẓām Māfi), 3 vols., Tehran, 1983. Ḥamid Šawkat, *Dar tir-ras-e ḥādaṯa: Zendegi-ye siāsi Qawām-al-Salṭana*, Tehran, 2007. Akram Šaybāni, *Ḵorāsān va naqš-e ostāndārān dar dawra-ye pahlavi-e avval*, Mashhad, 2013. Mahdi Sayyidi, *Tāriḵ-e šahr-e Mašhad*, Tehran, 1999. Sāzmān-e modiriyat va barnāma-rizi-e Ḵorāsān-e Rażawi (Khorasan Razavi Province Management and Planning Organization), website, khrazavi.mporg.ir. Mirzā Moḥammad-Taqi Lesān-al-Molk Sepehr, *Nāseḵ al-tawāriḵ: Tāriḵ-e qājāriyya*, ed. Jamšid Kiānfar, 3 vols. in 2, Tehran, 1998. A. Reza Sheikholeslami, *The Structure of Central Authority in Qajar Iran 1871-1896*, Atlanta, Ga., 1997. Clarmont P. Skrine, *World War in Iran*, London, 1962, tr. Ḡolāmḥosayn Mirzā Ṣāleḥ, as *Jang-e jahāni dar Irān: Ḵāterāt-e Ser Kalarmunt Iskrin*, Tehran, 1984. Francis Henry Skrine and Edward Denison ross, *The Heart of Asia*, London, 1899. Moḥammad-ʿAli Šuštari, *Ḵaṭerāt-e siāsi-ye Sayyed Moḥammad-ʿAli Šuštari: Ḵofiya-nevis-e Reżā Šāh Pahlavi*, ed. Ḡolām-Ḥosayn Mirzā Ṣāleḥ, Tehran, 2000. Percy Sykes, *A History of Persia*, 2 vols., London, 1951. Abu'l-Ḥasan Tafrišiān, *Qiām-e afsarān-e Ḵorāsān*, 2nd ed., Tehran, 1998. Kalim-Allāh Tavaḥḥodi, *Esfarāyen diruz, emruz*, Mashhad, 1996. Sinā Vāḥed, *Qiām-e Gowhar-šād*, Tehran 1366/1987. Mikhail Volodarsky, "Persia's Foreign Policy between the Two Herat Crises, 1831-56," *Middle Eastern Studies*, 21/2, 1985, pp. 111-51. Joseph Wolff, *Narrative of a Mission to Bokhara, in the Years 1843-1845, to Ascertain the Fate of Colonel Stoddart and Captain Conolly*, New York, 1845. Marżiya Yazdāni, *Asnād-e mohājerat-e yahudiān-e Irān beh Falasṭin*, Tehran, 1996. Zayn-al-ʿĀbedin Mirzā Qājār, *Nofus-e arż-e aqdas yā mardom-e Mašhad-e qadim*, ed. Mahdi Sayyedi, Mashhad, 2003.

(YOUSEF MOTAVALLI HAGHIGHI)

xii. HISTORY IN THE ISLAMIC REPUBLIC PERIOD. See Supplement.

xiii. KHORASAN IN MODERN ISLAMIST IDEOLOGY

Khorasan in modern Islamist ideology is a byproduct of the influx of Muslim fighters (*mojāhedin*) into Afghanistan after the Soviet Union invaded the country in 1979 during the Cold War. For the varied groups contesting Soviet presence, the revival of the pre-modern concept of Khorasan held specific, and at times contradictory, meaning. Leveraged by the Islamist militant network Al-Qaeda (al-Qāʿeda) in the mid-1990s and adopted by a unit of the Islamic State of Iraq and Syria (ISIS), the militant group that came to prominence in Iraq and Syria in 2013 and gained followers in its proclaimed caliphal province (*welāya*) of Khorasan including parts of Afghanistan, Pakistan and adjacent areas, the term saw a resurgence in its political currency, which had been dormant since the early 20th century.

The concept of Khorasan as a geographical space and its political, cultural, and historical references have continually changed since the former Sasanian region became part of the Omayyad Muslim empire in the 1st/7th century (see KHORASAN i.-iv.). The history of the region between the Muslim conquest and the 6th/13th centuries "is the history of a marginal region becoming a center and then again a margin" (Durand-Guédy, p. 2). In the 13th/20th century, the region once again gained prominence, this time in Afghanistan's historical narrative, beginning with an article in 1932 by Mir Ḡolam Mohammad Ḡobār that positioned the country as part of Āryānā, "Land of the Aryans," in pre-Islamic times (see ARYANS, ĒRĀN WĒZ; i.e., present-day Afghanistan and parts of Iran and Pakistan) and as Khorasan, "The Place where the Sun Rises," after the Islamic conquests (Ḡobār, 1932, pp. 7-40). In this narrative, Abu Moslem Ḵorāsāni (q.v.), the prominent 2nd/8th-century leader of the ʿAbbasid Revolution (see KHORASAN v.), is revered as an Afghan resistance leader who donned black clothing and raised a black banner against foreign (Omayyad) oppression. The symbolisms associated with Abu Moslem's movement have resonated in Afghan historical consciousness, a notable example being the color of the national flag that, until 1928, was all black with a white seal in the middle (see FLAGS ii.). To situate Abu Moslem further within modern Afghanistan's geographical boundaries, Afghan narratives designate the village of Sapid Dāž near the modern city of Sar-e Pol as his place of birth rather than the more conventional location near Marv or Isfahan (Dawlatābādi, pp. 198-99; Ḡobār, 1956, pp. 1-113; Kohzad).

From the initial phases of the Afghan *mojāhedin* political campaigns against the Soviets (1979-89) to the internal conflict with the Taliban (Ṭālebān) (1994-2001), Khorasan became a term of reference used by some of the local, mainly non-Pashtun, groups to propagate the idea that their armed struggle went beyond freeing the country from the foreign yoke and communism or the Taliban. For them, it was a call to return the country to its pre-1747 political makeup, the time before modern-day Afghanistan emerged as a political unit ruled by Dorrāni (q.v.) Pashtuns (Afḡān proper; see AFGHANISTAN x.). In this construct, the concept of Khorasan serves as a counterbalance to the Pashtun domination of the country, providing a more inclusive or Tajik-centric national construct than the exclusivity of Afghanistan as the "Land of the Afghans/ Pashtuns" (Tarzi, 2018, pp. 124-26).

The focus of the Arab jihadists in Afghanistan in the early part of the 1980s was principally on fighting the Soviets in Afghanistan (see also ISLAM IN IRAN xi. JIHAD IN ISLAM). After the formation of Al-Qaeda in the late 1980s and the departure of the Soviets from Afghanistan, this focus began to change to global jihadist agendas, culminating in the return of the former *mojāhed* Osama Bin Ladin (Osāma b. Lāden; d. 2011) to Afghanistan as the head of Al-Qaeda's remodeled organization in 1996. At this juncture, Afghanistan served only as a base of operations for the larger, more elusive goals of establishing an Islamic caliphate, ousting the United States from Saudi

Arabia, and destroying Israel. This led to theological, mythical, and geographic symbolisms associated with the historical Khorasan being incorporated into Al-Qaeda's overall strategic propaganda.

The theological part of Al-Qaeda's connection to Khorasan is based on a few hadiths (q.v.) linking the geographical location to future events (see Bahari and Hassan, pp. 18-19). The most referenced hadith, of which there are various renditions, conveys the message that there would emerge from Khorasan an army carrying black banners that no one would repel until it raised its banners in Ilia (the name used in early Muslim sources for Jerusalem). In one of these hadiths, the Prophet Moḥammad is alleged to have stated that his followers must join that army even if they have to crawl over ice (Haqqani). The hadith served to amplify symbolism denoting Khorasan's prophetic role in the ultimate apocalyptic battle between Islam and its enemies. Bin Laden, aware of this connection, wrote in his 1996 declaration of war on the United States that "by the Grace of God" he had found "a safe base in Khorasan" (Bin Laden). This became a primary text for the jihadist movement. Al-Qaeda also created an online magazine, *Ṭalāʿi Ḵorāsān* (*Vanguard of Khorasan*), leveraging the name. In its undated (most probably 2005) inaugural issue, Al-Qaeda identified two additional hadiths that detailed the "virtues of Khorasan" and used them as the justification behind the magazine's title. One claimed that the Prophet said "When you see black banners coming from Khorasan, follow them, as 'the Caliph of Allah, the Mahdi' will be among them." The second hadith, roughly recounting the 'Abbasid revolt, narrates the Prophet saying that the deliverance of his own family from suffering will come from the East (another term associated with Khorasan). In most of the current online inquiries about the authenticity of the Khorasan hadiths (e.g., https://abuaminaelias.com/hadith-black-flags-al-mahdi or https://islamqa.info/en/answers/171131; both accessed 1 June 2020), the chains of transmissions for these sayings are contested by responding scholars, and they are categorized as *żaʾif* (weak). Paradoxically, *Ṭalāʿi Ḵorāsān* mentions that Moḥammad b. ʿIsā Termeḏi (d. 279/892), who compiled the hadith about Jerusalem, had categorized the hadith as *ḡarib* (strange).

The geographical understanding of Khorasan, which has always fluctuated, according to the archeologist Rocco Rante, "could often be associated with a territorial entity more than an administrative one." Even though under Samanids in the 4th/10th century (see KHORASAN vi.), Khorasan's unification with Transoxiana (see MĀ WARĀʾ AL-NAHR) became "official," in no instance had this region or Greater Khorasan included territories south of the Hindu Kush mountains in Central Afghanistan (Rante, pp. 10, 14). However, in Al-Qaeda's understanding, Khorasan included Pakistan and parts of northern and northeastern India. The base of operations for Al-Qaeda was the seamless border regions between Afghanistan and Pakistan that they crisscrossed without any regard to the international administrative divisions. This transnational geographical delineation supported not only its physical territorial claims but also its political agenda: Its disregard for international borders emphasized that the Islamic world was a community of believers rather than states with distinct boundaries. This latter construct aligned with most of Al-Qaeda's local Pakistani jihadist groups, which were purposed to oppose Afghanistan's territorial claims over Pakistan's northwestern regions and its notion that these divided geographical spaces were one contiguous Pashtun land. Since the establishment of Pakistan as a separate state in 1947, Afghanistan has regarded its southeastern neighbor as a usurper of Afghan territory. Pakistan on the other hand has tried to defuse the irredentist claims of its neighbor with a series of policies designed to keep Afghanistan weak while replacing "Afghan nationalism with a more Pakistani-controlled pan-Islamism, thus rendering Afghan nationalistic territorial claims irrelevant" (Tarzi, 2012). In 2013, a new online magazine emerged promoting "Khorasan" as the staging grounds for the establishment of a pan-Islamic caliphate. Published by the "Taliban in Khorasan," *Āzān* promoted radicalization, global jihad, and the fomenting of anti-Shiʿite sentiments. The magazine most probably belonged to Tahrik-e Taliban Pakistan (TTP) and not the Afghan Taliban, who did not have an internationalist orientation and did not pay much attention to the Khorasan construct, preferring an Afghan nationalist agenda. Further indication of TTP authorship is that *Āzān* is published by the "Taliban in Khorasan"; the Afghan Taliban refers to itself as the "Islamic Emirate of Afghanistan" or simply as *mojāhedin* (Ingram).

The U.S.-led invasion of Iraq in 2003 prompted jihadist organizations, including many in the ranks of Al-Qaeda, to shift their focus westward from Afghanistan and to align with splinter local groups and more independent groups in Iraq and elsewhere in the Arab countries. In Iraq, Abu Moṣʿab Zarqawi (d. 2006) established Al-Qaeda in Iraq based on a vision of the revival of a Sunni caliphate and the elimination of Shīʿism. In a letter to Bin Ladin and his deputy, Ayman Zawāhiri, Zarqawi urged them join him in his modus operandi by prioritizing the targeting of Shī'as before all other enemies. Zarqawi reminded the two Al-Qaeda leaders that "the greatest benefit" of his activities in Mesopotamia "is that this is jihad in the Arab heartland, a stone's throw" from Mecca, Medina, and al-Aqṣā Mosque (Kepel and Milelli, pp. 251-67). In 2014, for the Sunnis in Iraq who were becoming increasingly marginalized and threatened by the Shiʿa administration in Baghdad, Zarqawi's message resonated, and his vision gave birth to the establishment of the Islamic State of Iraq and Syria (ISIS). The breakdown of the Syrian state that began in 2011 allowed ISIS to expand westward, gaining territorial strategic depth and significant economic strength (Gerges, pp. 15-18). With its capital in Raqqa, ISIS transformed itself into a state.

The reestablishment of a Sunni caliphate and territoriality changed the notion of Khorasan for ISIS. Being based in Syria and Iraq, and referring to itself since 2014 as Islamic State (IS), ISIS no longer looked to the East for an army to fulfill its destiny because the army had already arrived. Most of the founders of IS, including Zarqawi, had begun their jihadist careers in "Khorasan." They were the army with black banners, and they had already moved toward their target, the West, which symbolized Rome. IS preserved the black banner as its reference to the hadith about the army with black flags originating in Khorasan. Naming one of its online magazines *Dabiq* and its news agency Amaq, IS banked on another eschatological hadith, that the last hour would come when an army from Rome (Constantinople) would come to Amaq (present-day Turkey) or Dabiq (a city in northwestern Syria) and would be opposed with an army from Medina. After the Medinan army conquered Rome, they would become voracious and cavalier, leading to the appearance of Dajjāl (q.v.), "the great deceiver." The Medinan forces would regroup in Syria to fight Dajjāl and be led in prayer by Jesus, son of Mary, who would defeat Dajjāl. Zarqawi wrote in his letter that "[w]e know from God's religion that the true, decisive battle between unbelief and Islam is in Syria and its surrounding" (Kepel and Milelli, p. 251). Ironically, there are different hadiths concerning where Dajjāl will appear. Some state Dajjāl will appear in Khorasan, Sistan, and, more commonly, Yahudiya, the Jewish quarter of Isfahan in Iran. As IS gained in prominence over Al-Qaeda, the role of Khorasan in organizational narratives waned, as the Greater Syria traditions were more fitting to its geographical positioning and political agenda.

In 2014, usage of Khorasan resurfaced both in Syria and in and around the historical region. The U.S. Department of Defense in September issued a statement announcing the expected expansion of air campaigns beyond Iraq to include attacking "Khorasan Group targets west of Aleppo" (Lund). In this case, the usage of Khorasan most likely was due to the presence of veteran Al-Qaeda fighters in Syria who sought to identify themselves as those originally from the core Al-Qaeda areas and as members of the army with black banners. This group disappeared very quickly, or perhaps it never existed as an organized group, as it may have been more of a media invention resulting from a lack of understanding of some nameless group of Sunni fighters with alleged jihadist credentials from Afghanistan.

As an example of the contradictory understandings of "Khorasan" in modern Islamist ideology, one may note another group that surfaced in September 2013 in Iraq. The Khorasani Brigades (Sarāyā al-Ḵorāsāni), led by ʿAli Yasiri, was a well-armed and effective fighting Shiʿite group that opposed the Islamic State and had direct support from Iran's Islamic Revolution Guard Corps (IRGC; Sepāh-e pāsdarān-e enqelāb-e eslāmi). It was considered one of most closely linked groups to the IRGC and also had ties to Iraq's Islamic Vanguard Party (Hezb al-taliʿa al-eslāmiya) and became part of Iraq's Popular Mobilization Units (al-Hašd al-šaʿbi) (Heras, pp. 5, 10). The Khorasani Brigades displayed its affiliation with the IRGC very openly on its symbols (Figure 1) and, according to some sources, was named after either Abu Moslem Ḵorāsāni or "al-Sayyed al-Ḵorāsāni," a reference to Iran's Supreme Leader Ayatollah Ali Khamenei (Puxton; Qaidaari).

In 2015, closer to geographic Khorasan (or more accurately "Greater Khorasan"), another group, an IS affiliate, employing one of the many symbolisms attached to "Khorasan," appeared in the fluid border lands between Afghanistan and Pakistan. Individuals and small groups of disgruntled jihadists in Afghanistan and Pakistan pledged their allegiance to the IS leader, Abu Bakr al-Baghdādi (d. 2019), and created the Islamic State Khorasan Province (ISKP). The geographical limits of the Islamic State Khorasan Province, true to the region's history, remained fluid and corresponded to the locations where the group's forces were operational, countries it targeted for enlisting more recruits, and, finally, the regions that were of utmost importance to its central leadership. In most reports, ISKP's territorial claims encompassed Afghanistan, Pakistan, Iran, the Central Asian republics, northwestern (or all of) India, and part of Russia (Giustozzi, p. 2). The majority of the ISKP leadership came from Pakistani jihadist groups such as TTP, Laškar-e Ṭāʾeba, or Ḥarakat al-Mojāhedin. Early in ISKP's formative period, it was joined by the Islamic Movement of Uzbekistan (IMU) and also attracted a number of dissatisfied Afghan Ṭaliban members. While Afghanistan and Pakistan continued to be understood as Khorasan for Islamists of all stripes, the group expanded it to include Central Asia due to the large number of Uzbeks, Tajiks, and Uighurs among its ranks who aspired to extend the movement to their home regions. Additionally, the Pakistani jihadist outfits involved wanted Kashmir in particular and India in general included, as they sought to gain control over these lands. Both the Afghan government and the United States took military action against ISKP, but its most ardent opponent was the Taliban. By 2018, ISKP had lost most of its territorial holdings. The Taliban meanwhile gained greater acceptancy in international circles, including in Iran and Russia, for its opposition to ISKP and its internationalist agendas (Tarzi, 2018).

The idea of "Khorasan" or "Greater Khorasan" has held different and at times conflicting meanings to different groups that emerged as part of the local and international

Figure 1. Khorasani Brigades (Sarāyā al-Ḵorāsāni) logo.

resistance to the Soviet invasion of Afghanistan. For the local non-Pashtun groups in Afghanistan, "Khorasan" rekindled the region's pre-Pashtun-dominated identity and the glories associated with Abu Moslem. The idea entered modern Islamist mythology and information operations with the establishment of Al-Qaeda in Afghanistan and Pakistan and through the convenience of a series of eschatological hadiths. For Pakistan and its proxy militant Islamist groups, "Khorasan" countered Afghanistan's nationalism and its irredentist claims on Pakistani territory and brought India into an Islamist construct. In Iraq and Syria, the symbolisms associated with "Khorasan" are used by the Shiᶜite Islamists to resist Sunni domination and to link to the Islamic Republic of Iran. For the Islamic State, "Greater Khorasan" became a province in a geopolitical scheme to redraw state boundaries. For Al-Qaeda ideologues, "Khorasan" represented the mythical region from which pan-Islamism would begin and a useful tool to counter Shiᶜite Iran's influence in Central Asia. With the emergence of the Islamic State in Iraq and Syria and the subsequent geographic shift of the operational base to Syria, the hadiths associated with "Khorasan" as a locus of Islamist militancy lost their political currency. For the Islamist ideologies in the late 20th and early 21st centuries, as had happened in the past, Khorasan literally and figuratively loomed first on the margins of the Islamic world, later became central to it, and then returned again to the margins.

Bibliography: Mustazah Bahari and Muhammad Haniff Hassan, "The Black Flag Myth: An Analysis from Hadith Studies," *Counter Terrorist Trends and Analyses* 6/8, 2014, pp. 15-20. Osama bin Laden, "Eᶜlān al-jehād ᶜalā al-Amrikiin al-moḥtallin le-belād al-ḥaramayn," 1996; available at Combating Terrorism Center at West Point (https://ctc.usma.edu/wp-content/uploads/2013/10/Declaration-of-Jihad-against-the-Americans-Occupying-the-Land-of-the-Two-Holiest-Sites-Original.pdf). B. A. Dawlatābādi, *Šenās-nāma-ye Afḡānestān*, Qom, 1992. David Durand-Guédy, "Pre-Mongol Khurasan: A Historical Introduction" in R. Rante, ed., *Greater Khorasan*, Berlin, 2015, pp. 1-7. Fawaz A. Gerges, *ISIS: A History*, Princeton, 2016. M. G. M. Ghobār, "Tāriḵča-ye moḵtaṣar-e Afḡānestān," in *Sālnāma-ye Majalla-ye Kābol*, Kabul, 1311/1932, pp. 7-40. Idem, "Ẓohur wa nofuẓ-e Eslām wa 'Arab dar Afḡānestān" *Tāriḵ-e Afḡānestān* III/1, Kabul, 1956. Antonio Giustozzi, *The Islamic State in Khorasan: Afghanistan, Pakistan and the New Central Asian Jihad*, London, 2018. Husain Haqqani, "Prophecy and the Jihad in the Indian Subcontinent," *Current Trends in Islamist Ideology*, Vol. 18, 2015, pp. 5-17. Nicholas A. Heras, "Iraq's Fifth Column: Iran's Proxy Network," Middle East Institute Policy Paper 2017, No. 2, October 2017. Harold J. Ingram, "An Analysis of the Taliban in Khurasan's *Azan* (Issues 1-5)," *Studies in Conflict and Terrorism* 38, 2015, pp. 560-79. Ahmad Ali Kohzad, *Afḡānestān dar Šāhnāma: Šāhnāma dar Ḵorāsān yā Šāhnāma dar Āryānā*, Kabul, 1976. Gilles Kepel and Jean-Pierre Milelli, eds., *Al Qaeda in Its Own Words*, trans. P. Ghazaleh, Cambridge, Mass., 2008. Aron Lund, "What is the 'Khorasan Group' and Why Is the U.S. Bombing It in Syria?" Carnegie Middle East Center, 23 September 2014 (https:carnegie-mec.org/diwan/56707). Matteo Puxton, "Bataille de Mossoul: Saraya al-Khorasani, la milice chiite soutenue et armée par l'Iran" *France Soir*, 6 March 2017 (www.francesoir.fr/politique-monde/saraya-al-khorasani-milice-chiite-irakienne-soutien-syrie-iran-bataille-de-mossoul-combats-alep-guerre-etat-islamique-ei-daech-al-yasiri). Abbas Qaidaari, "Iran's New Group in Iraq: Saraya al-Khorasani," *Al-Monitor*, 11 January 2015 (www.al-monitor.com/pulse/fr/contents/articles/originals/2015/01/iran-iraq-saraya-al-khorasani.html). Rocco Rante, "'Khorasan Proper' and 'Greater Khorasan' within a Politico-Cultural Framework" in R. Rante, ed., *Greater Khorasan*, Berlin, 2015, pp. 9-25. M. A. Shaban, *The 'Abbāsid Revolution*, Cambridge, U.K., 1970. Amin Tarzi, "Political Struggles over the Afghanistan-Pakistan Borderlands" in S. Bashir and R. D. Crews, eds., *Under the Drones*, Cambridge, Mass., 2012, pp. 17-29. Idem, "Islamic State—Khurasan Province" in F. al-Istrabadi and S. Ganguly, eds., *The Future of ISIS: Regional and International Implications*, Washington, D.C., 2018, pp. 119-147. Joby Warrick, *Black Flags: The Rise of ISIS*, New York, 2015.

(AMIN TARZI)

xiv. ETHNOLOGY OF QAJAR AND PAHLAVI KHORASAN

Ethnically speaking, the population of modern Khorasan (i.e., northeastern Iran in the 19th and early 20 Century) is extremely varied. It consists principally of Persians, Arabs, Turks, Kurds, Mongols, Baluch, and smaller groups of Jews, Gypsies, and Lors.

Persians. The Persians appear to have been the first ethnic group to populate the province, but, in time, they mixed with an increasing number of foreign invaders and, as a result, their proportionate number was reduced. According to W. Ivanov (q.v.), by the 1920s few Persians remained in the province. Some "comparatively old Persian populations" dwelt in villages on the northern slopes of the Jaḡatāy mountain range in the district of Jovayn, as well as in the hills and the vicinity of cities in the districts of Sabzavār, Nishapur, Toršiz (Kāšmar) and Torbat-e Ḥaydari, on the other side of the Jaḡatāy range, and in the Mashhad region. There were also Persians who had emigrated from various provinces of the realm to Khorasan "after the Turkmen raids were stopped by the Russian occupation of Transcaspia." These had settled down in the districts of Esfarāyen and Jājarm, and along the Russian frontier. Finally, there was "a very thin Persian population" on the arid hills and in the desert oases of the districts of Arišk and Bošruya (southwest of Ferdows, earlier Ṭus), the district of Bejestān (north of Ferdows), the district of Kāḵk (northeast of Ferdows), the districts of Bāḵarz and Jām (east of Torbat-e Ḥaydari), and the districts of Ḵᵛāf and Tayebād (southeast of Torbat-e Ḥaydari) (pp. 146-47). According to the *Military Report on Persia*, in 1929 Persians predominated only in the villages of the Mashhad plain and in the districts of Nishapur and Qāʾen (p. 48).

Arabs. The Arab influx into Khorasan started with the garrisoning of Arab troops in Nishapur and Marv (and probably also in Herat and Balḵ) following the campaign of ʿAbdallāh b. ʿĀmer in 651, and continued throughout the Omayyad and ʿAbbasid Caliphates. This process has been described *ad extensio* in ARAB SETTLEMENTS IN IRAN and ARAB TRIBES OF IRAN.

Turks. The Turkic influx into the province started with the Saljuq invasions of the 11th century. The principal Turkic tribes in the province are the Afšār, the Karāʾi, the Gerāyli, the Qarā Bayāt, the Jalāyer, the Qarāqoyunlu, and the Boḡāyri.

The Afšār dwell mostly in the Darragaz (q.v.), Abivard (q.v.) and Kalāt-e Nāderi regions; the Karāʾi in the Torbat-e Ḥaydari region; the Gerāyli (q.v.) in Širvān, as well as in the Jājarm, Jovayn (Jaḡatāy), and Sabzavār regions.

The Qarā Bayāt dwell in the Nišāpur area. When Shah Esmāʿil I (r. 1501-24) conquered Khorasan in 1510-11, they acknowledged Safavid sovereignty (see BAYĀT). During the reign of Moḥammad Ḵodābanda (1578-88), the Qarā Bayāt resisted the Uzbek incursions with such vigor that the whole tribe was absolved from payment of *divān* dues and tribal warriors were enrolled as regular soldiers in the Safavid army (Eskandar Beg, p. 1035). In 1582, their amir, Moḥammad Beg, became embroiled in an intrigue to seize control of Kandahar, in Afghanistan, in the course of which he lost his life (Yate, p. 74).

During the reign of Shah ʿAbbās I (1588-1629), the Qarā Bayāt amir, Moḥammad Solṭān Bayāt (d. 1610), was successively governor of Esfarāyen, Sabzavār, and Nishapur (Eskandar Beg, p. 1035). Thereafter, Qarā Bayāt amirs continued to rule Nishapur until the fall of the Qajar dynasty.

When Malek Maḥmud, the ruler of Sistān, captured Nishapur in 1722, during the reign of Shah Ṭahmāsp II (1722-32), the Qarā Bayāt amir, Fatḥ ʿAli Khan Bayāt, submitted to him. He later rebelled against the Sistāni ruler and was beheaded (Yate, pp. 84-86).

Upon the death of Nāder Shah in 1747, the Qarā Bayāt amir, ʿAbbāsqoli Khan, backed by some 10,000 families of his tribe, established a semi-independent state in the Nishapur region. In 1751, Nishapur was sacked by Aḥmad Shah Dorrāni (r. 1747-72), who took ʿAbbāsqoli Khan to Kabul as his prisoner. ʿAbbāsqoli Khan succeeded in ingratiating himself with his captor to such an extent that a marriage was arranged between Aḥmad Shah and his sister, as well as between the daughter of the Afghan ruler and ʿAbbās Qoli Khan's eldest son. ʿAbbāsqoli Khan was then allowed to return to Nishapur, and he devoted the remainder of his life to improving that town and the districts dependent upon it (Malcolm, II, pp. 149-41).

In 1793, the Qarā Bayāt submitted to Āqā Moḥammad Khan Qajar (Bellew, p. 374). Nevertheless, their amir, Jaʿfar Khan, who had succeeded his father, ʿAbbāsqoli Khan, remained intractable. In spring 1799, the forces of Fatḥ ʿAli Shah Qajar (r. 1797-1834) besieged Nishapur. Even though Jaʿfar Khan's second son, who had been held as a hostage in the shah's camp, was put to death and the city was bombarded by artillery, the Qarā Bayāt leader fought on for forty days. When Jaʿfar Khan finally surrendered, the shah forgave him, bestowed on him a robe of honor, and reinstated him as governor of Nishapur. He assigned his own troops, however, to man the fort (Brydges, pp. 79-82; Ḥasan Fasāʾi I, p. 247) and, later, he forced Jaʿfar Khan to reside at his court in Tehran (Malcolm II, p. 331).

The Jalāyer (or Jalaʾer) dwell in Kalāt-e Nāderi. According to Faruk Sümer, they are of Chaghatay origin (*Oğuzlar*, p. 360). ʿAli Mirniā includes them in his list of Afšār *tiras*, or clans (II, p. 20). Two Jalāyer leaders are included on Eskandar Beg's list of the great amirs of the time of Shah ʿAbbās I: Šāhvali Sultan Jalāyer (who was governor of Pasākuh, a district in the vicinity of Kalāt) and Oḡurlu Sultan Jalāyer (p. 1314). The Jalāyer were also faithful allies of Nāder Shah (r. 1736-47), and their leader, Ṭahmāsp Khan Wakil-al-Dawla, was one of that ruler's most important generals (Marvi, pp. 356-60, 582-99, 605-9, 1009-11; Mirniā I, pp. 70-75).

For many years, the Jalāyer ruling family held sway over Kalāt and its fort. During the reign of Moḥammad Shah Qajar (1835-48), the tribe's chief, Yalāntuš Khan, rebelled against the central government, as a result of which he was stripped of all his titles and possessions. Under his son and successor, who remained chief of the tribe until his death in 1883, the Jalāyer again flourished. This leader's son and successor, however, another Yalāntuš Khan, "was a man of no ability, and was deprived of the chiefship two years later," putting a permanent end to Jalāyer rule in Kalāt (Yate, p. 157). Lady Sheil, in 1856, estimated the number of Jalāyer at 1,500 houses (p. 400); Yate, in 1900, at 400 families (p. 157).

The Qarāqoyunlu dwell in the Darragaz region. They were probably moved there from Azerbaijan during Safavid times to help protect the northeastern frontier of Persia against Uzbek and Turkmen incursions. Today, most of them are to be found in Moḥammadābād, Nowḵandān and three villages southeast of Nowḵandān: Kāhu (also known as Kāhuhā), Saʿadābād and Qarāqoyunlu, and the summer pastures of those who are still sedentary are in the Hezār Masjed Mountains (Mirniā II, pp. 21-22).

The Boḡāyri dwell in a region southwest of Qučān. During the reign of Nāder Shah, two of their leaders participated in tribal rebellions, Manṣur Khan Beg and Moḥammad Taqi Khan (Marvi, pp. 1094-95, 1175-79). In the 1890s, one group of them, numbering some 800 families, was located in Bām, and another group, called Saraḵsi and numbering some 500 families, was located in Ṣafiābād (Yate, p. 370).

According to the *Military Report*, "The northern frontier [of Khorasan], especially the district of Kalat-i-Nadiri, is inhabited by Turks, who are found scattered all over the northern part of the province. Their centre may be said to be the Jam valley" (p. 48). The Turks of Khorasan are, for the most part, Shiʿite and speak a wide variety of Turkic dialects.

Kurds. Ivanov tells us that there may have been Kurds in Khorasan before the 16th century, for one encounters the surname of Kurt in the historical data of previous centuries, and there was a dynasty by that name south of Herat (1245-1389). If there were Kurds in the province at that time, however, they left no trace (p. 150). Most of the Kurds in Khorasan claim descent from tribes that were transferred to the province from western Persia by the Safavids for the purpose of protecting the northeastern frontier of the country from inroads by Uzbek and Turkmen tribes. According to Ivanov, some of these tribes were moved as early as the middle of the 16th century (p. 150). But by far the largest transfer was carried out by Shah ʿAbbās I at the very beginning of the 17th century (Ivanov, p. 150; Papoli-Yazdi, pp. 24-25). The principal Kurdish tribes of Khorasan are the Zaʿfarānlu, the Šādlu, the Keyvānlu, and the ʿAmārlu.

The Zaʿfarānlu dwell in northern Khorasan, having been transplanted there from western Persia around 1600. According to Yate, they were first settled in an area to the north of the Atrak river, but during the reign of Shah Ḥosayn I (1694-1722) they moved into a mountainous region south of the Atrak that was less exposed to attack from tribes beyond the Persian border (p. 181). In their new habitat they occupied a swath of territory that stretched from Reżāābād, 15 kilometers northwest of Širvān, to Čenārān, 60 kilometers northwest of Mashhad, and included the towns of Širvān and Qučān, and they displaced the Gerāyli who had been living there (Yate, p. 181; also Napier, pp. 83-87, 97, 101-2; MacGregor II, pp. 86, 143).

From the time of Shah ʿAbbās I to the beginning of the reign of Reżā Shah Pahlavi, the Zaʿfarānlu leaders were hereditary governors of Qučān and headed a principality that stretched about 90 miles from east to west and about forty miles from north to south (MacGregor II, p. 87; for a list of the Zaʿfarānlu chiefs, who, after 1735-36, bore the title of *ilḵāni*, see Afšār-Sistāni, pp. 985-87). According to the *Military Report*, in 1929 around 50,000 Zaʿfarānlu lived in the Qučān district and some 12,000 of them lived in the Širvān district, roughly 13,000 of them being still nomadic (p. 52). According to British Naval Intelligence, in 1945 some 10,000 families of them lived in the Qučān district and around 2,400 families lived in the Širvān district, 2,600 families of them being still nomadic (*Persia*, p. 388).

The Šādlu (or Šādilu) also dwell in northern Khorasan. Like the Zaʿfarānlu, they were transplanted from western Persia by Shah ʿAbbās I around 1600 and were first settled in an area to the north of the present border of Persia. When raids by Turkmen and other marauding tribes forced them to move into the Persian hinterland, they settled in and around Bojnurd. There, until the beginning of the reign of Reżā Shah, they formed a principality that extended about 90 miles from east to west, and about 50 miles from north to south. This included the districts of Samalqān and Māna on the Atrak River in the north, and the towns of Jājarm and Esfarāyen in the south (MacGregor II, p. 142). Until 1832-33 the Zaʿfarānlu and Šādlu formed a unified tribal confederacy under the Zaʿfarānlu *ilḵani*, but when during that year Reżā Qoli Khan, the confederacy's *ilḵāni*, rebelled and the Šādlu leader, Najaf Qoli Khan, did not come to his aid when requested to do so, the two tribes split. After that, the Šādlu had their own *ilḵāni* (Afšār-Sistāni, p. 1003). According to the *Military Report*, in 1929 the Šādlu of Bojnurd alone numbered some 75,000 individuals, all of whom were sedentary (p. 51). According to Masʿud Kayhān, in 1932-33 they numbered some 18,000 households (II, p. 105). According to British Naval Intelligence, in 1945 they numbered around 15,000 families, all of which were sedentary (*Persia*, p. 388; for additional information, see Mirniā, II, p. 38).

Like the Zaʿfarānlu and Šādlu, the Keyvānlu dwell in northern Khorasan and were sent to the province by Shah ʿAbbās I in around 1600. Yate, who lived in the province from 1893 to 1898, wrote that at that time three sections of the tribe controlled the Rādkān district as far south as Čašma Gilās and spent the summers on the Hezār Masjed Mountains. Five other sections lived in the hills on the border of the Darra-gaz valley, and 300 or 400 more families were in the Jovayn district (p. 364). Rādkān is their chief center. Although the Keyvānlu were once led by an *ilḵāni*, by the 1890s they no longer had a ruling chief (Yate, p. 364). According to Henry Field, they numbered around 8,000 individuals in 1929 (p. 252; for additional information, see Mirniā, II, pp. 32-33).

The ʿAmārlu dwell northwest of Nishapur, in and around the village of Mārusk, having been moved to Khorasan by Nāder Shah (Ivanov, p. 150). According to the *Military Report*, they numbered some 500 families in 1924 (p. 51).

Other important Kurdish tribes in Khorasan are: Bāčevānlu, Bādalānlu, Bičarānlu, Pahlavānlu, Tupkānlu, Jalāli, Ḥamzakānlu, Rešvānlu, Ravatkānlu, Zeydānlu, Sil Saparānlu, Sivkānlu, Šaʿrānlu, Amirānlu, Šeyḵkānlu, Ṣufiānlu, Qāčakānlu, Qarā Čorlu, Qaramānlu, Kaviānlu, Guliānlu, Maždagānlu, Milānlu, Verānlu, Hizulānlu, and Heyvadānlu (Afšār-Sistāni, pp. 988-1001).

Most of the Kurds of Khorasan are Shiʿite. According to Ivanov, the language of the Khorasani Kurds belongs to the "northern" or "real Kurdish" family, and resembles that of the Mokri, but the vocabulary "is either replete with Persian terms in the south, or with Turkish in the north" (p. 152).

Mongols. The Mongols of Khorasan are divided into two major groups: the Hazāra (q.v.) and the Timuri. Most of the Hazāra (or "Berberi" as they are called by their Persian neighbors) dwell in northeastern Khorasan. According to the *Military Report*, they emigrated from the Hazārajāt region in central Afghanistan when Amir ʿAbd-al-Raḥmān seized their grazing lands in 1891. We know, however, that there were already Hazāra in Khorasan several decades earlier. Colonel MacGregor, who visited the province in 1875, noted that at that time the population of Esfarāyen in northern Khorasan and Čahār Deh in eastern Khorasan were Hazāra who allegedly had been transplanted from the Herat mountains in 1857 after the occupation of that city by Persian forces during the war with Great Britain (II, pp. 142, 146). Whatever the case, during the relatively few years since their arrival in Persia, they have spread over a wide area, settling down in the Borujerd, Širvān, Darra-gaz, and Saraḵs regions and in the valleys of the Kašaf and Jām rivers (p. 53). According to Ivanov, they "gradually ousted Persians and Turks from the eastern extremity of the Hezar Masjed range" and "the districts of Meshed and Quchan have many villages with a Barbari population, especially in the lands belonging to the Shrine of Imam Riza at Meshed" (p. 155).

Also according to Ivanov, the most important Hazāra tribes in northeastern Khorasan are: Uruzgāni (near Čahār Deh and in the Hezār Masjed range), Jāguri (in the Hezār Masjed range and in Sar-e Jām), Bisud, Daizāngi, and Daikundi (east of Sar-e Jām), Laljāngi (east of Sar-e Jām and in Sarak̲s). Ivanov claims that all of the Hazāra are "fanatical Shi'ites" and reports that their language is "a jargon of Persian" (p. 155; for the origin and early history of the Hazāra, see Jarring, pp. 79-81).

The Timuri dwell in eastern Khorasan. According to Yate, Moḥammad Shah Qājār (r. 1834-48) moved some 8,000 families of them to the province from the Herat region in 1838, following the siege of that city by Persian forces. They settled in the districts of Torbat-e Jām, Bāk̲arz, K̲ᵛāf, and Zurābād and their chief, Qilič Khan, was made governor of Torbat-e Jām, Bāk̲arz, and K̲ᵛāf, bearing the title *amir* (p. 38). In 1867, Nāṣer-al-Din Shah gave their leader, Mir ʿAli Mardān Shah Noṣrat-al-Molk, the rank of *amir-e tumān* (division commander) for his zeal in combating the Turkmen. Subsequently, he was appointed deputy to the governor-general and commander-in-chief of Persian forces in Khorasan, but, in 1895, he was abruptly dismissed and exiled to Tehran (Yate, pp. 45-47). Mir Asad-Allāh Khan Šawkat-al-Dawla, who was the leader of a group of 300 families of Timuri who had moved into Persia from the Herat region in 1858, had been given the rank of *amir-e tuman* in 1893, and then made governor of Torbat-e Jām and Zurābād (Yate, p. 46). In 1900, Yate estimated the Timuri population at 6,000 families (p. 38; for a list of the 70 Timuri tribes in Khorasan, see Adamec, pp. 329-31). Most of the Timuri are Sunni; they speak Persian and intermarry only with the Baluch (Ivanov, p. 153; for the connection between the Timuri and Timur Leng, see Yate, p. 38).

Baluch. The Baluch dwell mostly in northeastern Khorasan. An analysis of Ḥosayn ʿAli Razmārā's *Farhang-e jog̲rāfia-ye Irān* IX shows that the vast majority of Baluch villages are located in the districts of Fadiša (near Nishapur), Sarak̲s (on the Russian border), and Jannatābād (on the Afghan border). According to the *Military Report*, the principal Baluch tribes in northeastern Khorasan are: Sālār K̲āni, Ebrāhim K̲āni, Zardād K̲āni, Jān Begi, and Morād K̲āni (pp. 55-56). There are also Baluch, namely the Bahluli, who live in the Birjand region in southern Khorasan (Razmārā, pp. 363, 370, 371, 419). In 1936, their number was estimated at some 5,400 families (Afšār-Sistāni, p. 1016). In the 1920s, the Baluch of northeastern Khorasan had already lost their original language. Only those in the south still used their traditional Makrāni dialect (Ivanov, p. 152). The Baluch are Sunni and intermarry only with the Timuri (Ivanov, p. 153).

Jews. There are very few Jews in Khorasan, and, according to Ivanov, nothing remains of the large Jewish communities that once inhabited the cities in the province (p. 156). The few Jews remaining in the 1920s dwelt in Mashhad and some of them were "Jadids," i.e., descendents of Jews who were forced to convert to Islam in 1839 but continued, in secret, to observe their traditional rituals (Ivanov, p. 156).

Gypsies. The Gypsies of Khorasan are mostly itinerant craftsmen, employed by peasants as blacksmiths, carpenters, sieve-weavers, etc. According to Ivanov, in the 1920s there were also Gypsy quarters in Nishapur and Sabzavār in the north of the province. In the south of the province, Gypsies tended to congregate in the large village of Sarbiša, south of Birjand, during the winter months (p. 157). Ivanov published several studies of the Gypsies of Khorasan and their language (see Ivanov, p. 157n). For more information, see GYPSIES OF PERSIA and GYPSY DIALECTS.

Lors. According to British Naval Intelligence, Reżā Shah Pahlavi (r. 1925-41) moved a large number of Lors to Khorasan (*Persia*, pp. 370, 387). These were nomads belonging to the Bālā Gariva group of tribes in the Piš-e Kuh region of Lorestān, who had revolted against the central government in the late 1920s. Most of them probably returned to western Persia after World War II, for there is no trace of them in Khorasan today.

Bibliography: Ludwig W. Adamec, ed., *Historical Gazetteer of Iran* II, Graz, 1981. Iraj Afšār-Sistāni, *Ilhā, čādornešinān va ṭawāyef-e ʿašāyeri-e Irān*, Tehran, 1987. H. W. Bellew, *From the Indus to the Tigris*, London, 1874. British Intelligence and Policy on Persia 1900-1949, *Military Report on Persia* I: *Khurasan and Seistan*, Calcutta, 1930. British Naval Intelligence Division, *Persia*, 1945, n.p. Harford Jones Brydges, *The Dynasty of the Kajars*, London, 1833. Eskandar Beg Torkamān Monši, *Tārik̲-e ʿālamārā-ye ʿabbasi*, tr. R. Savory, as *History of Shah ʿAbbas the Great*, tr. R. Savory, 2 vols., Boulder, Colo., 1978. Ḥasan Fasāʾi, *Fārsnāma-ye nāṣeri,* lith., Tehran, 1895-96. W. Ivanov (also Ivanow), "Notes on the Ethnology of Khurasan," *The Geographical Journal* 67, 1926, pp. 143-58. Gunnar Jarring, *On the Distribution of Turk Tribes in Afghanistan*, Leipzig, 1939. Masʿud Kayhān, *Jog̲rāfiyā-ye mofaṣṣal-e Irān* II, Tehran, 1931. C. M. MacGregor, *Narrative of a Journey through the Province of Khorassan and of the N.W. Frontier of Afghanistan in 1875*, 2 vols., London, 1879. John Malcolm, *The History of Persia*, 2 vols., London, 1829. Moḥammad-Kāẓem Marvi, *ʿĀlamārā-ye nāderi*, ed. M.-A. Riāhi, 3 vols., Tehran, 1985. Vladimir Minorsky, *Tadhkirat al-Mulūk: A Manual of Safavid Administration*, Cambridge, 1943. ʿAli Mirniā, *Ilāt va ṭawāyef-e Darragaz*, 2 vols., Mashhad, 1982-83. G. C. Napier, "Extracts from a Diary of a Tour in Khorassan, and Notes on the Eastern Tract," *JRGS* 46, 1976, pp. 62-145. Moḥammad-Ḥosayn Papoli Yazdi, *Le nomadisme dans le nord du Khorassan*, Paris, 1991. Ḥosayn-ʿAli Razmārā, *Farhang-e jog̲rāfiā-ye Irān* IX, Tehran, 1951. Lady M. L. Sheil, *Glimpses of Life and Manners in Persia*, London, 1856. Faruk Sümer, "Bayatlar," *Istanbul Üniversitesi Edebiyat Fakültesi: Türk Dili ve Edebiyat Dergisi*, 1950, pp. 374-98. Idem, *Oğuzlar*, second edition, Istanbul, 1992. Charles Edward Yate, *Khurasan and Sistan*, London, 1900.

(†PIERRE OBERLING)